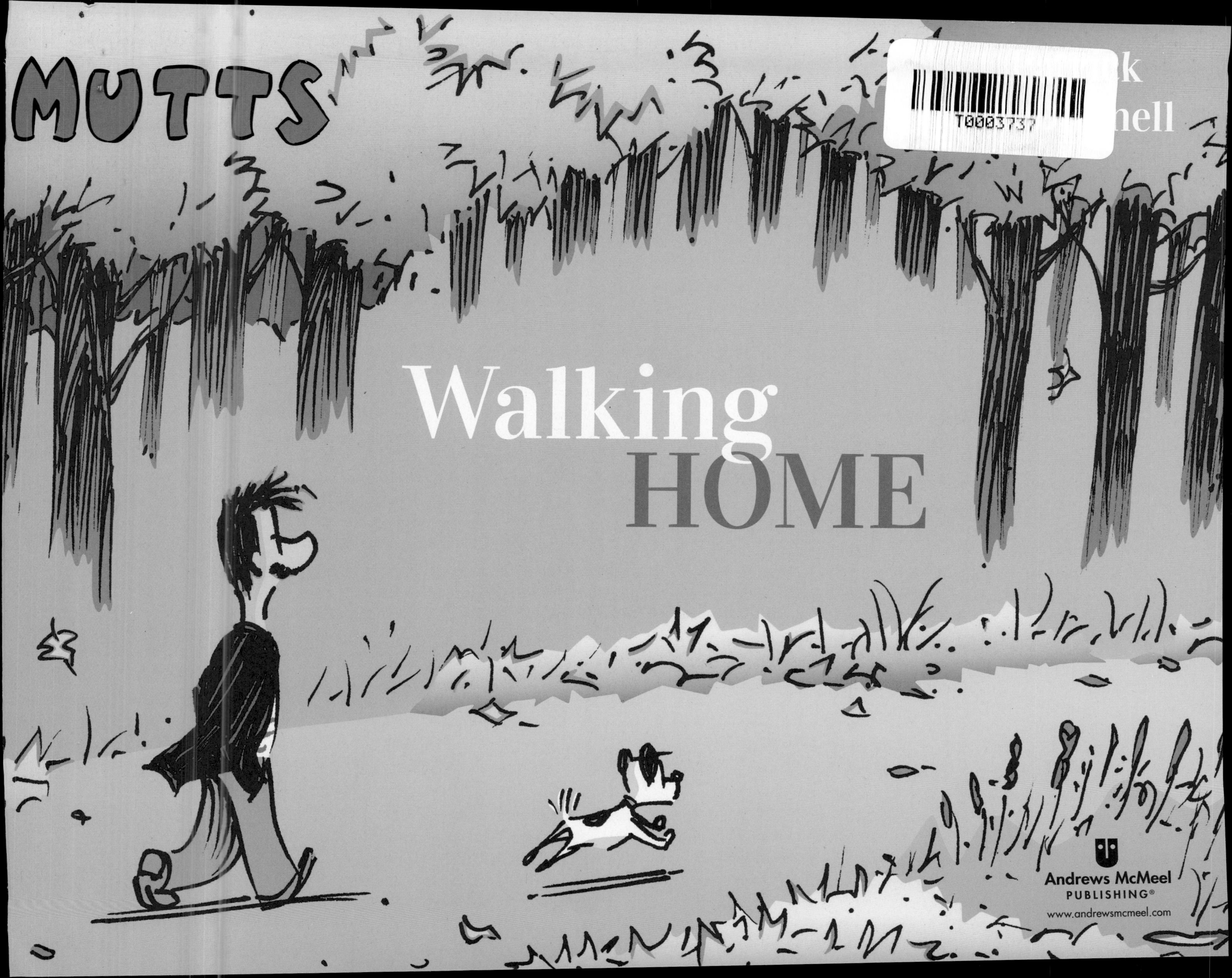
MUTTS
Walking
HOME
Andrews McMeel
PUBLISHING®
www.andrewsmcmeel.com

Other Books by Patrick McDonnell

Mutts
Cats and Dogs: Mutts II
More Shtuff: Mutts III
Yesh!: Mutts IV
Our Mutts: Five
A Little Look-See: Mutts VI
What Now: Mutts VII
I Want to Be the Kitty: Mutts VIII
Dog-Eared: Mutts IX
Who Let the Cat Out: Mutts X
Everyday Mutts
Animal Friendly
Call of the Wild
Stop and Smell the Roses
Earl & Mooch
Our Little Kat King
Bonk!
A Shtinky Little Christmas
Cat Crazy
Living the Dream
Playtime
Year of Yesh
#LoveMutts
You've Got Those Wild Eyes Again, Mooch
Mutts Sundays
Hot Dogs, Hot Cats
Sunday Mornings
Sunday Afternoons
Sunday Evenings
Mutts Go Green
Mutts Moments
Mutts Shelter Stories: Love. Guaranteed.

Mutts is distributed internationally by King Features Syndicate, Inc. For information, write to King Features Syndicate, Inc., 300 West Fifty-Seventh Street, New York, New York 10019, or visit www.KingFeatures.com.

Andrews McMeel Publishing, a division of Andrews McMeel Universal, 1130 Walnut Street, Kansas City, Missouri 64106.

22 23 24 25 26 POA 10 9 8 7 6 5 4 3 2 1

ISBN: 978-1-5248-7803-0

Library of Congress Control Number: 2022935506

Cover design: Nicole Tramontana

Printed on recycled paper.

Mutts can be found on the Internet at **www.mutts.com.**

Walking The Dog

Dogs are great. They get us out of the house and out of our head.
Taking your dog for a walk is like a shared meditation, a chance to
change the scenery, to be in the moment and enjoy the natural world.
But there's also a feeling of comfort when you head back home.
My rescue Jack Russell, Amelie, always picks up the pace
the closer we get to our house.

And why is it so rewarding to return home? That's where the cat is.

— PATRICK

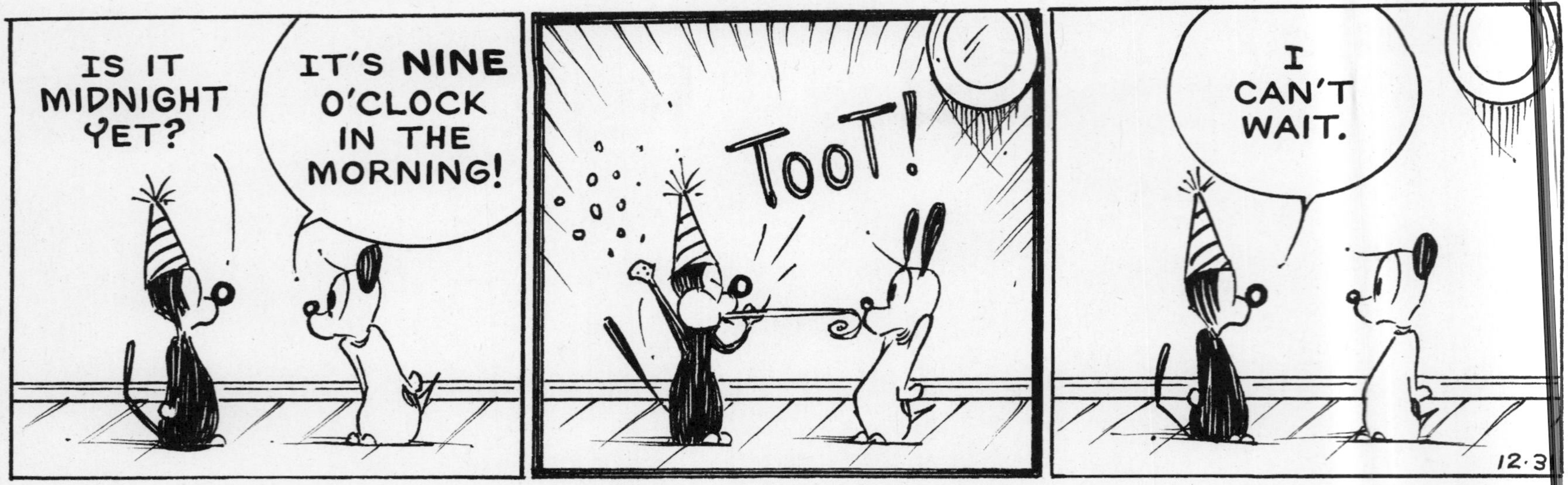
IS IT MIDNIGHT YET?
IT'S NINE O'CLOCK IN THE MORNING!
TOOT!
I CAN'T WAIT.
12·31

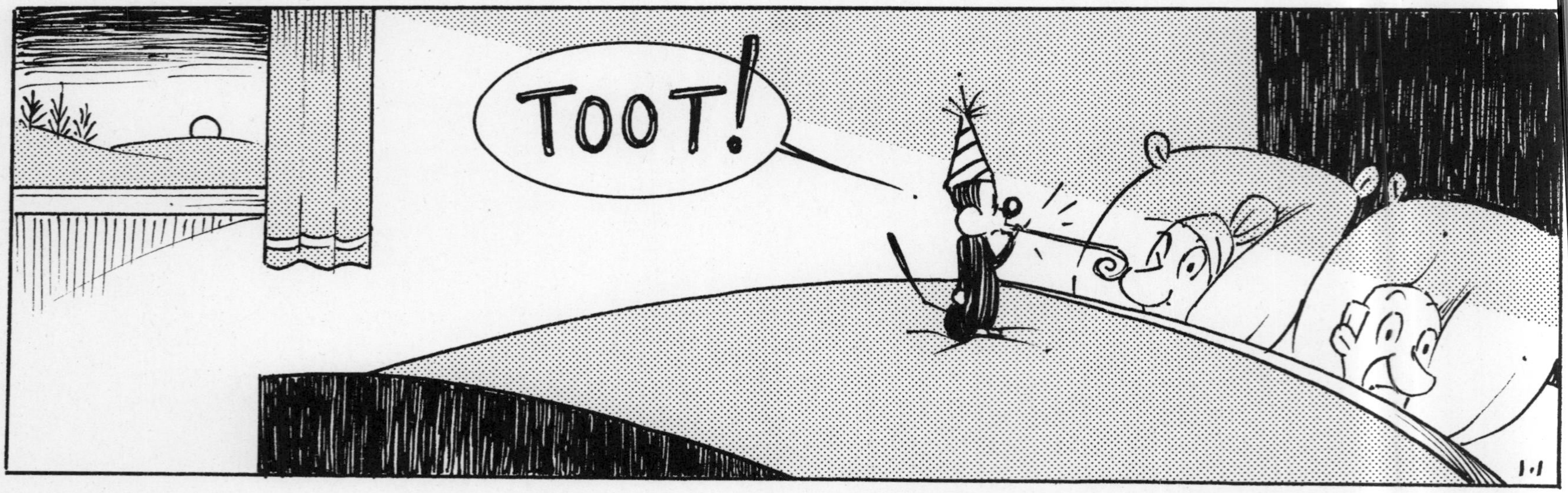
TOOT!
1·1

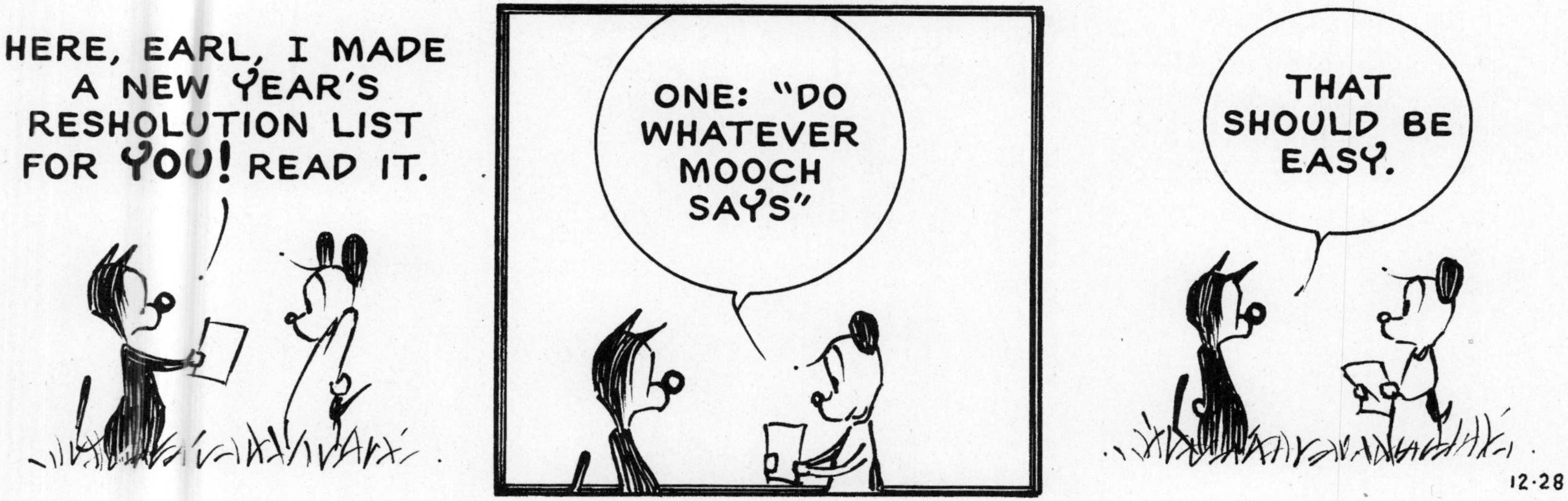
HERE, EARL, I MADE A NEW YEAR'S RESHOLUTION LIST FOR YOU! READ IT.
ONE: "DO WHATEVER MOOCH SAYS"
THAT SHOULD BE EASY.
12·28

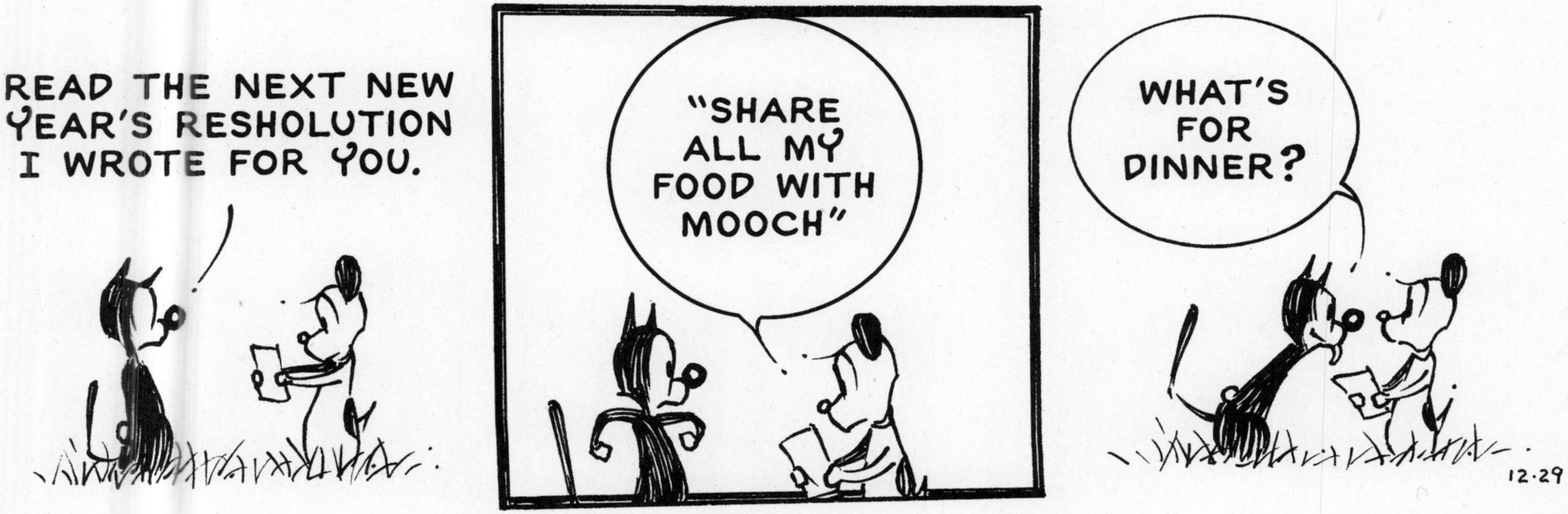
READ THE NEXT NEW YEAR'S RESHOLUTION I WROTE FOR YOU.
"SHARE ALL MY FOOD WITH MOOCH"
WHAT'S FOR DINNER?
12·29

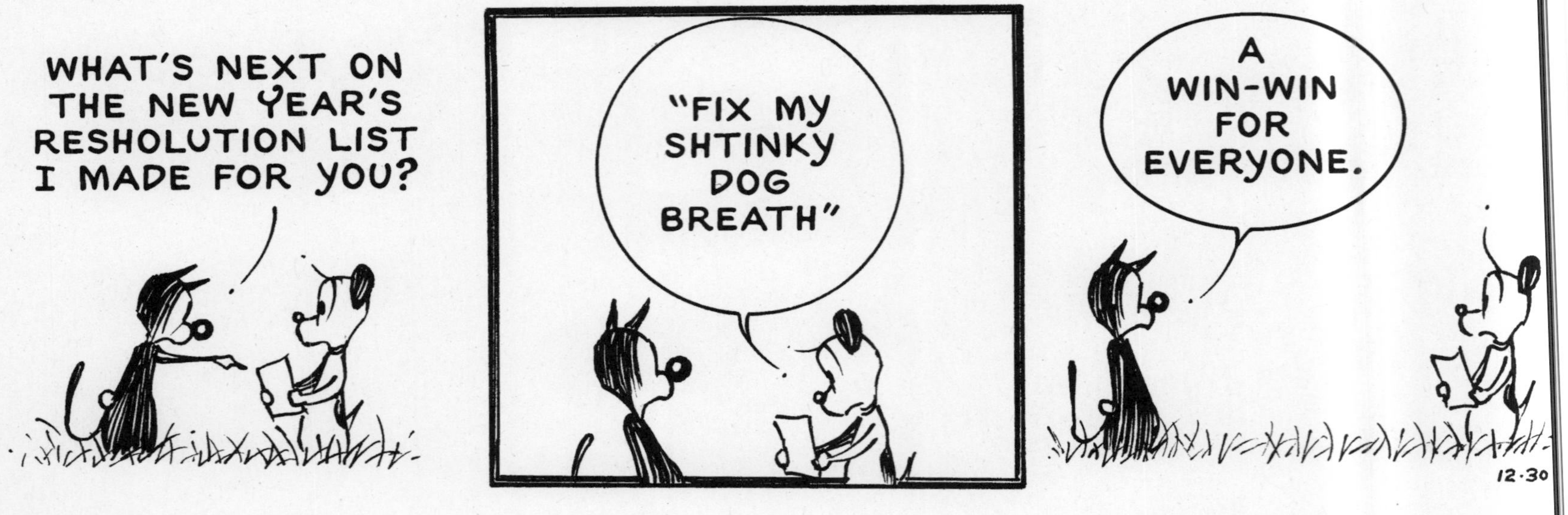
WHAT'S NEXT ON THE NEW YEAR'S RESHOLUTION LIST I MADE FOR YOU?
"FIX MY SHTINKY DOG BREATH"
A WIN-WIN FOR EVERYONE.
12·30

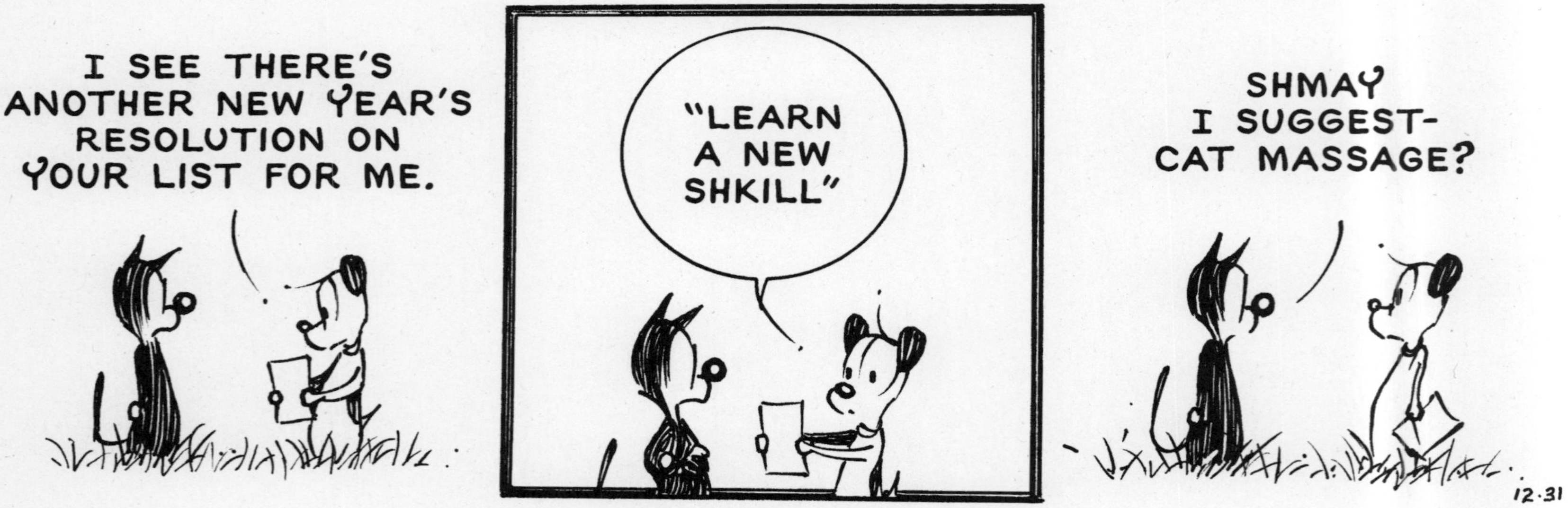
I SEE THERE'S ANOTHER NEW YEAR'S RESOLUTION ON YOUR LIST FOR ME.
"LEARN A NEW SHKILL"
SHMAY I SUGGEST-CAT MASSAGE?
12·31

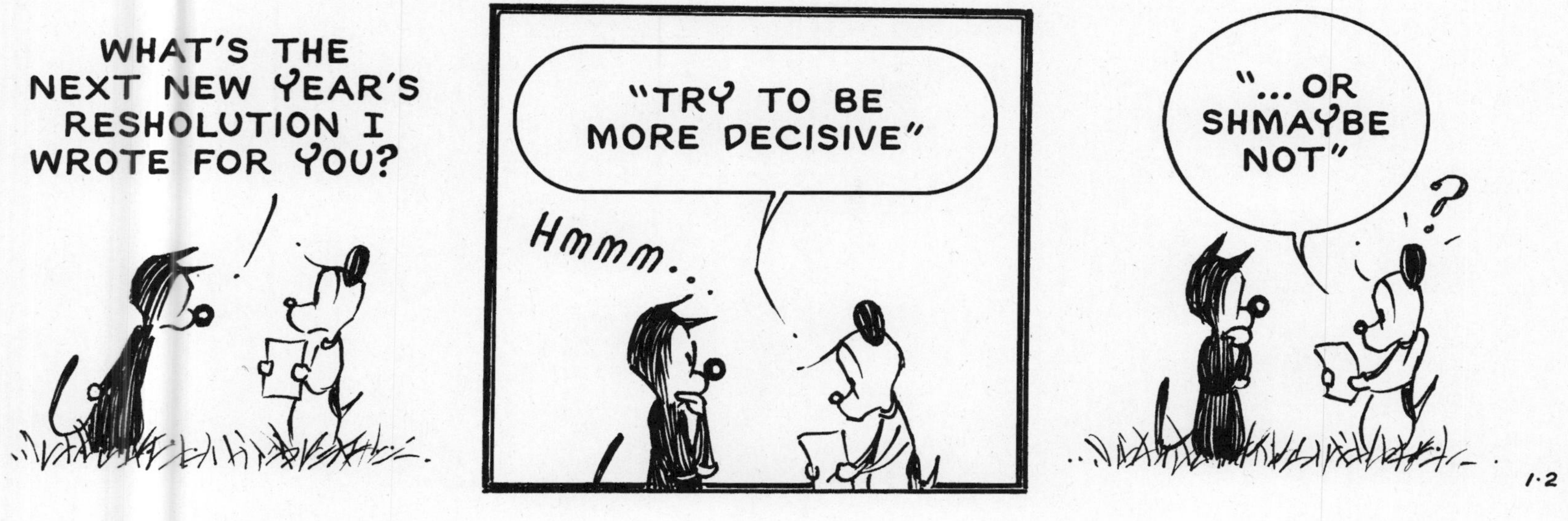
WHAT'S THE NEXT NEW YEAR'S RESHOLUTION I WROTE FOR YOU?
Hmmm..
"TRY TO BE MORE DECISIVE"
"...OR SHMAYBE NOT"
?
1·2

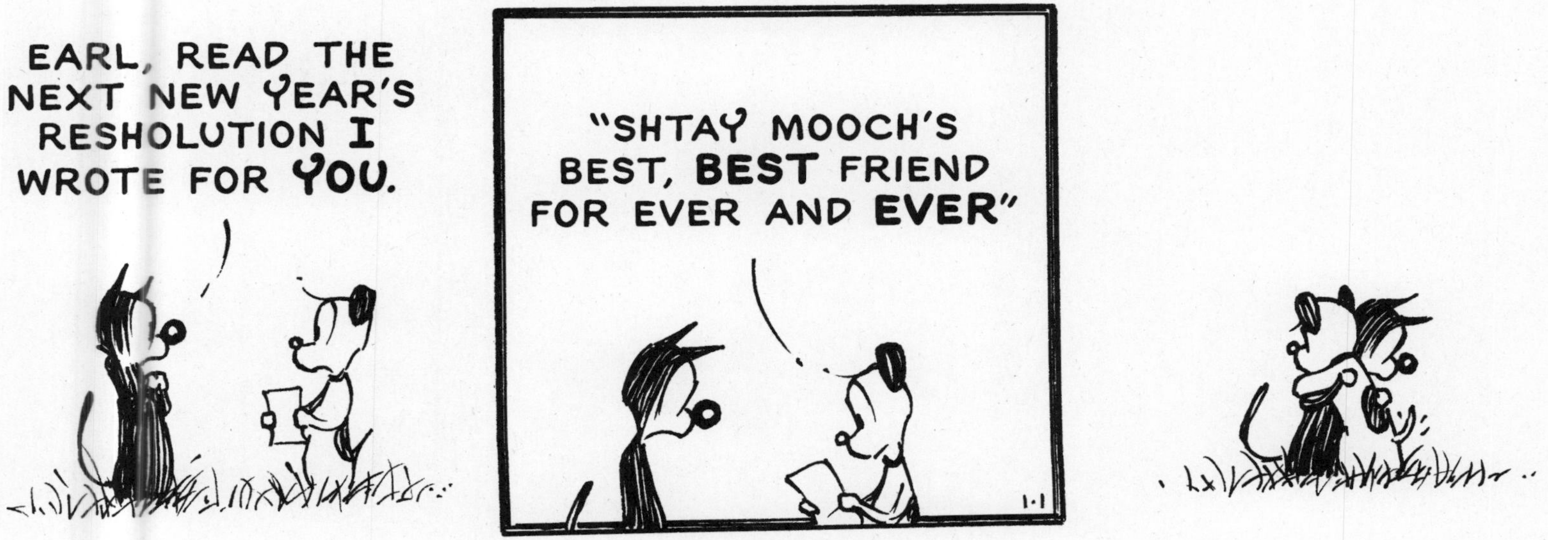
EARL, READ THE NEXT NEW YEAR'S RESHOLUTION **I** WROTE FOR **YOU**.
"SHTAY MOOCH'S BEST, **BEST** FRIEND FOR EVER AND **EVER**"
1·1

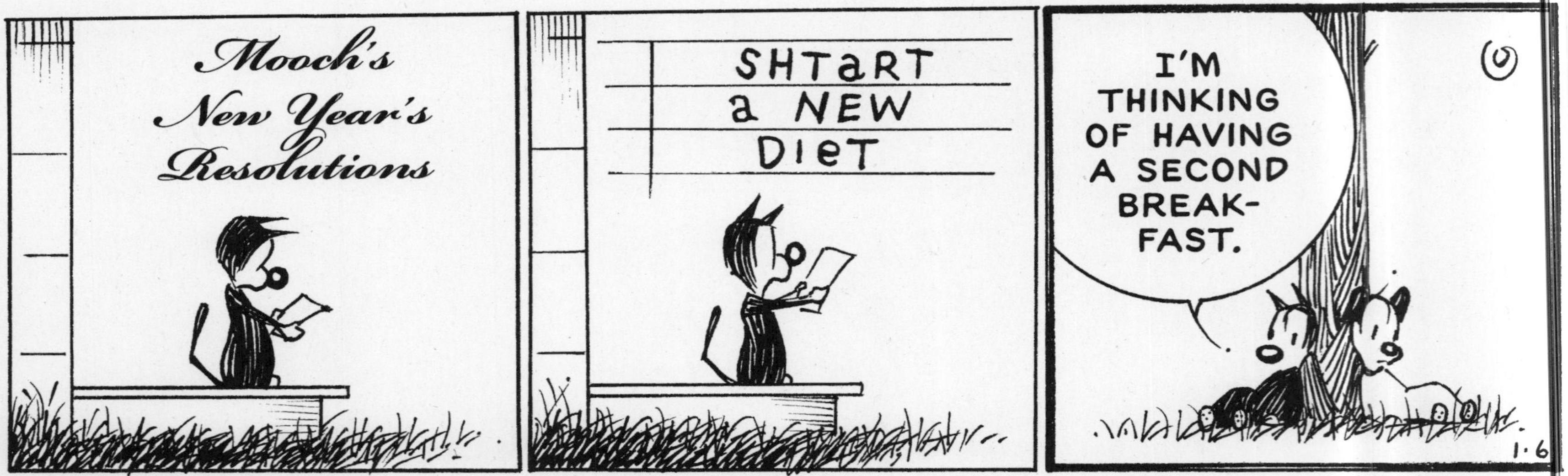
Mooch's New Year's Resolutions
SHTaRT a NEW DieT
I'M THINKING OF HAVING A SECOND BREAK-FAST.
1·6

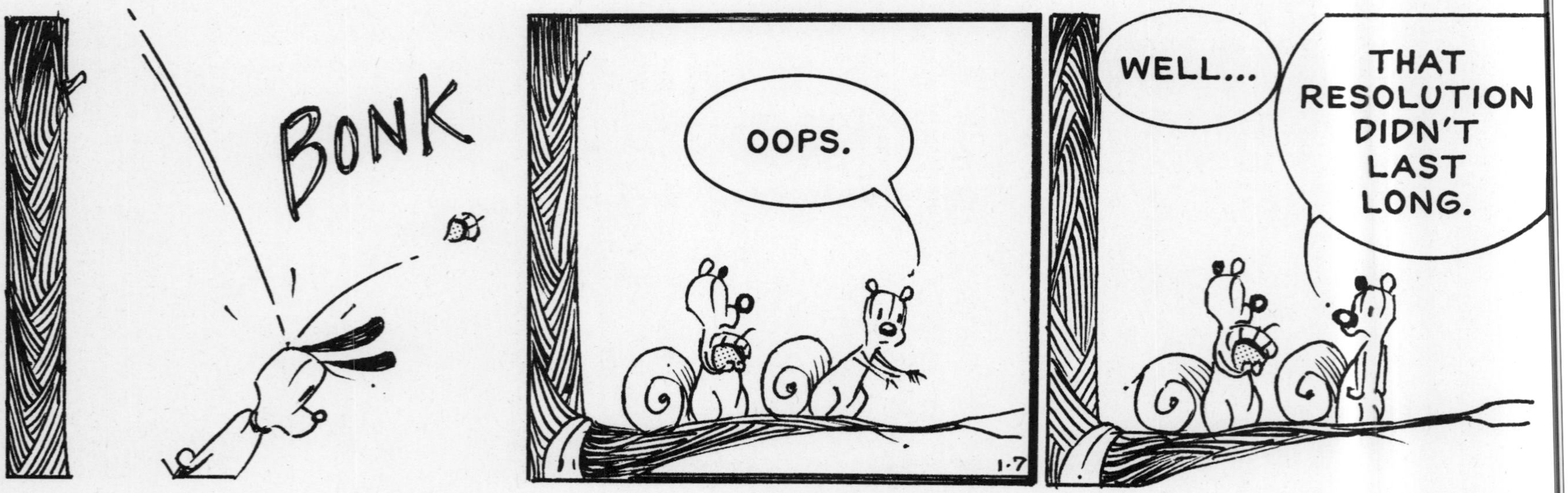
BONK
OOPS.
1·7
WELL...
THAT RESOLUTION DIDN'T LAST LONG.

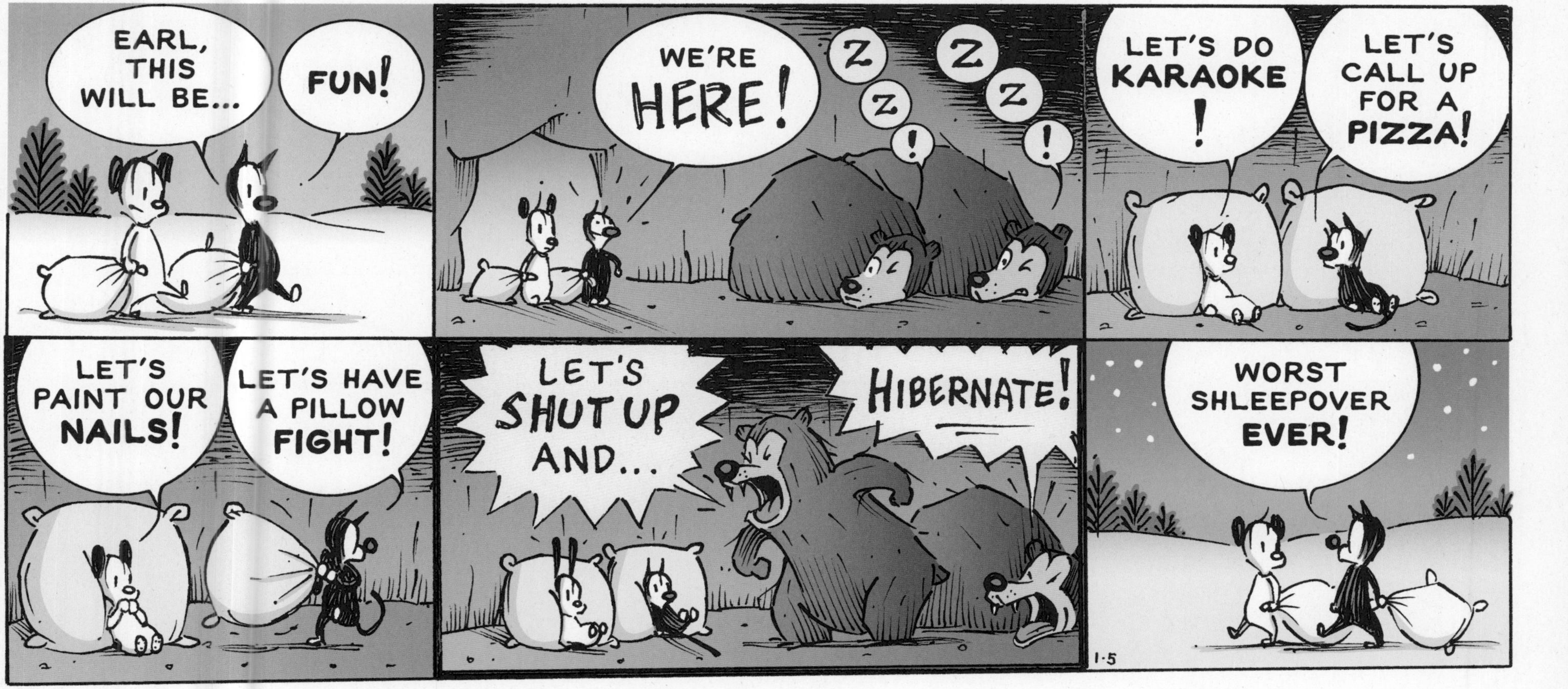
EARL, THIS WILL BE...
FUN!
WE'RE HERE!
Z Z !
Z Z !
LET'S DO KARAOKE!
LET'S CALL UP FOR A PIZZA!
LET'S PAINT OUR NAILS!
LET'S HAVE A PILLOW FIGHT!
LET'S SHUT UP AND...
HIBERNATE!
WORST SHLEEPOVER EVER!
1·5

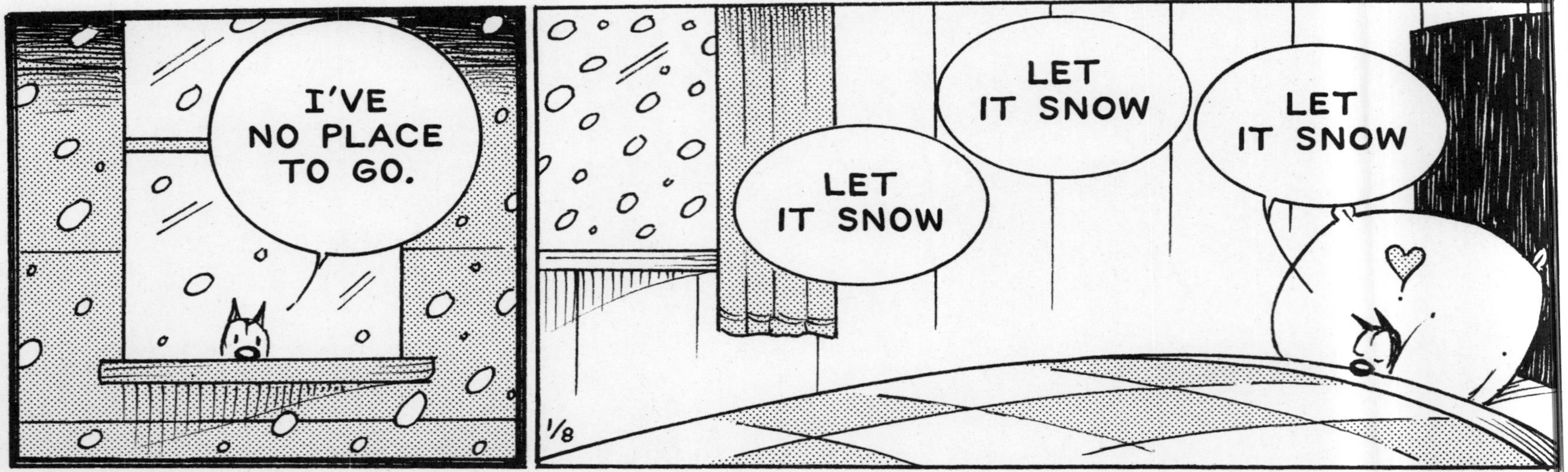
I'VE NO PLACE TO GO.
LET IT SNOW
LET IT SNOW
LET IT SNOW
1/8

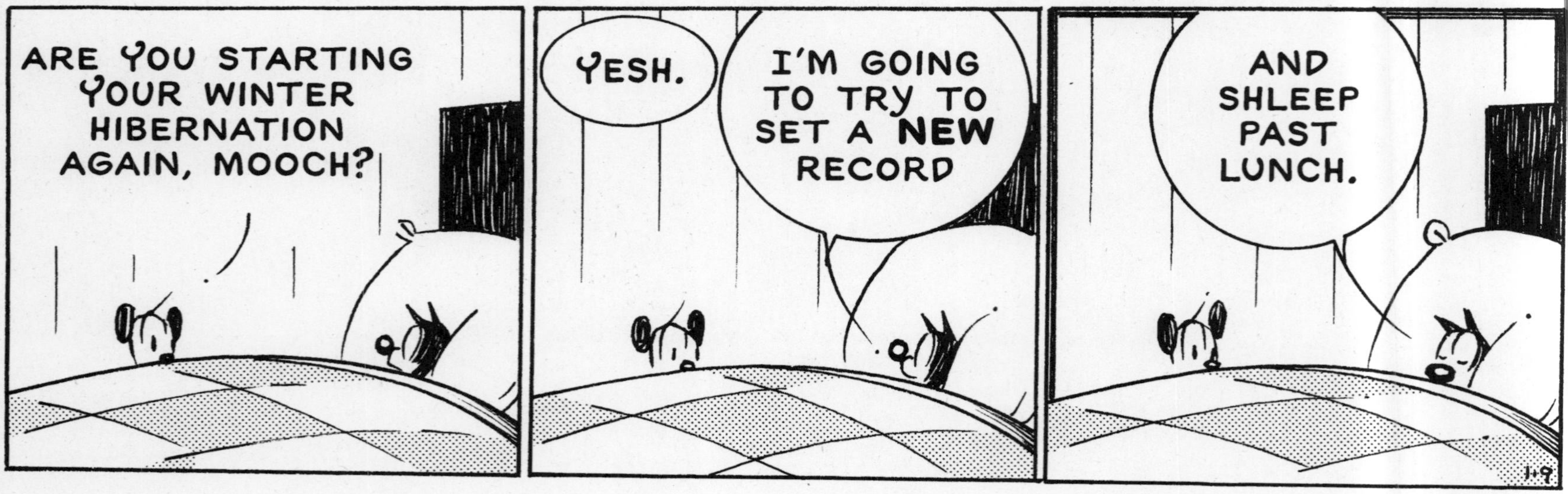
ARE YOU STARTING YOUR WINTER HIBERNATION AGAIN, MOOCH?
YESH.
I'M GOING TO TRY TO SET A **NEW** RECORD
AND SHLEEP PAST LUNCH.
1-9

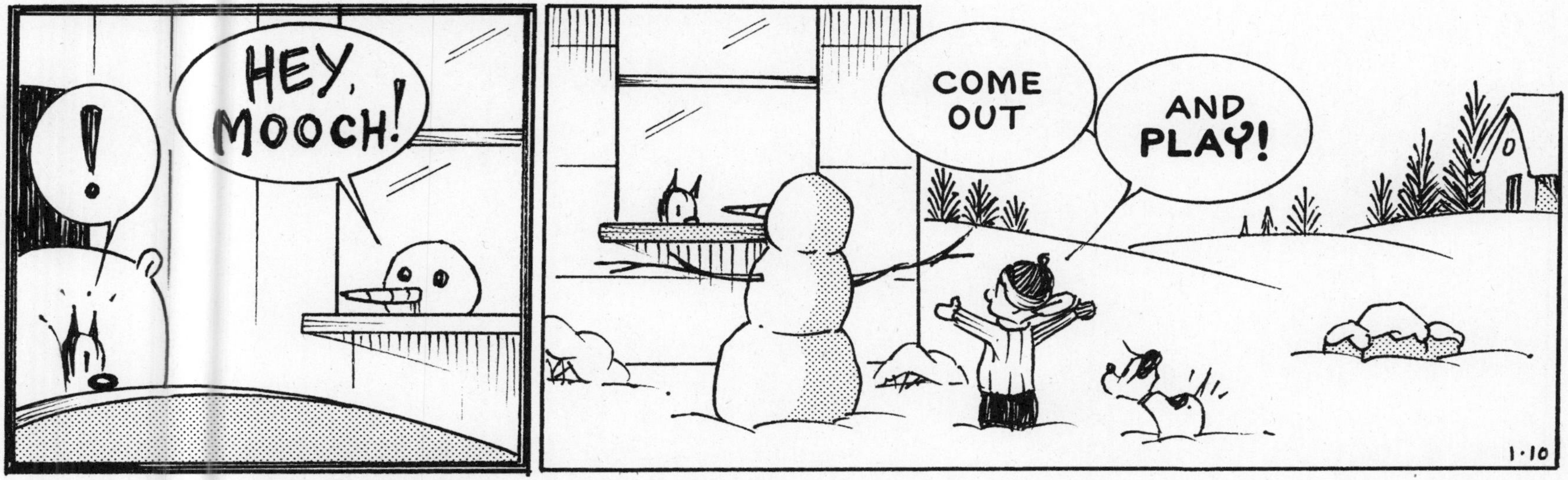
!
HEY, MOOCH!
COME OUT
AND PLAY!
1·10

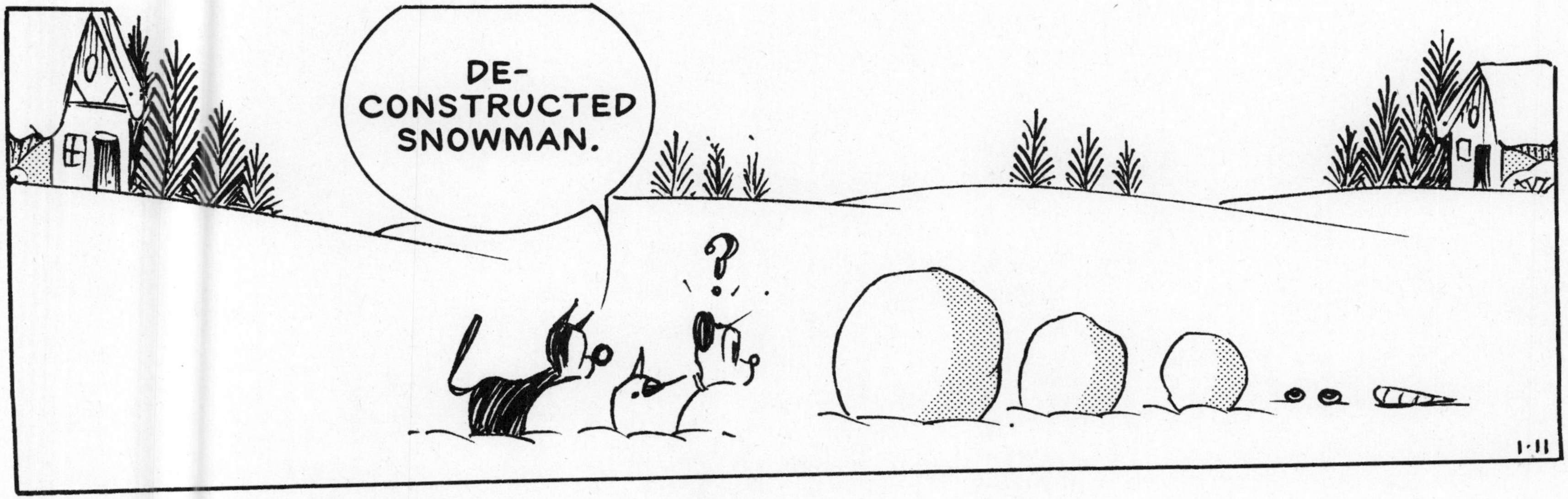
DE-CONSTRUCTED SNOWMAN.
?
1·11

MUTTS

Patrick McDonnell

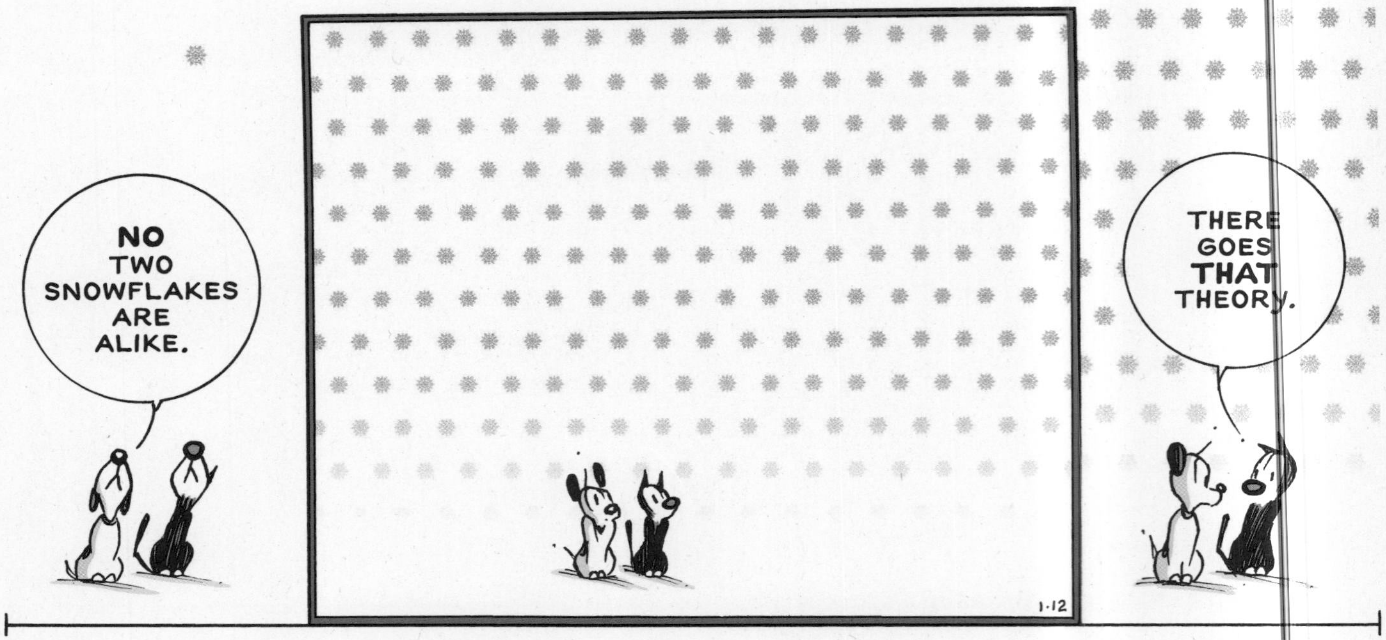
NO TWO SNOWFLAKES ARE ALIKE.
THERE GOES THAT THEORY.
1·12

MUTTS

Patrick McDonnell

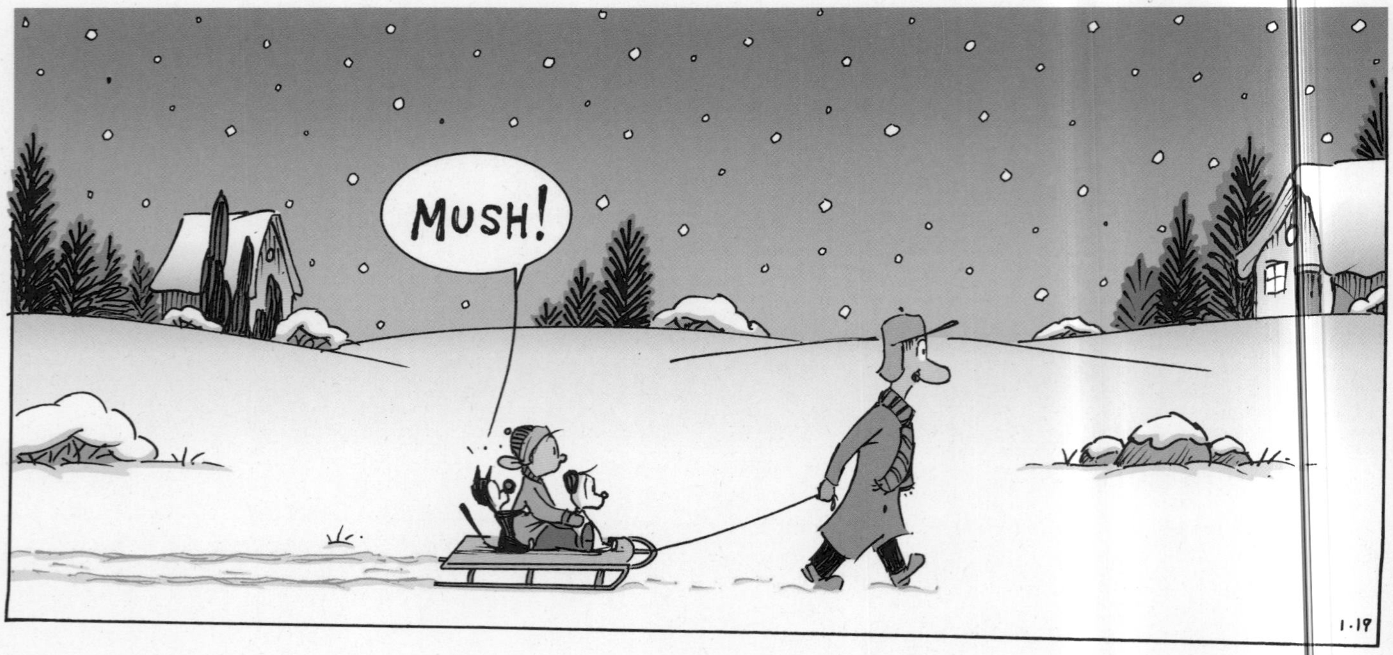
MUSH!
1·19

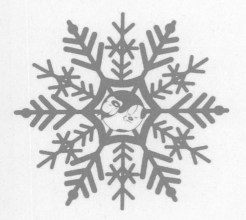

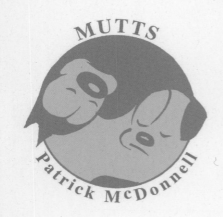

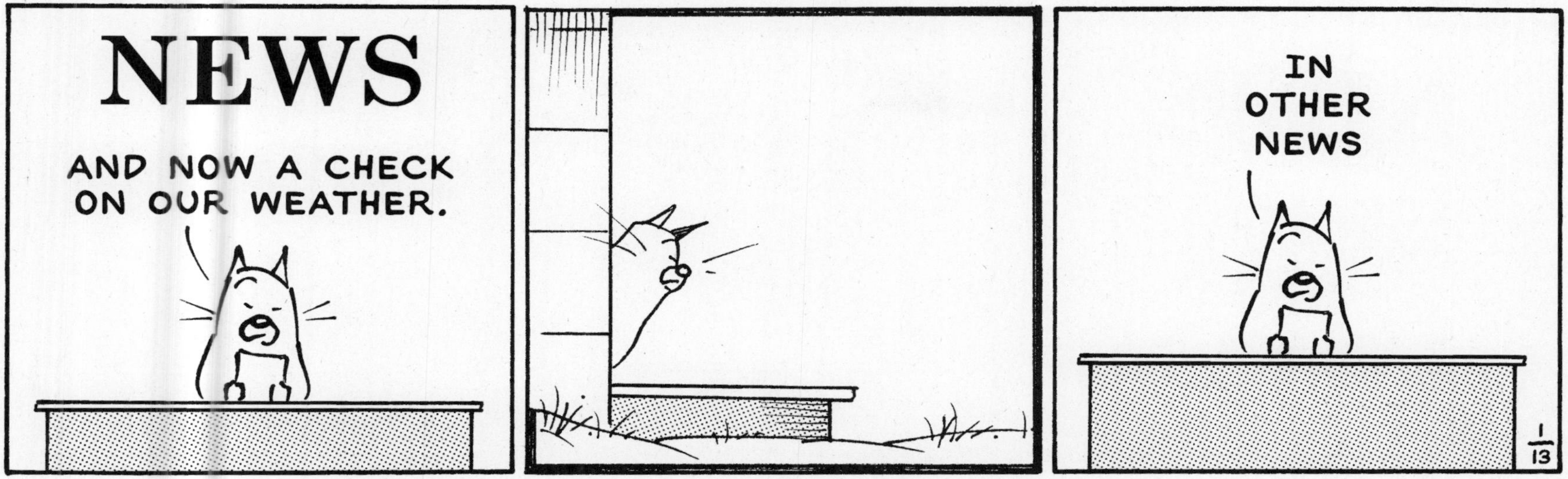
NEWS
AND NOW A CHECK ON OUR WEATHER.
IN OTHER NEWS
1/13

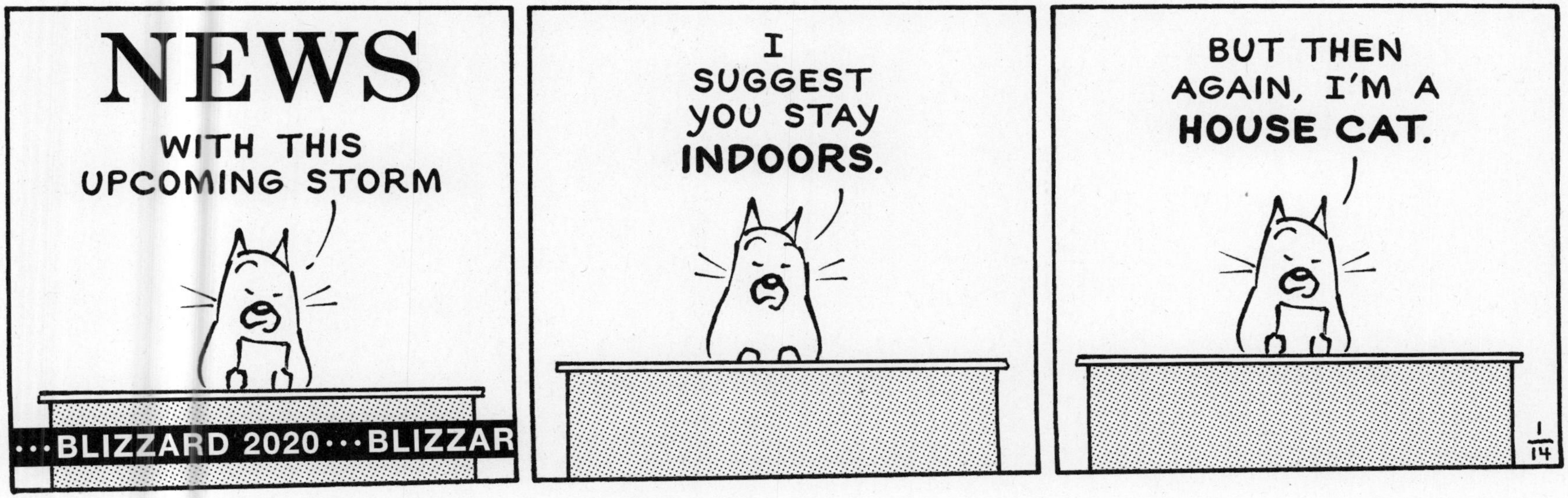
NEWS
WITH THIS UPCOMING STORM
···BLIZZARD 2020···BLIZZAR
I SUGGEST YOU STAY **INDOORS.**
BUT THEN AGAIN, I'M A **HOUSE CAT.**
1/14

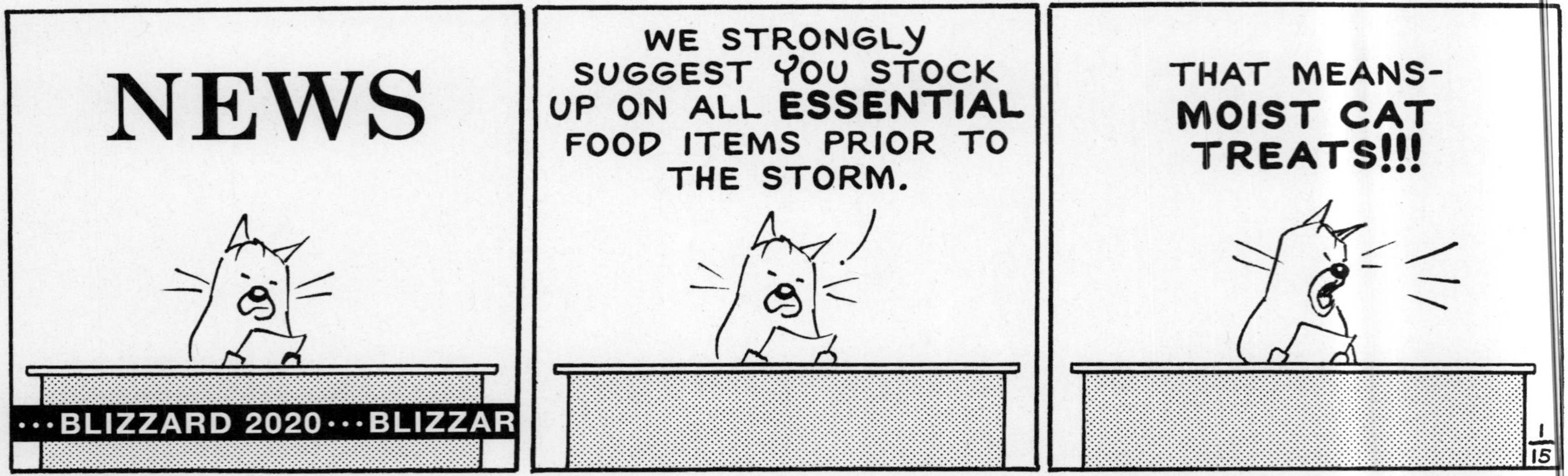
NEWS
•••BLIZZARD 2020•••BLIZZAR
WE STRONGLY SUGGEST YOU STOCK UP ON ALL ESSENTIAL FOOD ITEMS PRIOR TO THE STORM.
THAT MEANS- MOIST CAT TREATS!!!
1/15

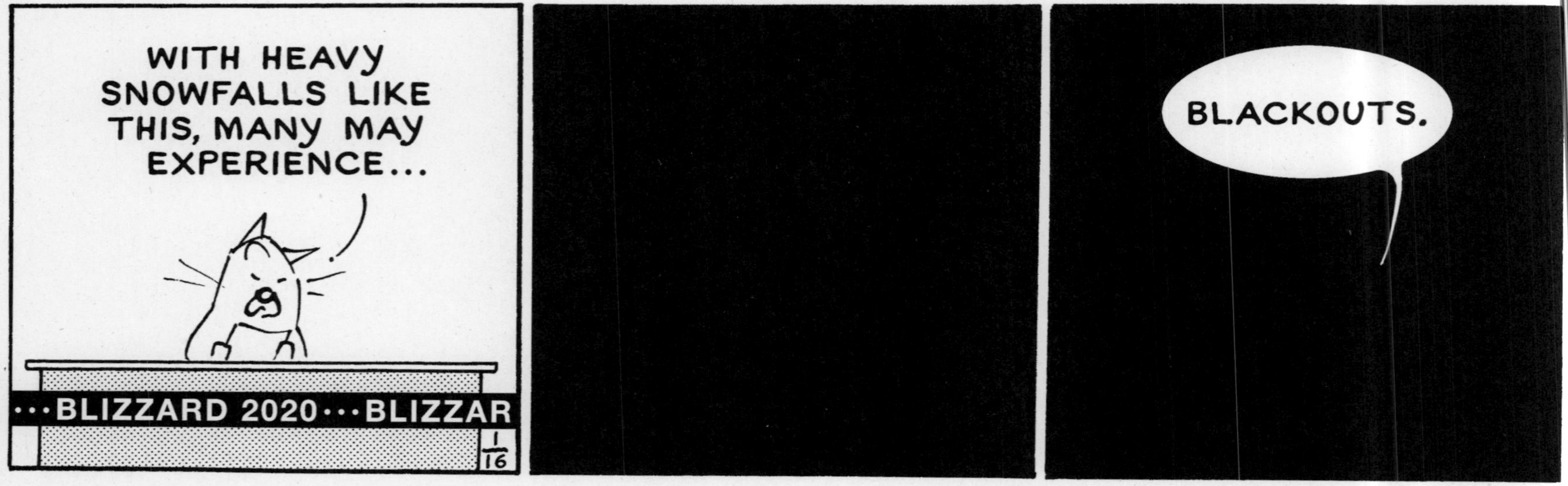
WITH HEAVY SNOWFALLS LIKE THIS, MANY MAY EXPERIENCE...
•••BLIZZARD 2020•••BLIZZAR
1/16
BLACKOUTS.

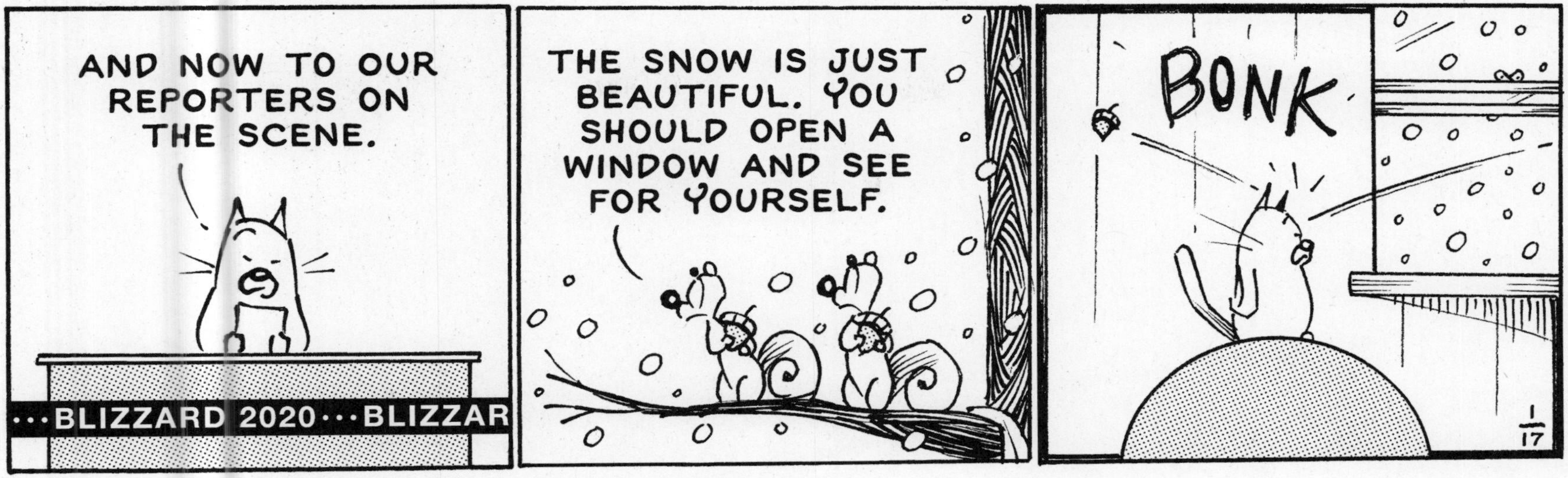
AND NOW TO OUR REPORTERS ON THE SCENE.
...BLIZZARD 2020...BLIZZAR
THE SNOW IS JUST BEAUTIFUL. YOU SHOULD OPEN A WINDOW AND SEE FOR YOURSELF.
BONK
1/17

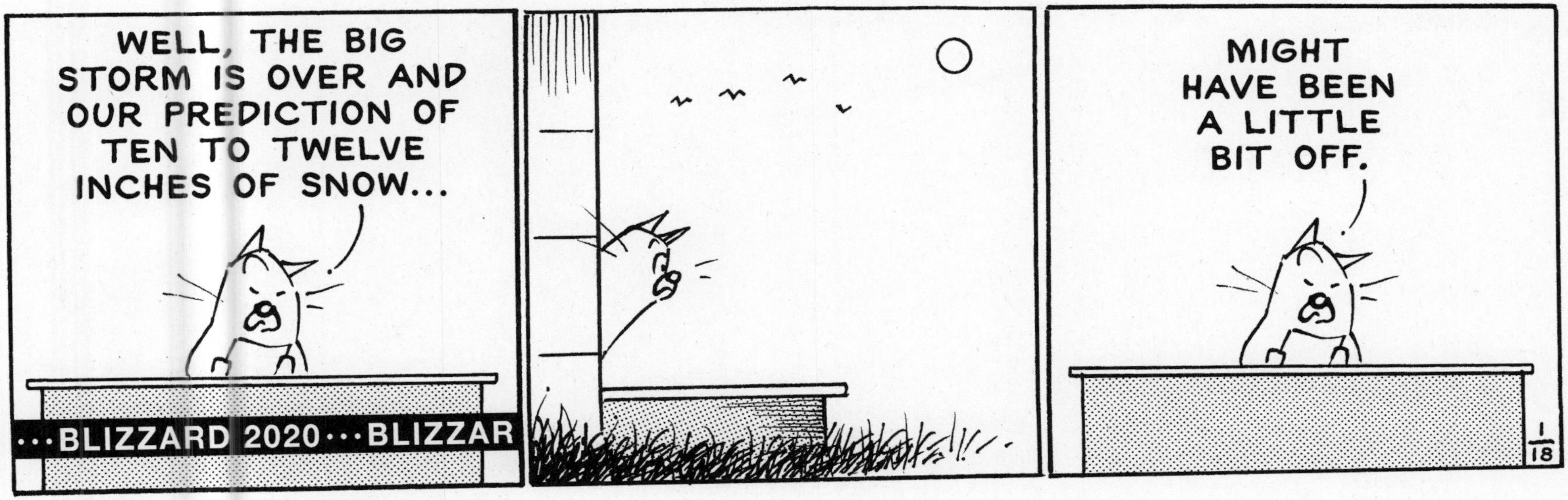
WELL, THE BIG STORM IS OVER AND OUR PREDICTION OF TEN TO TWELVE INCHES OF SNOW...
...BLIZZARD 2020...BLIZZAR
MIGHT HAVE BEEN A LITTLE BIT OFF.
1/18

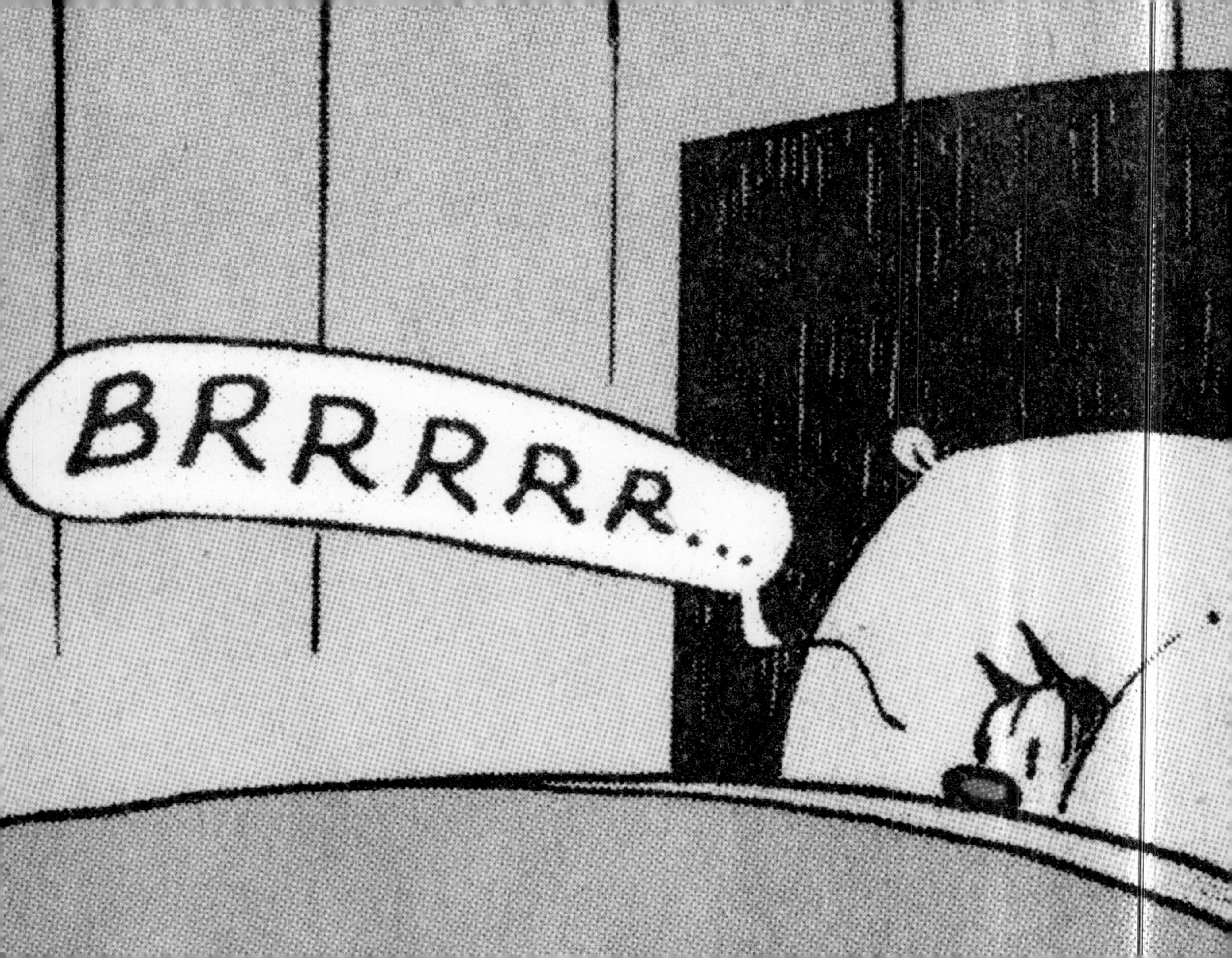
BRRRRRR...

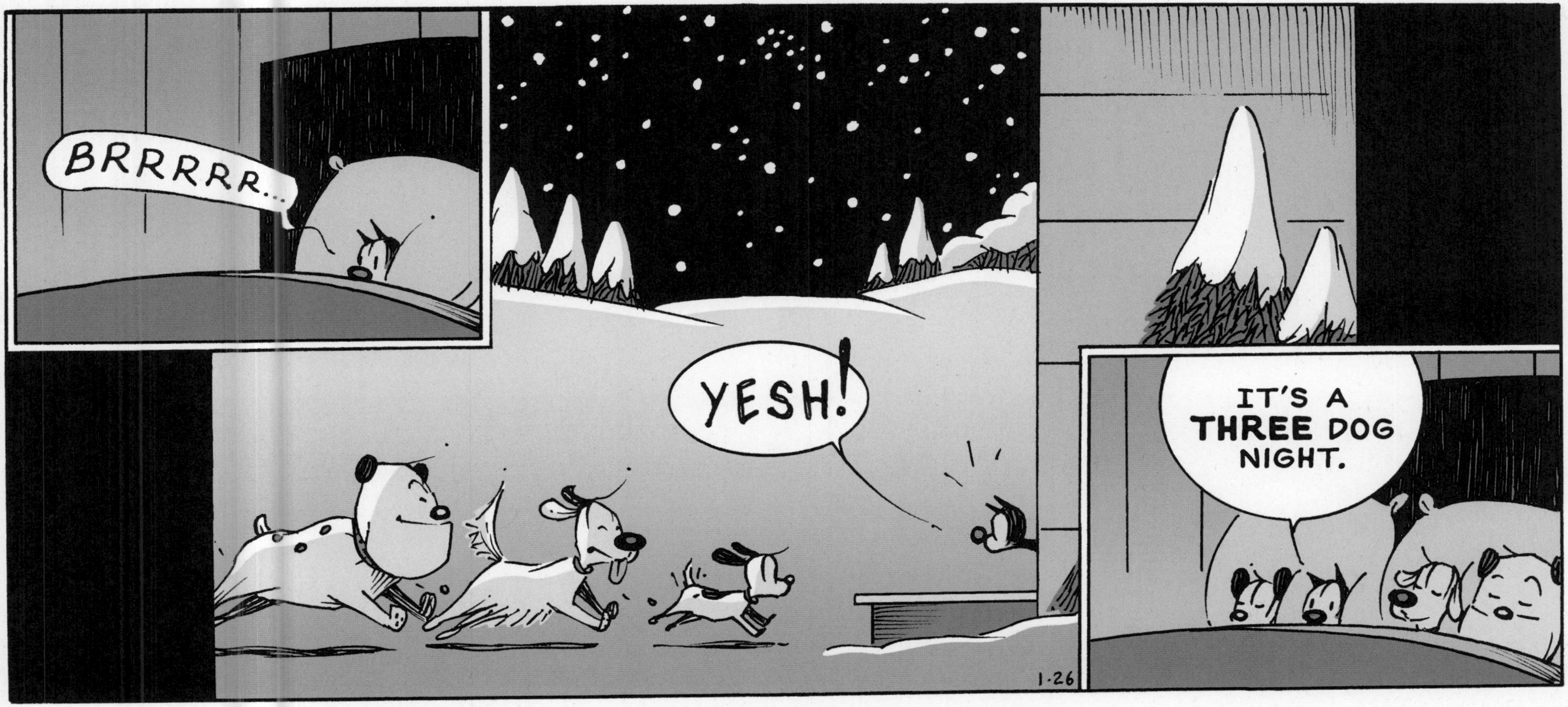
BRRRRRR...
YESH!
IT'S A **THREE** DOG NIGHT.
1·26

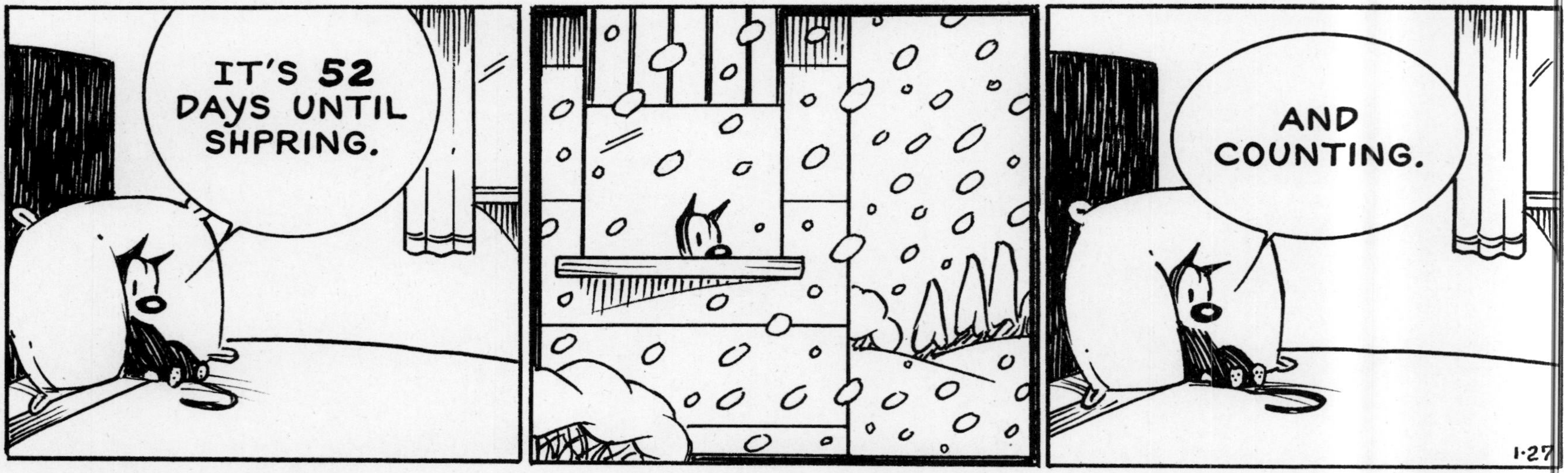
IT'S 52 DAYS UNTIL SHPRING.
AND COUNTING.
1·27

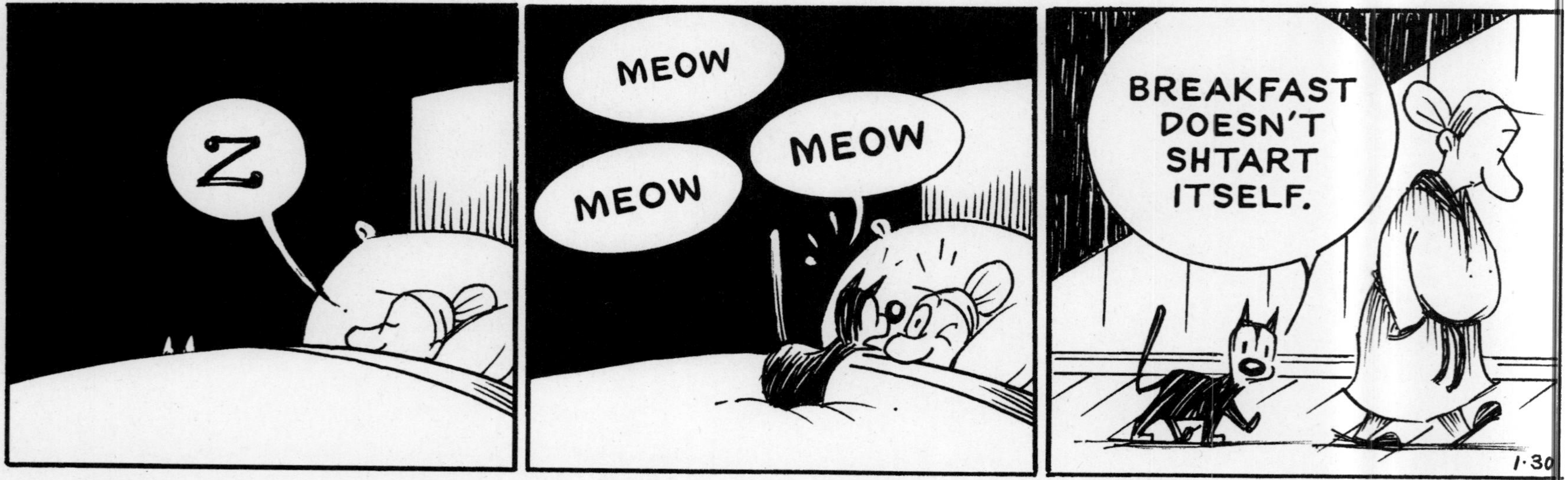
Z
MEOW
MEOW
MEOW
BREAKFAST DOESN'T SHTART ITSELF.
1·30

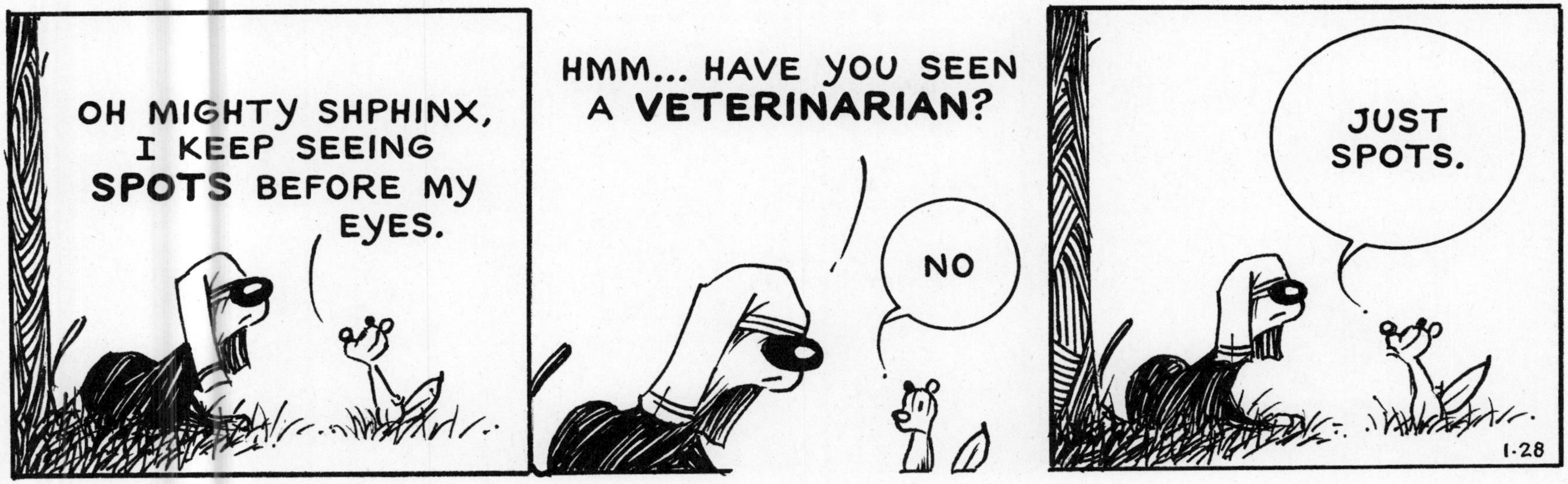
OH MIGHTY SHPHINX, I KEEP SEEING SPOTS BEFORE MY EYES.
HMM... HAVE YOU SEEN A VETERINARIAN?
NO
JUST SPOTS.
1-28

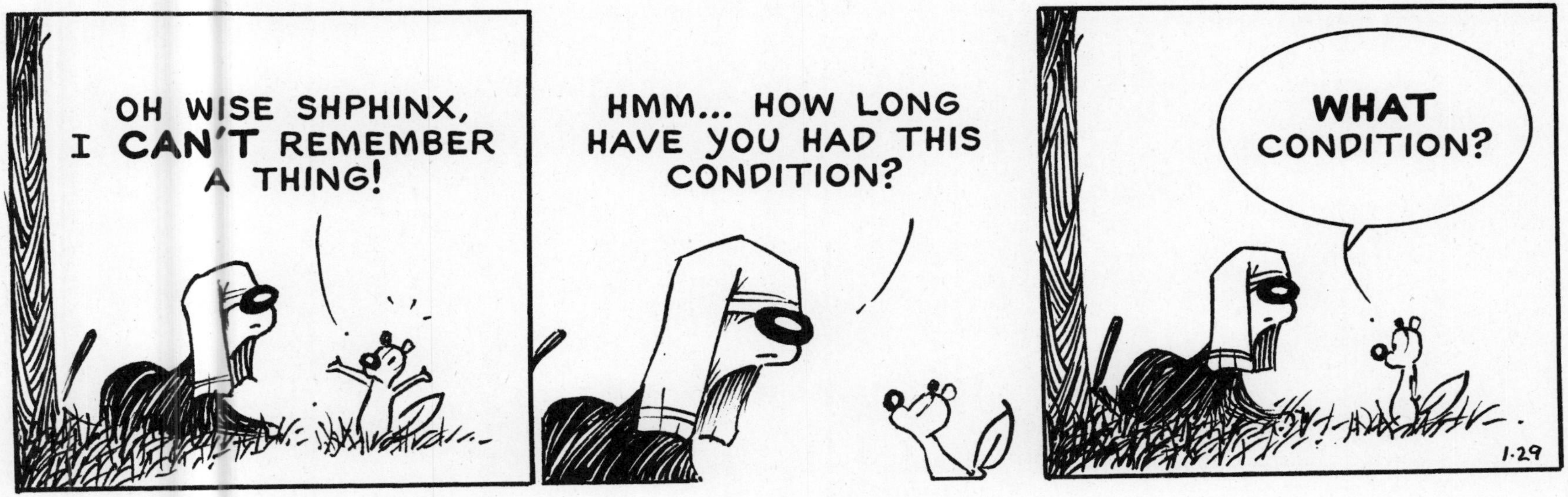
OH WISE SHPHINX, I CAN'T REMEMBER A THING!
HMM... HOW LONG HAVE YOU HAD THIS CONDITION?
WHAT CONDITION?
1-29

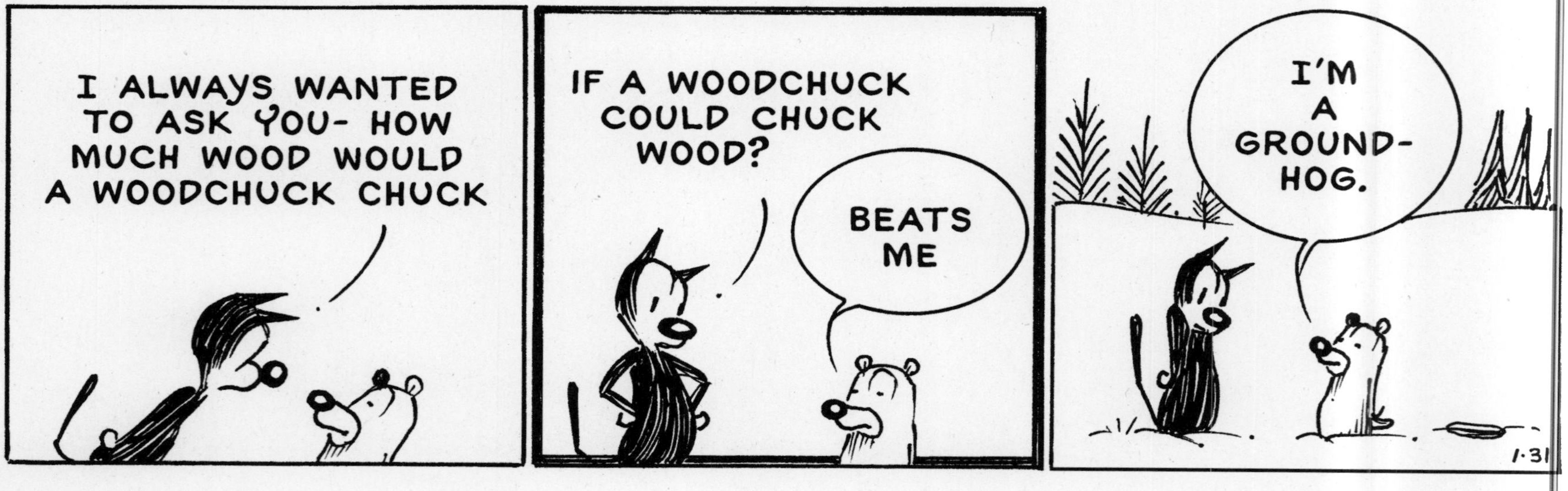
I ALWAYS WANTED TO ASK YOU- HOW MUCH WOOD WOULD A WOODCHUCK CHUCK
IF A WOODCHUCK COULD CHUCK WOOD?
BEATS ME
I'M A GROUND-HOG.
1·31

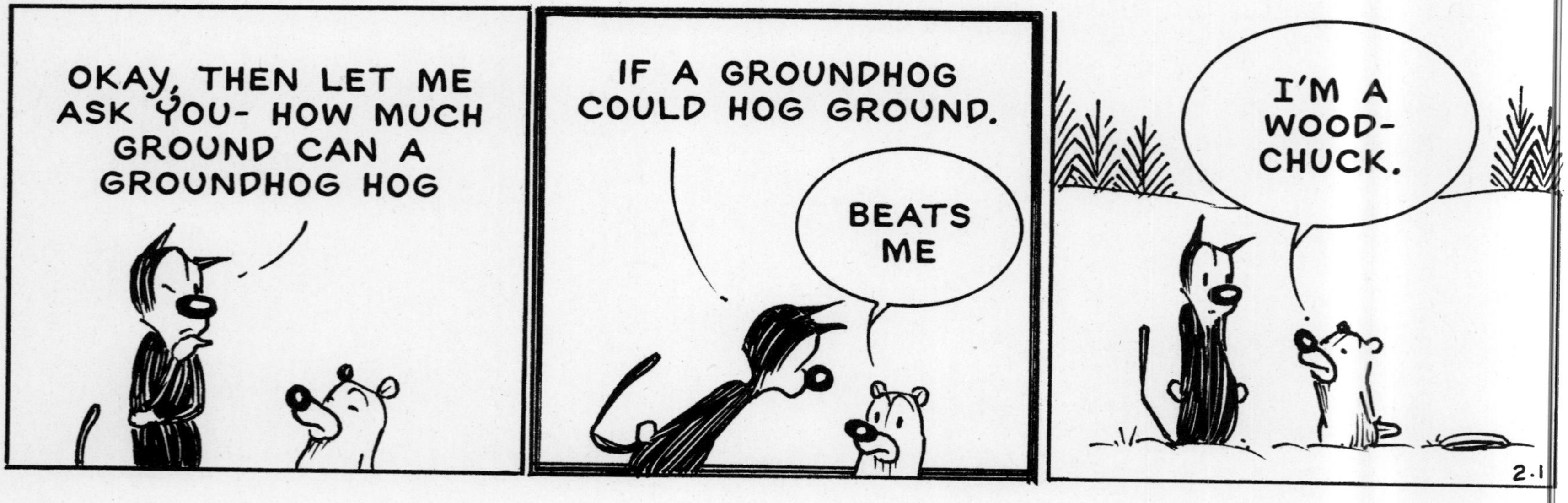
OKAY, THEN LET ME ASK YOU- HOW MUCH GROUND CAN A GROUNDHOG HOG
IF A GROUNDHOG COULD HOG GROUND.
BEATS ME
I'M A WOOD-CHUCK.
2·1

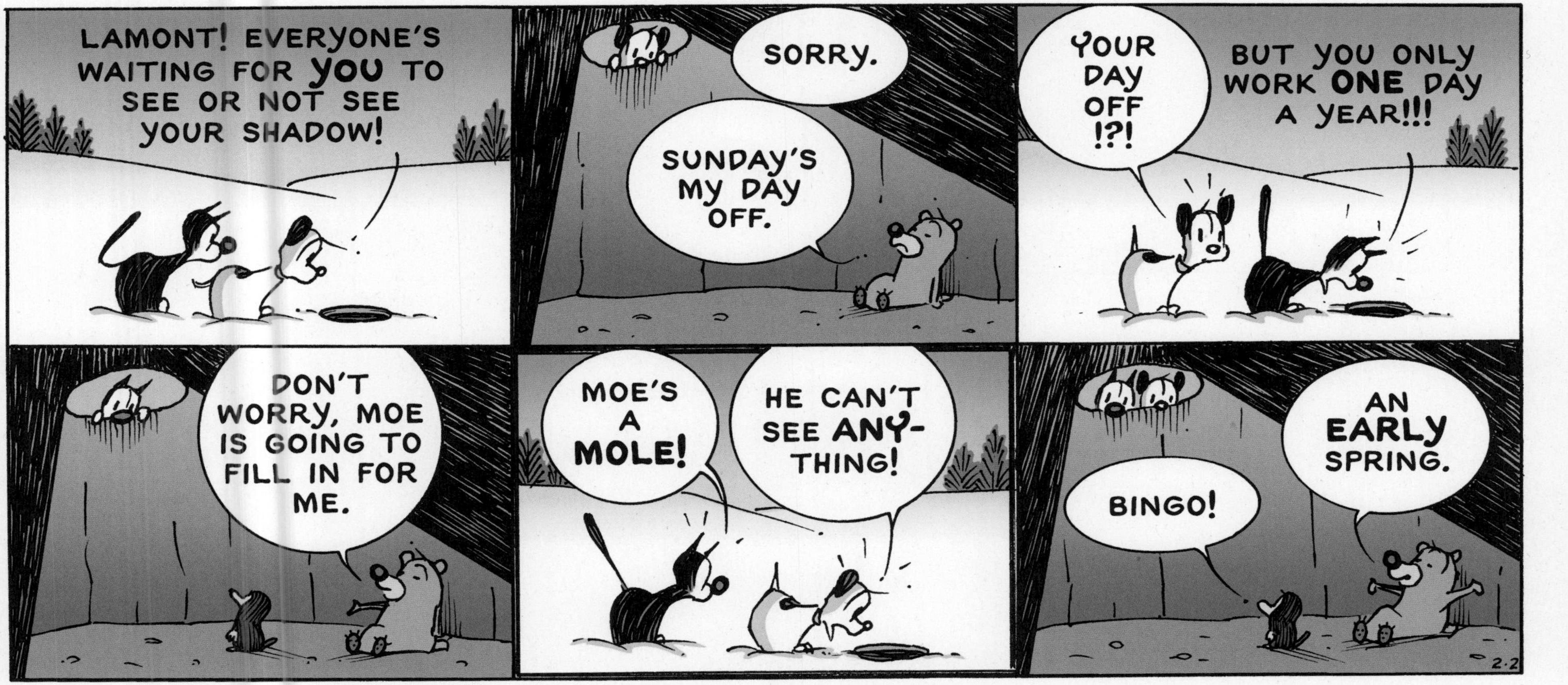
LAMONT! EVERYONE'S WAITING FOR YOU TO SEE OR NOT SEE YOUR SHADOW!
SORRY.
SUNDAY'S MY DAY OFF.
YOUR DAY OFF !?!
BUT YOU ONLY WORK ONE DAY A YEAR!!!
DON'T WORRY, MOE IS GOING TO FILL IN FOR ME.
MOE'S A MOLE!
HE CAN'T SEE ANY-THING!
BINGO!
AN EARLY SPRING.
2·2

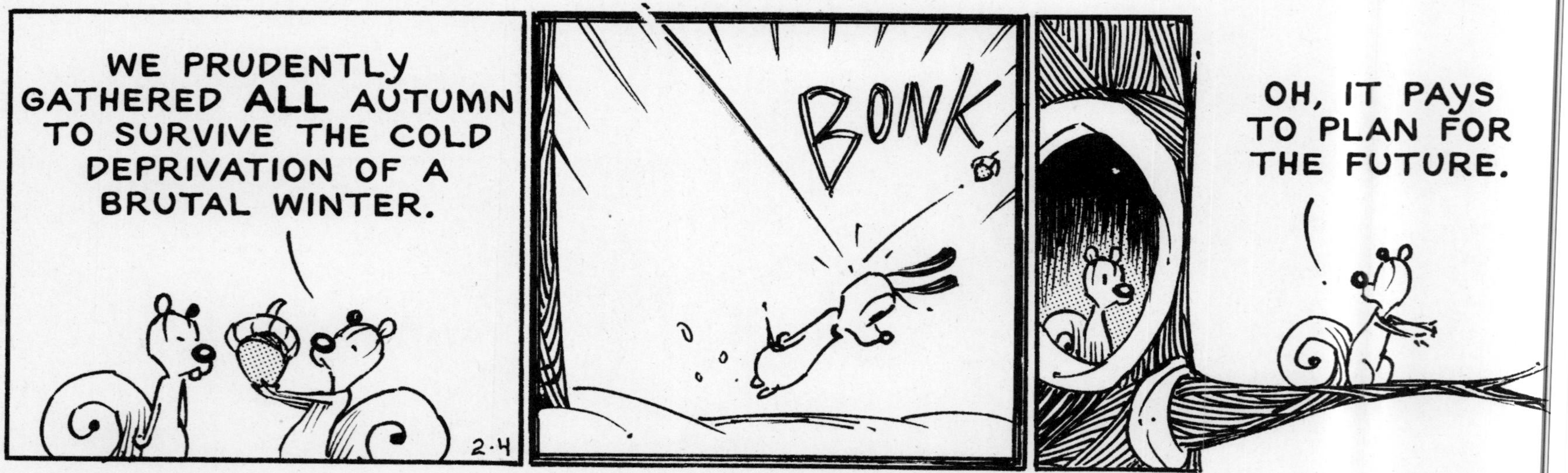
WE PRUDENTLY GATHERED ALL AUTUMN TO SURVIVE THE COLD DEPRIVATION OF A BRUTAL WINTER.
2·4
BONK
OH, IT PAYS TO PLAN FOR THE FUTURE.

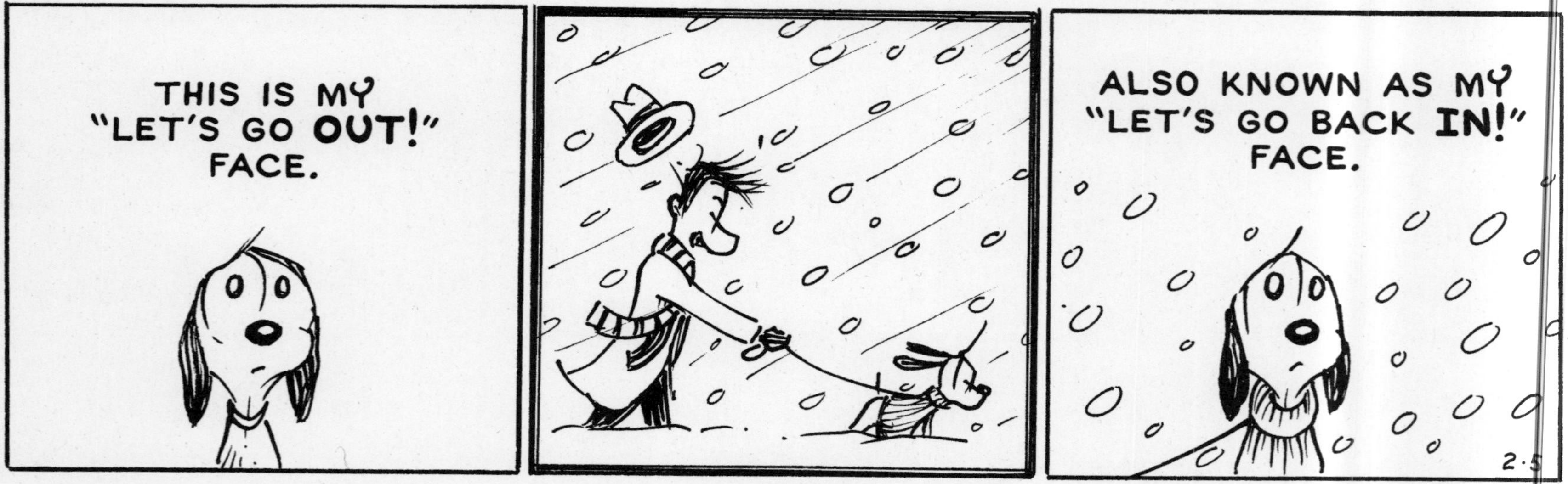
THIS IS MY "LET'S GO OUT!" FACE.
ALSO KNOWN AS MY "LET'S GO BACK IN!" FACE.
2·5

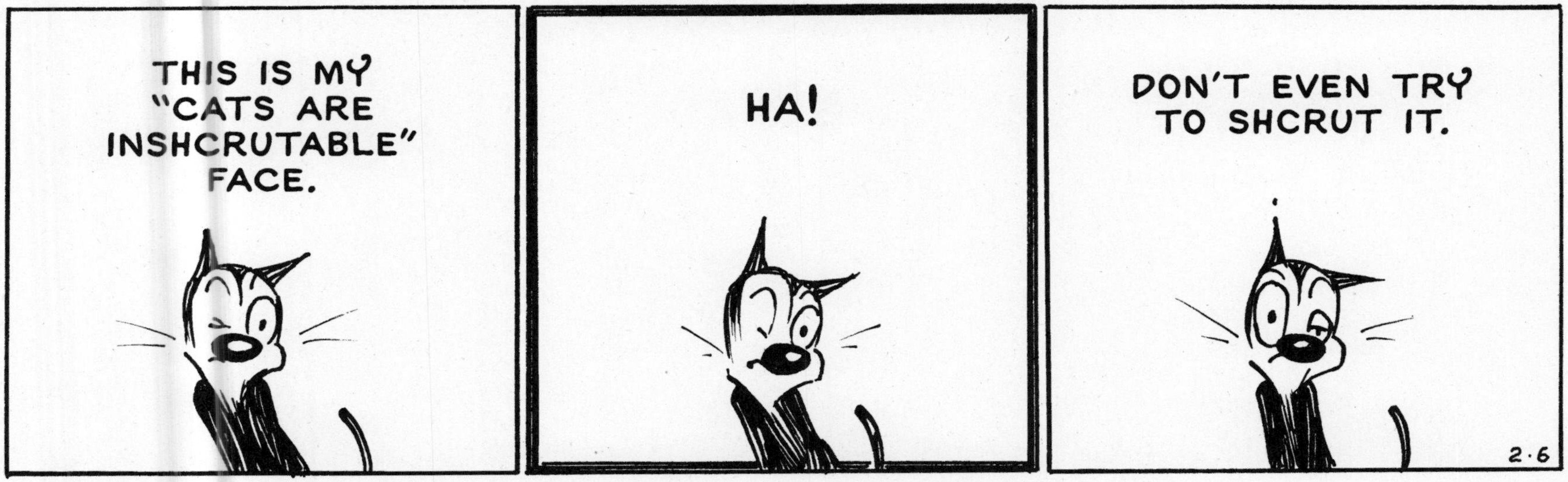
THIS IS MY "CATS ARE INSHCRUTABLE" FACE.
HA!
DON'T EVEN TRY TO SHCRUT IT.
2·6

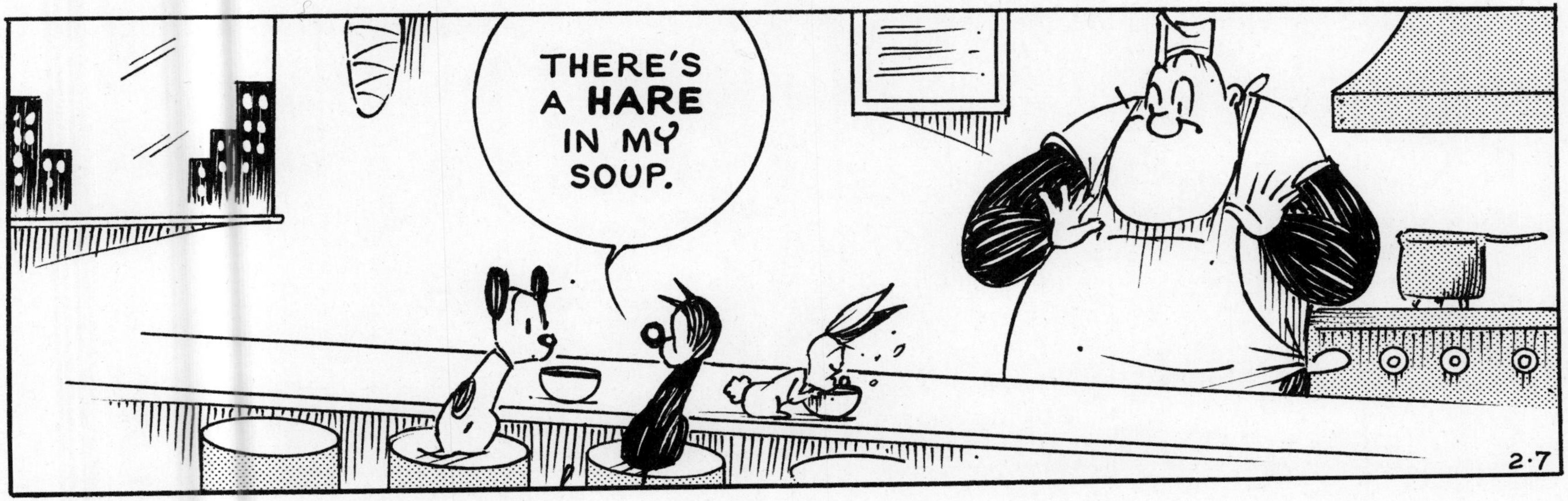
THERE'S A **HARE** IN MY SOUP.
2·7

MUTTS

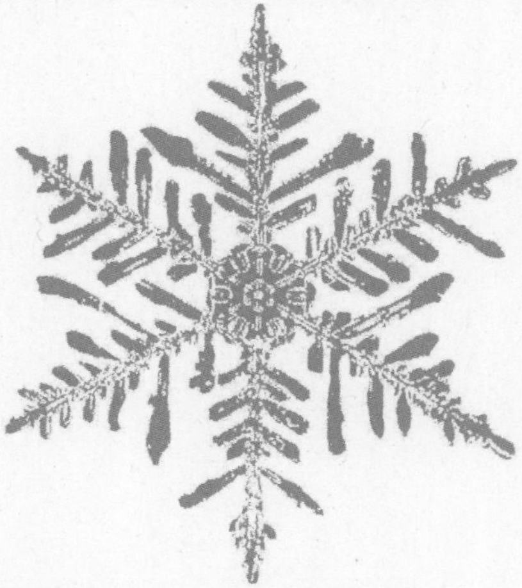

Patrick McDonnell

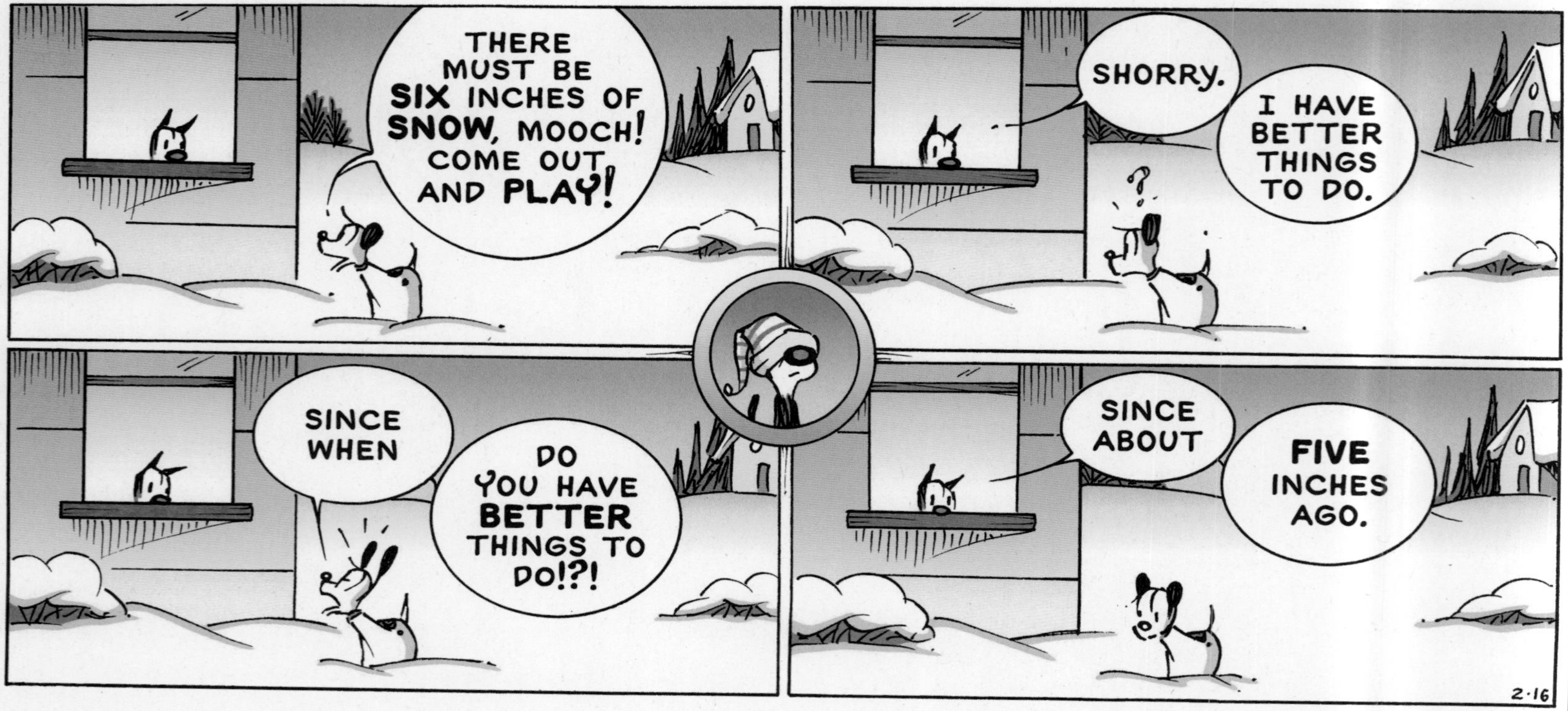
THERE MUST BE SIX INCHES OF SNOW, MOOCH! COME OUT AND PLAY!
SHORRY.
I HAVE BETTER THINGS TO DO.
?
SINCE WHEN
DO YOU HAVE BETTER THINGS TO DO!?!
SINCE ABOUT
FIVE INCHES AGO.
2·16

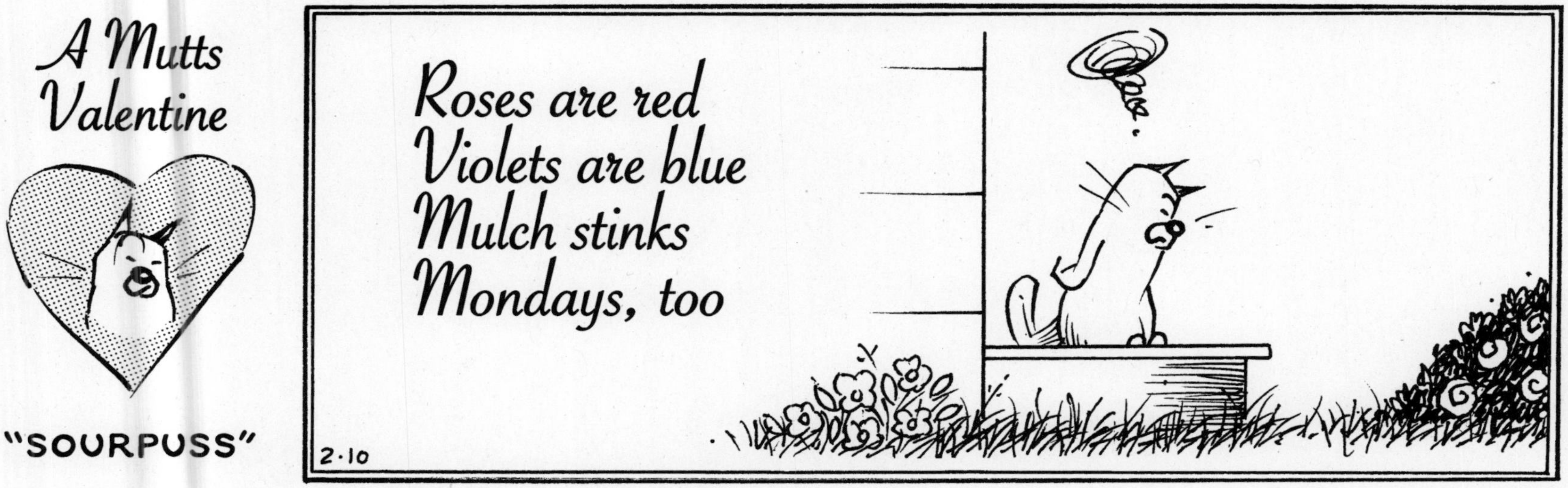
A Mutts Valentine
"SOURPUSS"
Roses are red
Violets are blue
Mulch stinks
Mondays, too
2·10

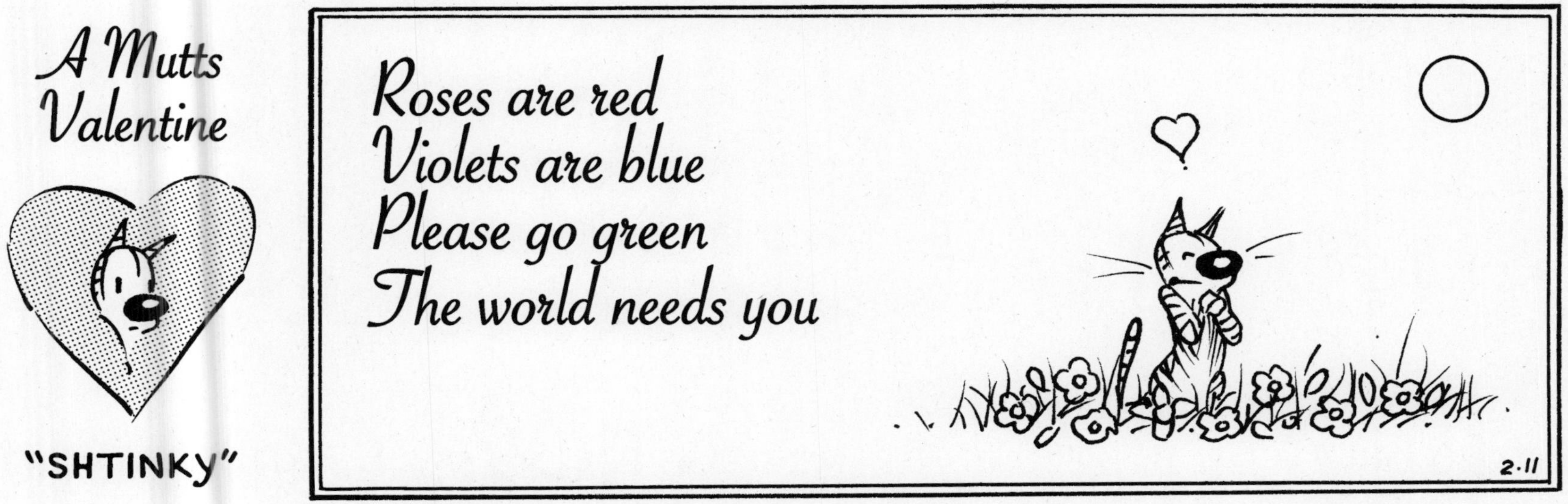
A Mutts Valentine
"SHTINKY"
Roses are red
Violets are blue
Please go green
The world needs you
2·11

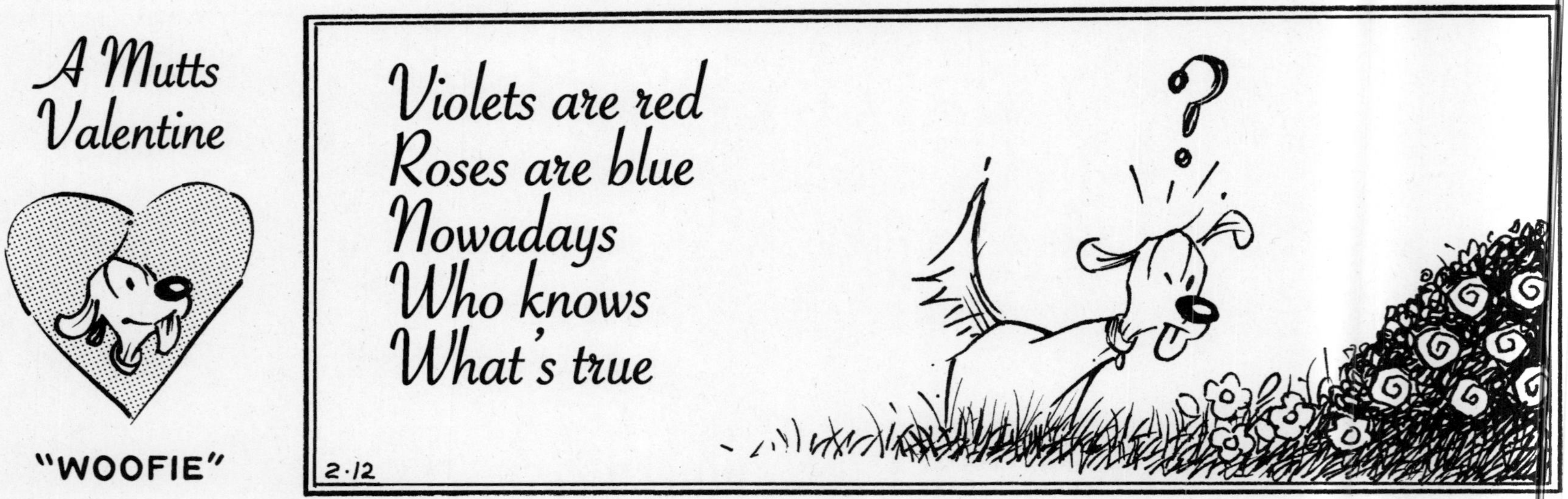
A Mutts Valentine
"WOOFIE"
Violets are red
Roses are blue
Nowadays
Who knows
What's true
2·12

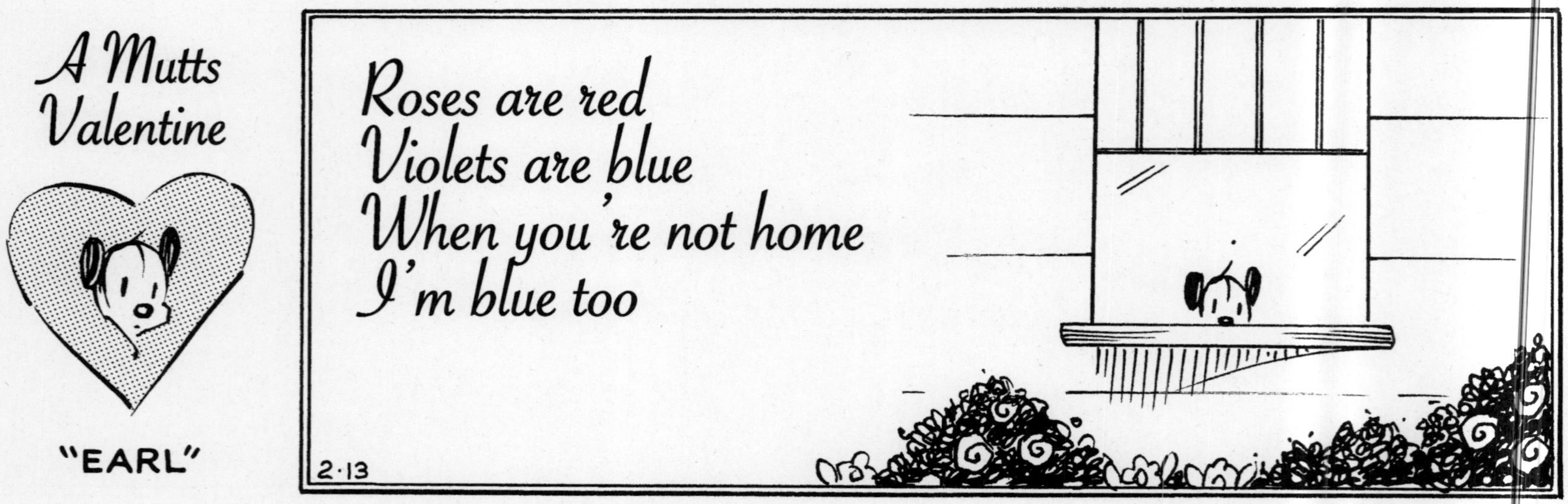
A Mutts Valentine
"EARL"
Roses are red
Violets are blue
When you're not home
I'm blue too
2·13

A Mutts Valentine

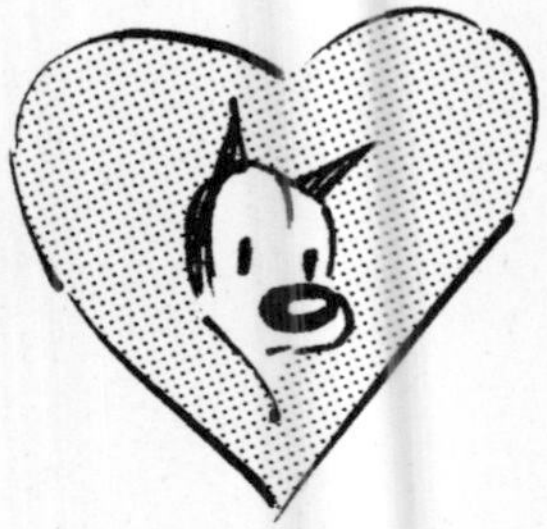

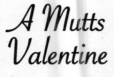

"MOOCH"

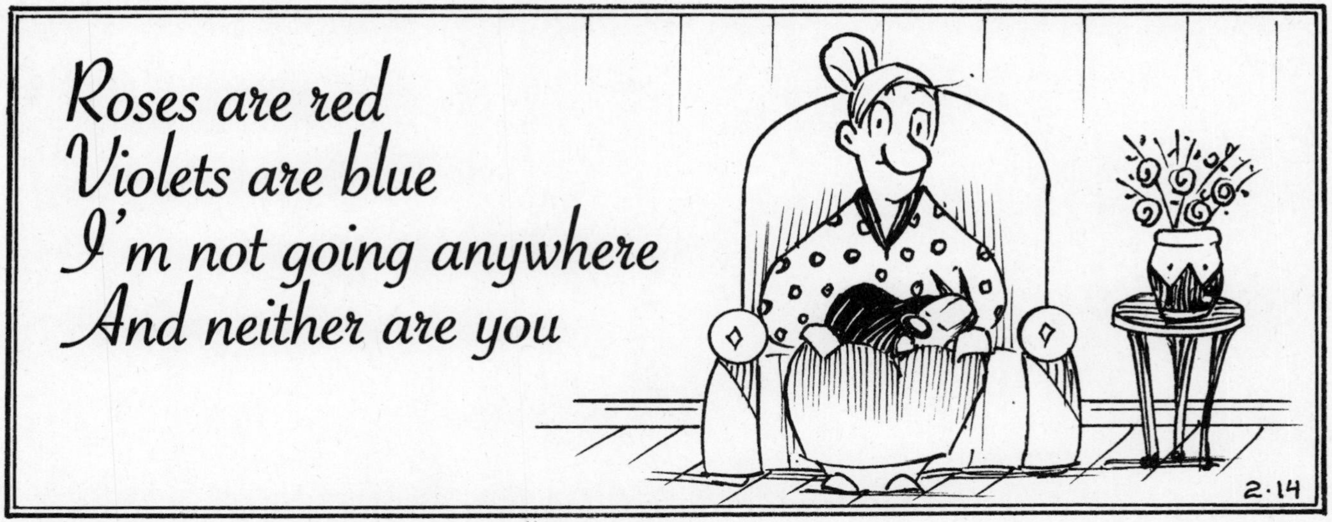
Roses are red
Violets are blue
I'm not going anywhere
And neither are you
2.14

A Mutts Valentine

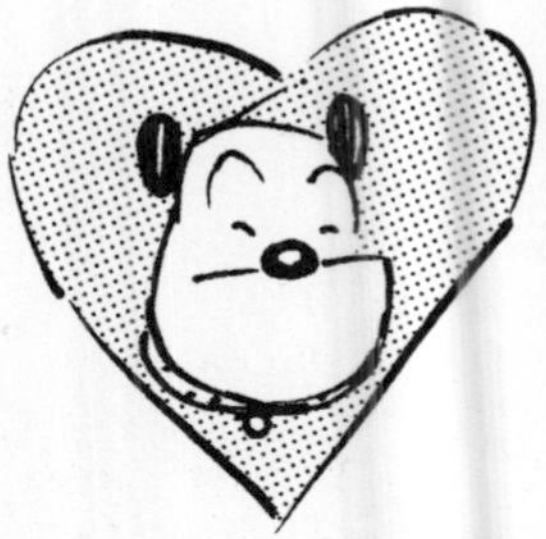

"GUARD DOG"

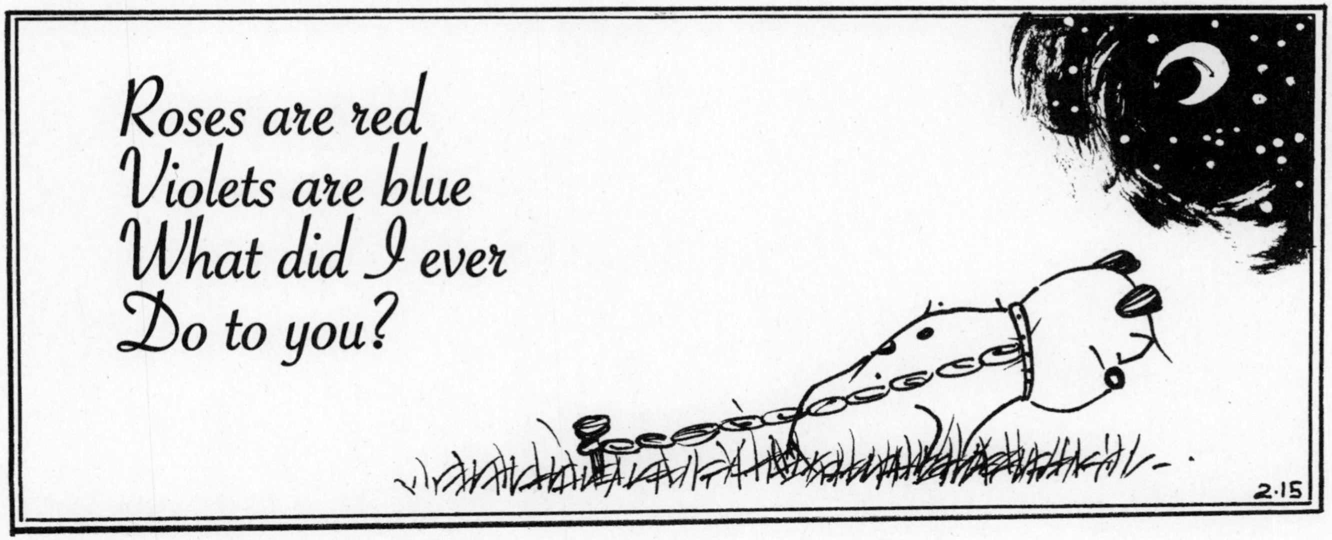
Roses are red
Violets are blue
What did I ever
Do to you?
2.15

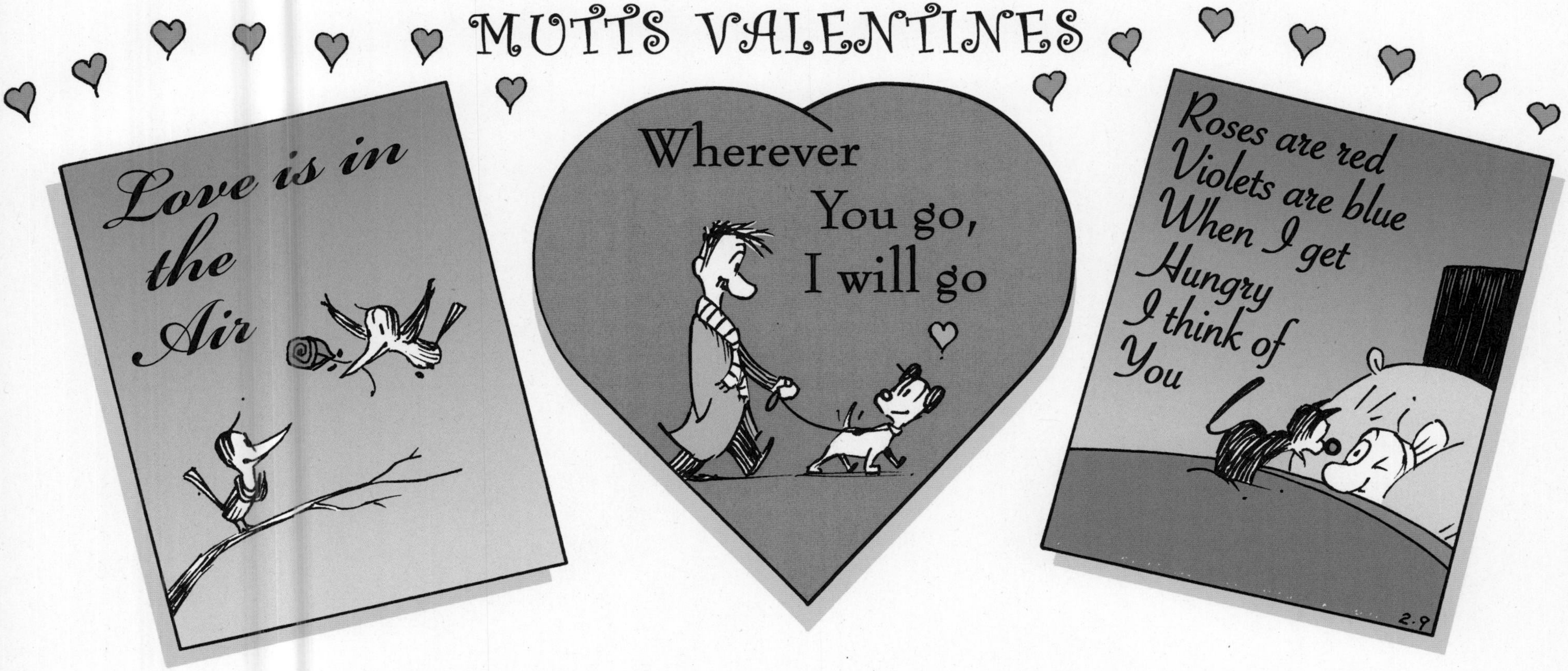
MUTTS VALENTINES
Love is in the Air
Wherever You go, I will go
Roses are red
Violets are blue
When I get
Hungry
I think of
You
2.9

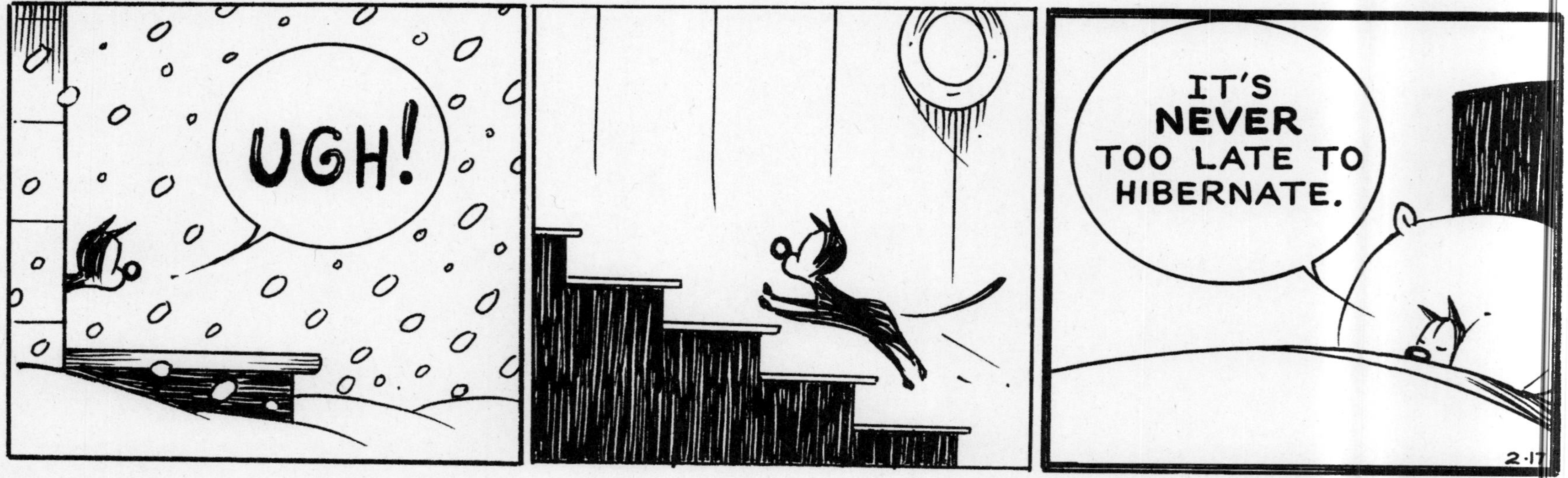
UGH!
IT'S NEVER TOO LATE TO HIBERNATE.
2·17

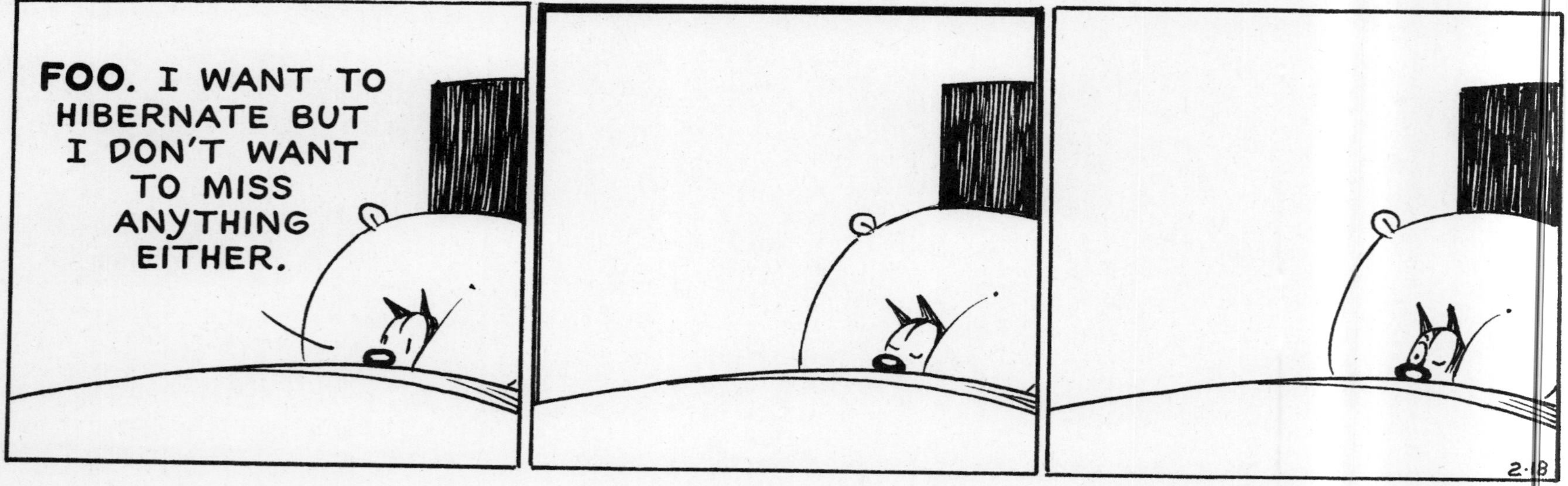
FOO. I WANT TO HIBERNATE BUT I DON'T WANT TO MISS ANYTHING EITHER.
2·18

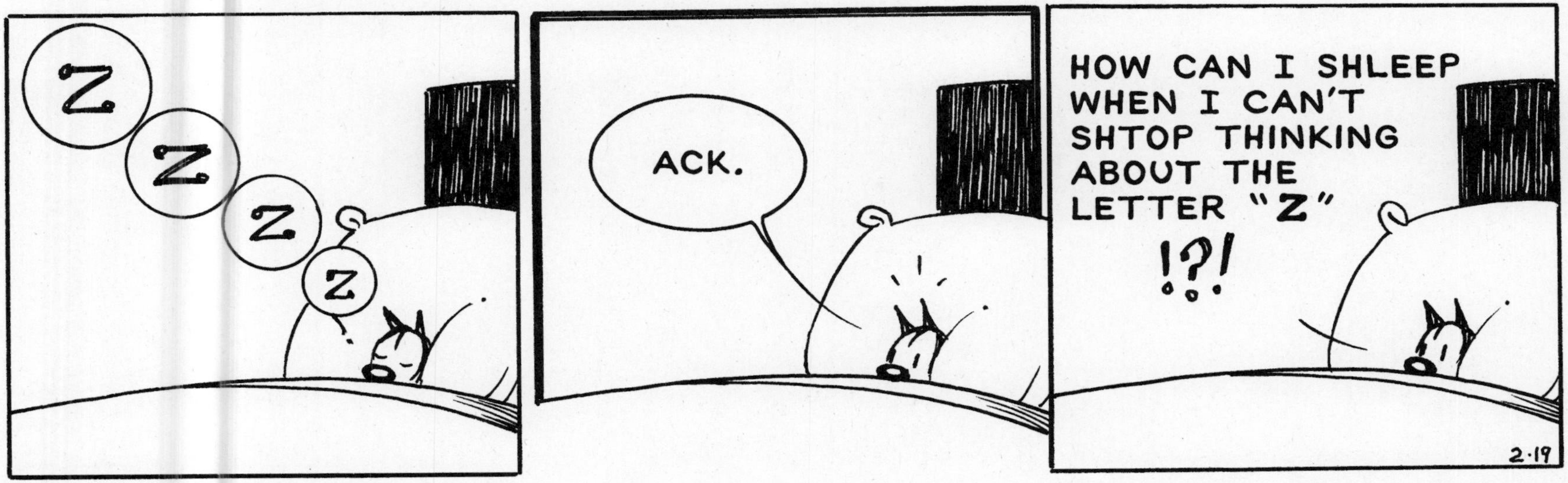
Z
Z
Z
Z
ACK.
HOW CAN I SHLEEP WHEN I CAN'T SHTOP THINKING ABOUT THE LETTER "Z"
!?!
2·19

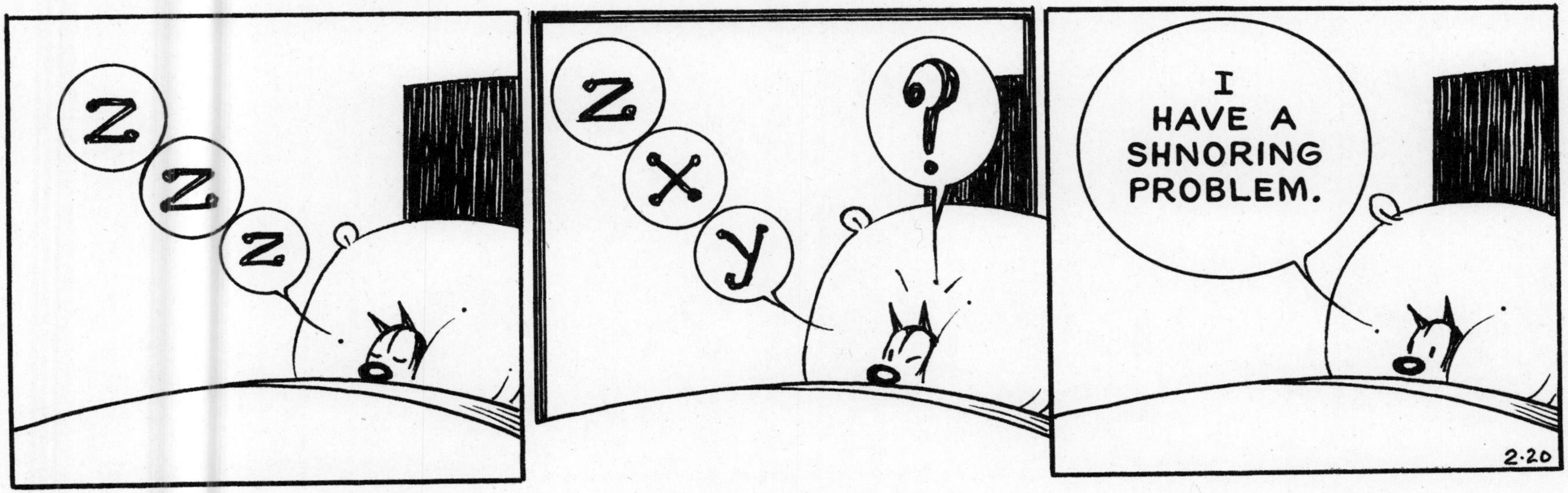
Z
Z
Z
Z
X
Y
?
I HAVE A SHNORING PROBLEM.
2·20

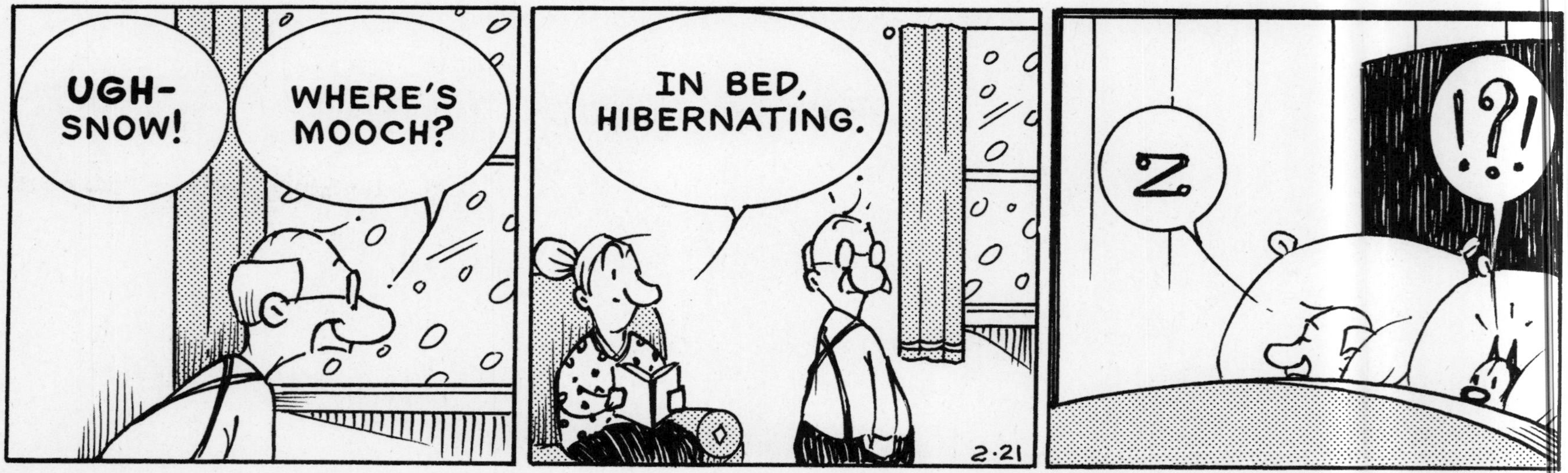
UGH-
SNOW!
WHERE'S
MOOCH?
IN BED,
HIBERNATING.
2·21
Z
!?!

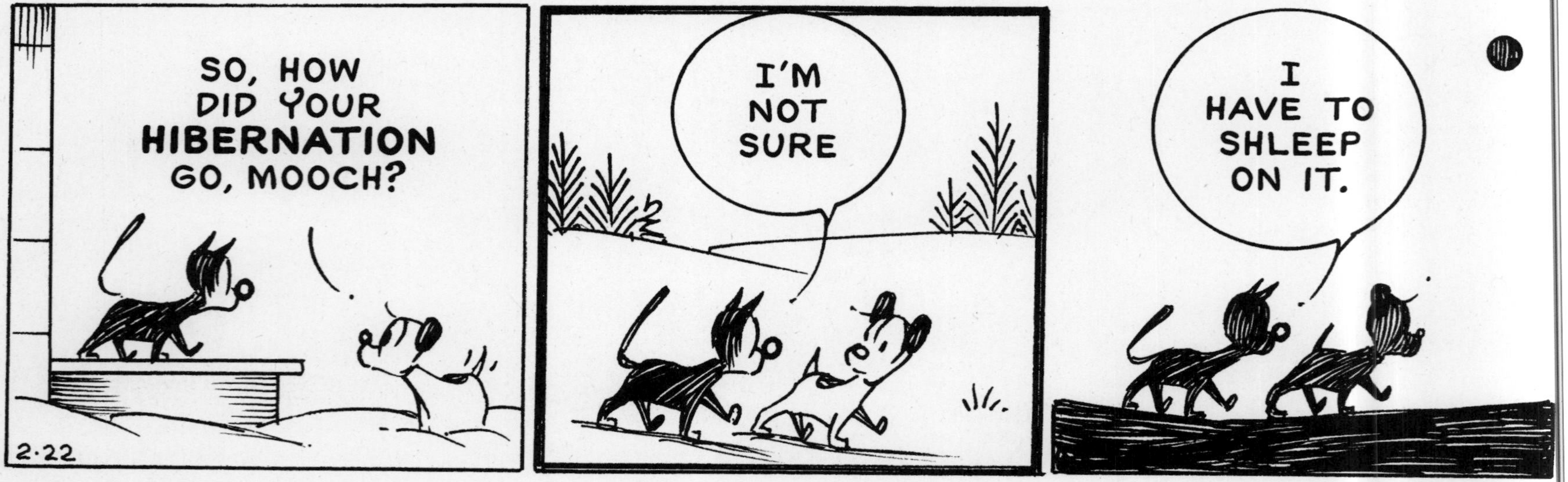
SO, HOW
DID YOUR
HIBERNATION
GO, MOOCH?
2·22
I'M
NOT
SURE
I
HAVE TO
SHLEEP
ON IT.

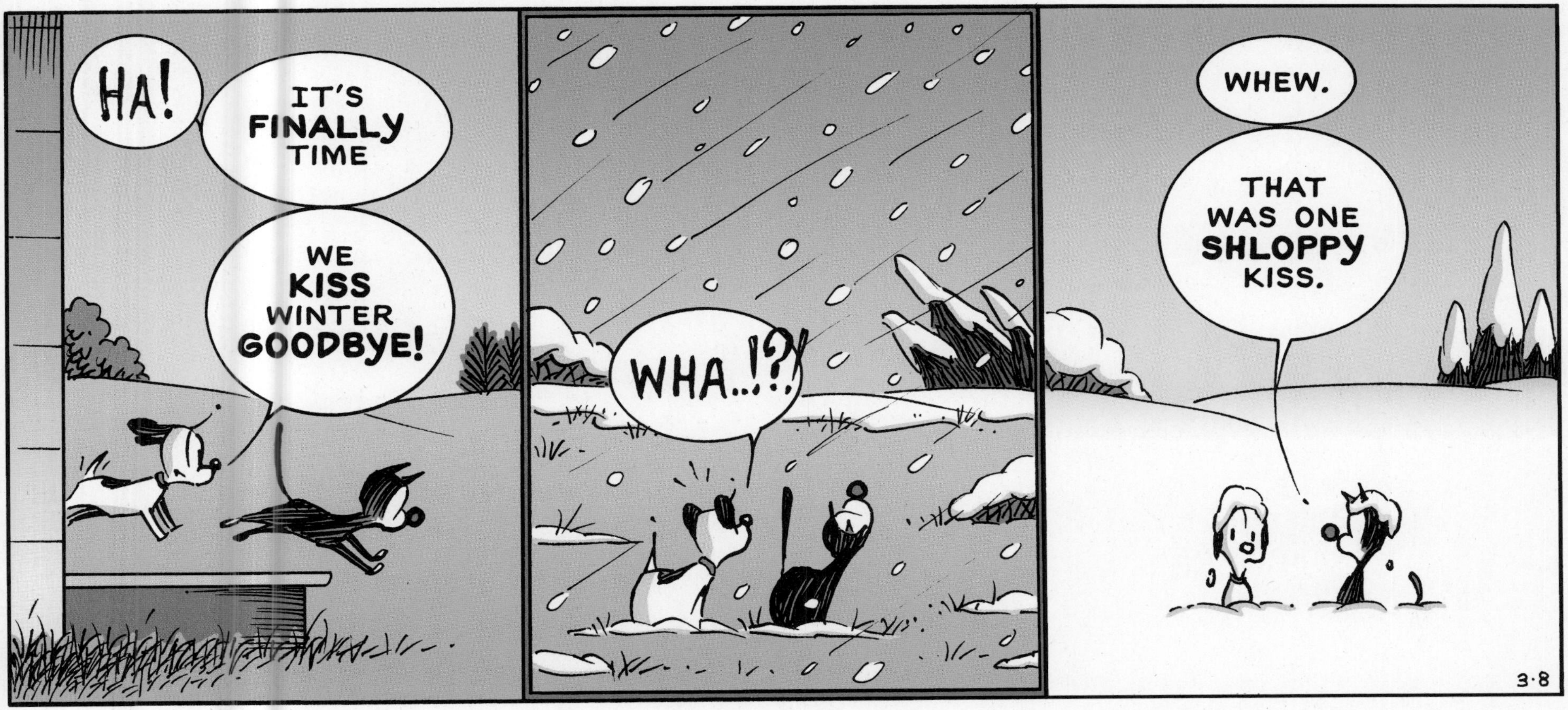
HA!
IT'S FINALLY TIME
WE KISS WINTER GOODBYE!
WHA..!?!
WHEW.
THAT WAS ONE SHLOPPY KISS.
3·8

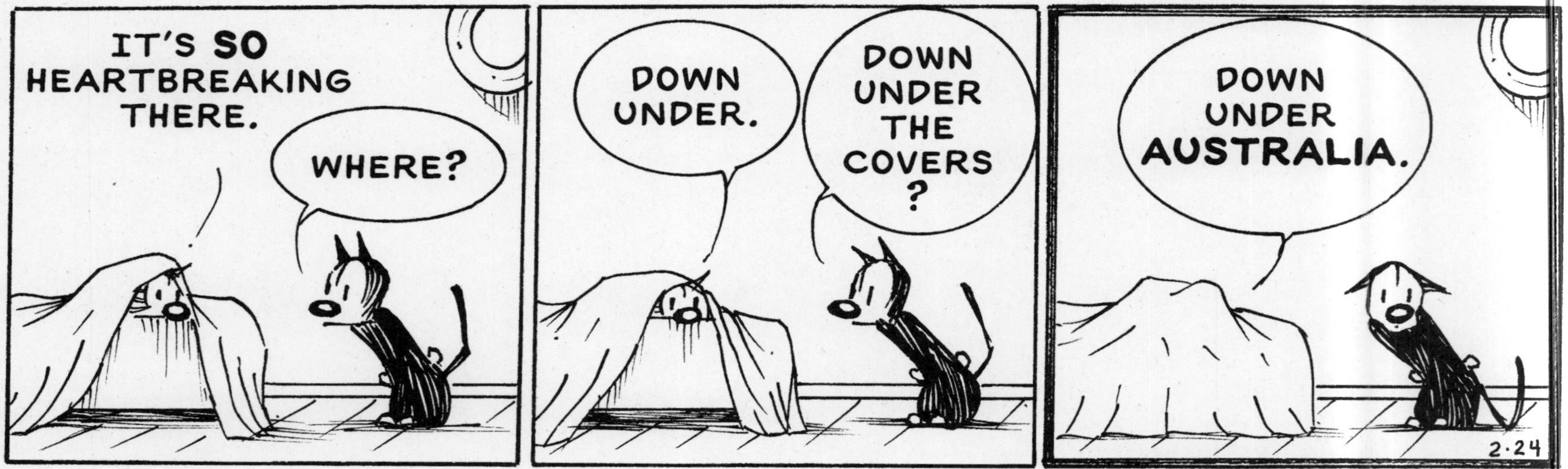
IT'S SO HEARTBREAKING THERE.
WHERE?
DOWN UNDER.
DOWN UNDER THE COVERS ?
DOWN UNDER AUSTRALIA.
2·24

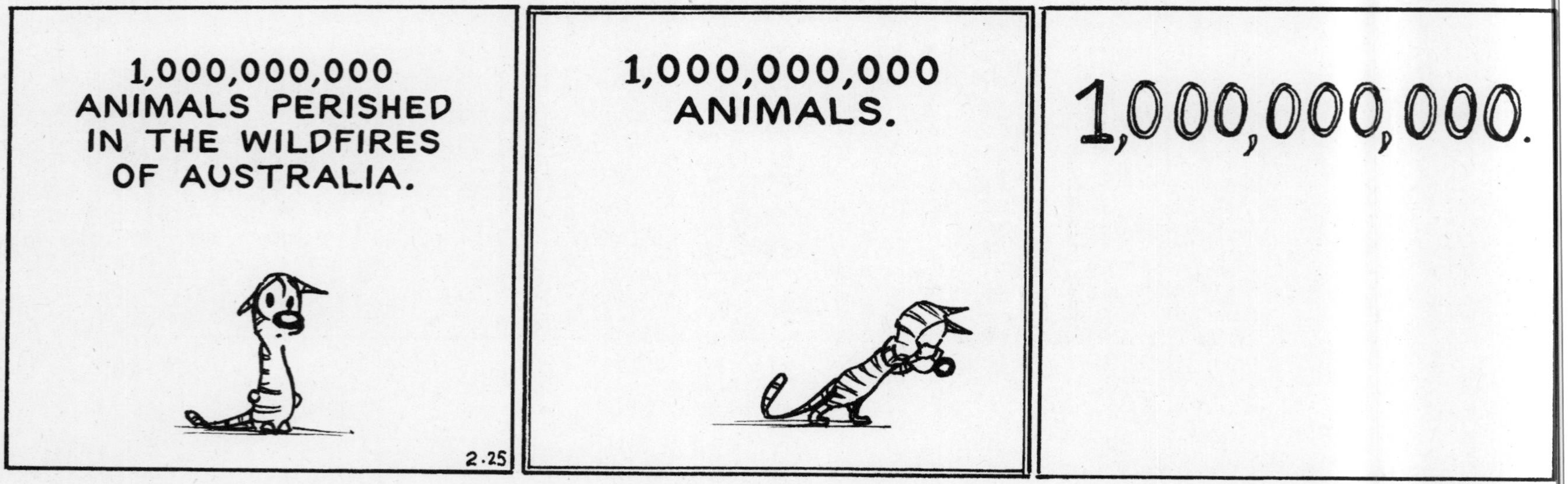
1,000,000,000 ANIMALS PERISHED IN THE WILDFIRES OF AUSTRALIA.
2·25
1,000,000,000 ANIMALS.
1,000,000,000.

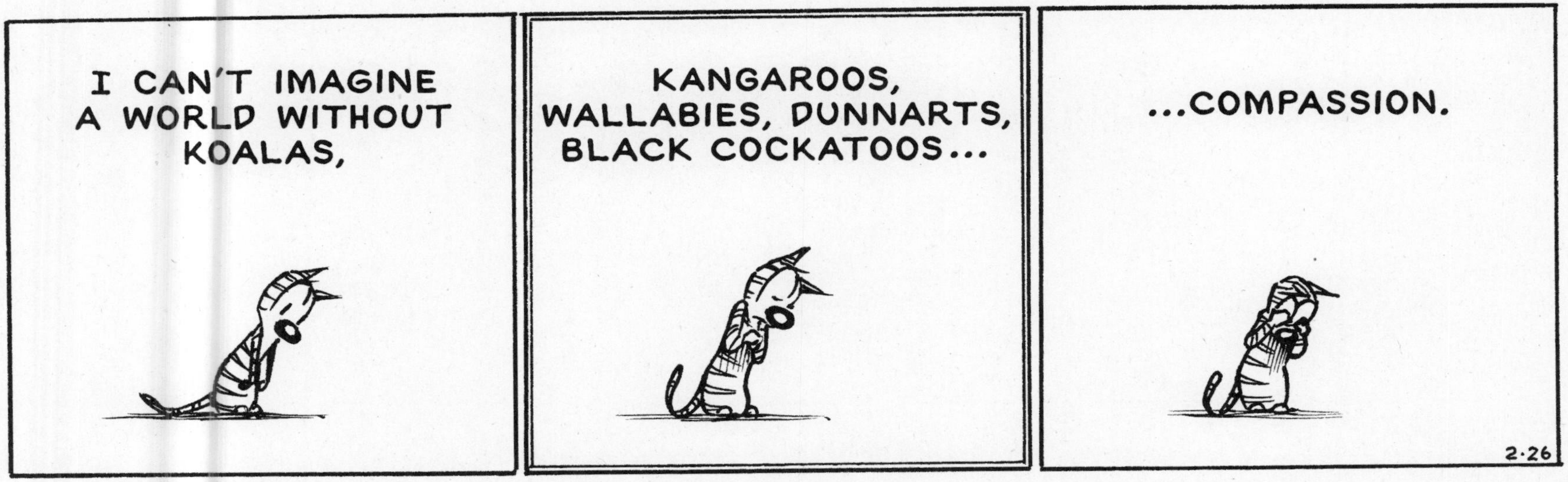
I CAN'T IMAGINE A WORLD WITHOUT KOALAS,
KANGAROOS, WALLABIES, DUNNARTS, BLACK COCKATOOS...
...COMPASSION.
2·26

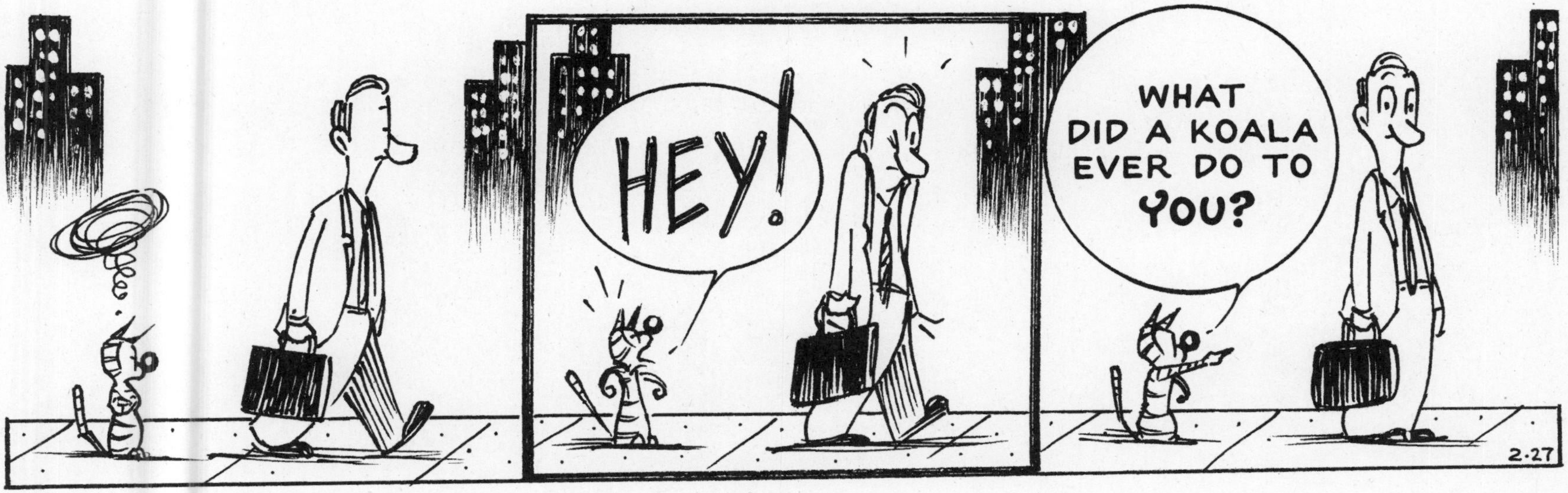
HEY!
WHAT DID A KOALA EVER DO TO YOU?
2·27

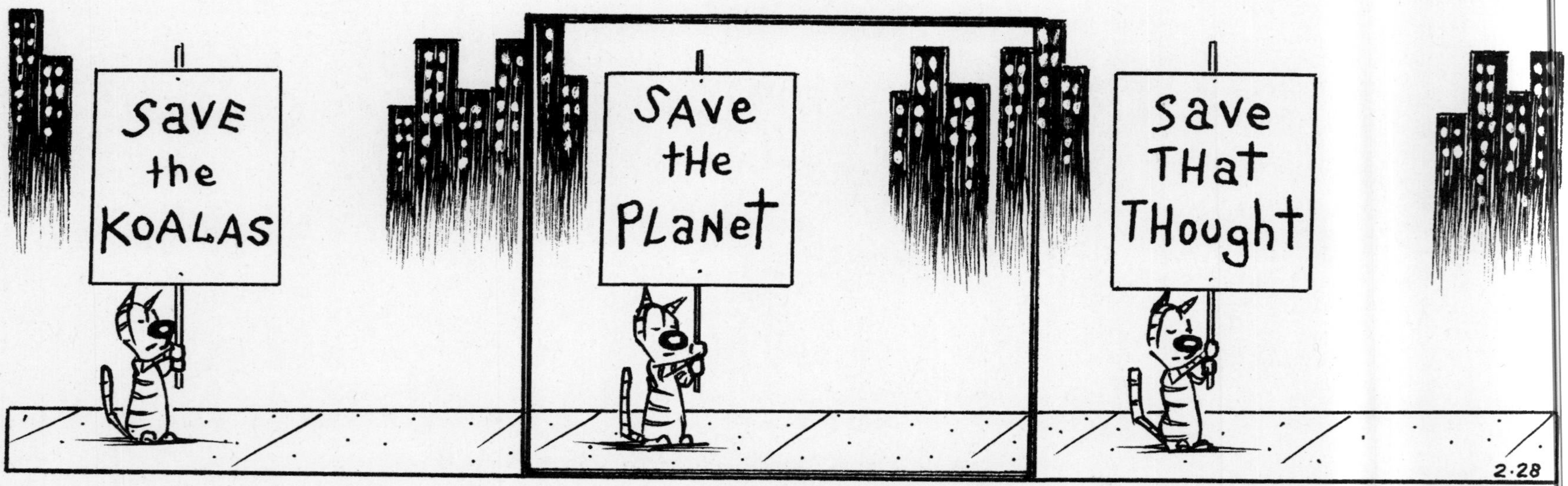
Save the KOALAS
Save the Planet
Save That Thought
2·28

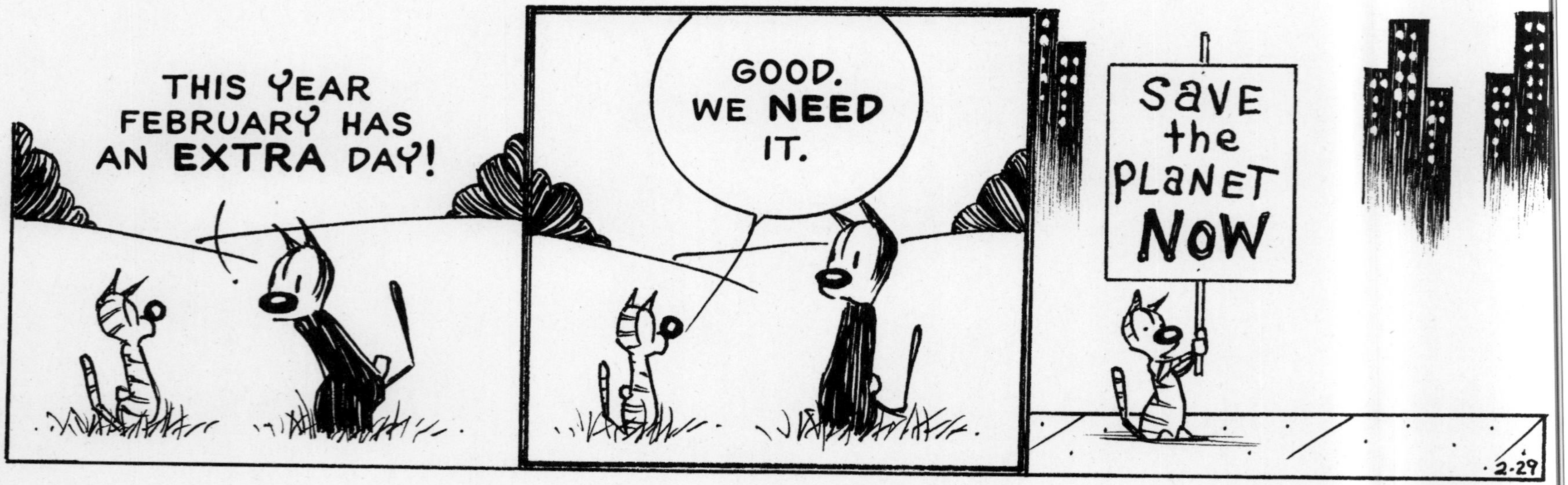
THIS YEAR FEBRUARY HAS AN **EXTRA** DAY!
GOOD. WE **NEED** IT.
Save the PLANET NOW
2·29

MUTTS
Patrick McDonnell

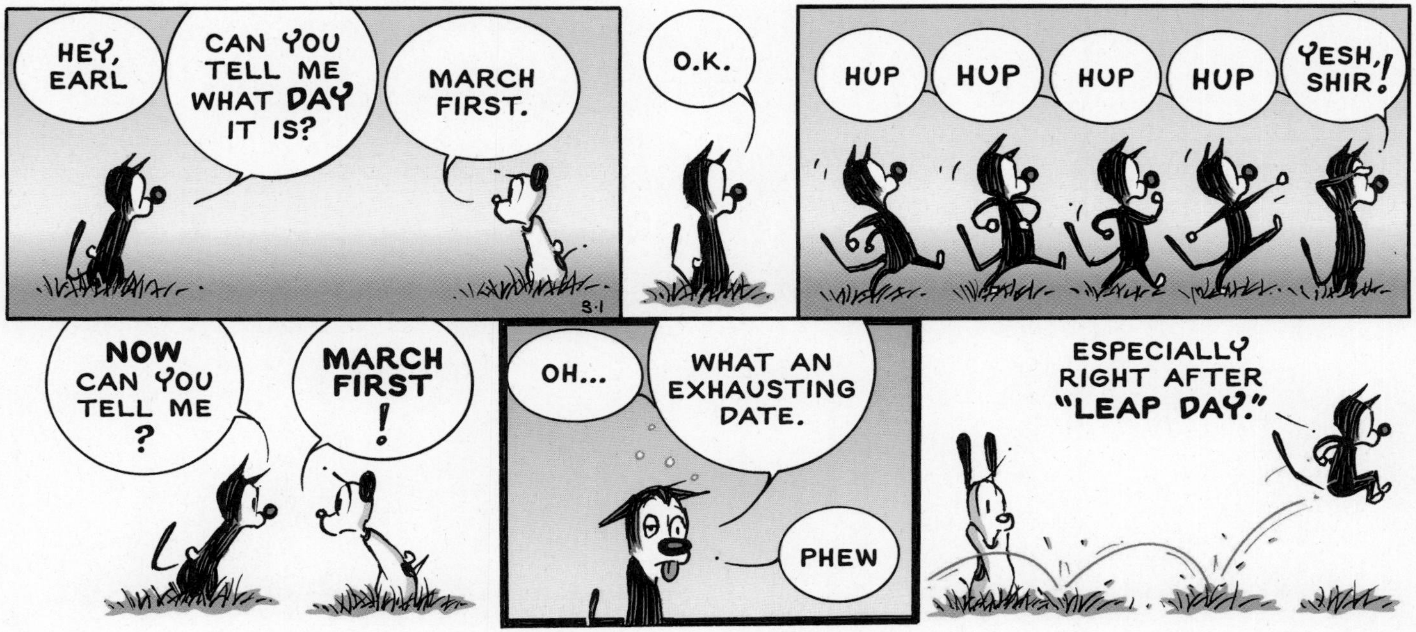
HEY, EARL
CAN YOU TELL ME WHAT DAY IT IS?
MARCH FIRST.
3·1
O.K.
HUP
HUP
HUP
HUP
YESH, SHIR!
NOW CAN YOU TELL ME ?
MARCH FIRST !
OH...
WHAT AN EXHAUSTING DATE.
PHEW
ESPECIALLY RIGHT AFTER "LEAP DAY."

MUTTS
Patrick McDonnell

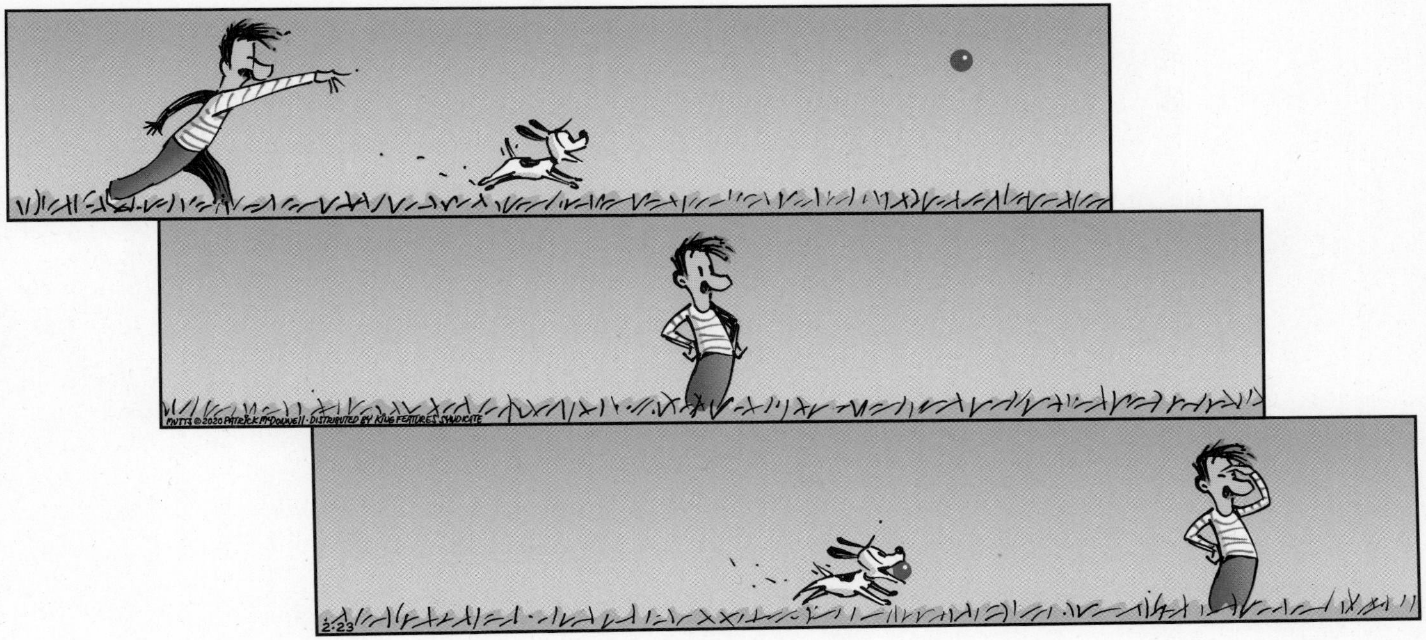
MUTTS © 2020 PATRICK McDONNELL · DISTRIBUTED BY KING FEATURES SYNDICATE
2·23

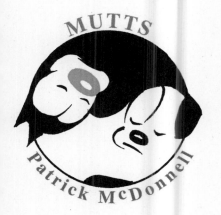

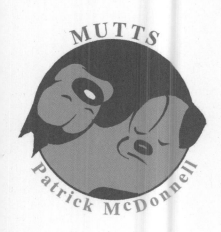

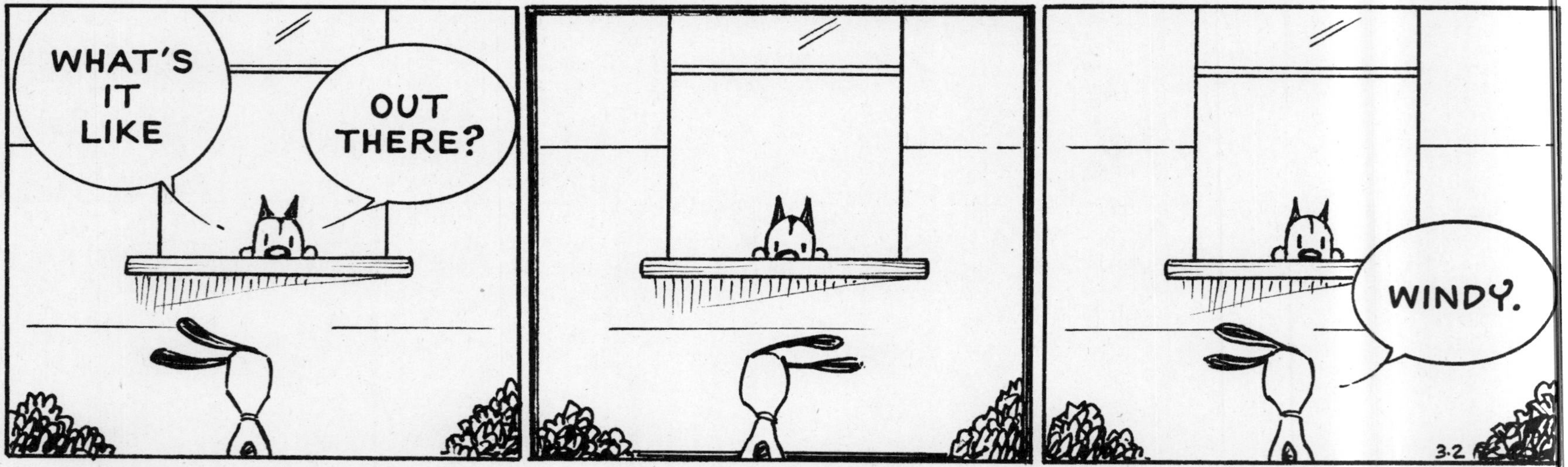
WHAT'S IT LIKE
OUT THERE?
WINDY.
3.2

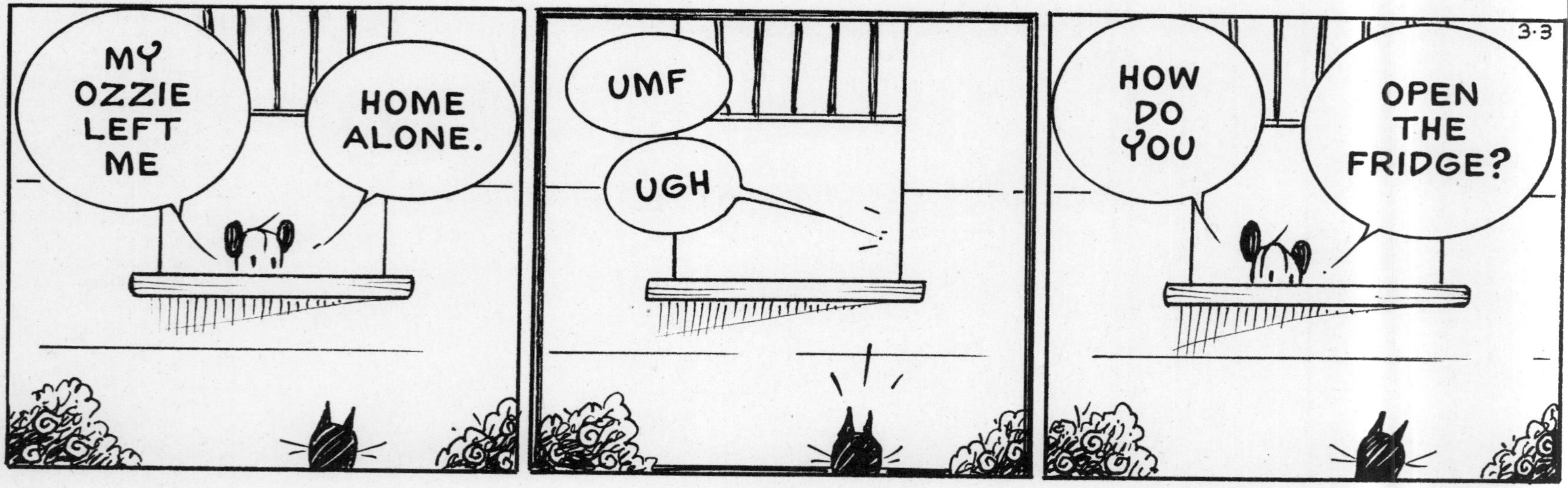
3.3
MY OZZIE LEFT ME
HOME ALONE.
UMF
UGH
HOW DO YOU
OPEN THE FRIDGE?

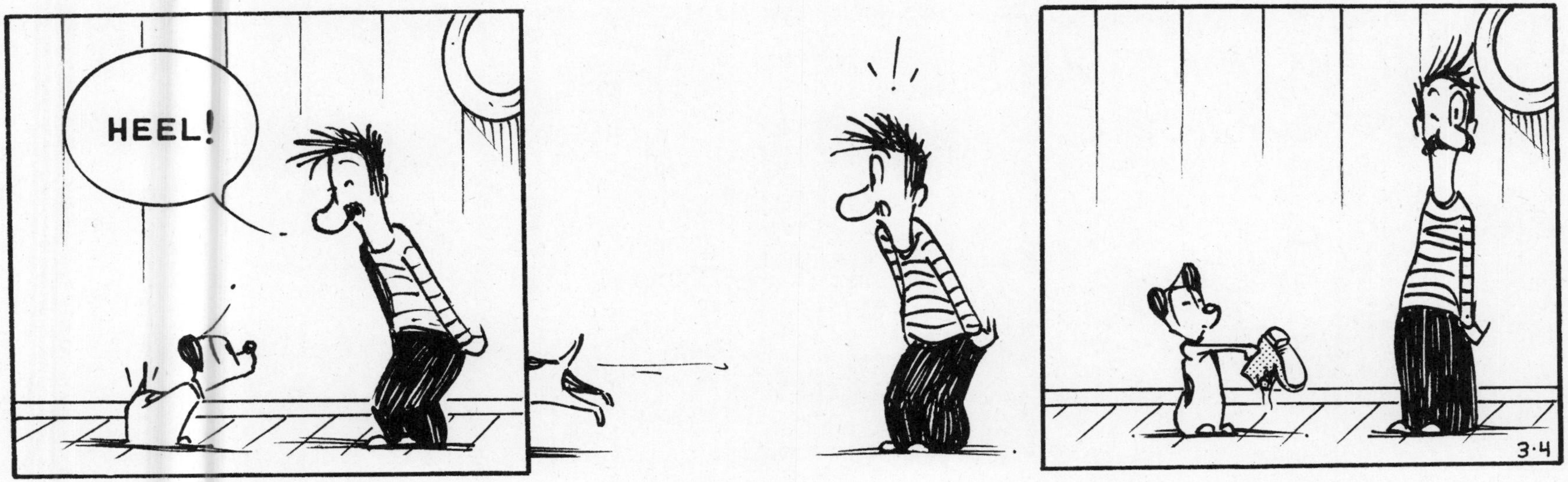
HEEL!
3·4

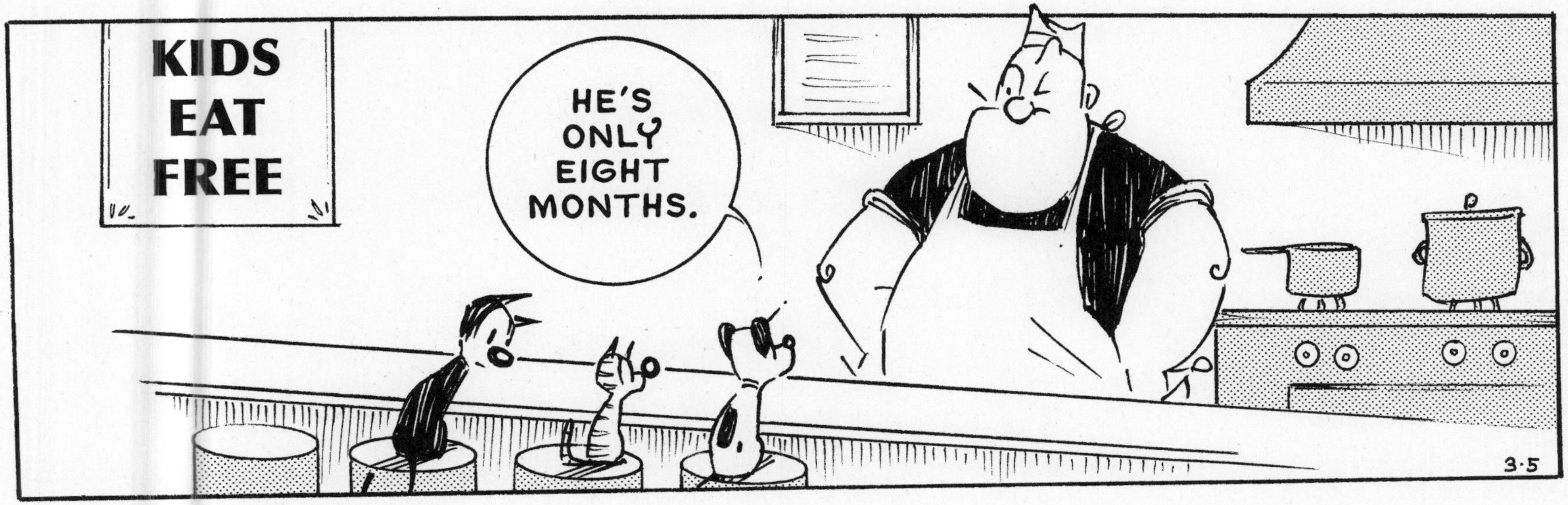
KIDS EAT FREE
HE'S ONLY EIGHT MONTHS.
3·5

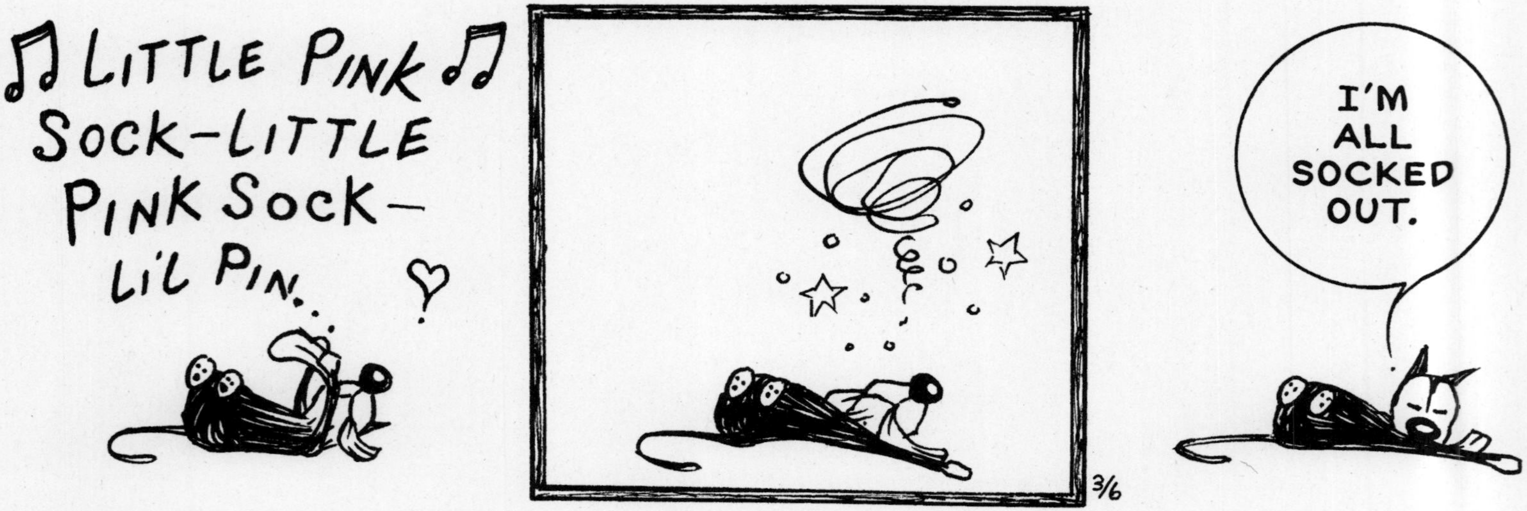
♫ LITTLE PINK ♫ SOCK–LITTLE PINK SOCK– LI'L PIN...
I'M ALL SOCKED OUT.
3/6

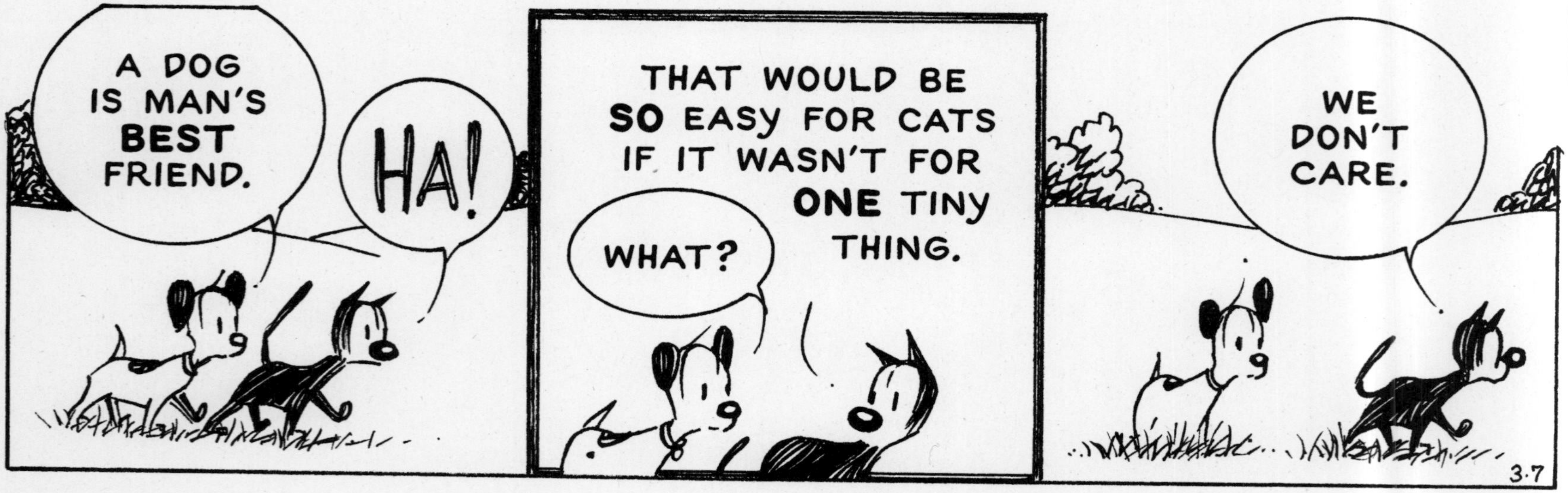
A DOG IS MAN'S BEST FRIEND.
HA!
THAT WOULD BE SO EASY FOR CATS IF IT WASN'T FOR ONE TINY THING.
WHAT?
WE DON'T CARE.
3·7

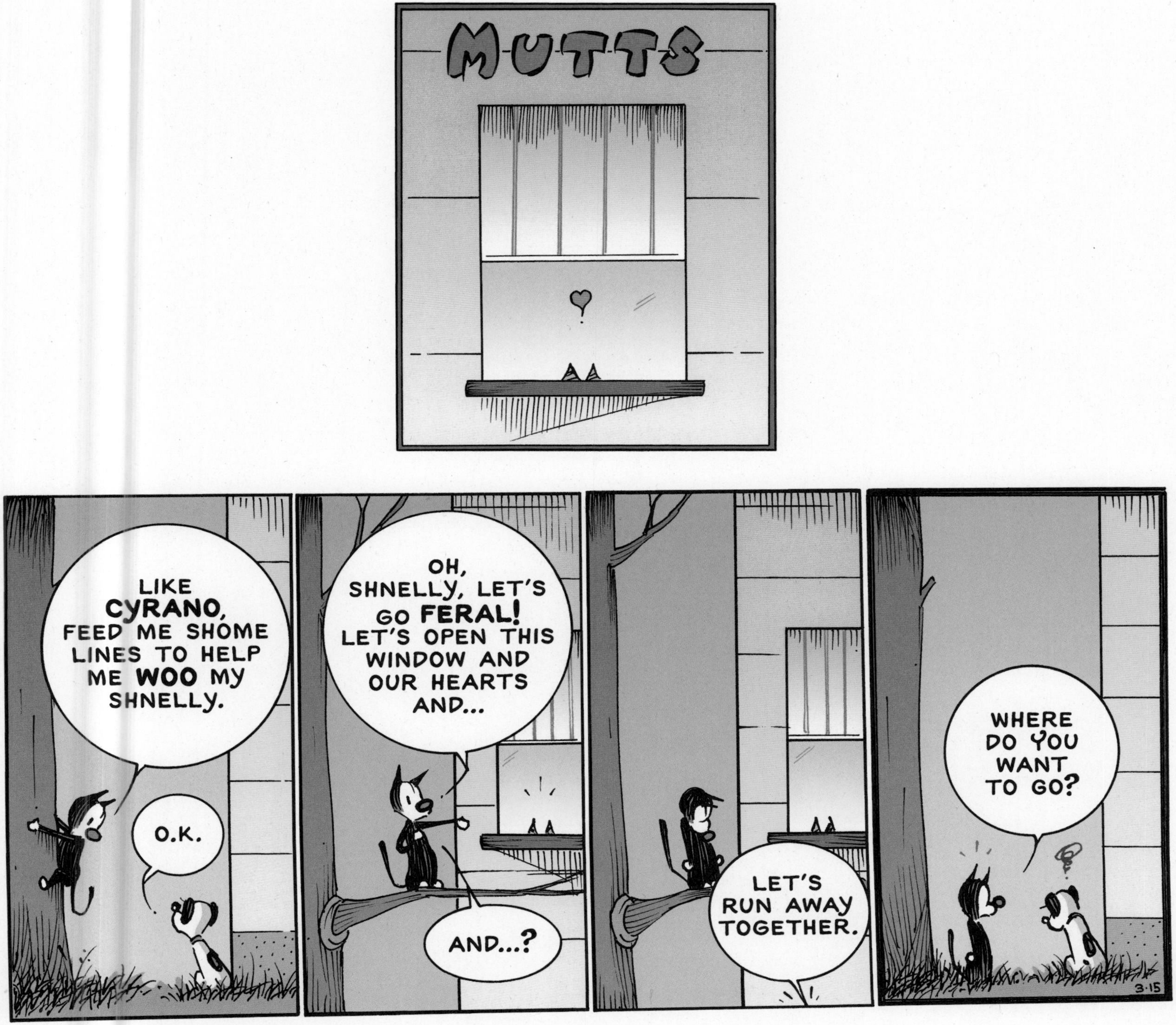
MUTTS
LIKE CYRANO, FEED ME SHOME LINES TO HELP ME WOO MY SHNELLY.
O.K.
OH, SHNELLY, LET'S GO FERAL! LET'S OPEN THIS WINDOW AND OUR HEARTS AND...
AND...?
LET'S RUN AWAY TOGETHER.
WHERE DO YOU WANT TO GO?
3·15

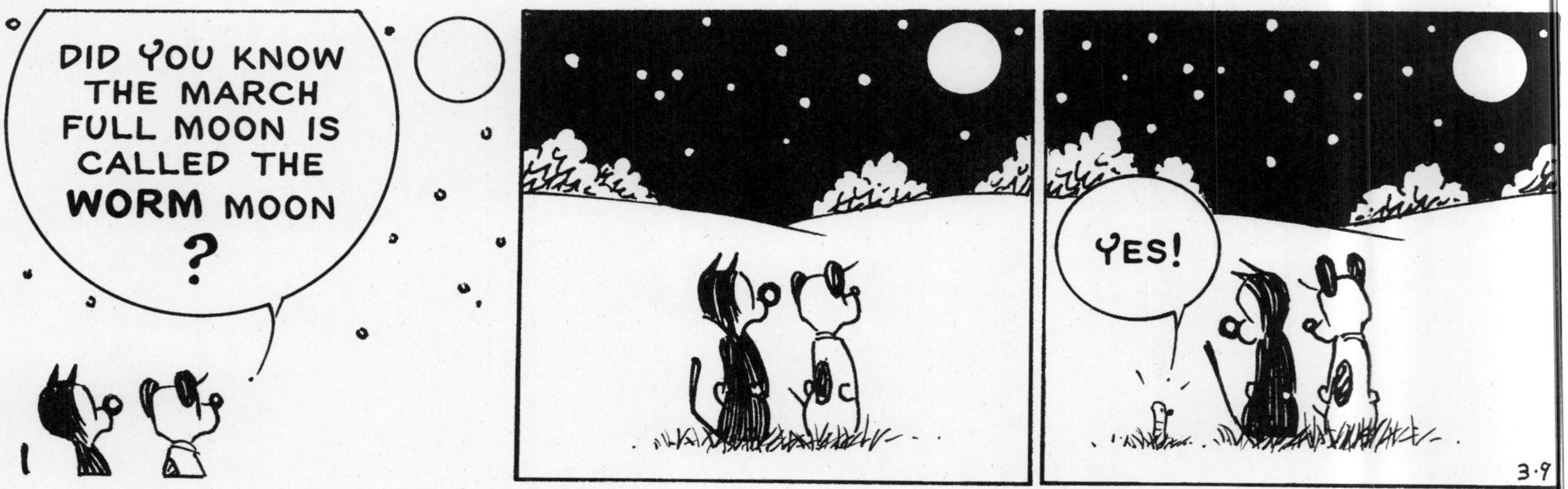
DID YOU KNOW THE MARCH FULL MOON IS CALLED THE **WORM** MOON ?
YES!
3·9

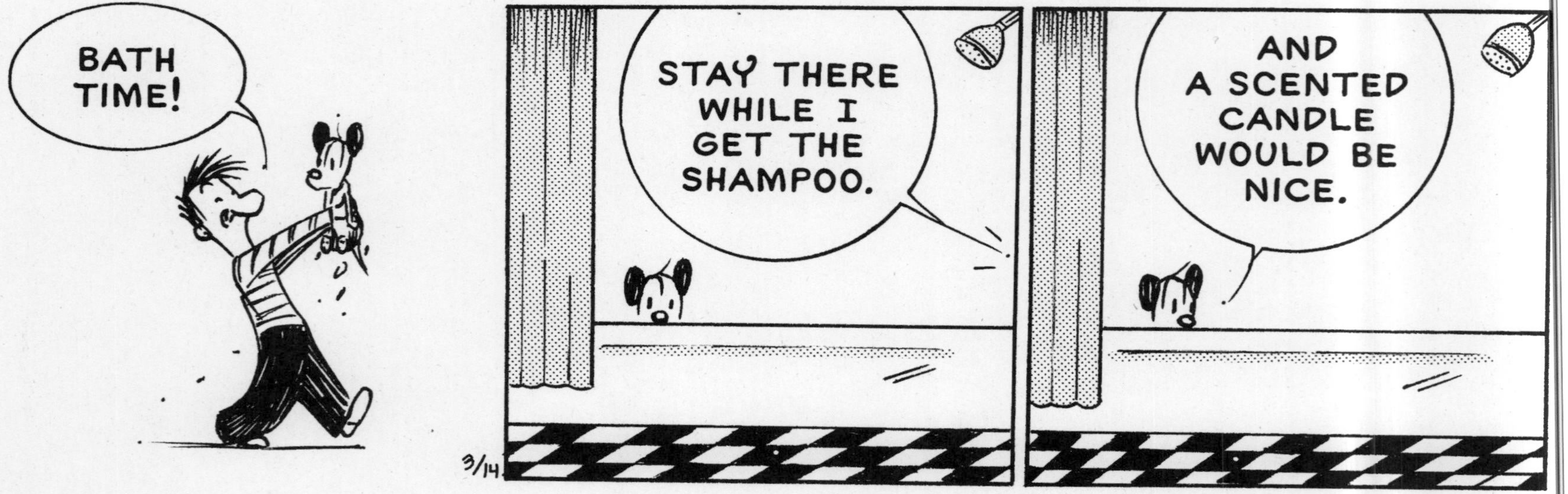
BATH TIME!
3/14
STAY THERE WHILE I GET THE SHAMPOO.
AND A SCENTED CANDLE WOULD BE NICE.

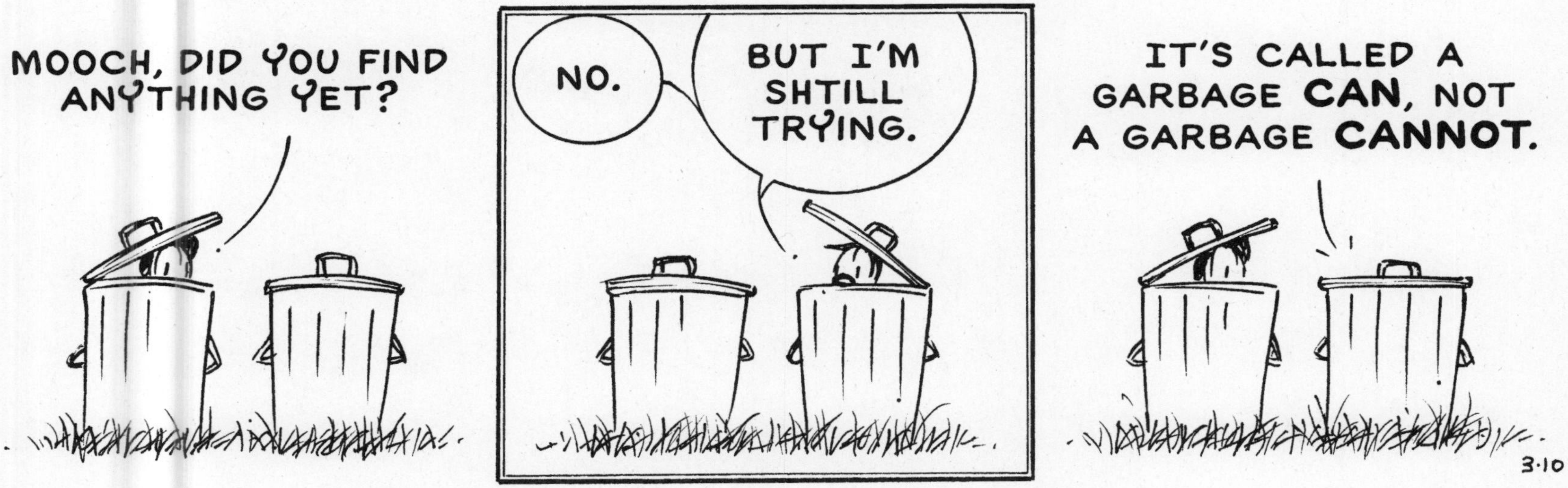
MOOCH, DID YOU FIND ANYTHING YET?
NO.
BUT I'M SHTILL TRYING.
IT'S CALLED A GARBAGE **CAN**, NOT A GARBAGE **CANNOT**.
3·10

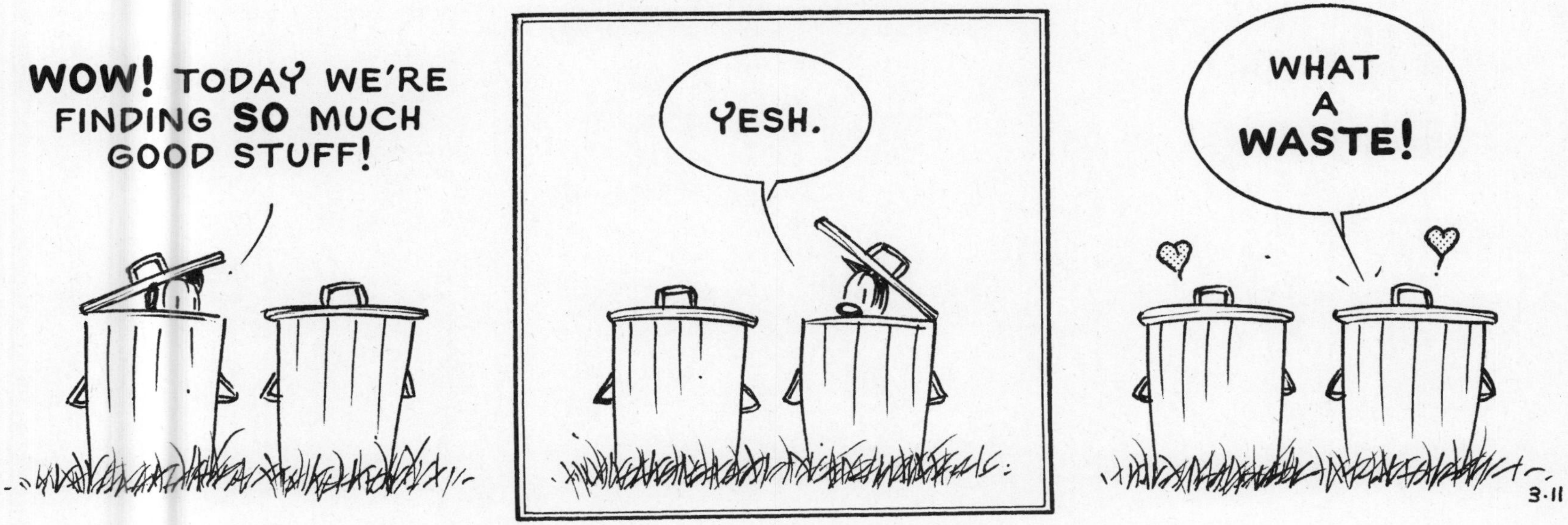
WOW! TODAY WE'RE FINDING **SO** MUCH GOOD STUFF!
YESH.
WHAT A **WASTE!**
3·11

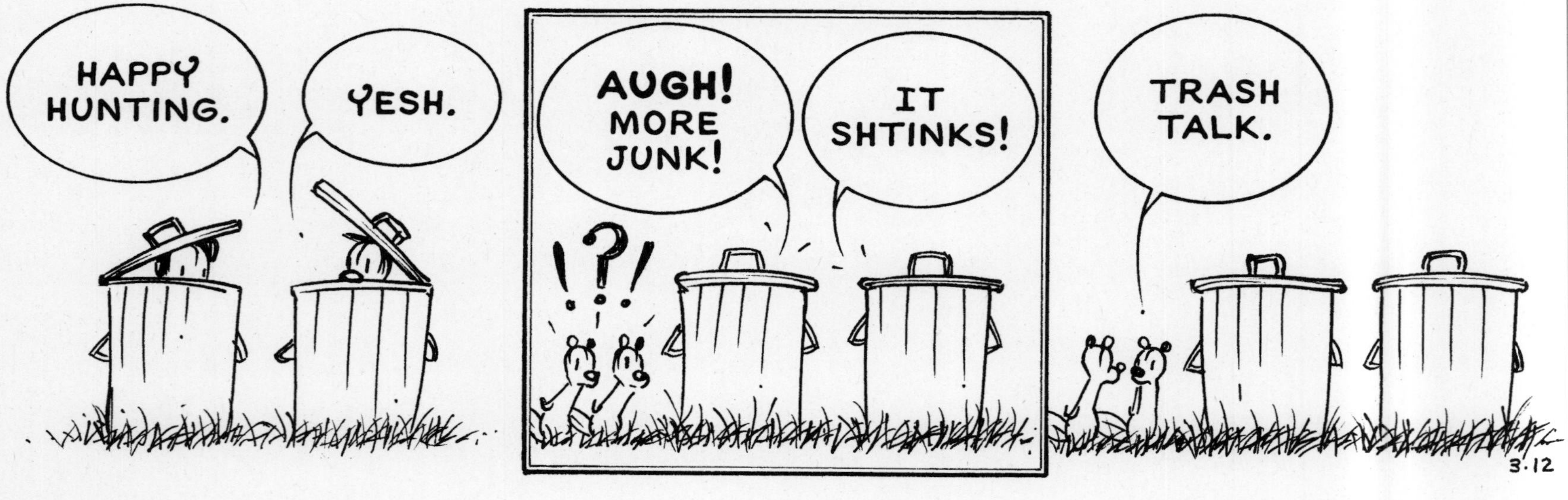
HAPPY HUNTING.
YESH.
AUGH! MORE JUNK!
IT SHTINKS!
TRASH TALK.
3·12

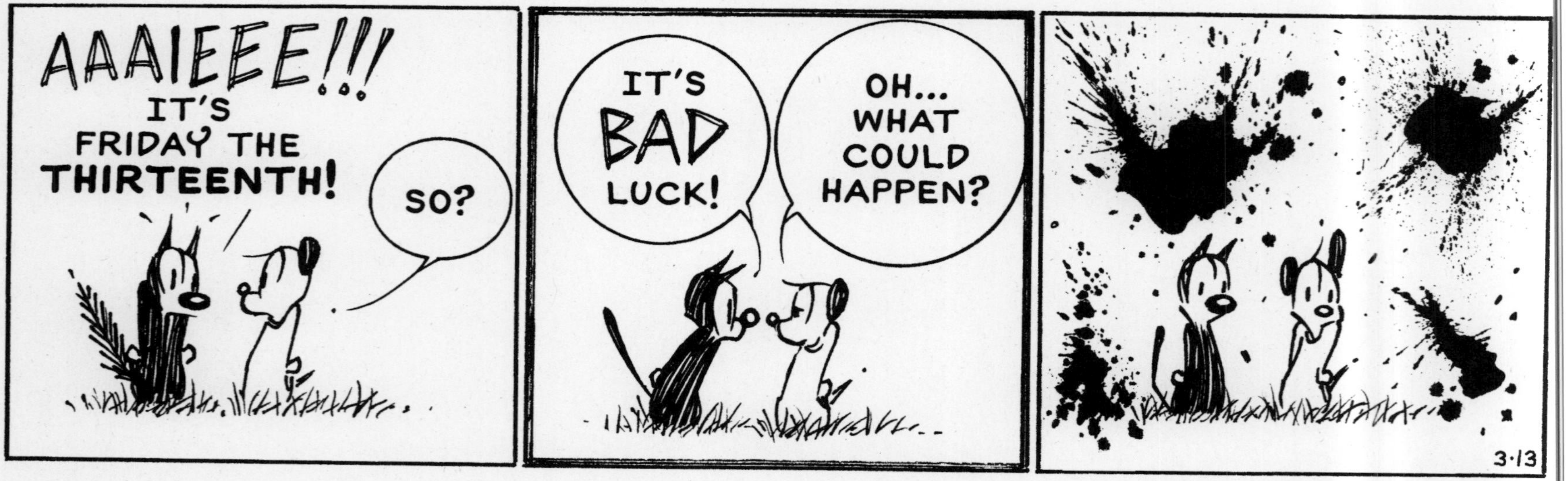
AAAIEEE!!! IT'S FRIDAY THE THIRTEENTH!
SO?
IT'S BAD LUCK!
OH... WHAT COULD HAPPEN?
3·13

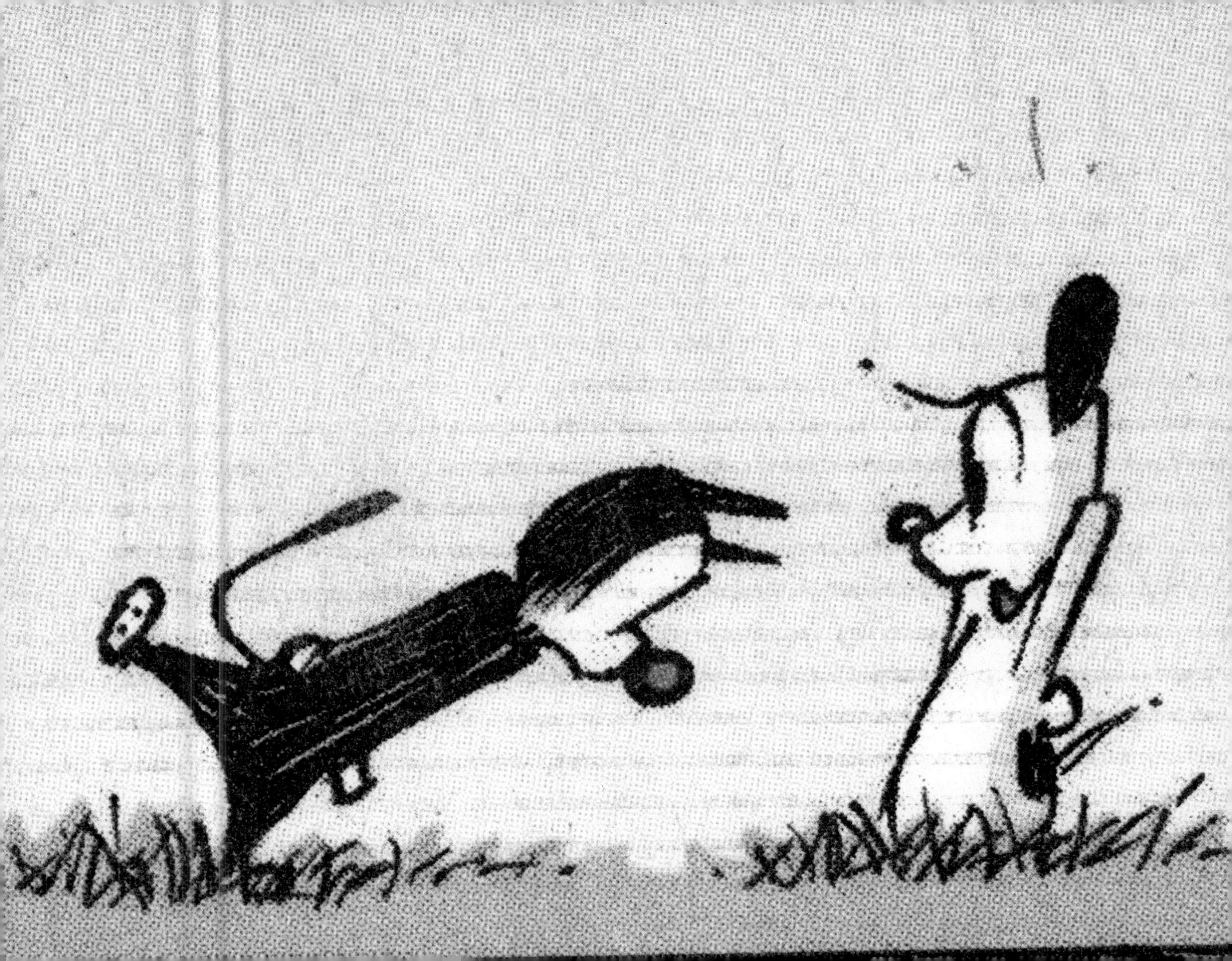

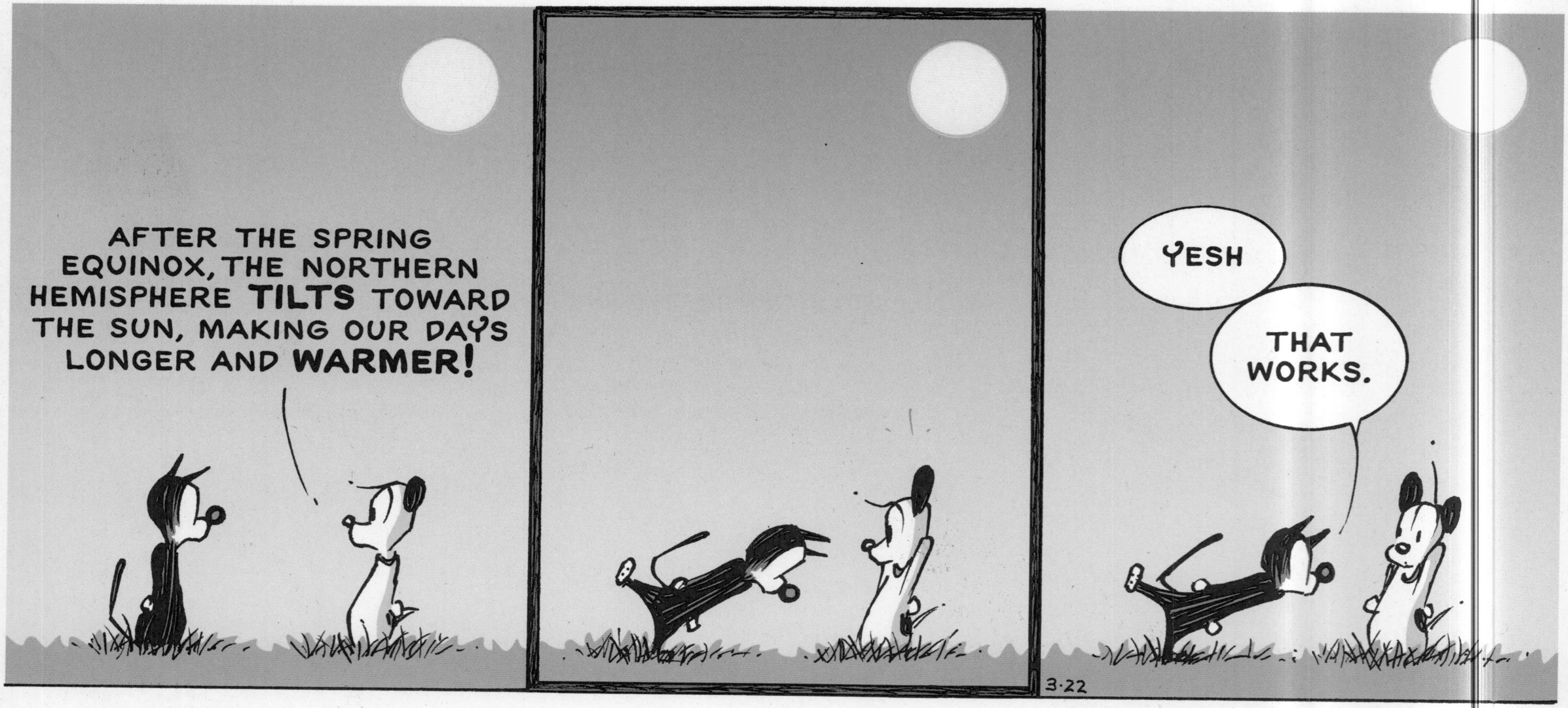
AFTER THE SPRING EQUINOX, THE NORTHERN HEMISPHERE **TILTS** TOWARD THE SUN, MAKING OUR DAYS LONGER AND **WARMER!**
YESH
THAT WORKS.
3·22

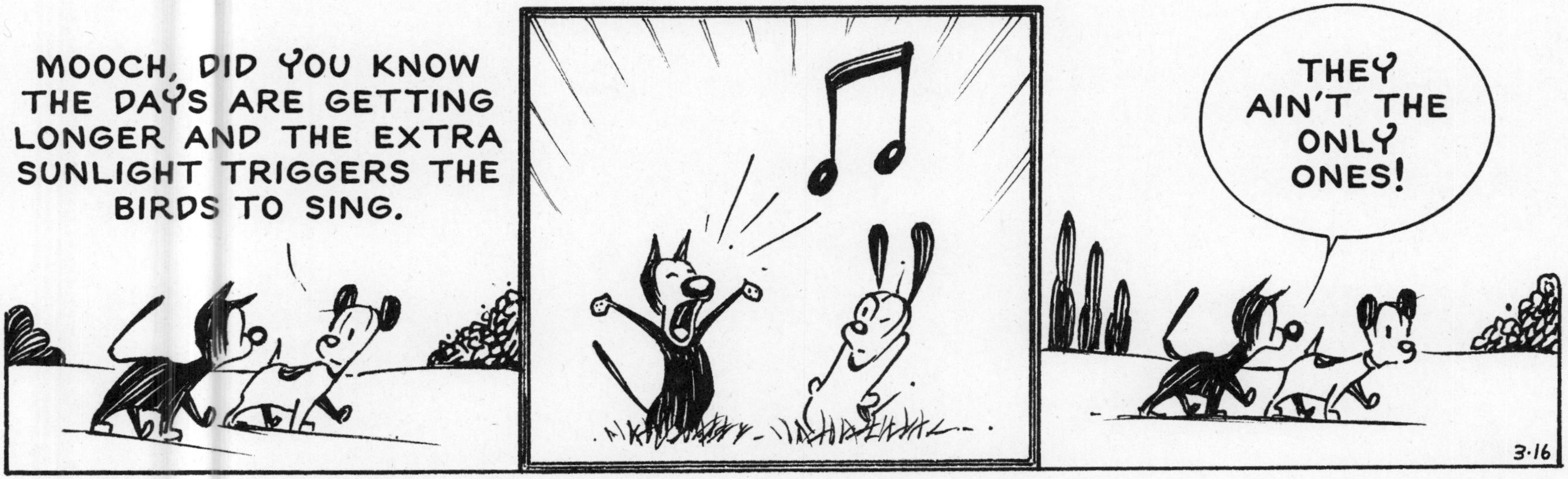
MOOCH, DID YOU KNOW THE DAYS ARE GETTING LONGER AND THE EXTRA SUNLIGHT TRIGGERS THE BIRDS TO SING.
THEY AIN'T THE ONLY ONES!
3·16

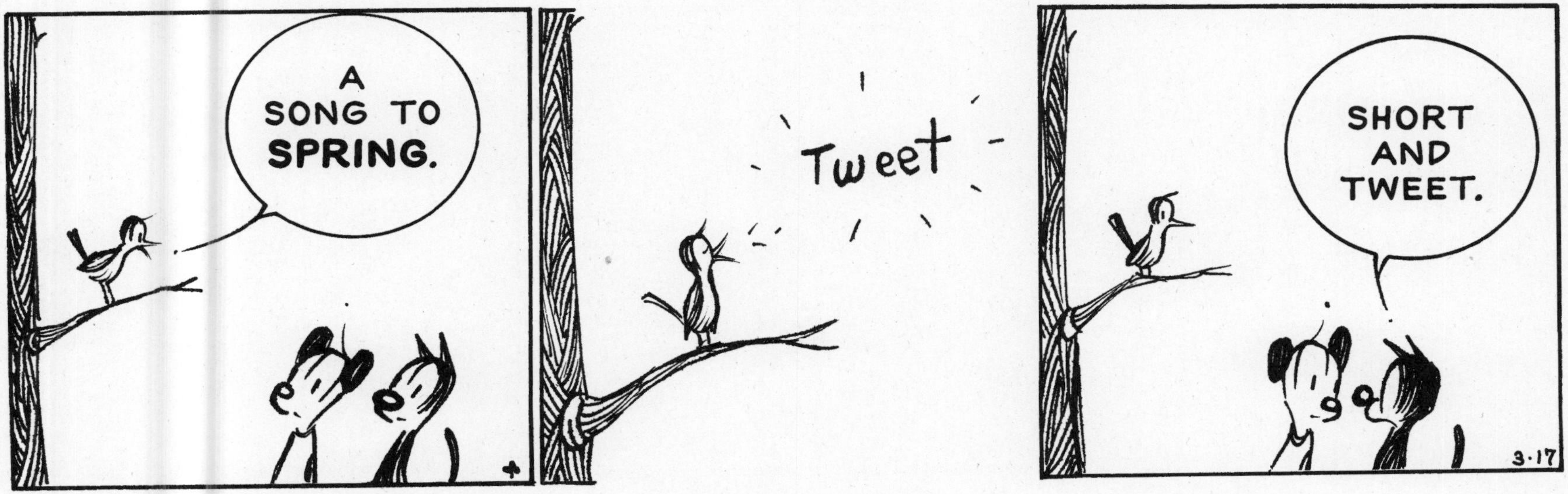
A SONG TO SPRING.
Tweet
SHORT AND TWEET.
3·17

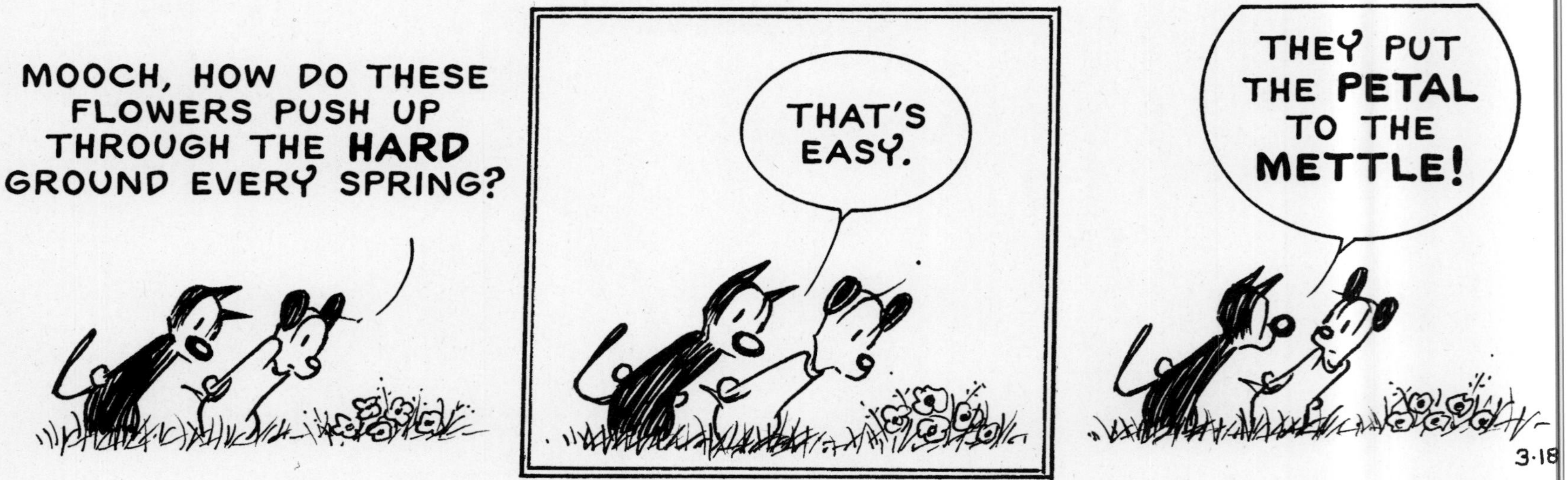
MOOCH, HOW DO THESE FLOWERS PUSH UP THROUGH THE **HARD** GROUND EVERY SPRING?
THAT'S EASY.
THEY PUT THE **PETAL** TO THE **METTLE!**
3·18

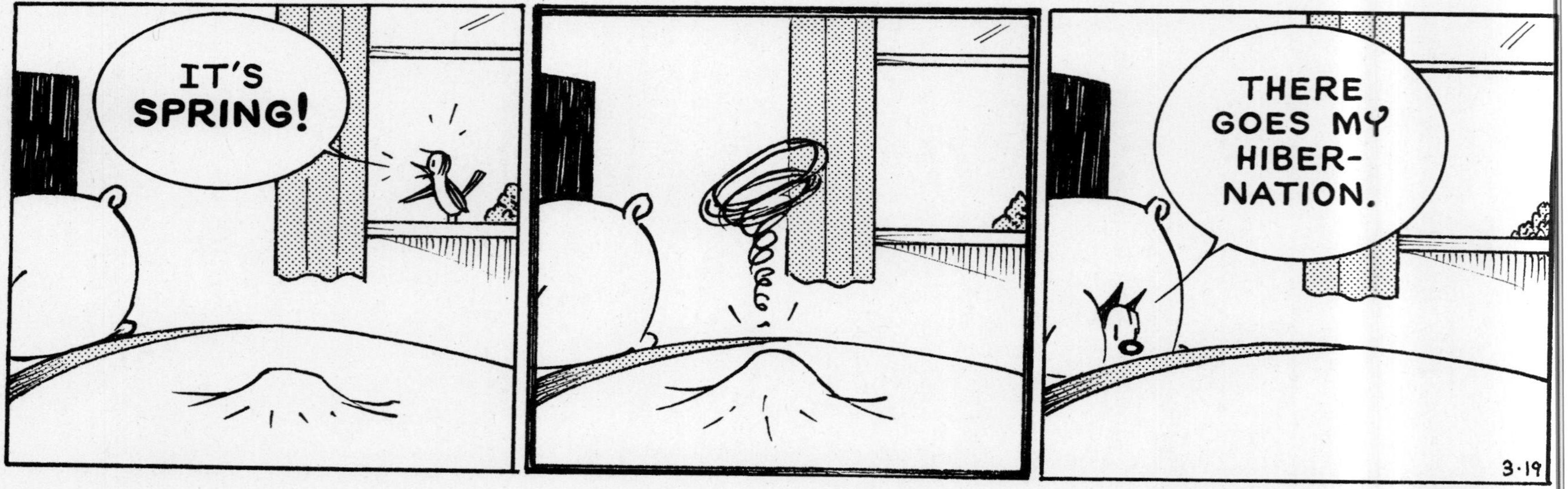
IT'S **SPRING!**
THERE GOES MY HIBER-NATION.
3·19

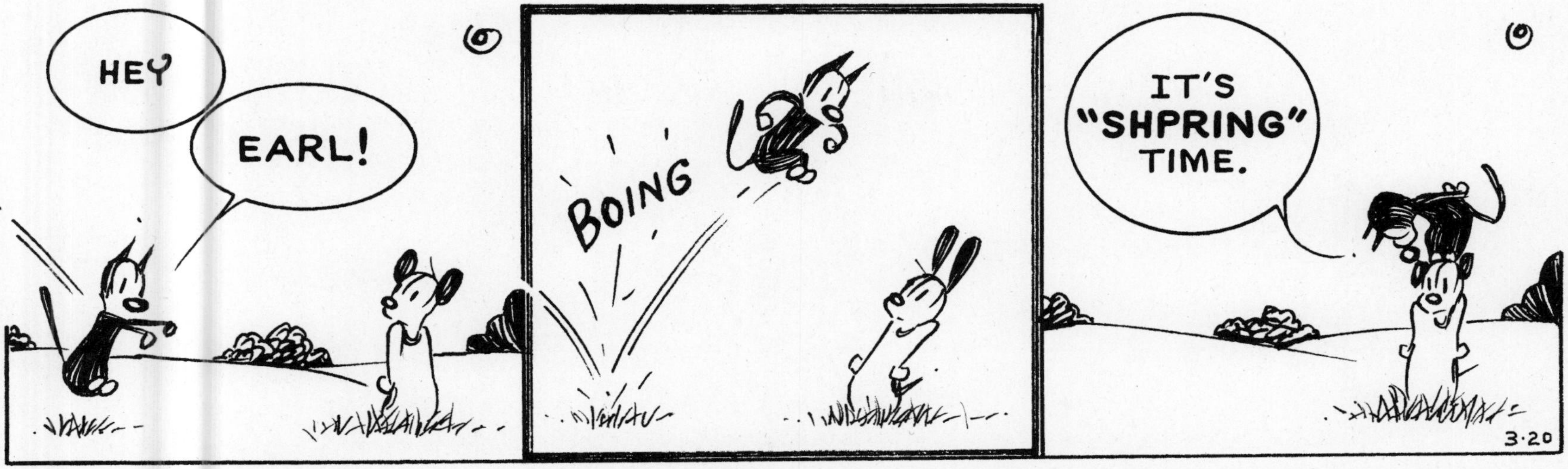
HEY
EARL!
BOING
IT'S "SHPRING" TIME.
3·20

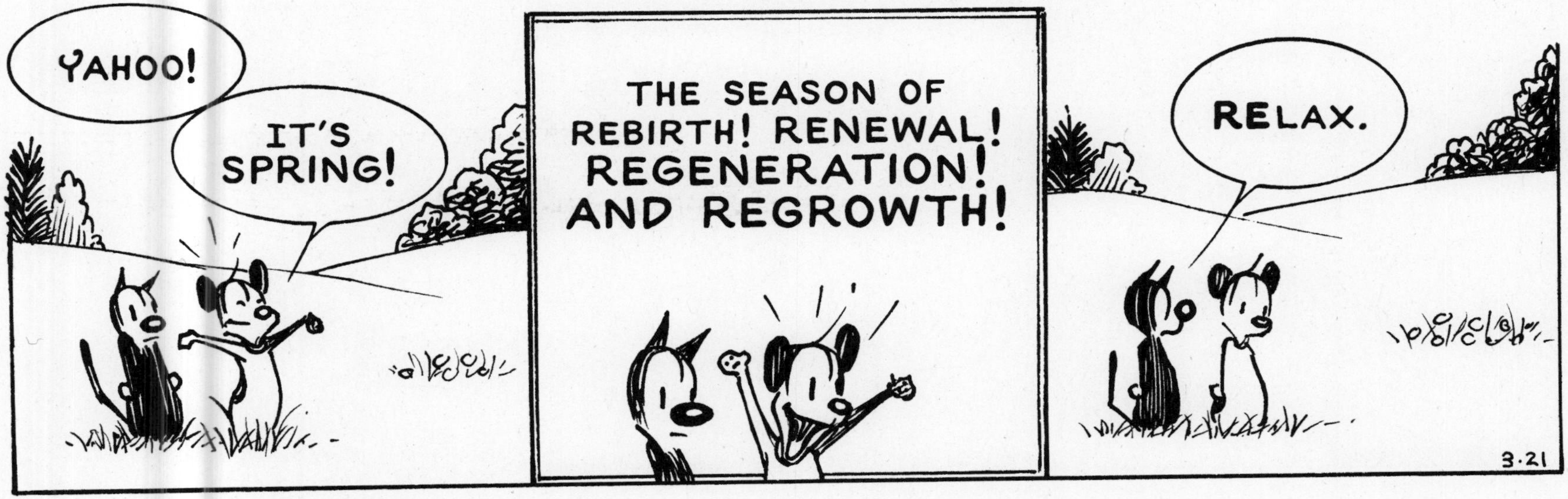
YAHOO!
IT'S SPRING!
THE SEASON OF REBIRTH! RENEWAL! REGENERATION! AND REGROWTH!
RELAX.
3·21

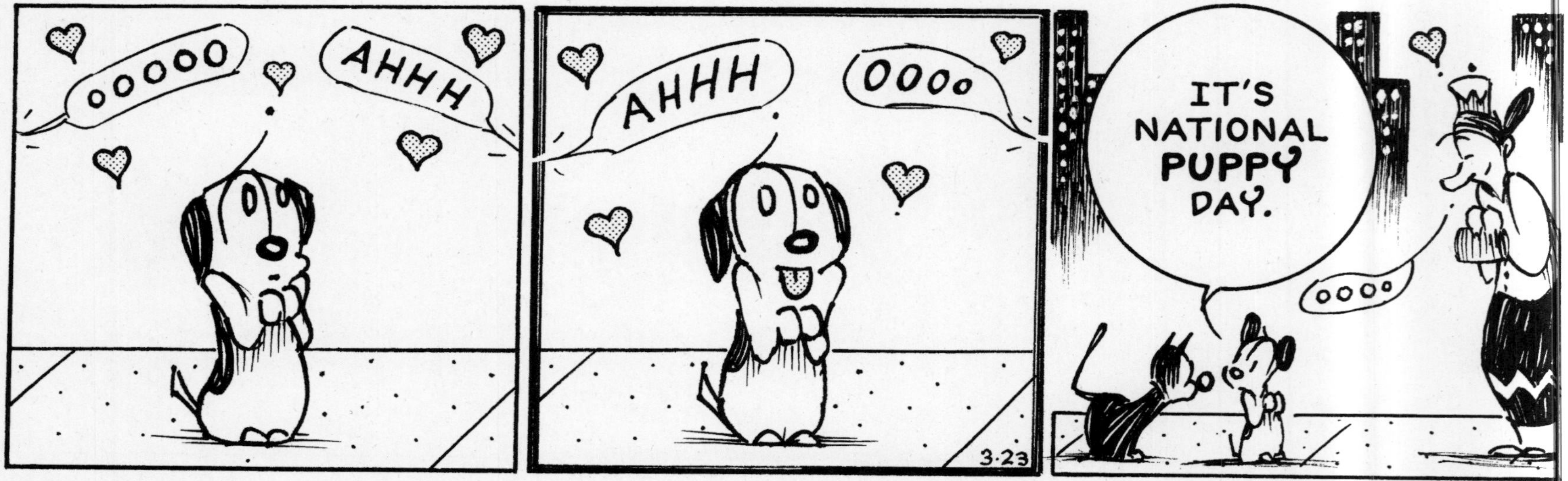
OOOOO
AHHH
AHHH
OOOo
3·23
IT'S NATIONAL PUPPY DAY.
OOOo

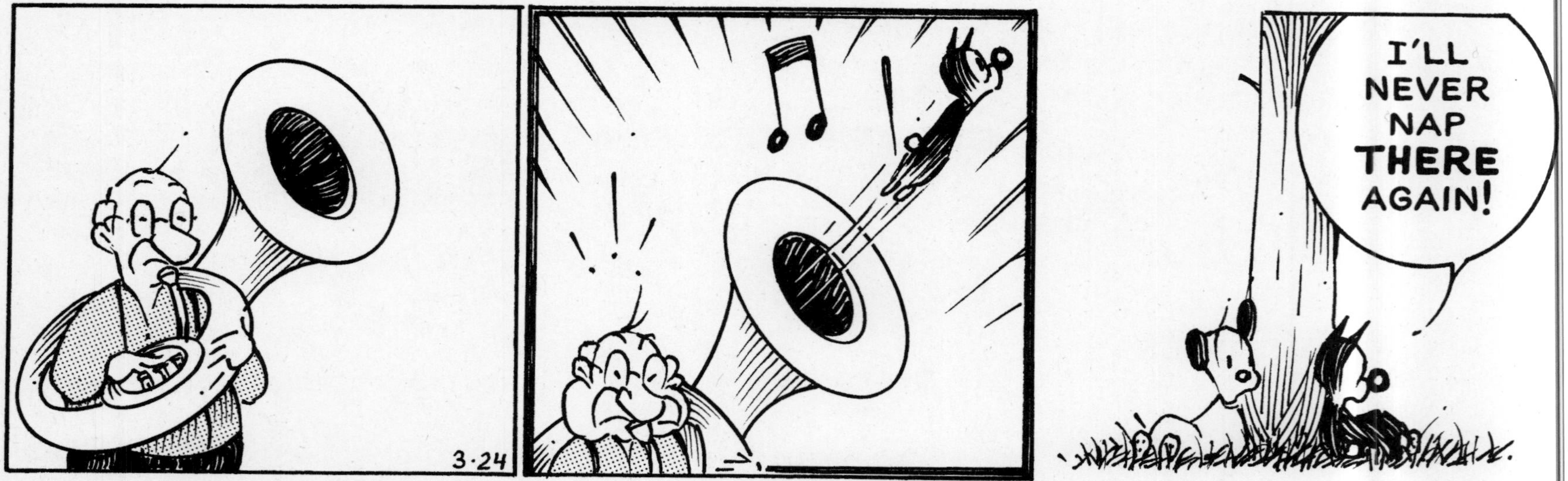
3·24
I'LL NEVER NAP THERE AGAIN!

I'M THE GUY
THAT PUT THE "NIP" IN CATNIP.
3·25

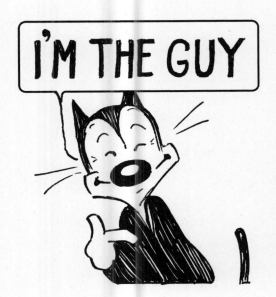

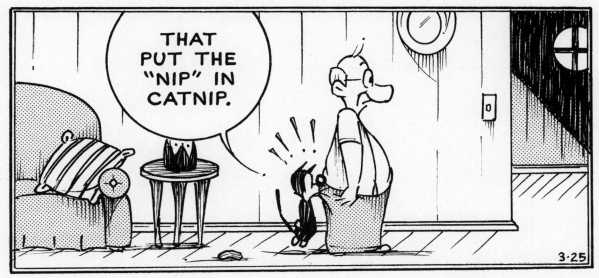

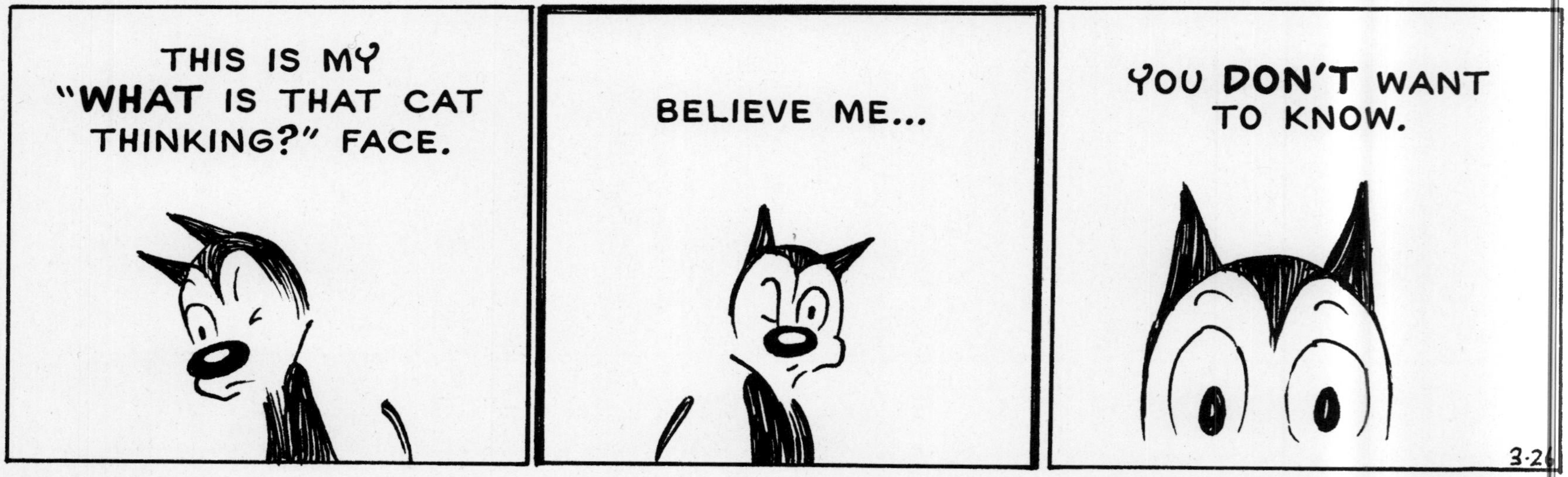
THIS IS MY "WHAT IS THAT CAT THINKING?" FACE.
BELIEVE ME...
YOU DON'T WANT TO KNOW.
3·26

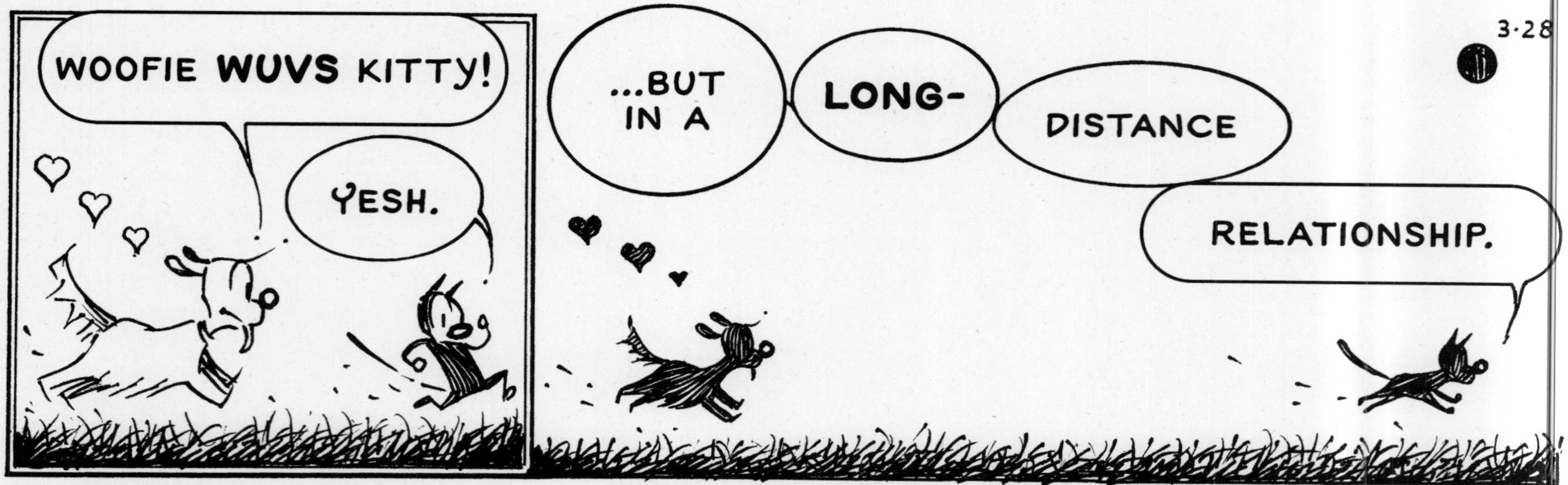
WOOFIE WUVS KITTY!
YESH.
...BUT IN A
LONG-
DISTANCE
RELATIONSHIP.
3·28

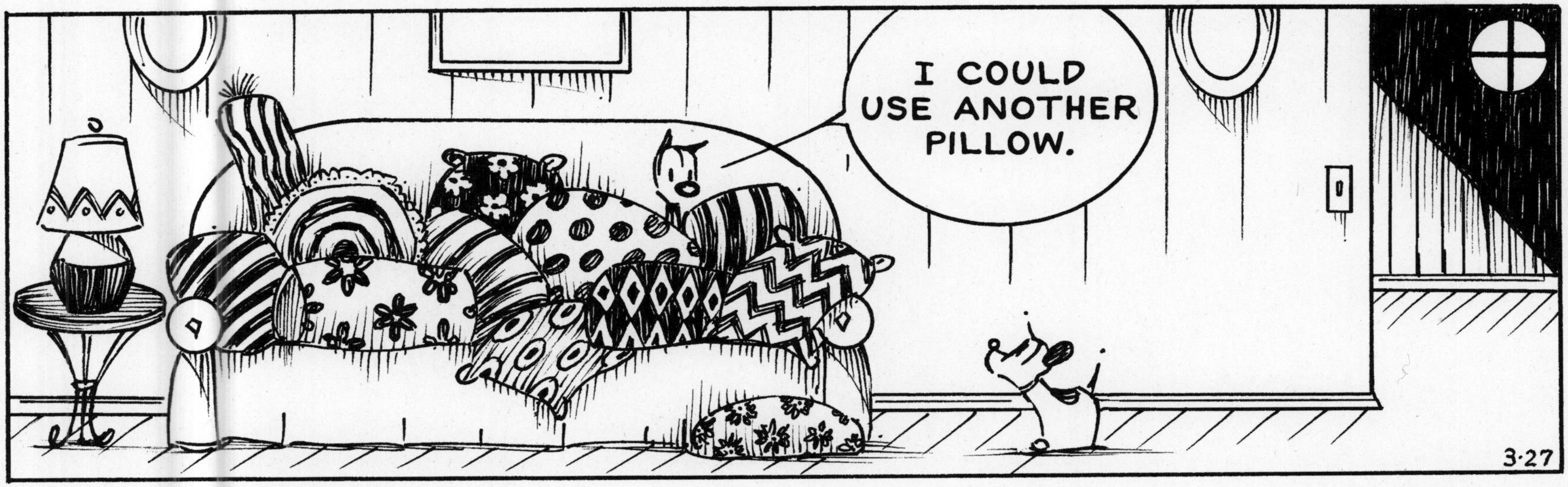
I COULD USE ANOTHER PILLOW.
3·27

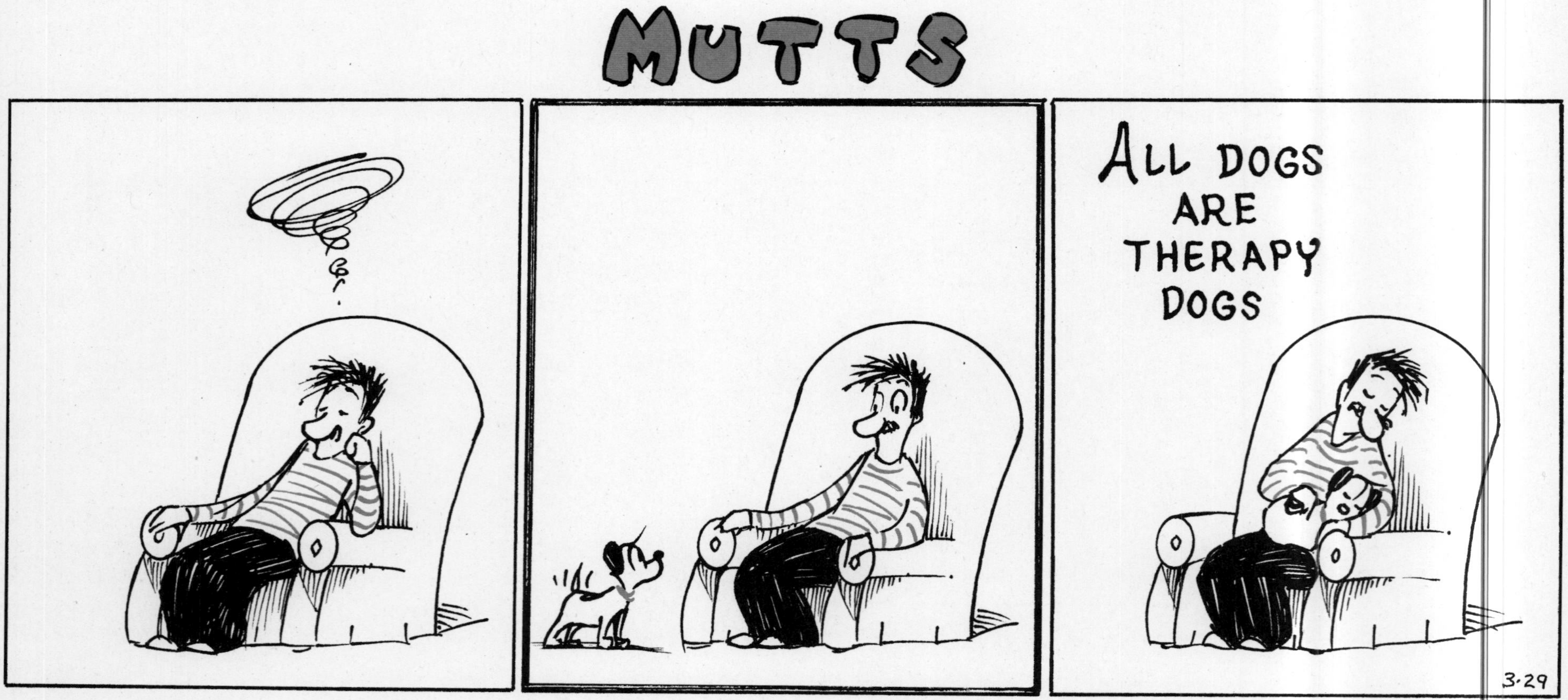
MUTTS
ALL DOGS ARE THERAPY DOGS
3·29

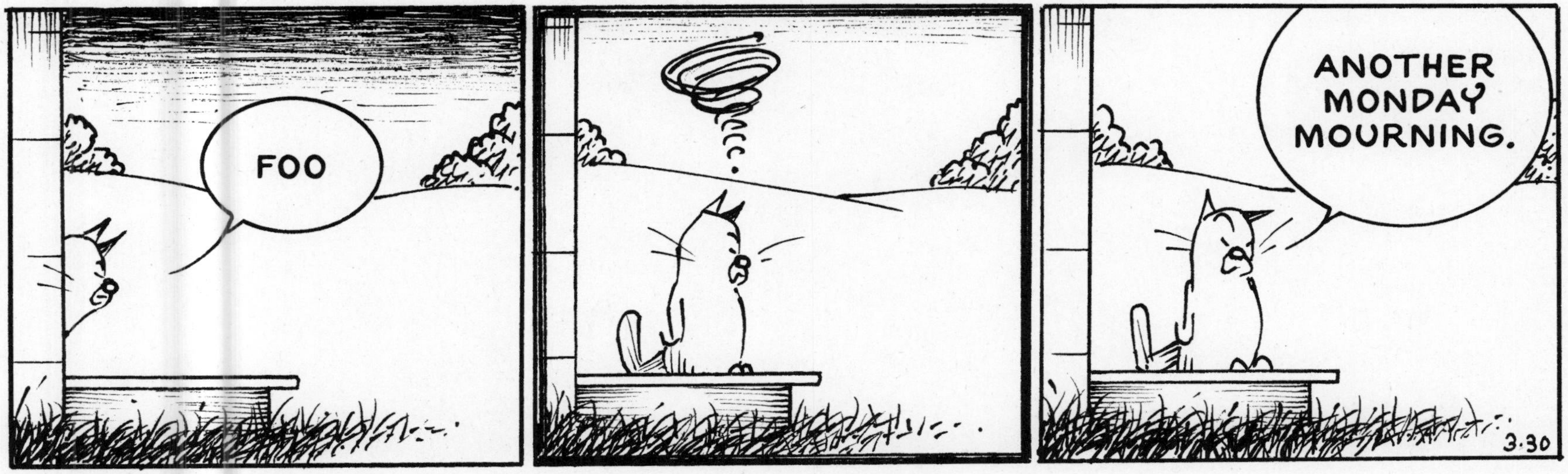
FOO
ANOTHER MONDAY MOURNING.
3·30

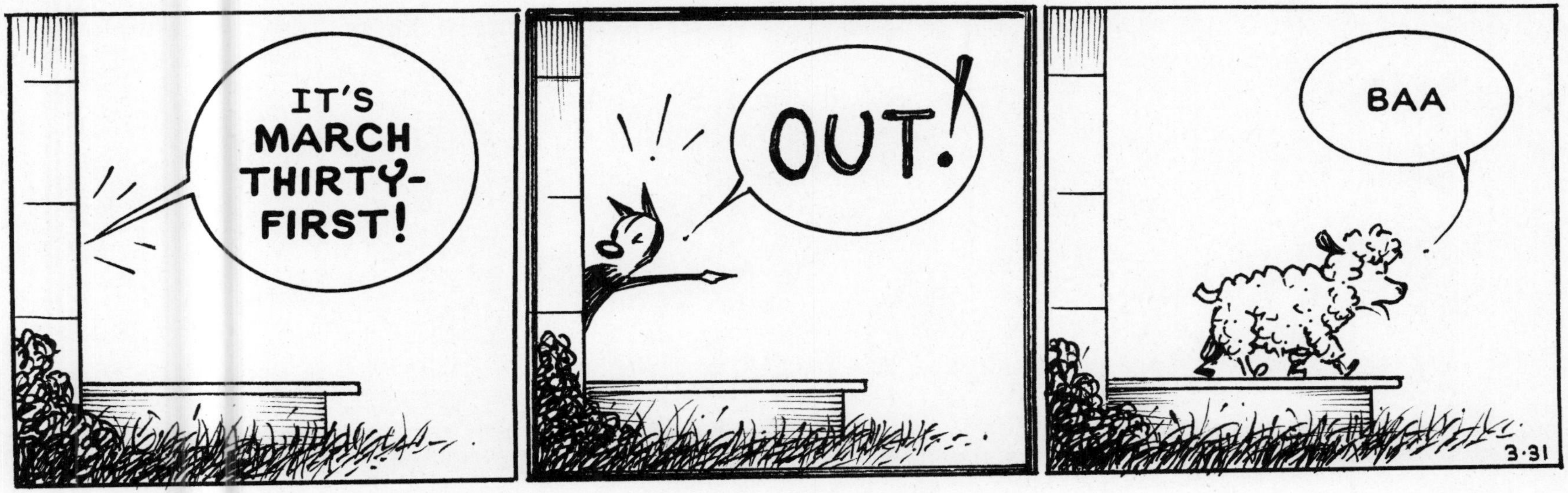
IT'S MARCH THIRTY-FIRST!
OUT!
BAA
3·31

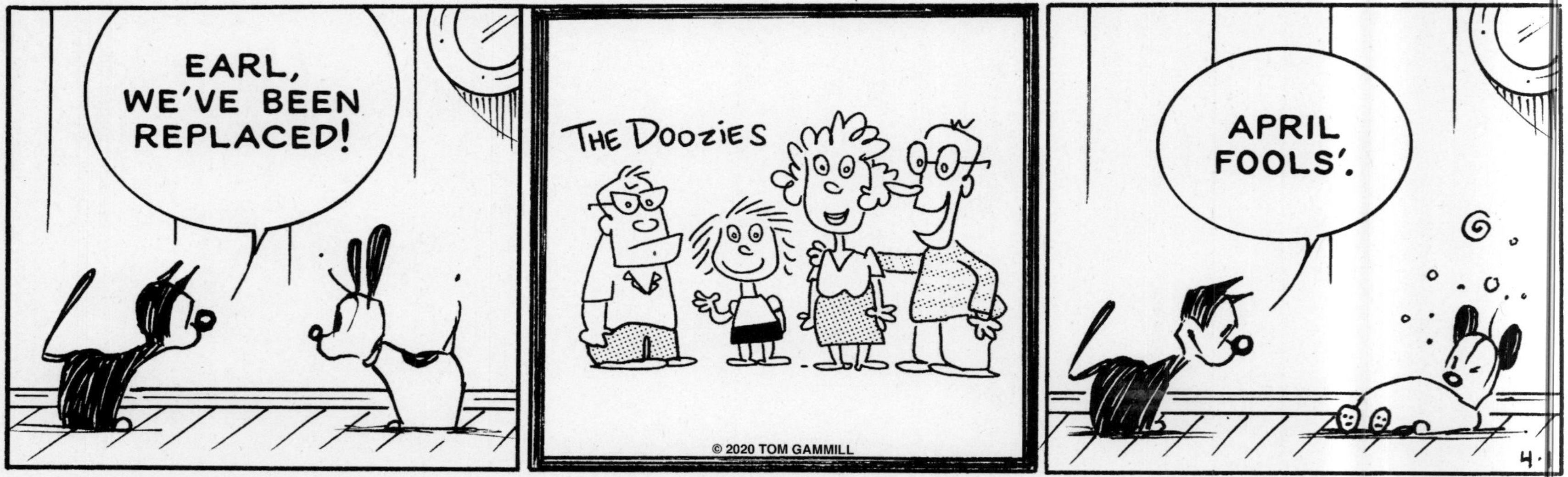
EARL, WE'VE BEEN REPLACED!
THE DOOZIES
© 2020 TOM GAMMILL
APRIL FOOLS'.
4.1

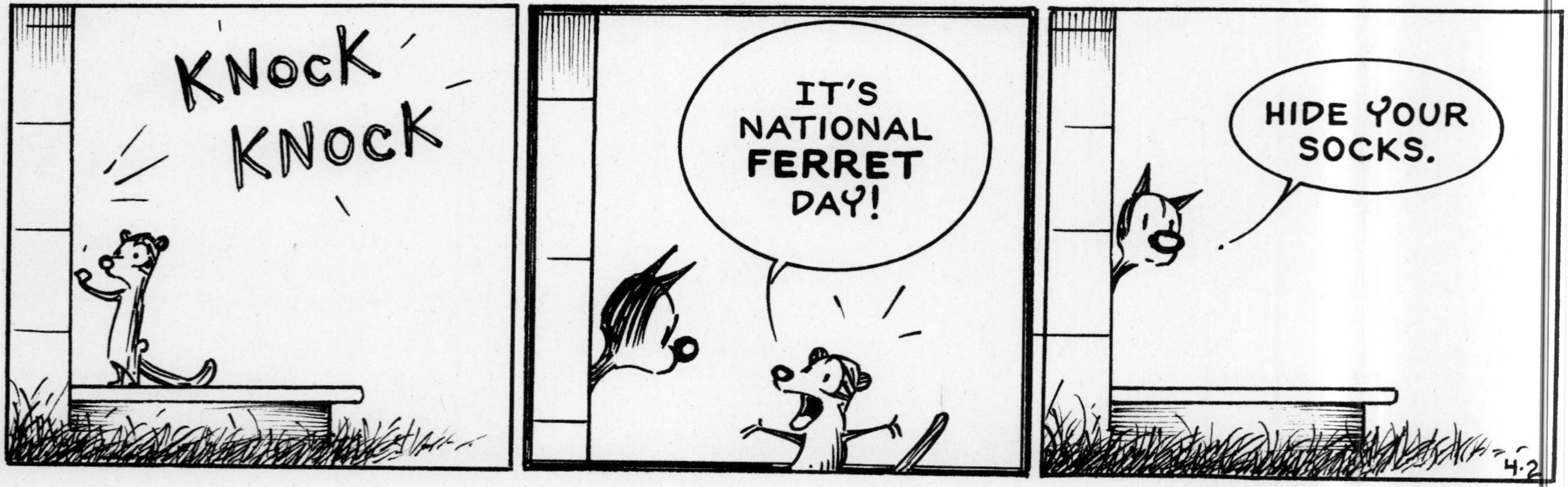
KNOCK KNOCK
IT'S NATIONAL FERRET DAY!
HIDE YOUR SOCKS.
4.2

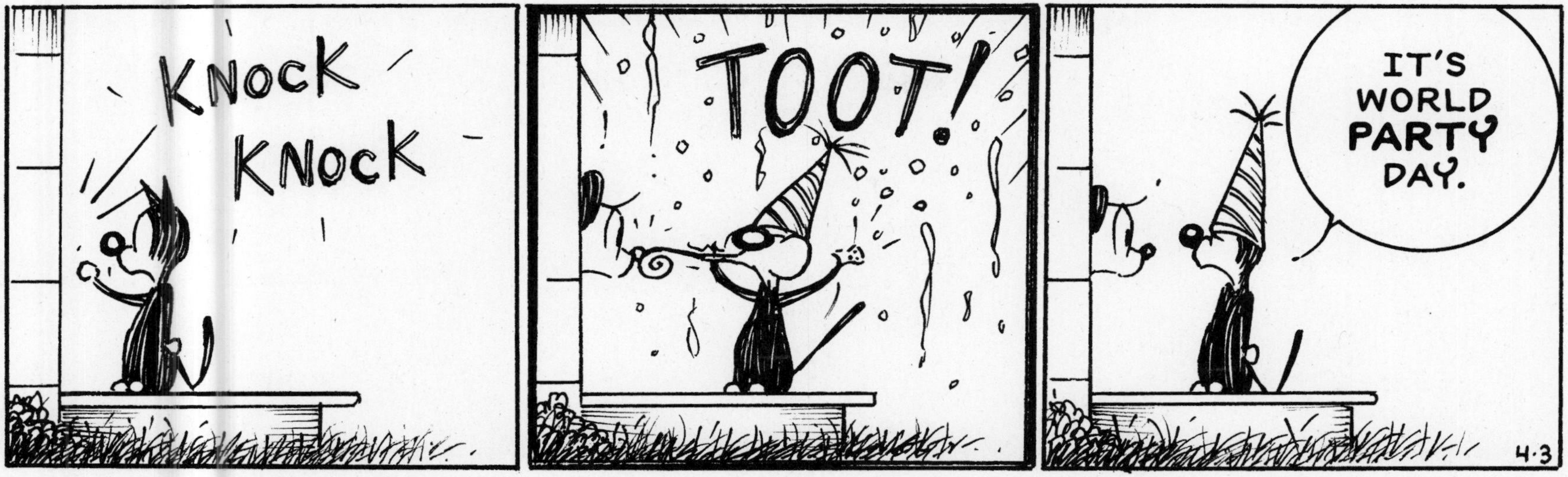
KNOCK KNOCK
TOOT!
IT'S WORLD PARTY DAY.
4·3

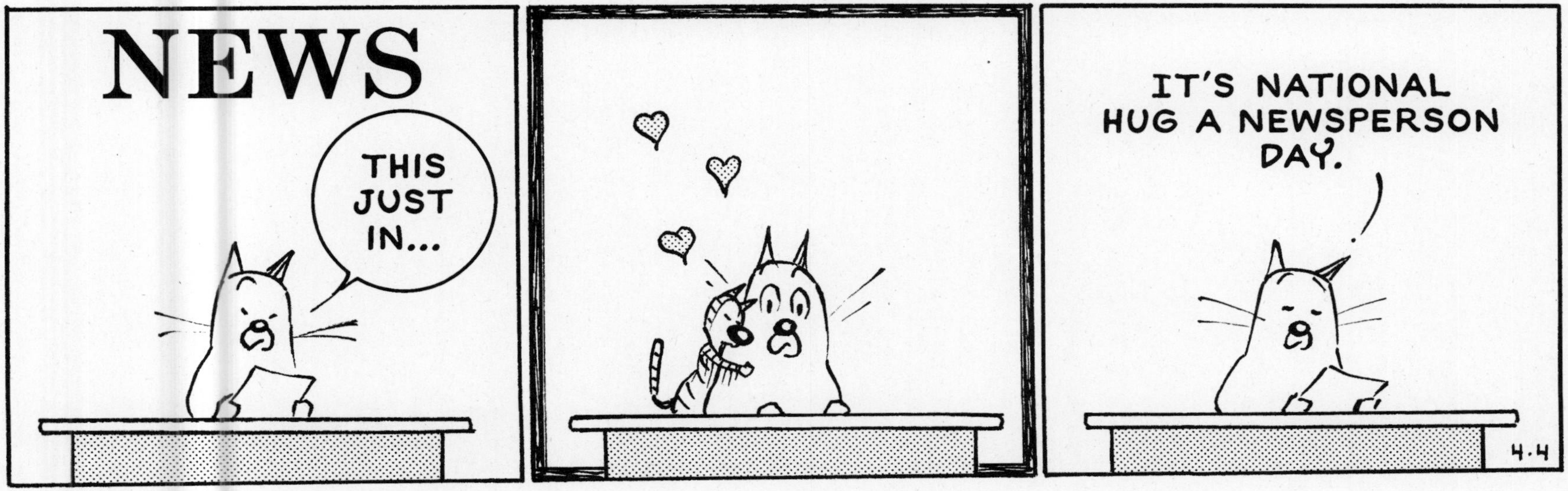
NEWS
THIS JUST IN...
IT'S NATIONAL HUG A NEWSPERSON DAY.
4·4

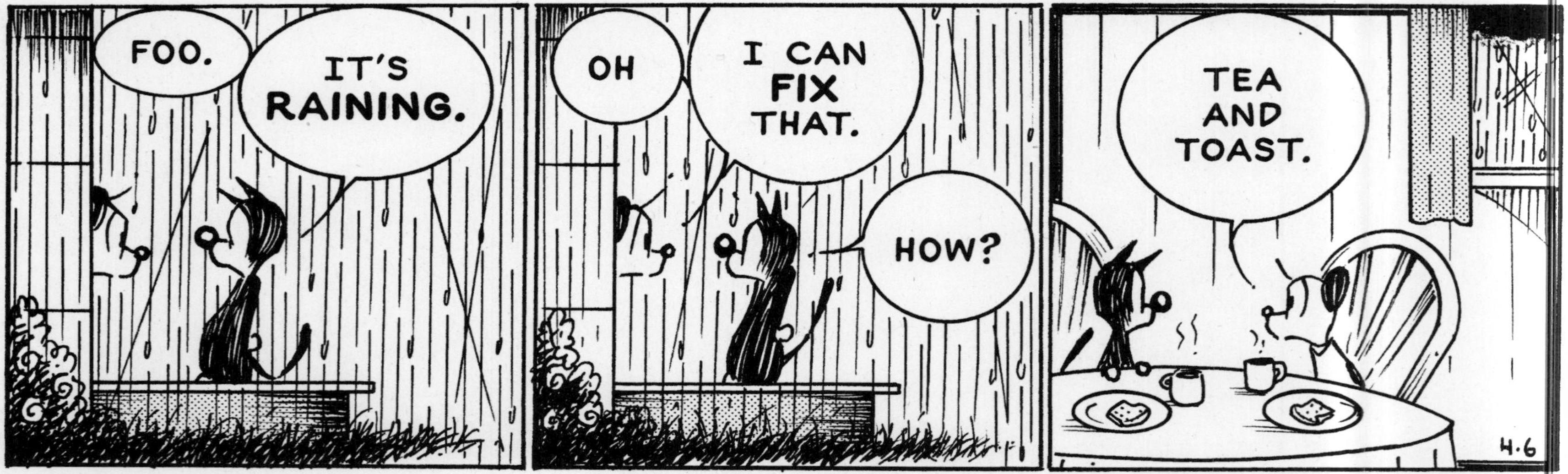
FOO.
IT'S RAINING.
OH
I CAN FIX THAT.
HOW?
TEA AND TOAST.
4·6

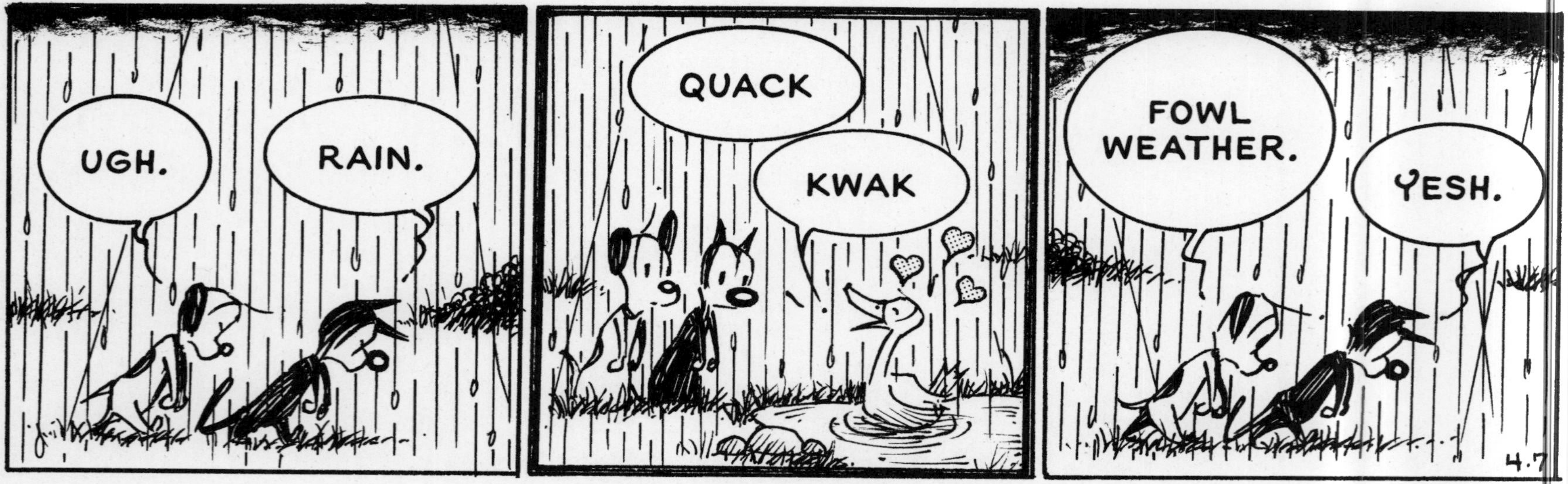
UGH.
RAIN.
QUACK
KWAK
FOWL WEATHER.
YESH.
4·7

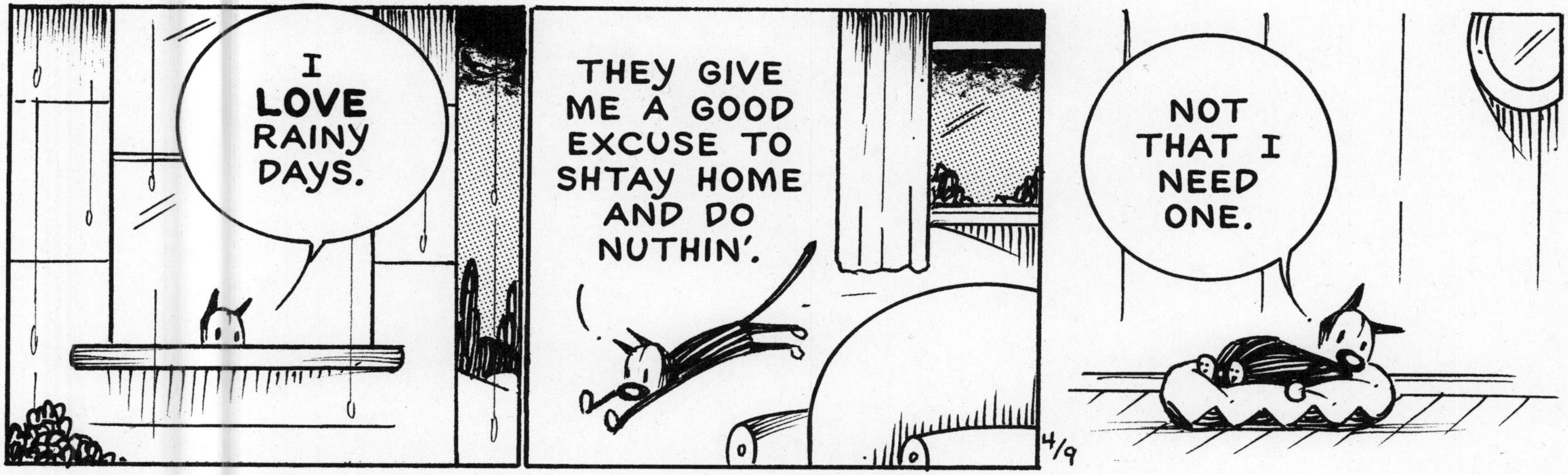
I **LOVE** RAINY DAYS.
THEY GIVE ME A GOOD EXCUSE TO SHTAY HOME AND DO NUTHIN'.
NOT THAT I NEED ONE.
4/9

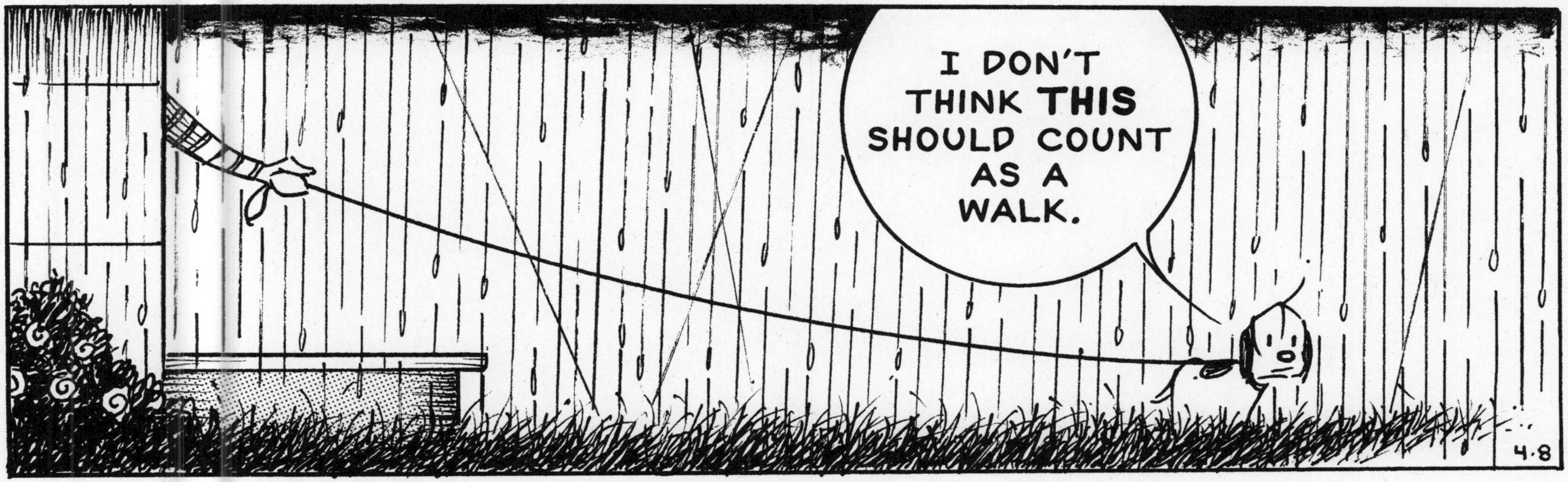
I DON'T THINK **THIS** SHOULD COUNT AS A WALK.
4·8

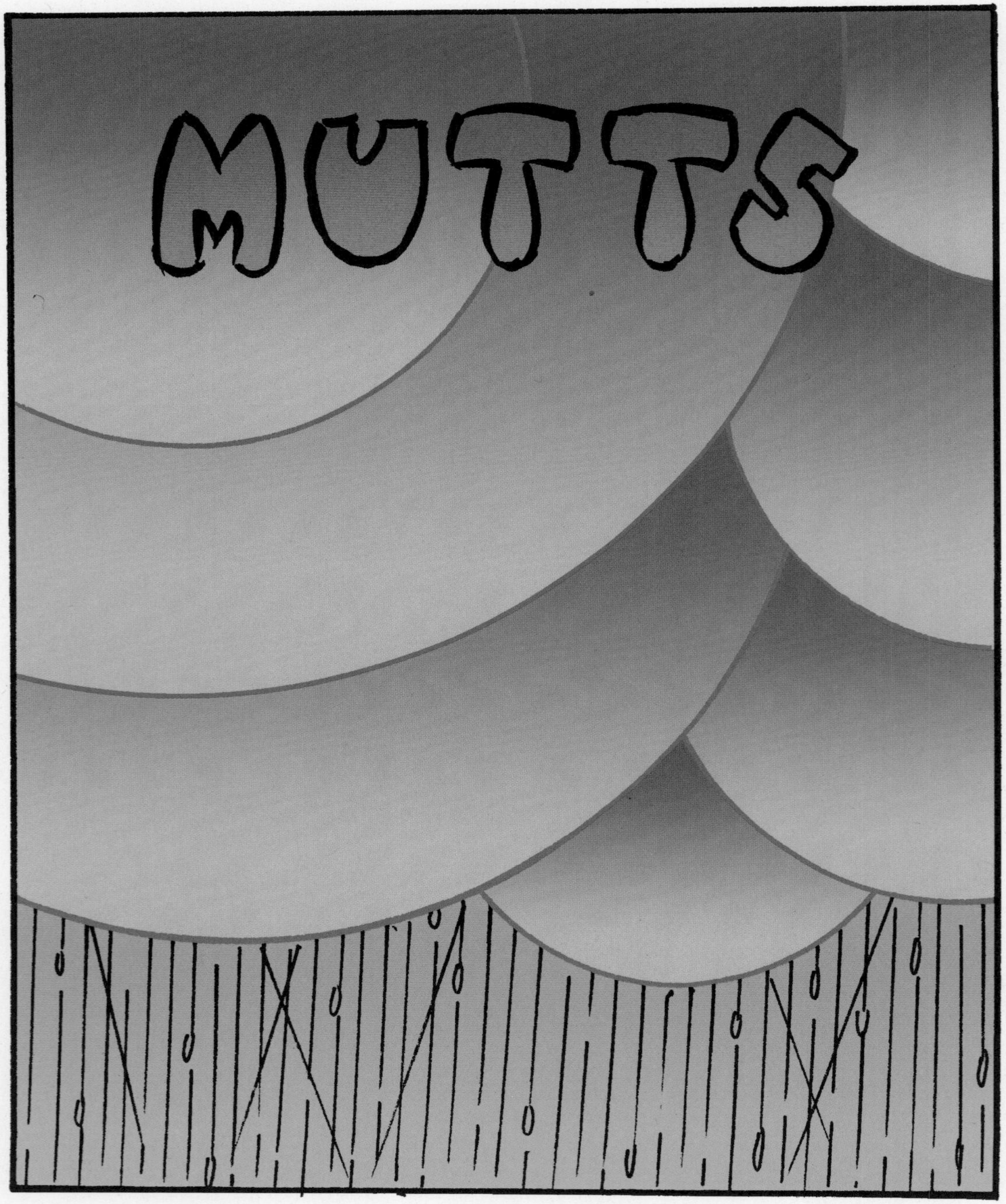
MUTTS

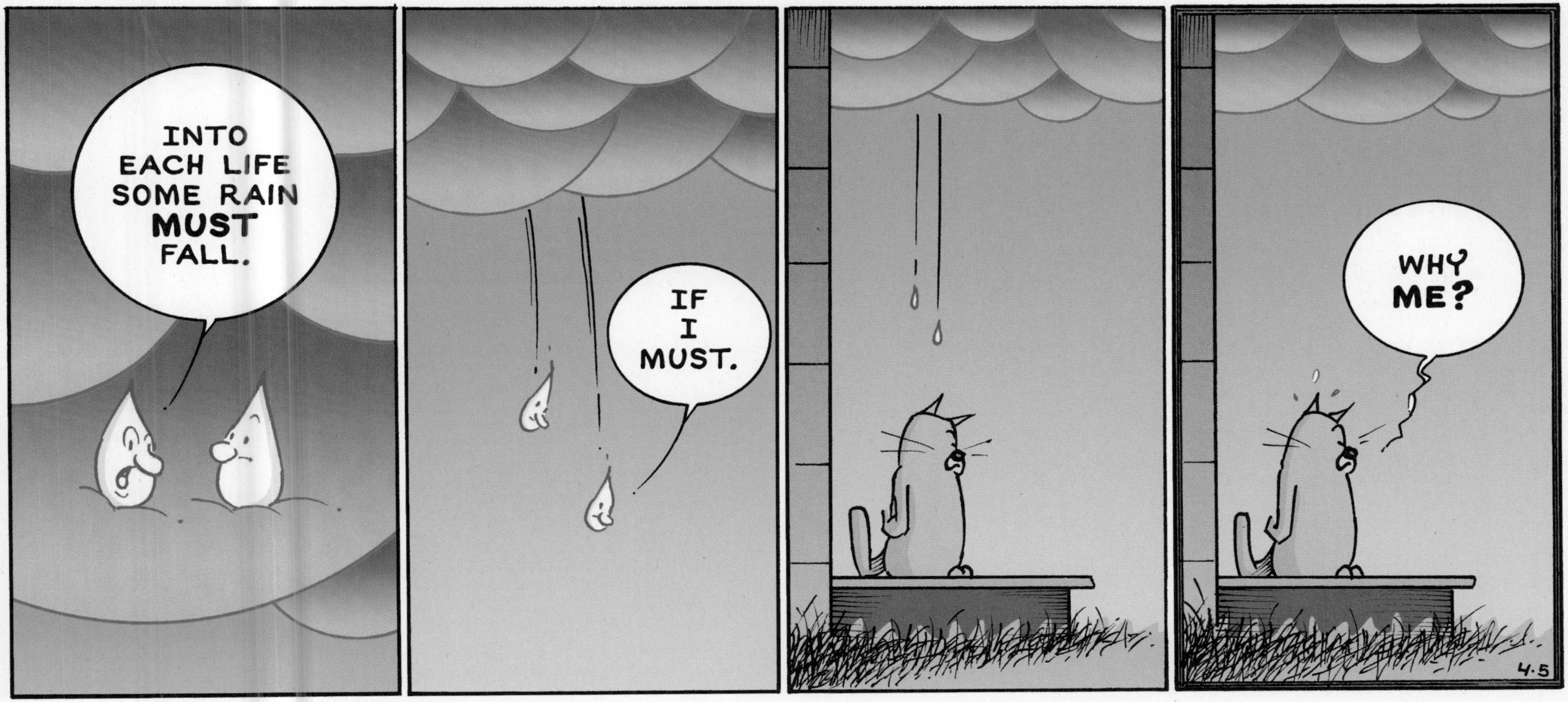
INTO EACH LIFE SOME RAIN **MUST** FALL.
IF I MUST.
WHY **ME?**
4.5

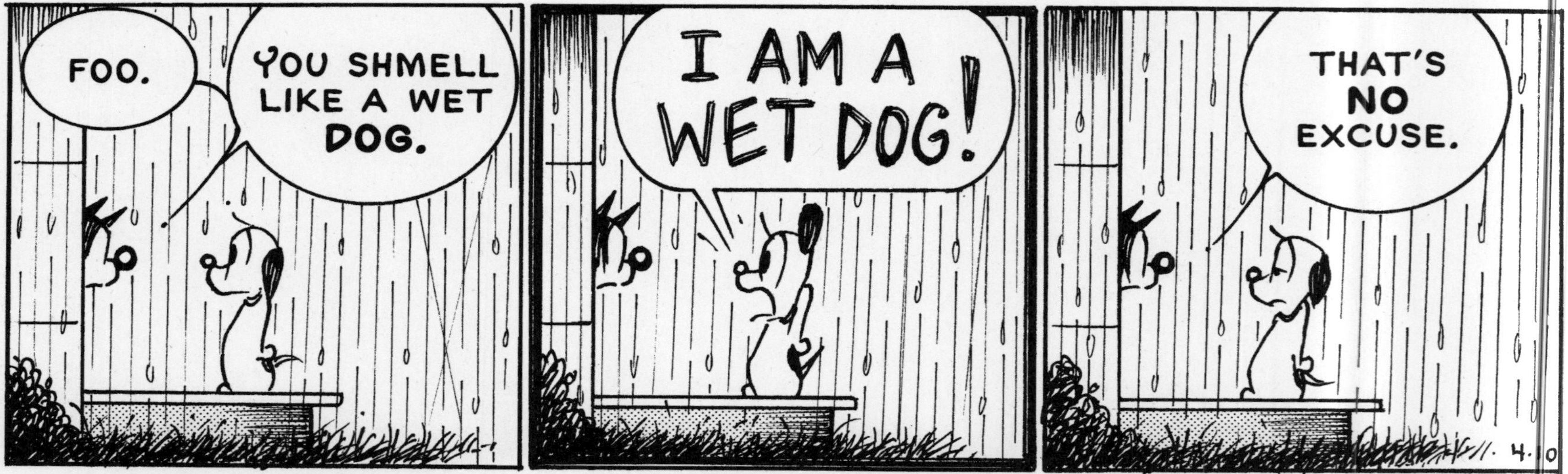
FOO.
YOU SHMELL LIKE A WET DOG.
I AM A WET DOG!
THAT'S NO EXCUSE.
4.10

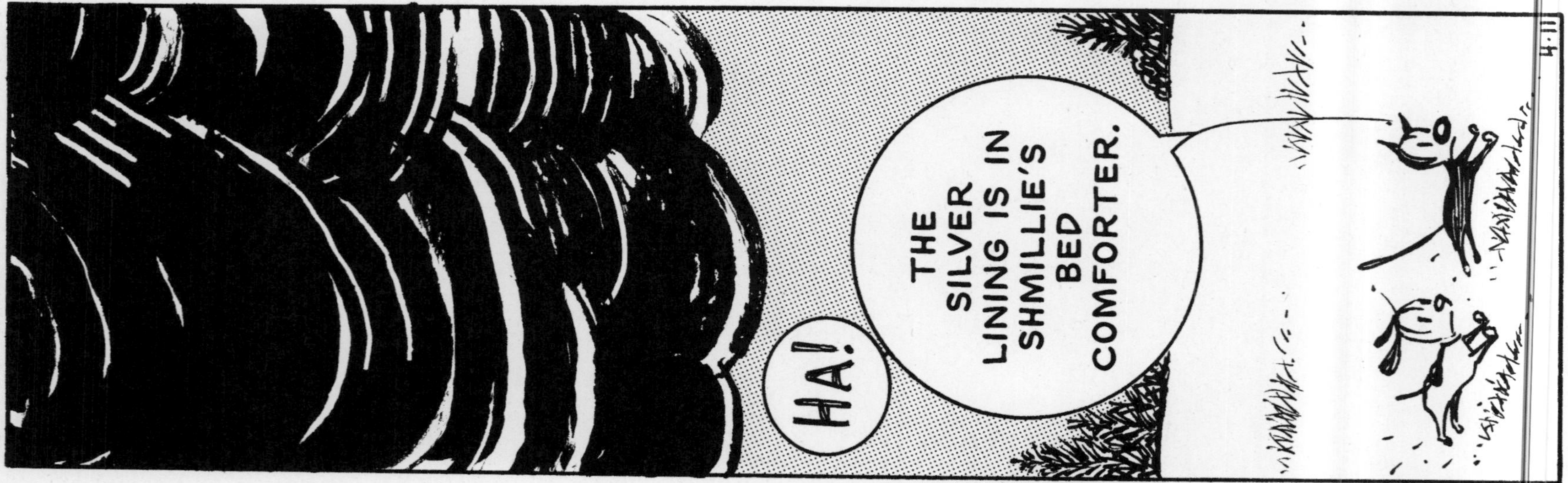
THE SILVER LINING IS IN SHMILLIE'S BED COMFORTER.
HA!
4.11

MUTTS

Patrick McDonnell

THAT'S IT.
NO MORE CATNIP.
4.12

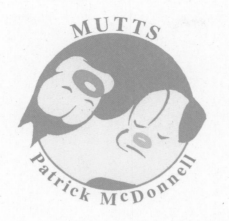

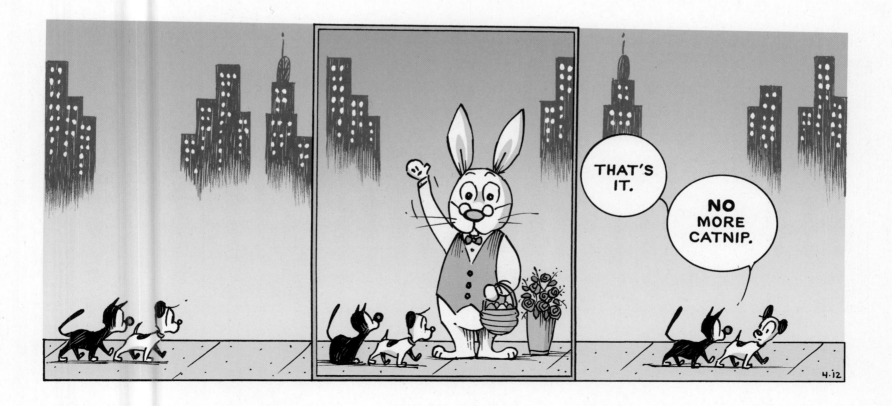

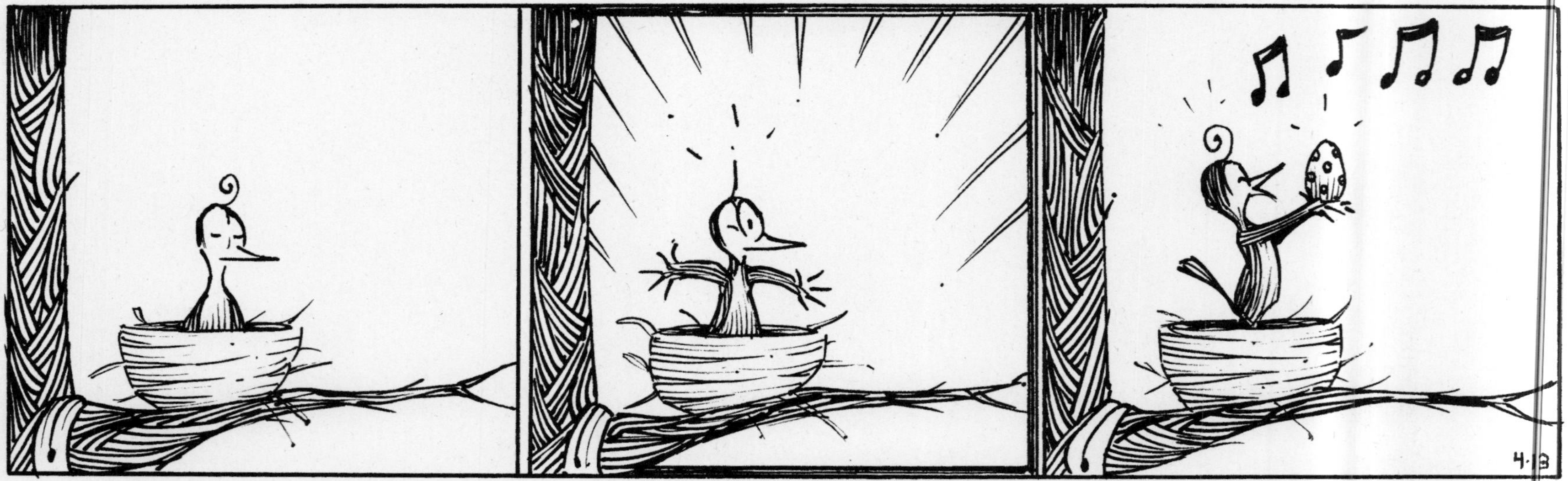
4·13

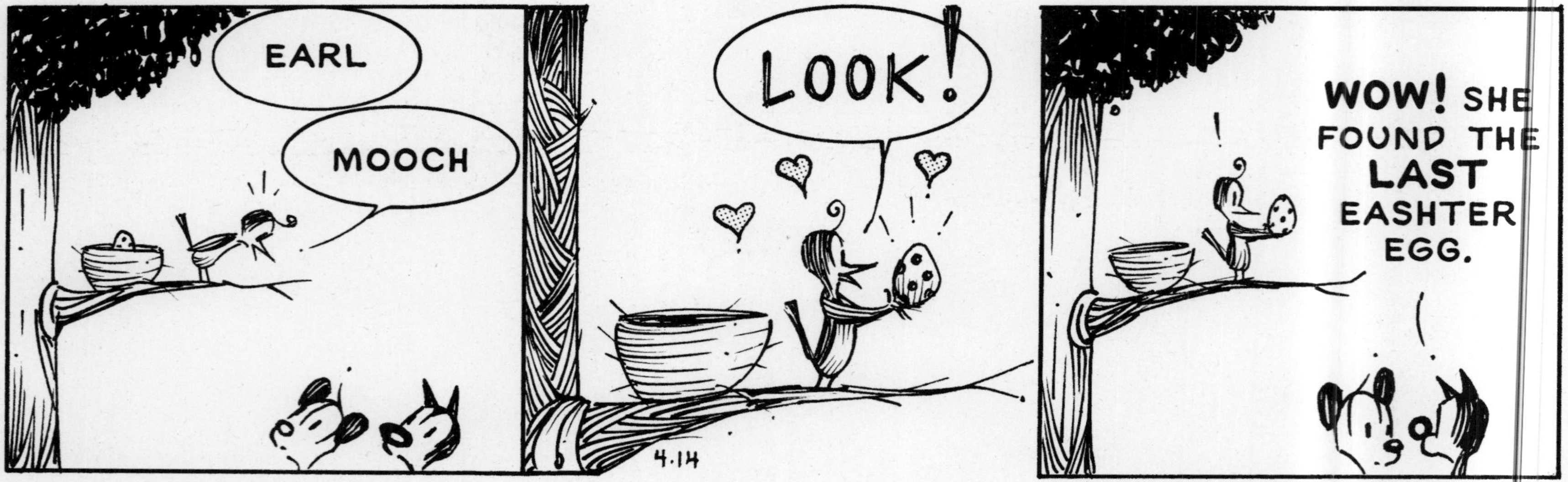
EARL
MOOCH
LOOK!
4·14
WOW! SHE FOUND THE LAST EASHTER EGG.

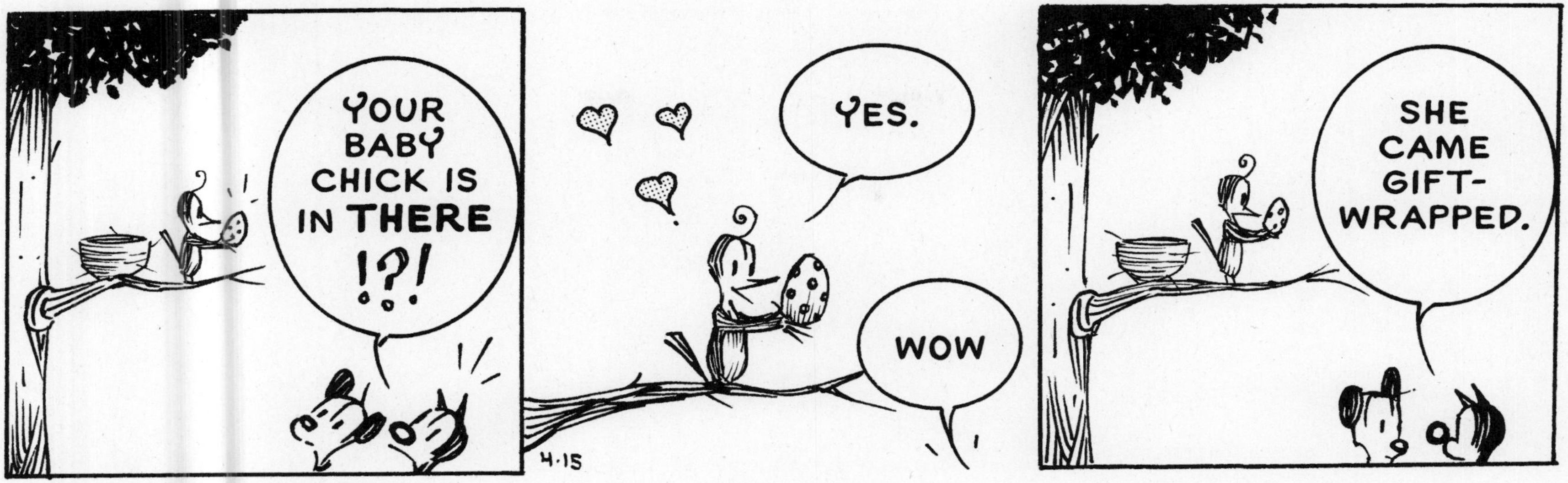
YOUR BABY CHICK IS IN THERE !?!
YES.
WOW
4.15
SHE CAME GIFT-WRAPPED.

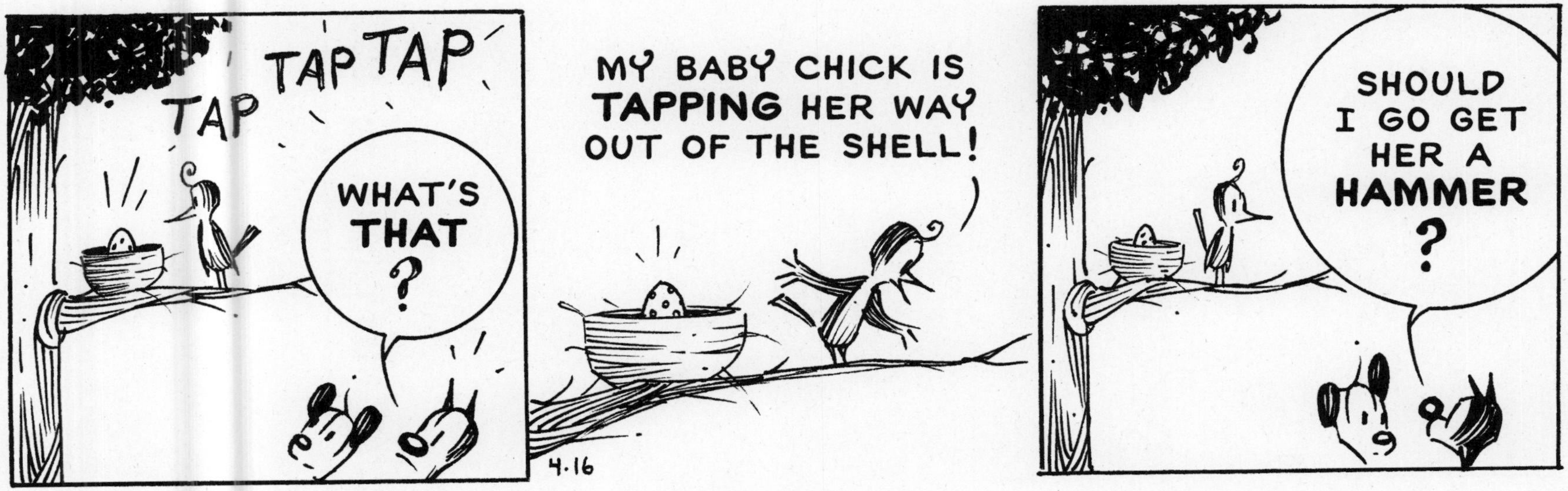
TAP TAP TAP
WHAT'S THAT ?
MY BABY CHICK IS TAPPING HER WAY OUT OF THE SHELL!
4.16
SHOULD I GO GET HER A HAMMER ?

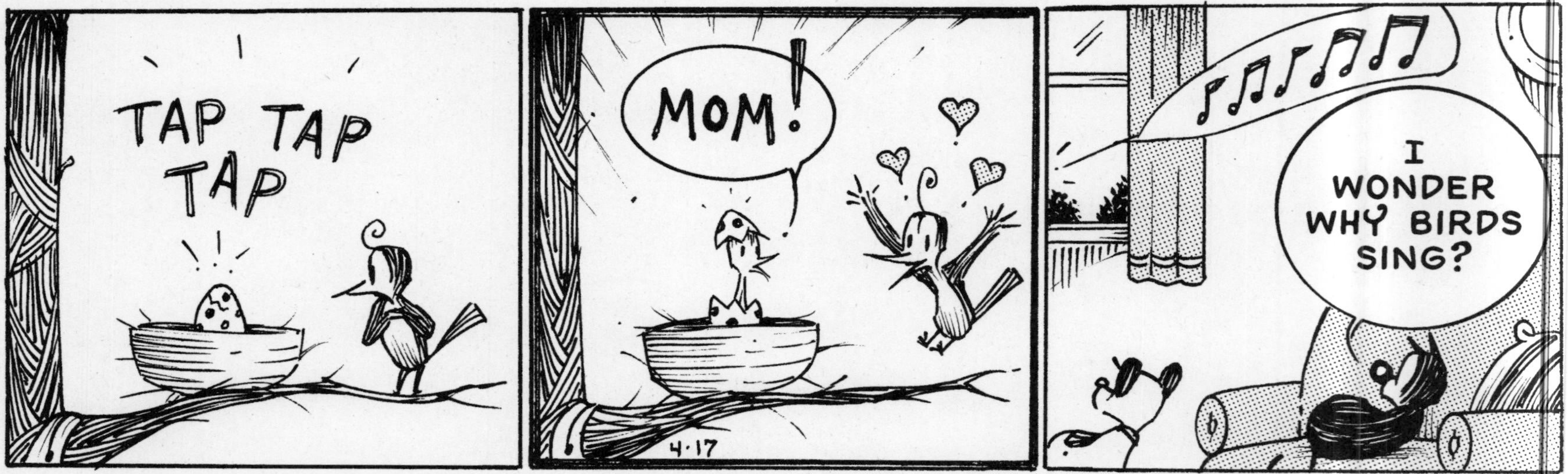
TAP TAP
TAP
MOM!
I WONDER WHY BIRDS SING?
4·17

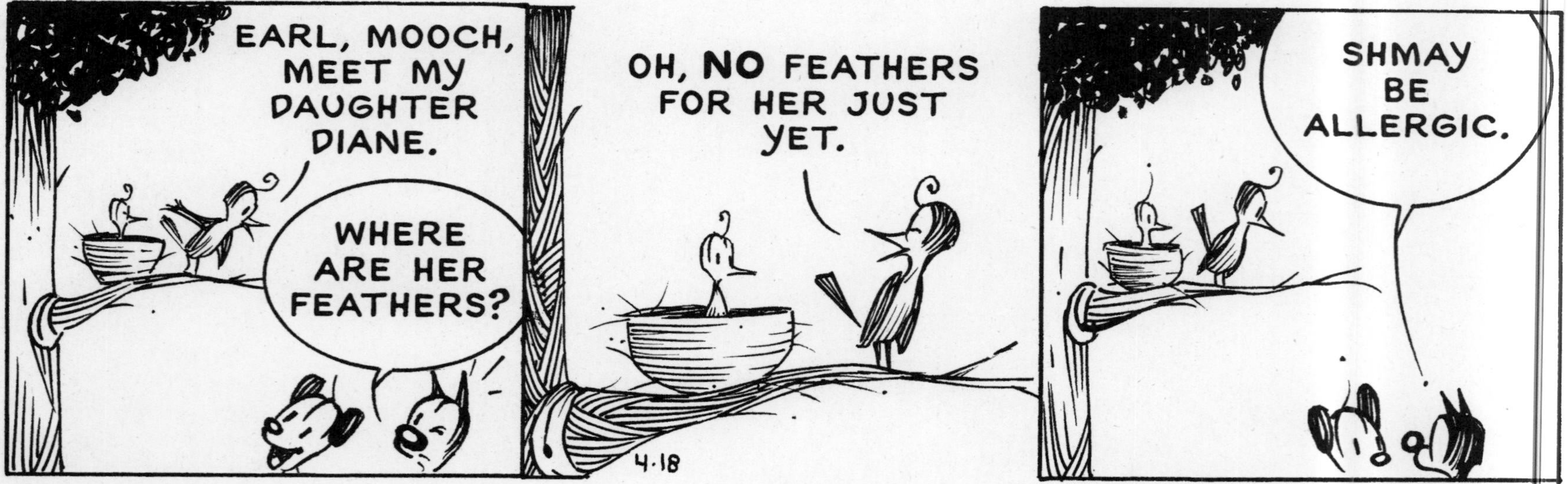
EARL, MOOCH, MEET MY DAUGHTER DIANE.
WHERE ARE HER FEATHERS?
OH, NO FEATHERS FOR HER JUST YET.
SHMAY BE ALLERGIC.
4·18

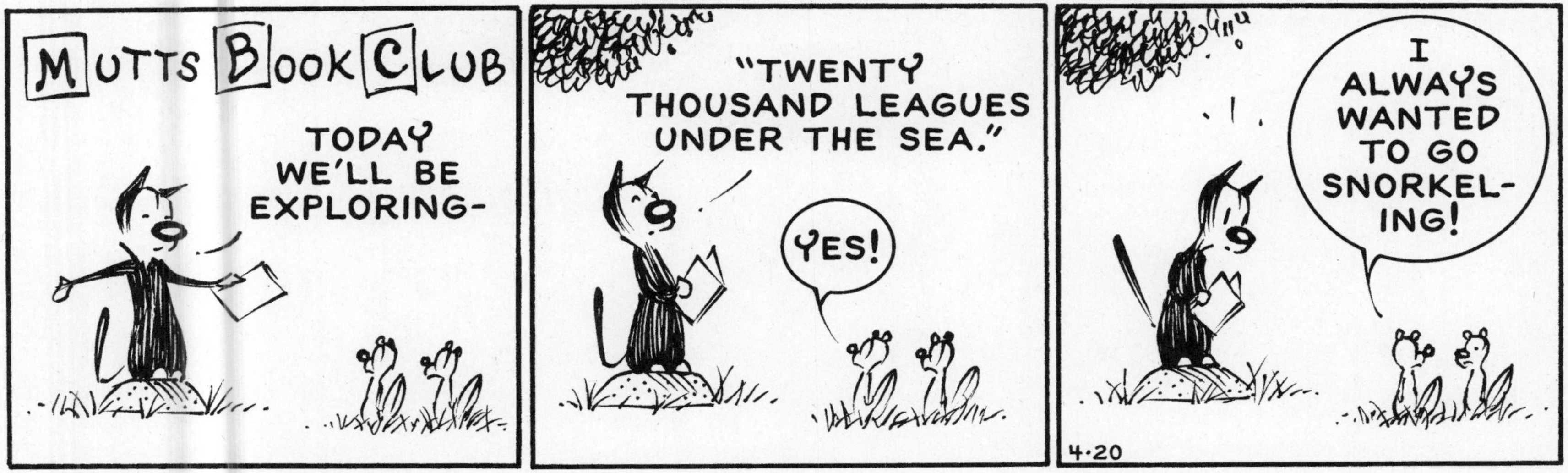
MUTTS BOOK CLUB
TODAY WE'LL BE EXPLORING-
"TWENTY THOUSAND LEAGUES UNDER THE SEA."
YES!
I ALWAYS WANTED TO GO SNORKEL-ING!
4·20

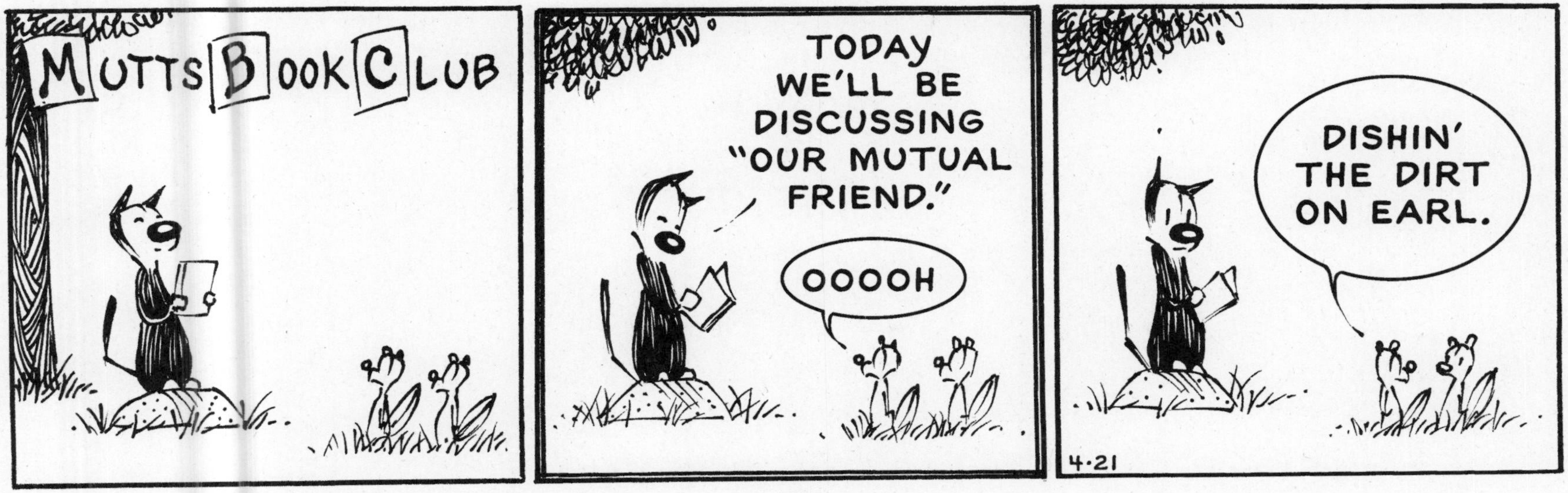
MUTTS BOOK CLUB
TODAY WE'LL BE DISCUSSING "OUR MUTUAL FRIEND."
OOOOH
DISHIN' THE DIRT ON EARL.
4·21

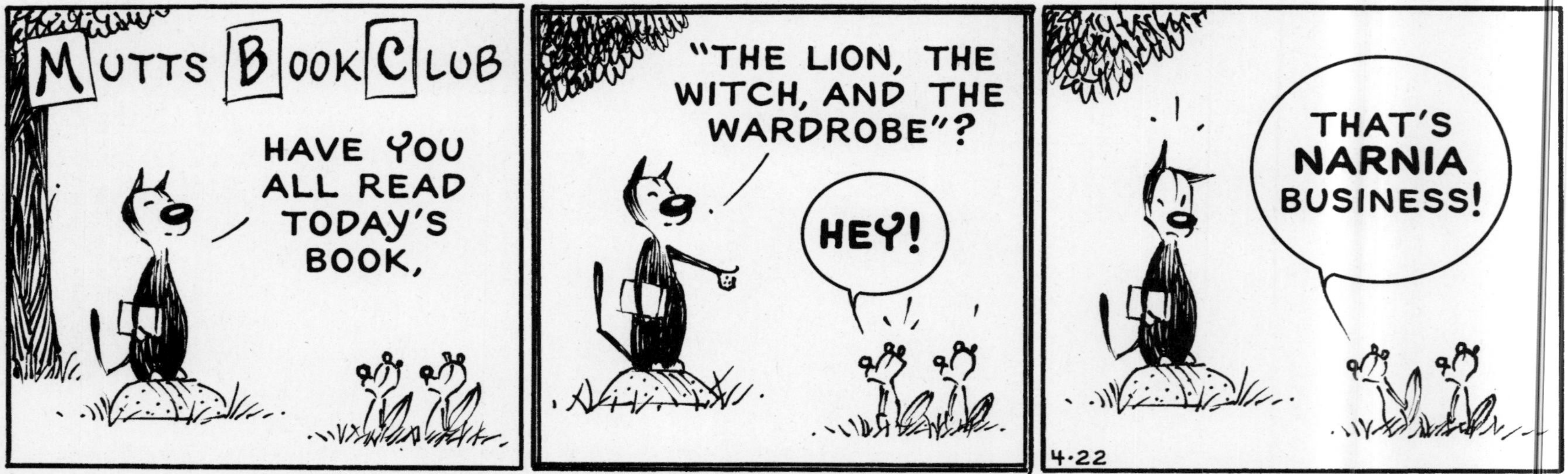
MUTTS BOOK CLUB
HAVE YOU ALL READ TODAY'S BOOK,
"THE LION, THE WITCH, AND THE WARDROBE"?
HEY!
THAT'S NARNIA BUSINESS!
4·22

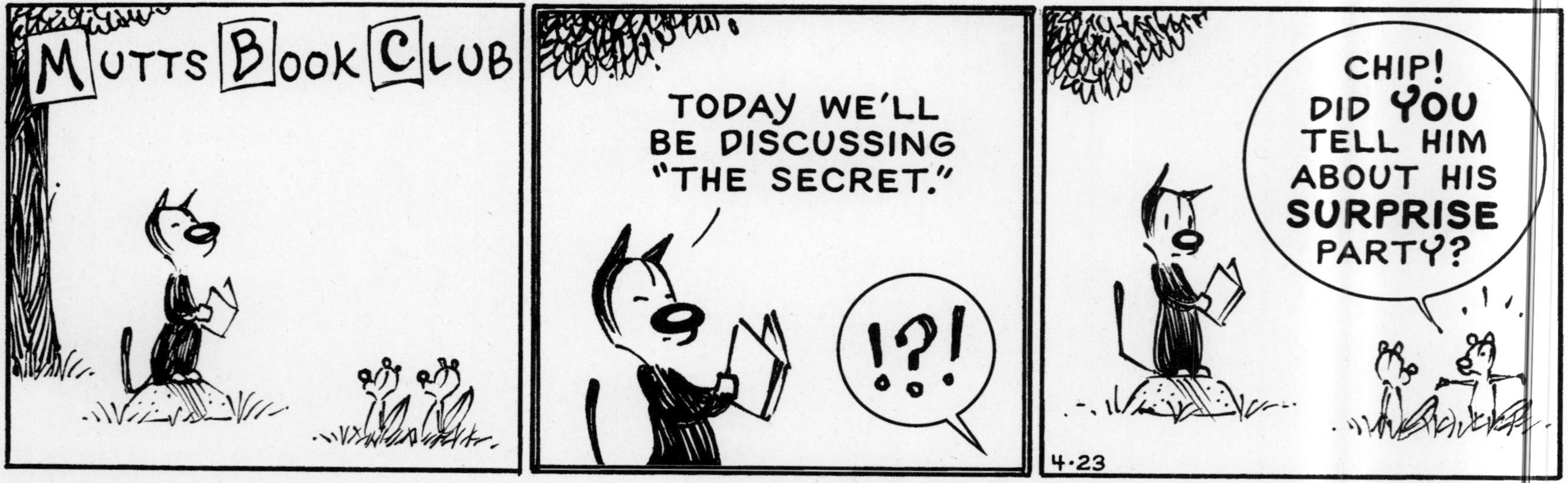
MUTTS BOOK CLUB
TODAY WE'LL BE DISCUSSING "THE SECRET."
!?!
CHIP! DID YOU TELL HIM ABOUT HIS SURPRISE PARTY?
4·23

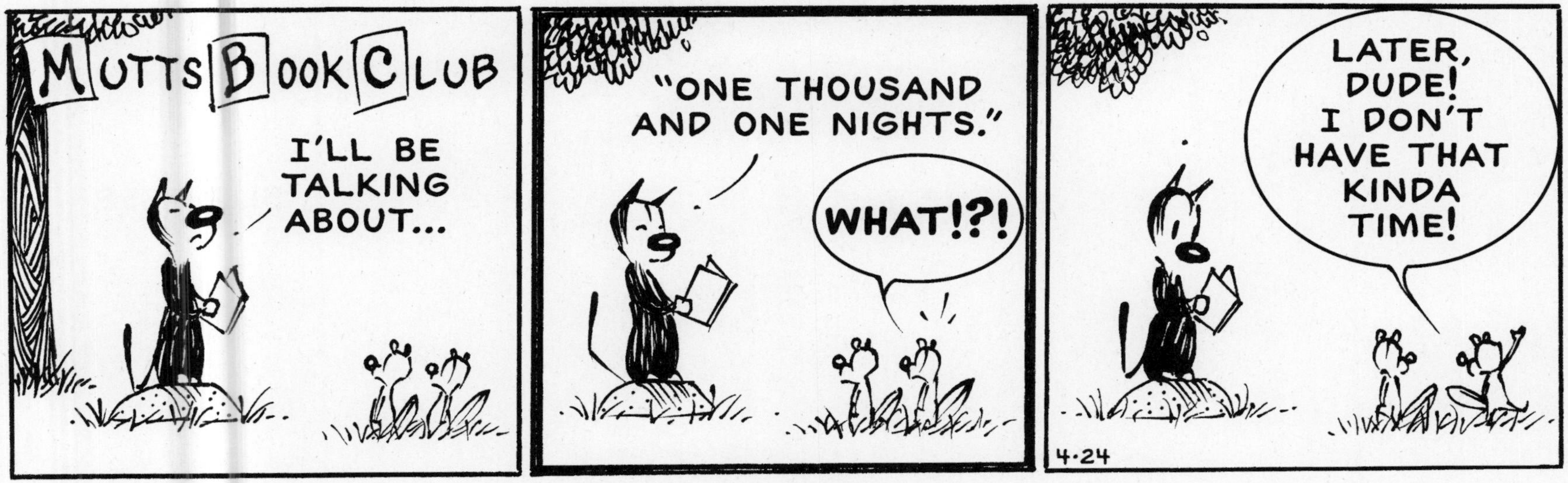
MUTTS BOOK CLUB
I'LL BE TALKING ABOUT...
"ONE THOUSAND AND ONE NIGHTS."
WHAT!?!
LATER, DUDE! I DON'T HAVE THAT KINDA TIME!
4·24

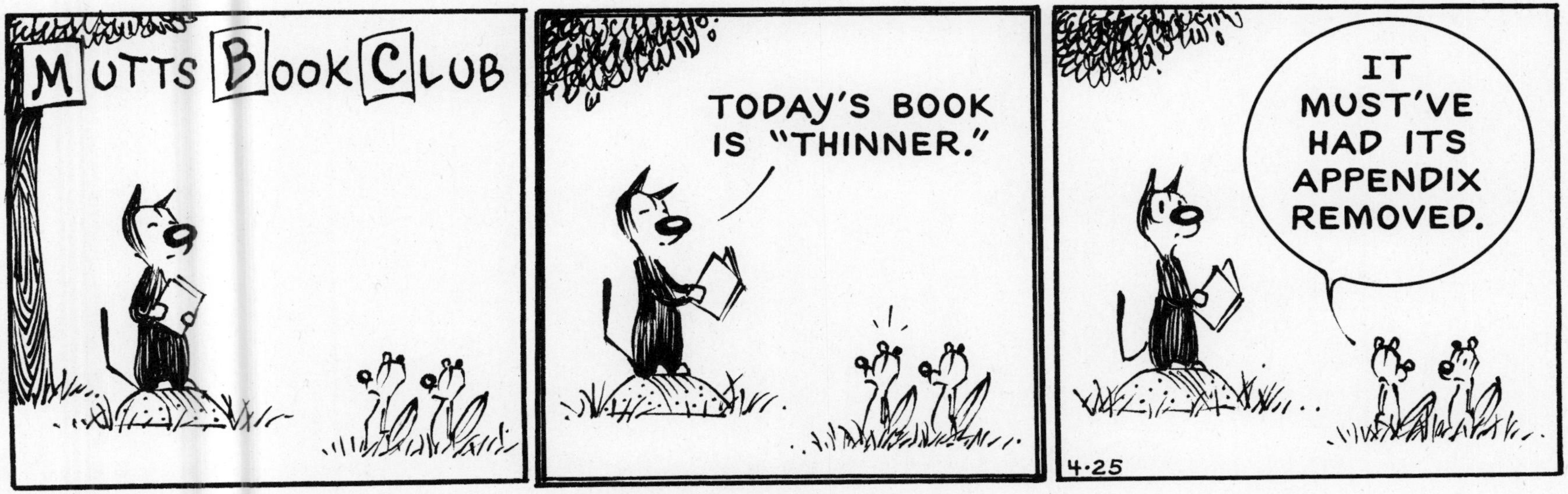
MUTTS BOOK CLUB
TODAY'S BOOK IS "THINNER."
IT MUST'VE HAD ITS APPENDIX REMOVED.
4·25

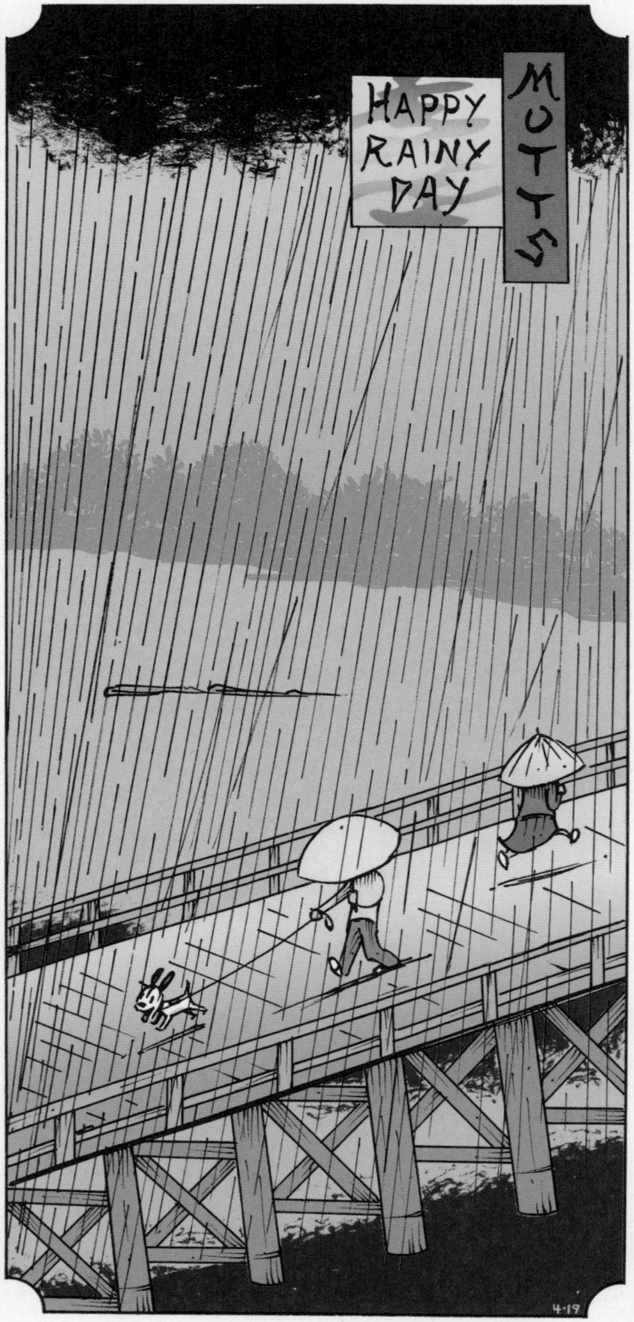
HAPPY RAINY DAY
MOTTS
4·19

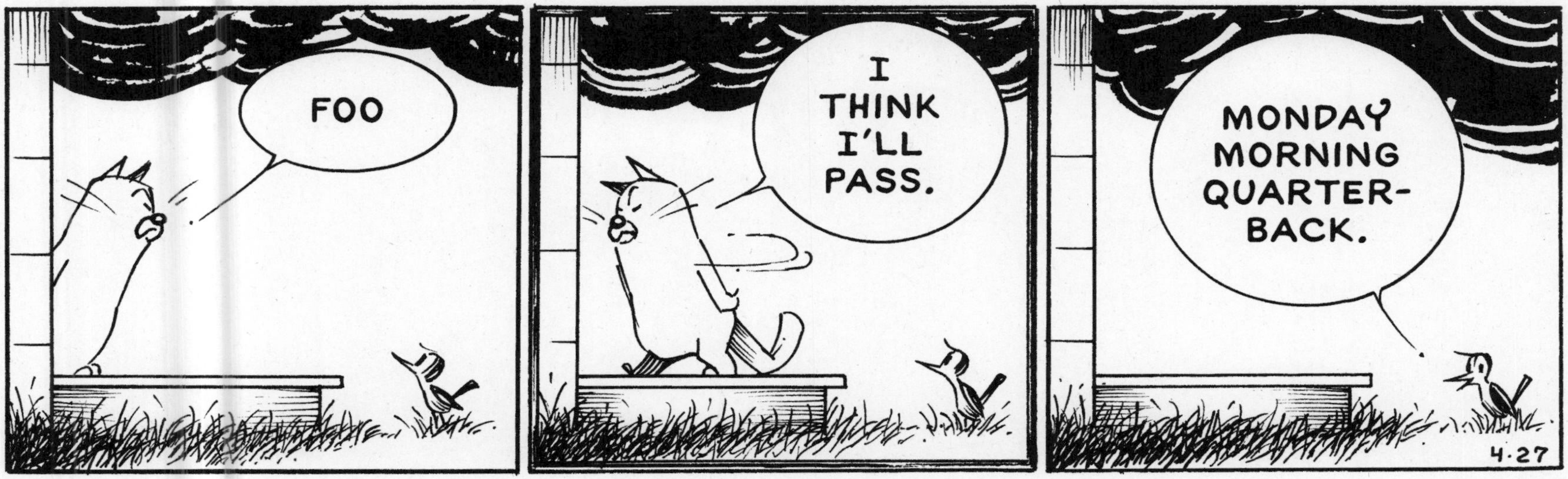
FOO
I THINK I'LL PASS.
MONDAY MORNING QUARTER-BACK.
4·27

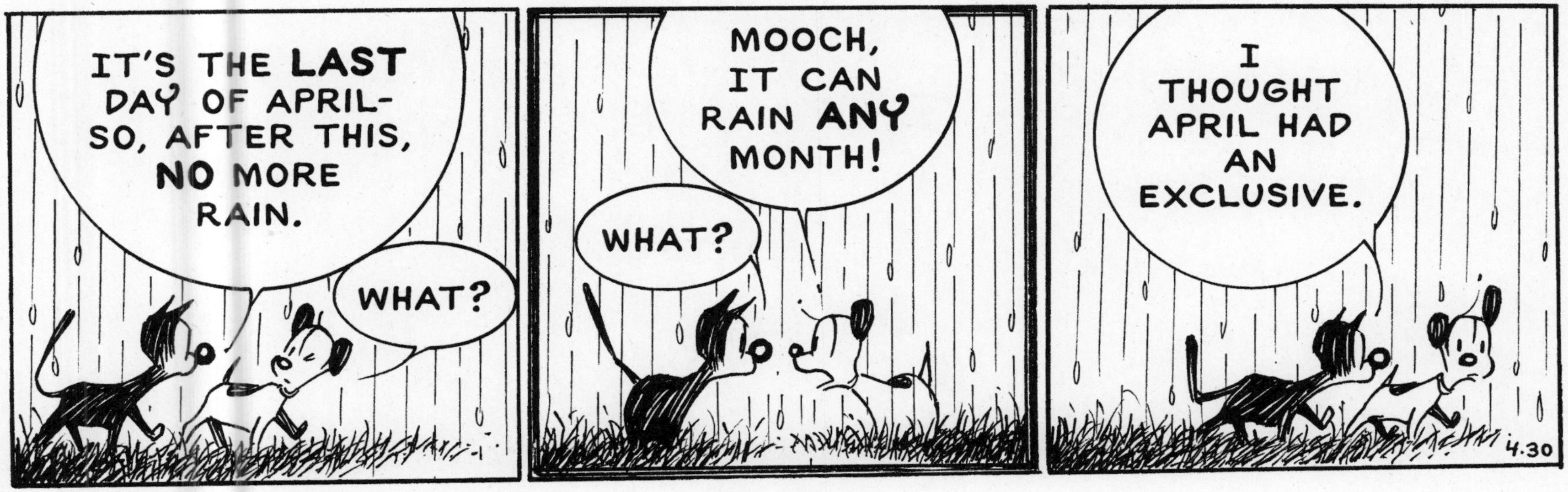
IT'S THE LAST DAY OF APRIL- SO, AFTER THIS, NO MORE RAIN.
WHAT?
WHAT?
MOOCH, IT CAN RAIN ANY MONTH!
I THOUGHT APRIL HAD AN EXCLUSIVE.
4·30

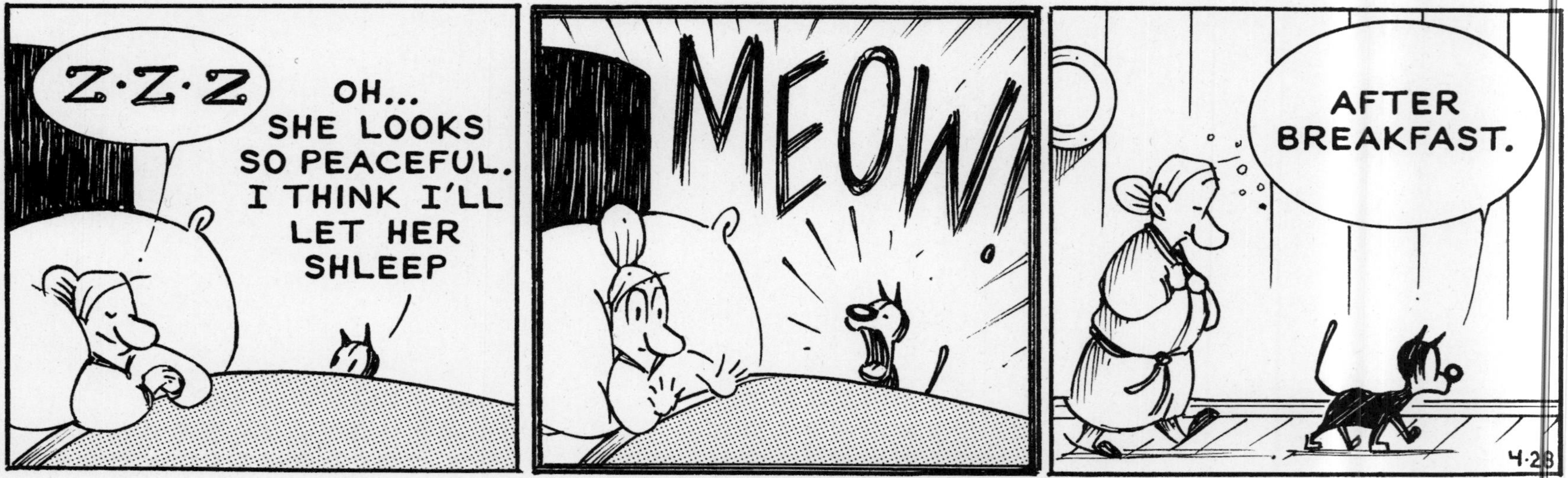
Z·Z·Z
OH... SHE LOOKS SO PEACEFUL. I THINK I'LL LET HER SHLEEP
MEOW!
AFTER BREAKFAST.
4·28

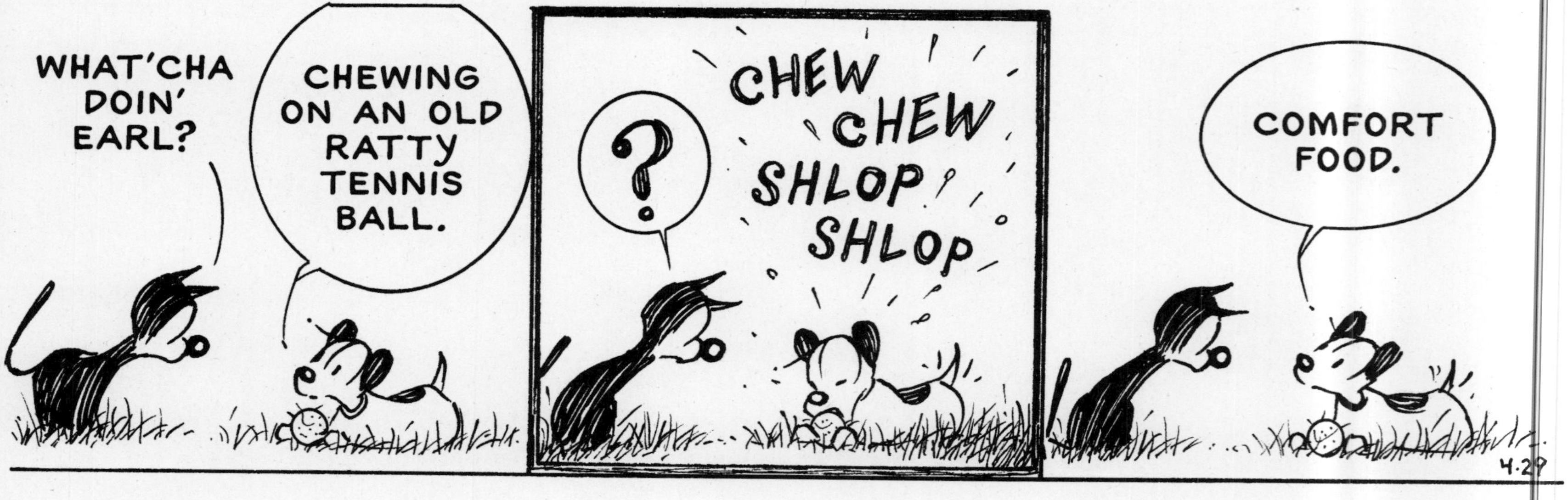
WHAT'CHA DOIN' EARL?
CHEWING ON AN OLD RATTY TENNIS BALL.
?
CHEW CHEW SHLOP SHLOP
COMFORT FOOD.
4·29

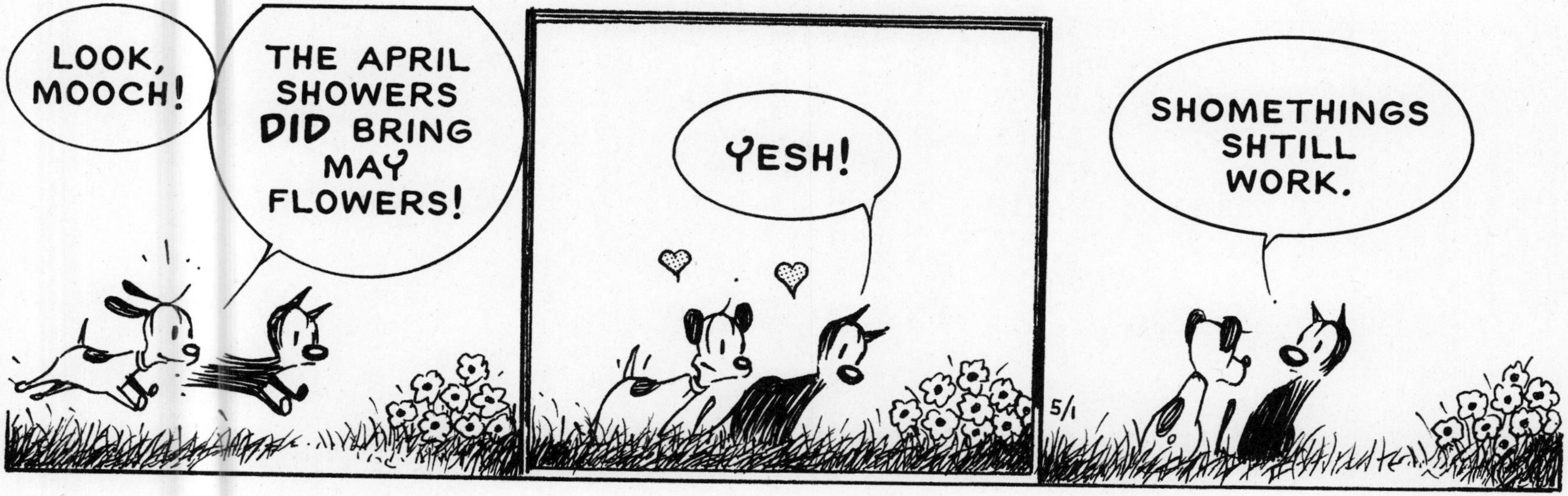
LOOK, MOOCH!
THE APRIL SHOWERS DID BRING MAY FLOWERS!
YESH!
SHOMETHINGS SHTILL WORK.
5/1

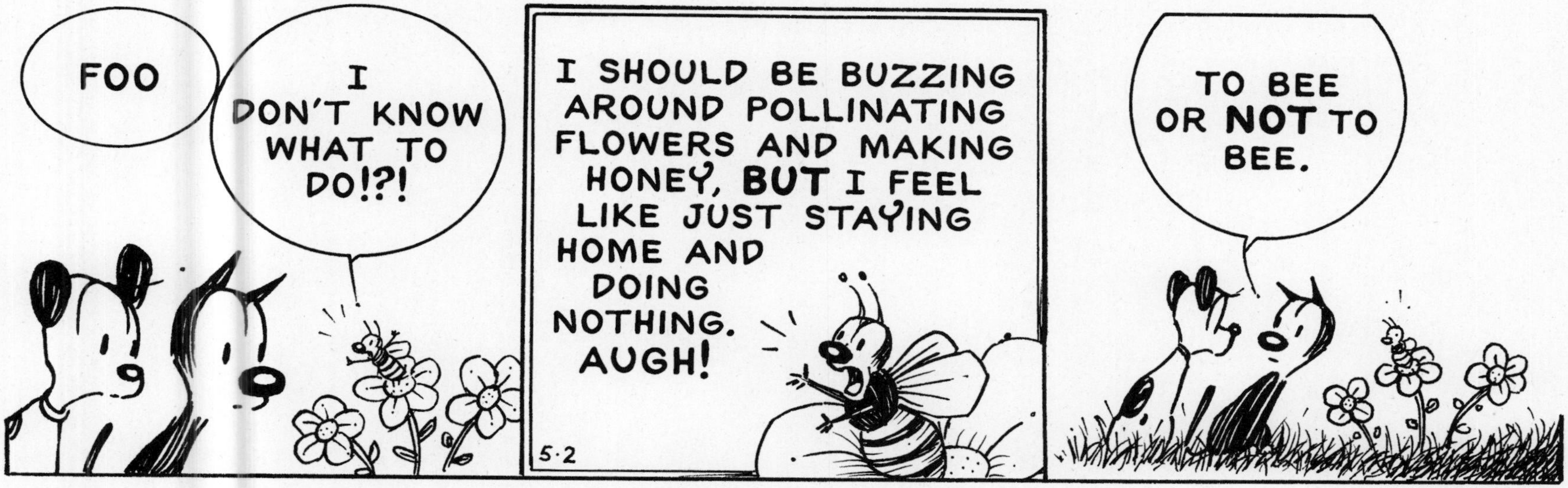
FOO
I DON'T KNOW WHAT TO DO!?!
I SHOULD BE BUZZING AROUND POLLINATING FLOWERS AND MAKING HONEY, BUT I FEEL LIKE JUST STAYING HOME AND DOING NOTHING. AUGH!
TO BEE OR NOT TO BEE.
5·2

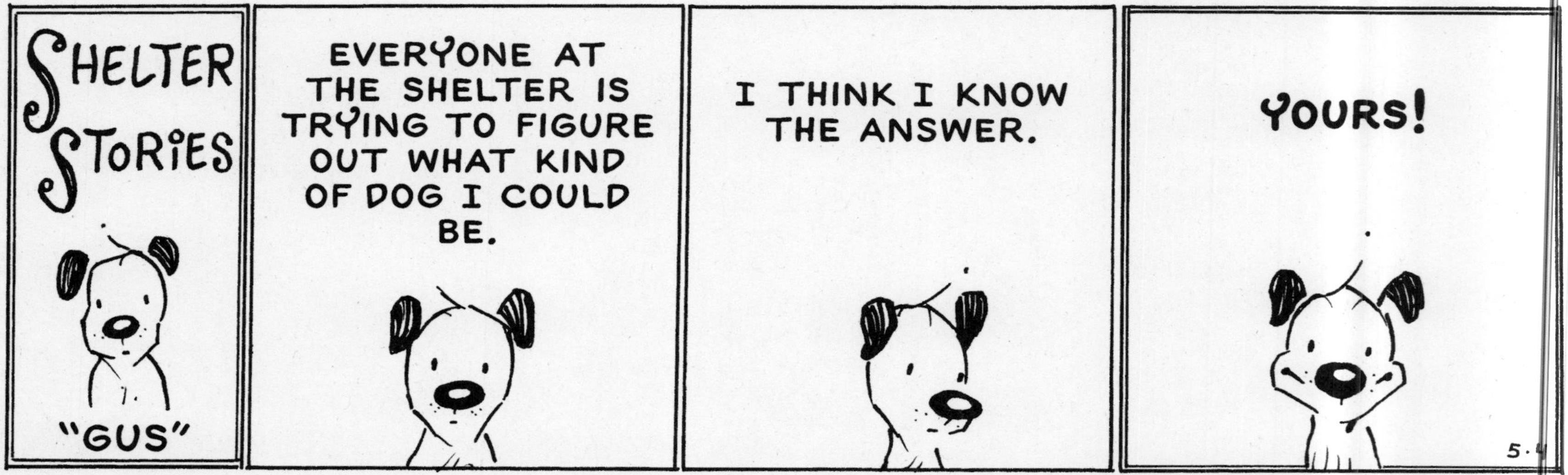
SHELTER STORIES
"GUS"
EVERYONE AT THE SHELTER IS TRYING TO FIGURE OUT WHAT KIND OF DOG I COULD BE.
I THINK I KNOW THE ANSWER.
YOURS!
5·4

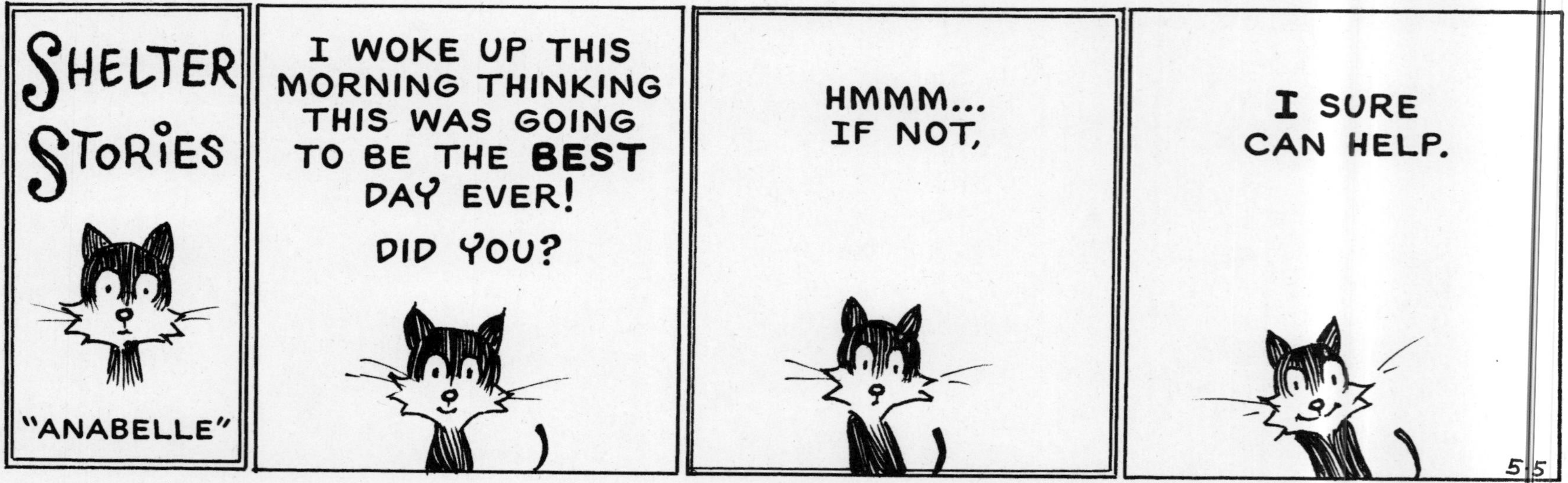
SHELTER STORIES
"ANABELLE"
I WOKE UP THIS MORNING THINKING THIS WAS GOING TO BE THE BEST DAY EVER!
DID YOU?
HMMM... IF NOT,
I SURE CAN HELP.
5·5

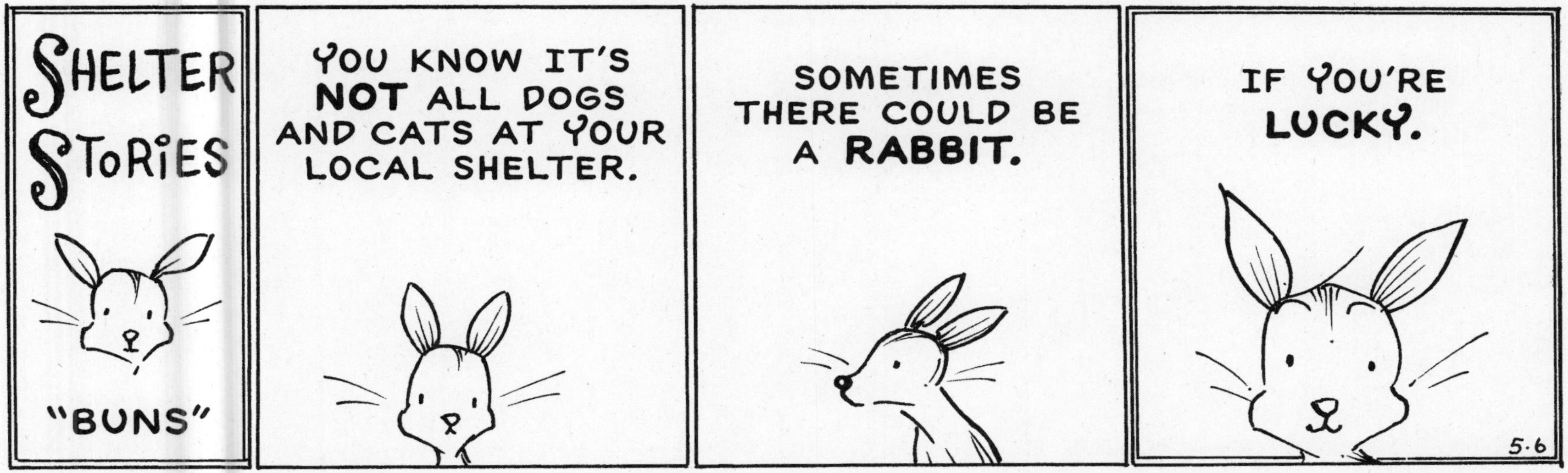
SHELTER STORIES
"BUNS"
YOU KNOW IT'S NOT ALL DOGS AND CATS AT YOUR LOCAL SHELTER.
SOMETIMES THERE COULD BE A RABBIT.
IF YOU'RE LUCKY.
5·6

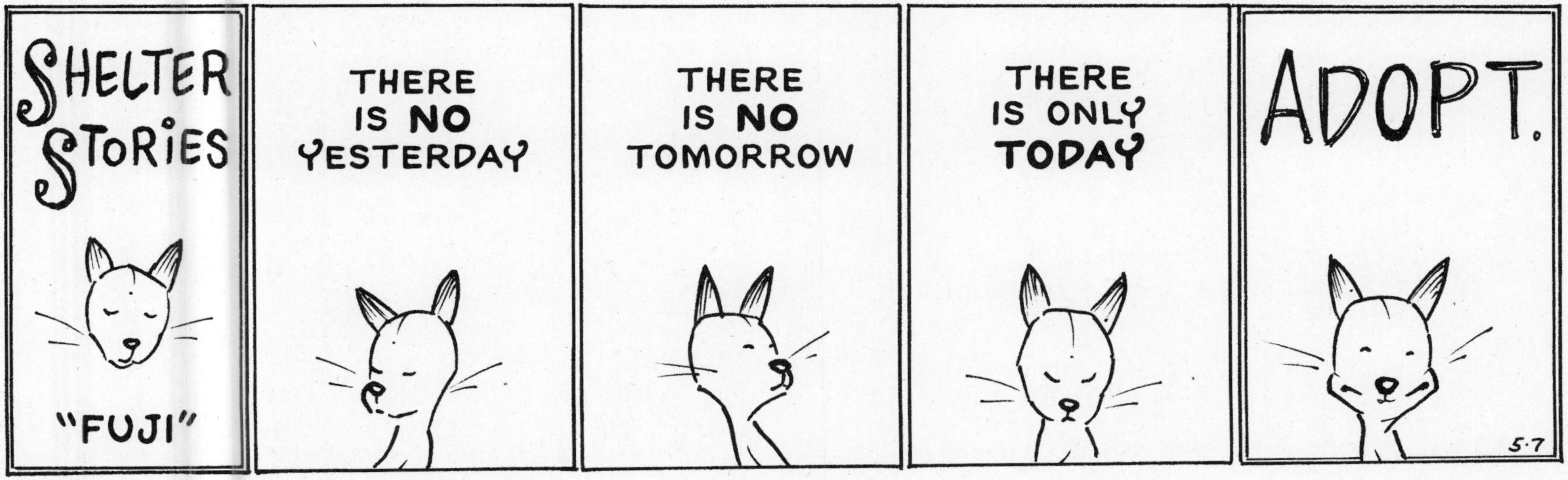
SHELTER STORIES
"FUJI"
THERE IS NO YESTERDAY
THERE IS NO TOMORROW
THERE IS ONLY TODAY
ADOPT.
5·7

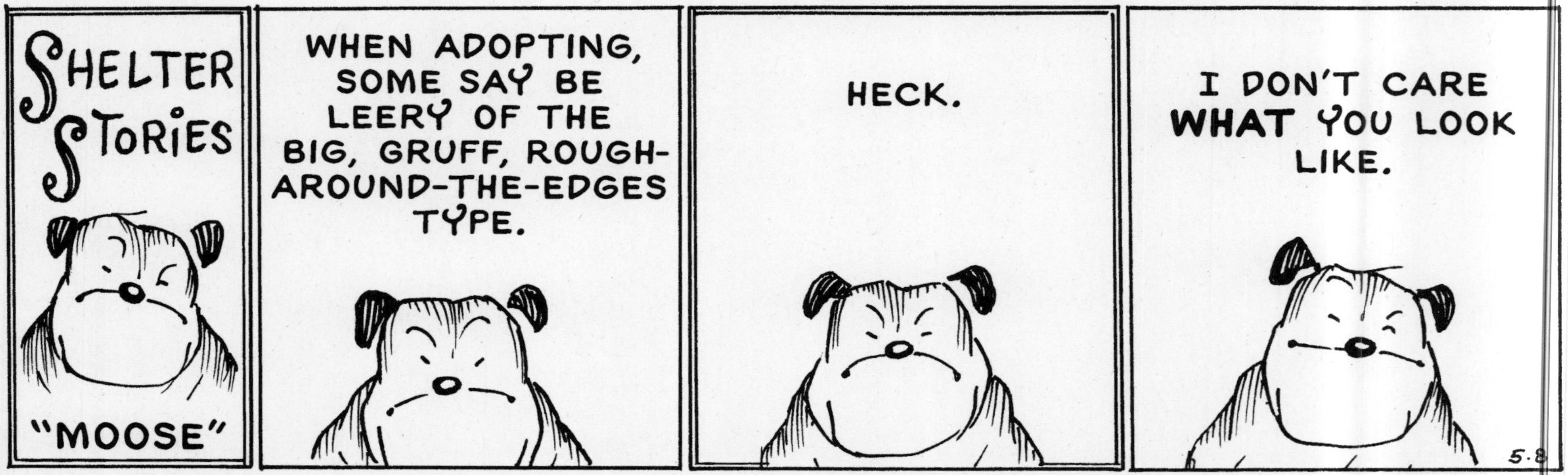
SHELTER STORIES
"MOOSE"
WHEN ADOPTING, SOME SAY BE LEERY OF THE BIG, GRUFF, ROUGH-AROUND-THE-EDGES TYPE.
HECK.
I DON'T CARE **WHAT** YOU LOOK LIKE.

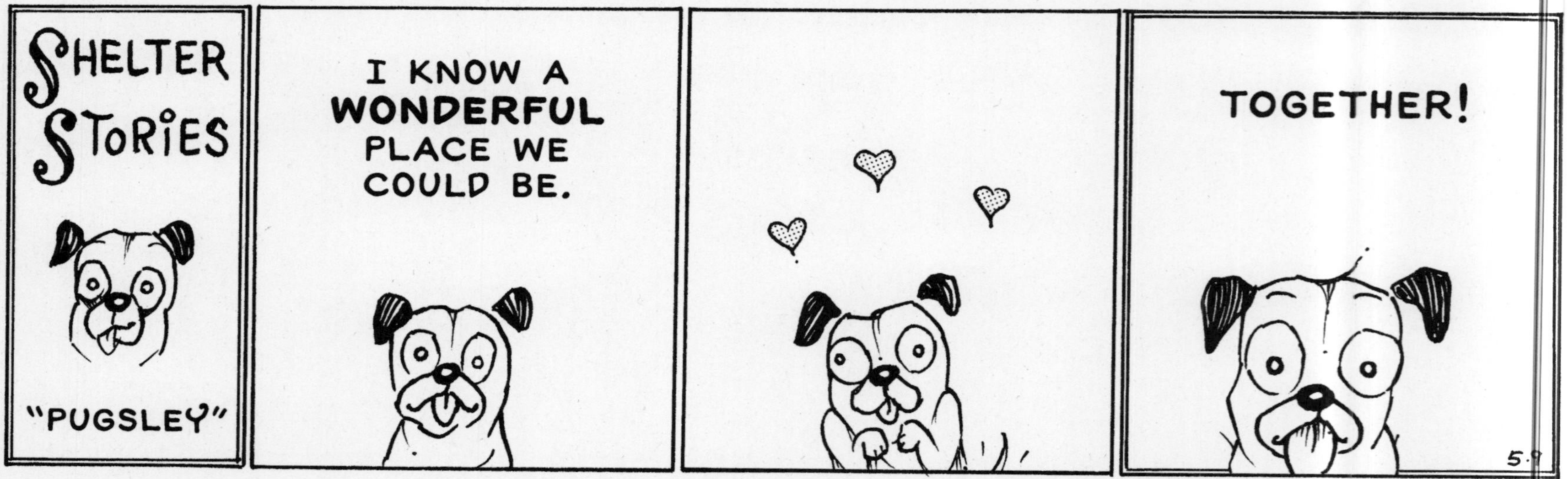
SHELTER STORIES
"PUGSLEY"
I KNOW A **WONDERFUL** PLACE WE COULD BE.
TOGETHER!

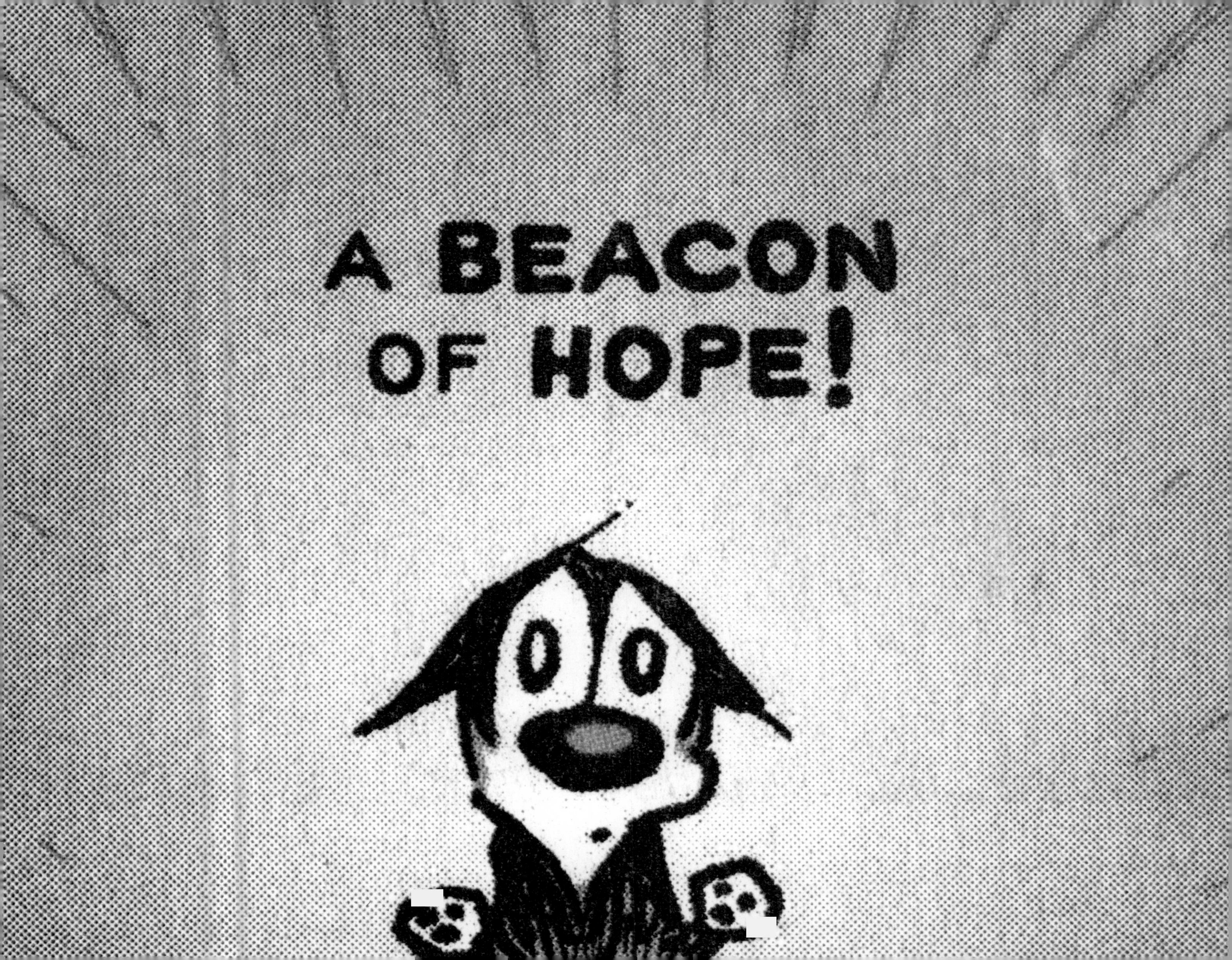
A BEACON
OF HOPE!

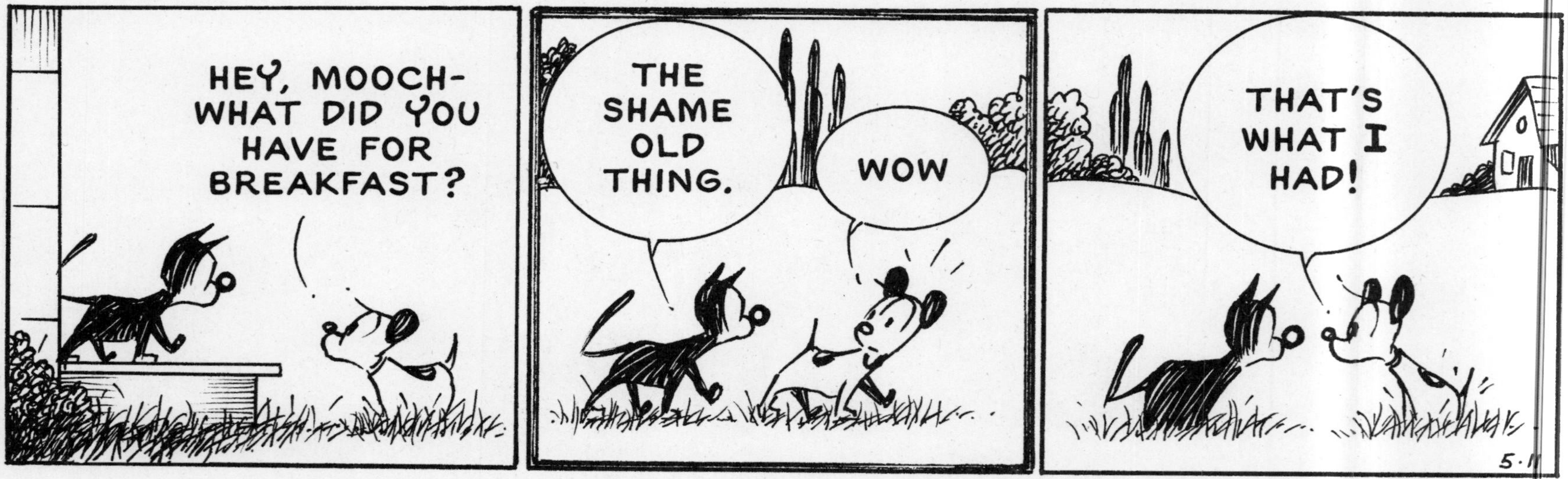
HEY, MOOCH-
WHAT DID YOU
HAVE FOR
BREAKFAST?
THE
SHAME
OLD
THING.
WOW
THAT'S
WHAT I
HAD!
5-11

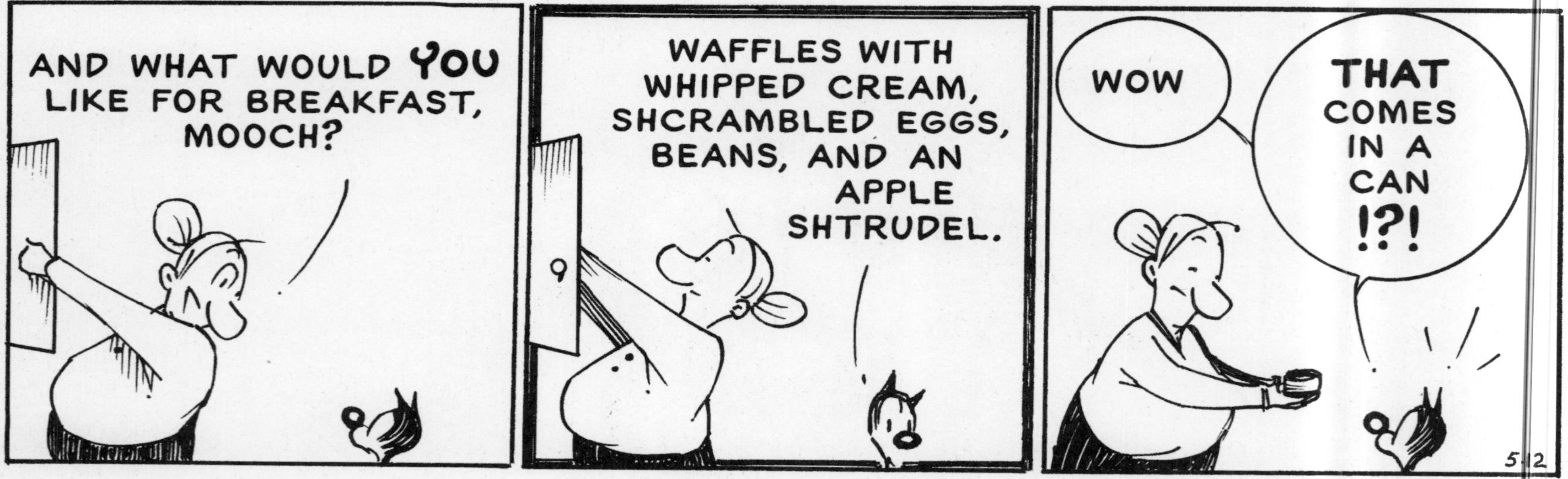
AND WHAT WOULD YOU
LIKE FOR BREAKFAST,
MOOCH?
WAFFLES WITH
WHIPPED CREAM,
SHCRAMBLED EGGS,
BEANS, AND AN
APPLE
SHTRUDEL.
WOW
THAT
COMES
IN A
CAN
!?!
5-12

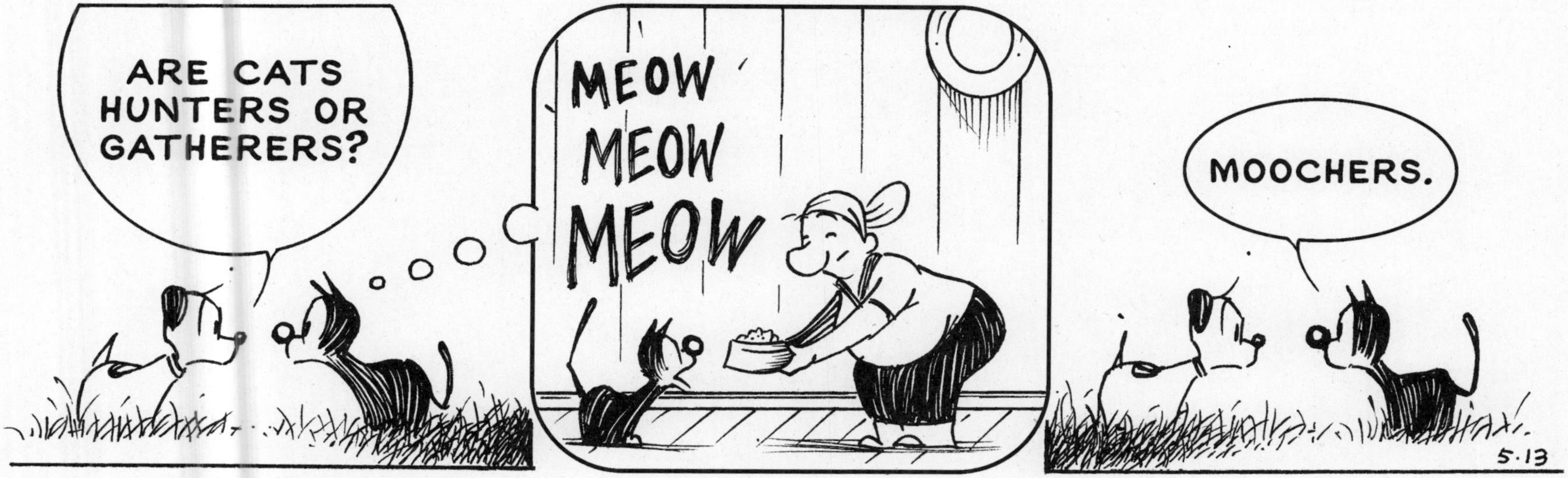
ARE CATS HUNTERS OR GATHERERS?
MEOW MEOW MEOW
MOOCHERS.
5·13

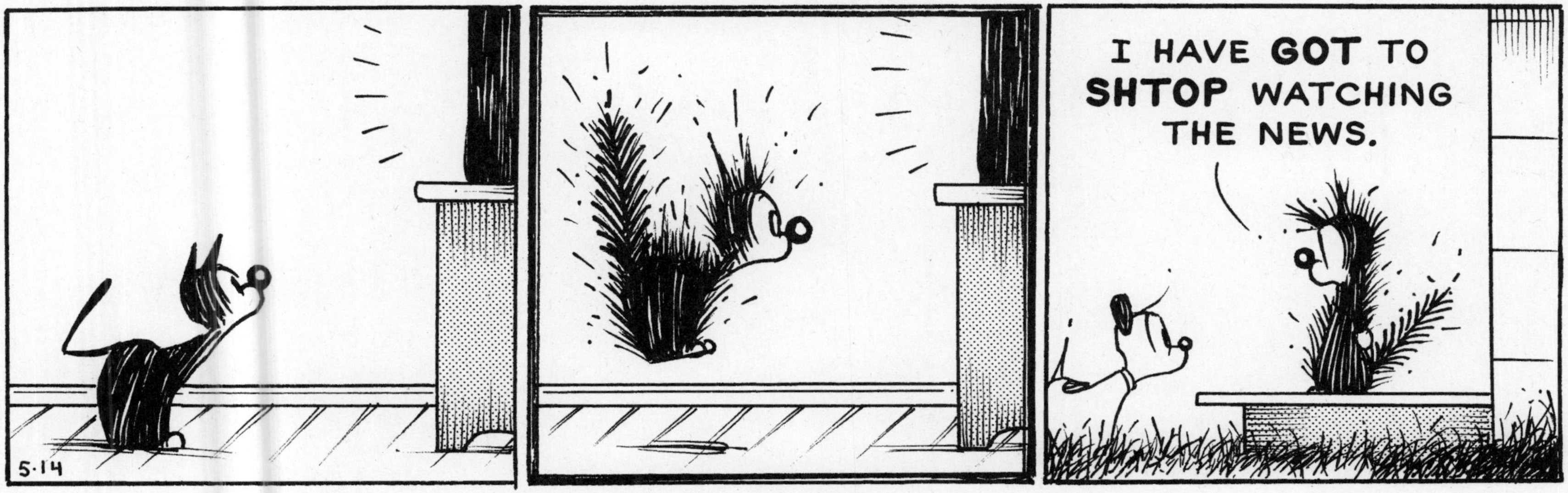
5·14
I HAVE **GOT** TO **SHTOP** WATCHING THE NEWS.

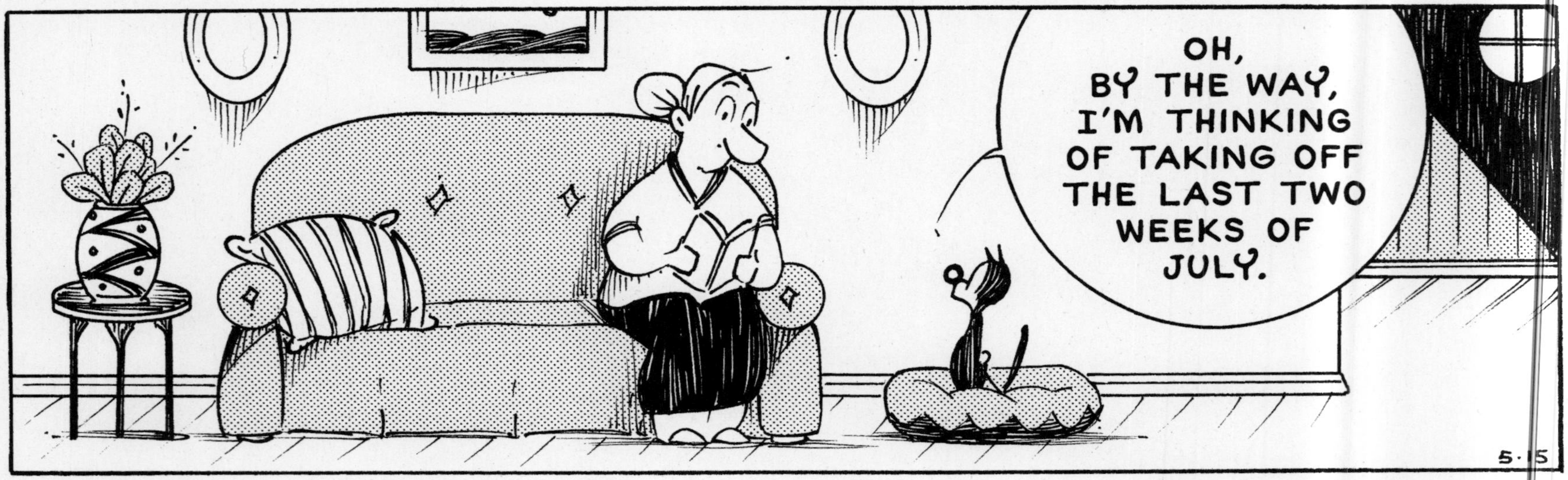
OH, BY THE WAY, I'M THINKING OF TAKING OFF THE LAST TWO WEEKS OF JULY.
5·15

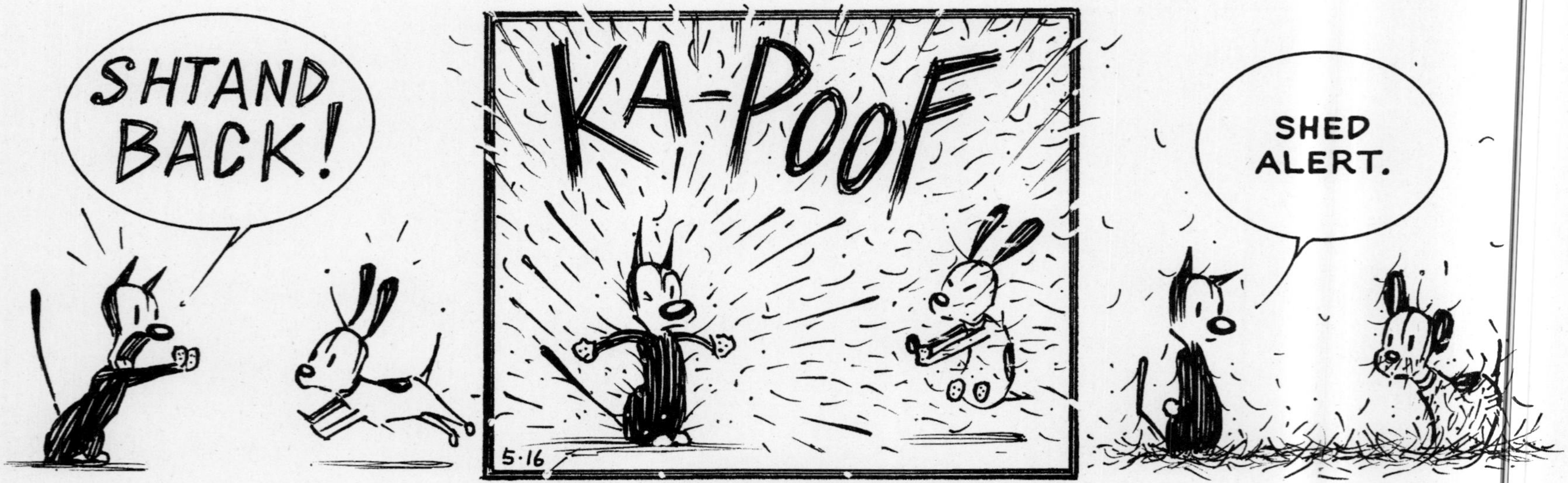
SHTAND BACK!
KA-POOF
5·16
SHED ALERT.

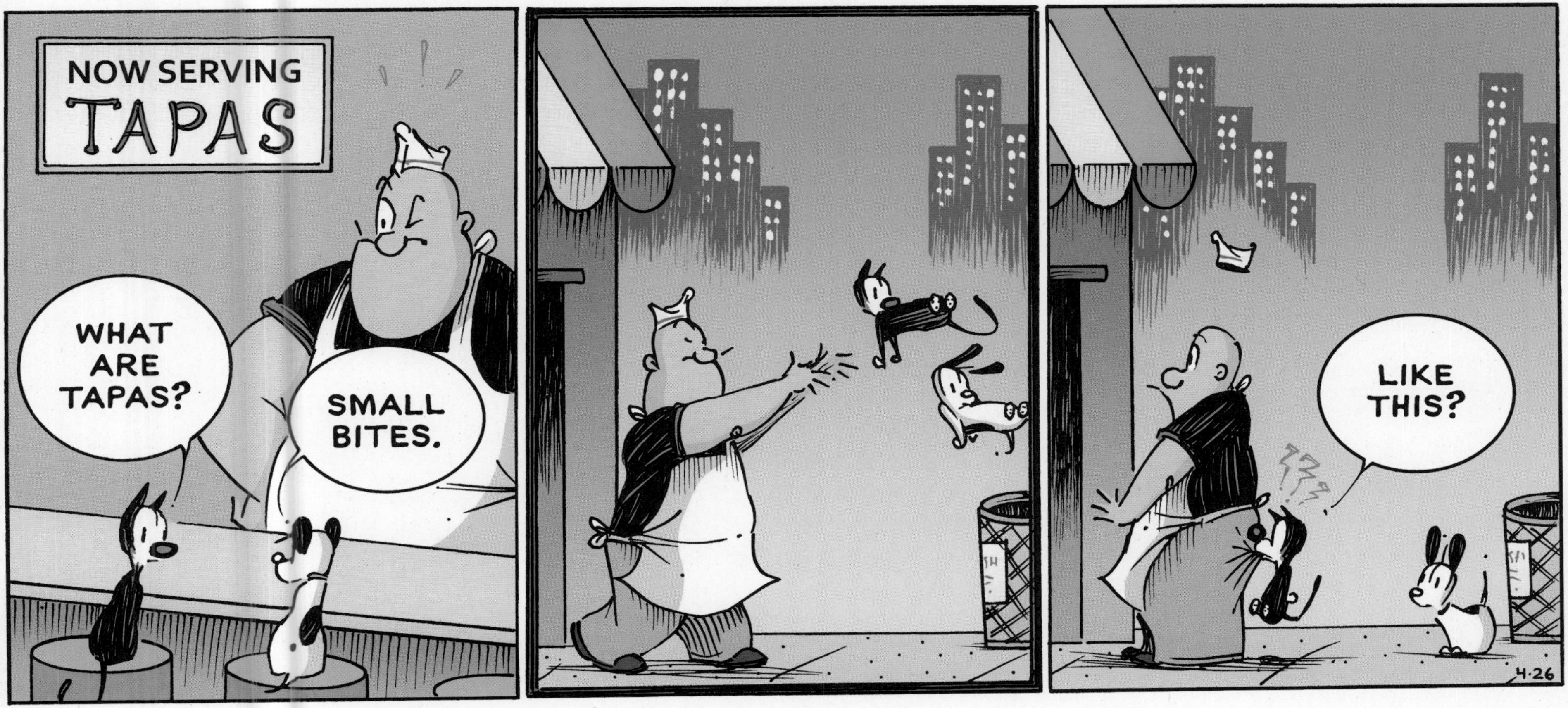
NOW SERVING
TAPAS
WHAT ARE TAPAS?
SMALL BITES.
LIKE THIS?
4·26

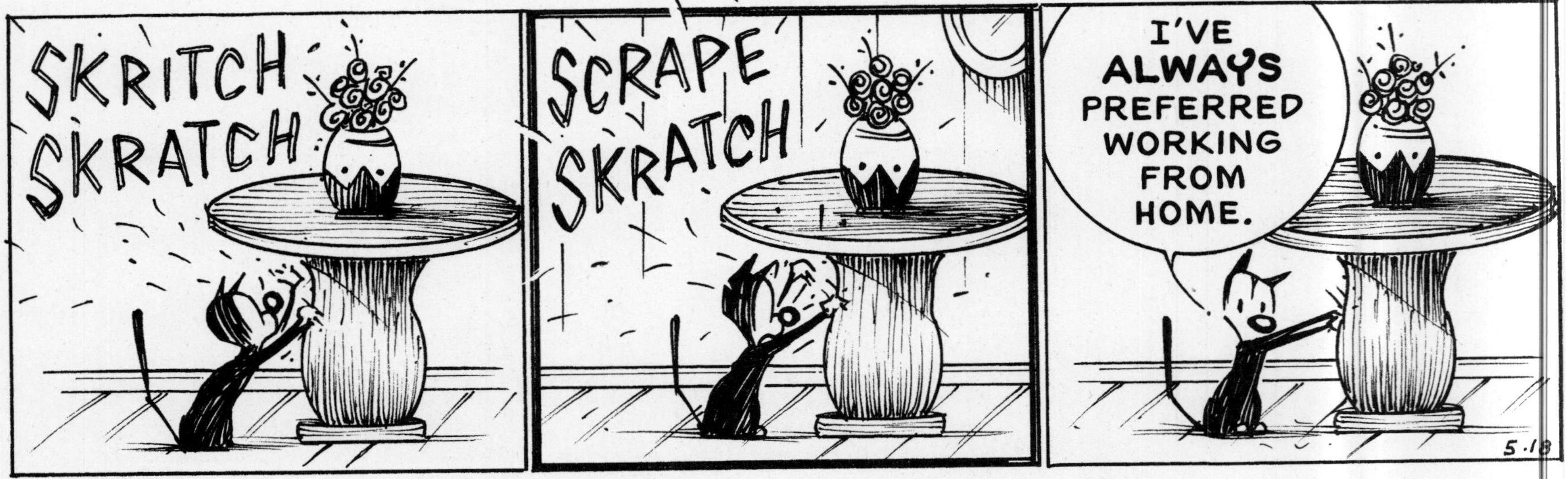
SKRITCH SKRATCH
SCRAPE SKRATCH
I'VE ALWAYS PREFERRED WORKING FROM HOME.
5.18

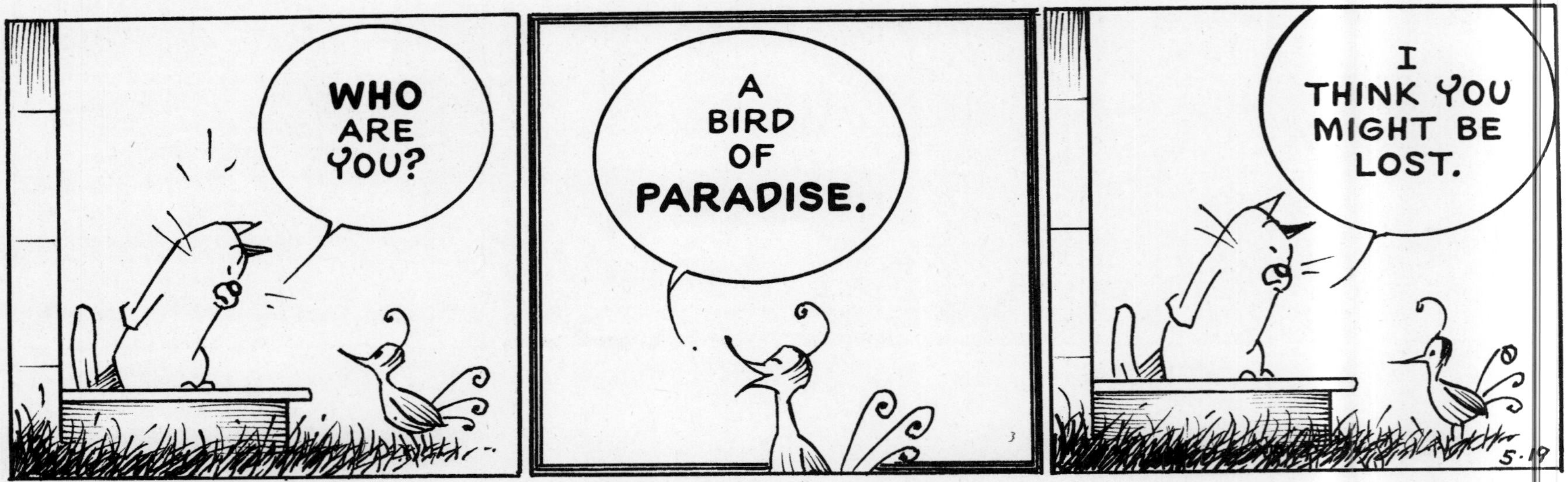
WHO ARE YOU?
A BIRD OF PARADISE.
I THINK YOU MIGHT BE LOST.
5.19

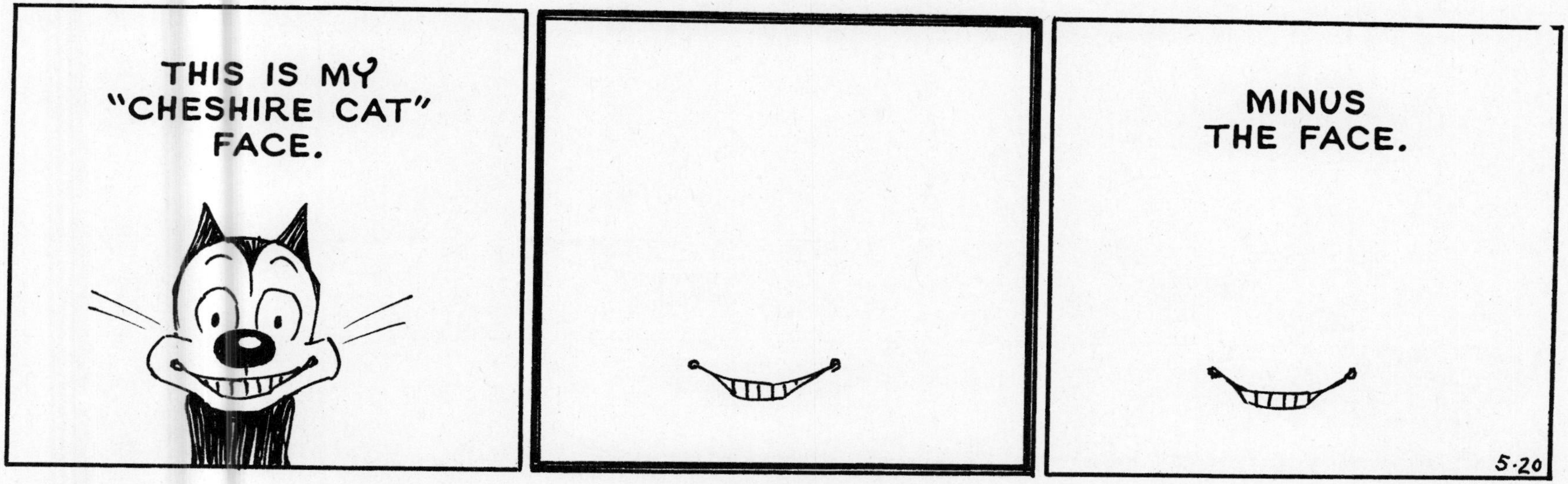
THIS IS MY "CHESHIRE CAT" FACE.
MINUS THE FACE.
5·20

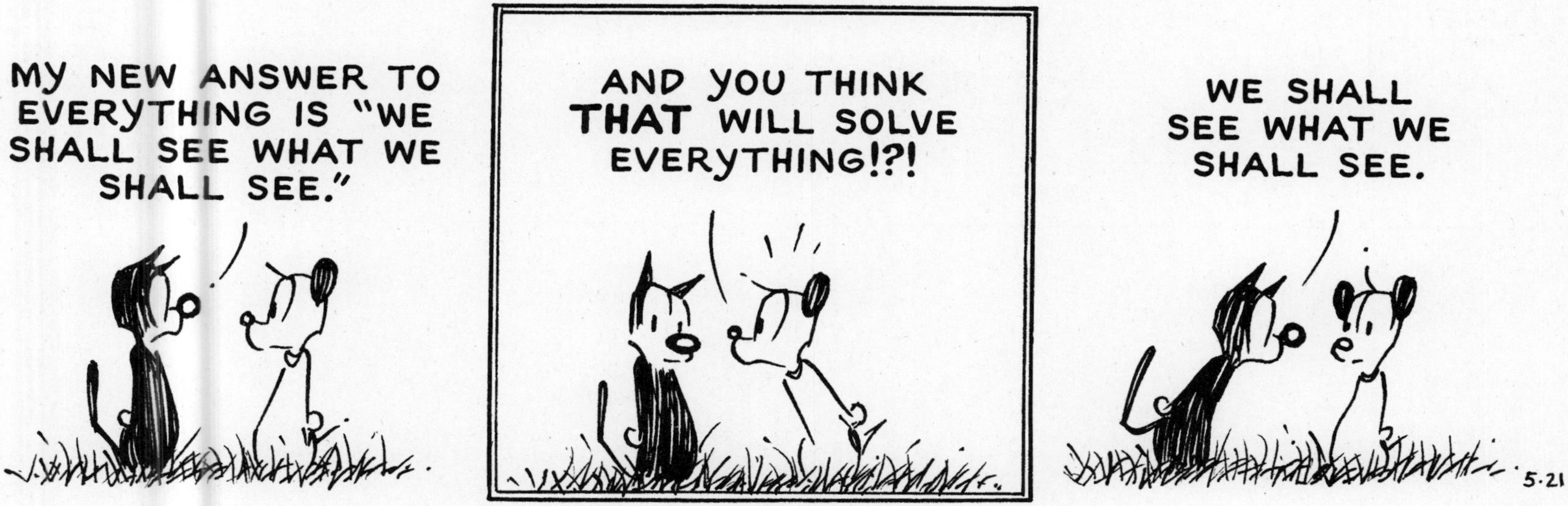
MY NEW ANSWER TO EVERYTHING IS "WE SHALL SEE WHAT WE SHALL SEE."
AND YOU THINK **THAT** WILL SOLVE EVERYTHING!?!
WE SHALL SEE WHAT WE SHALL SEE.
5·21

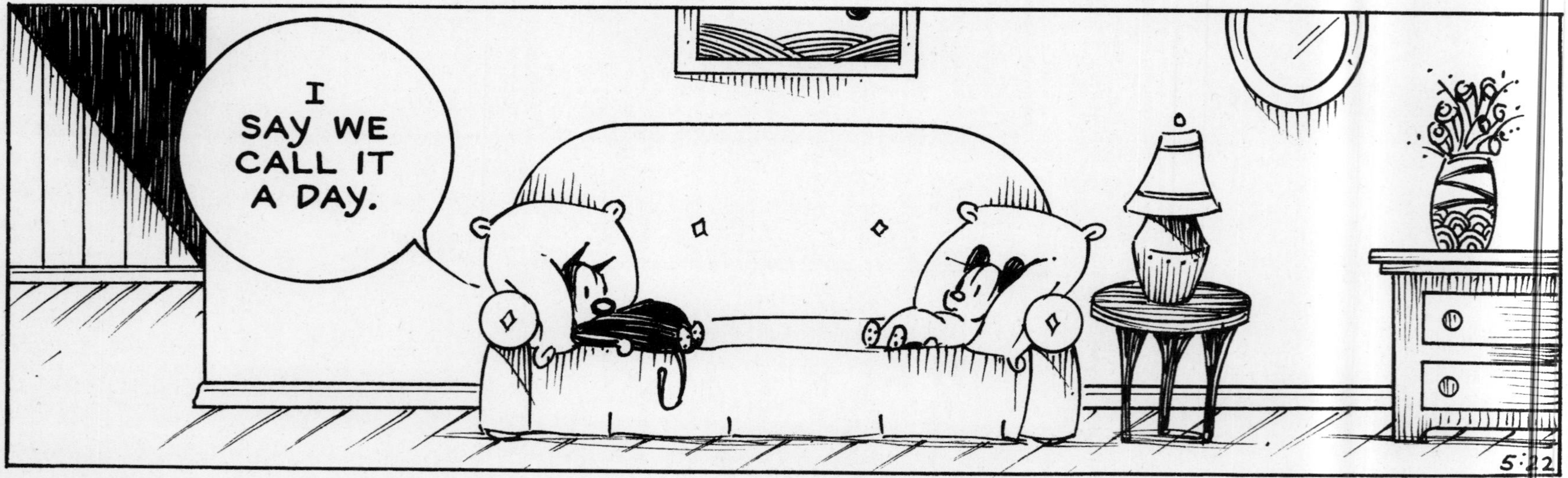
I SAY WE CALL IT A DAY.
5·22

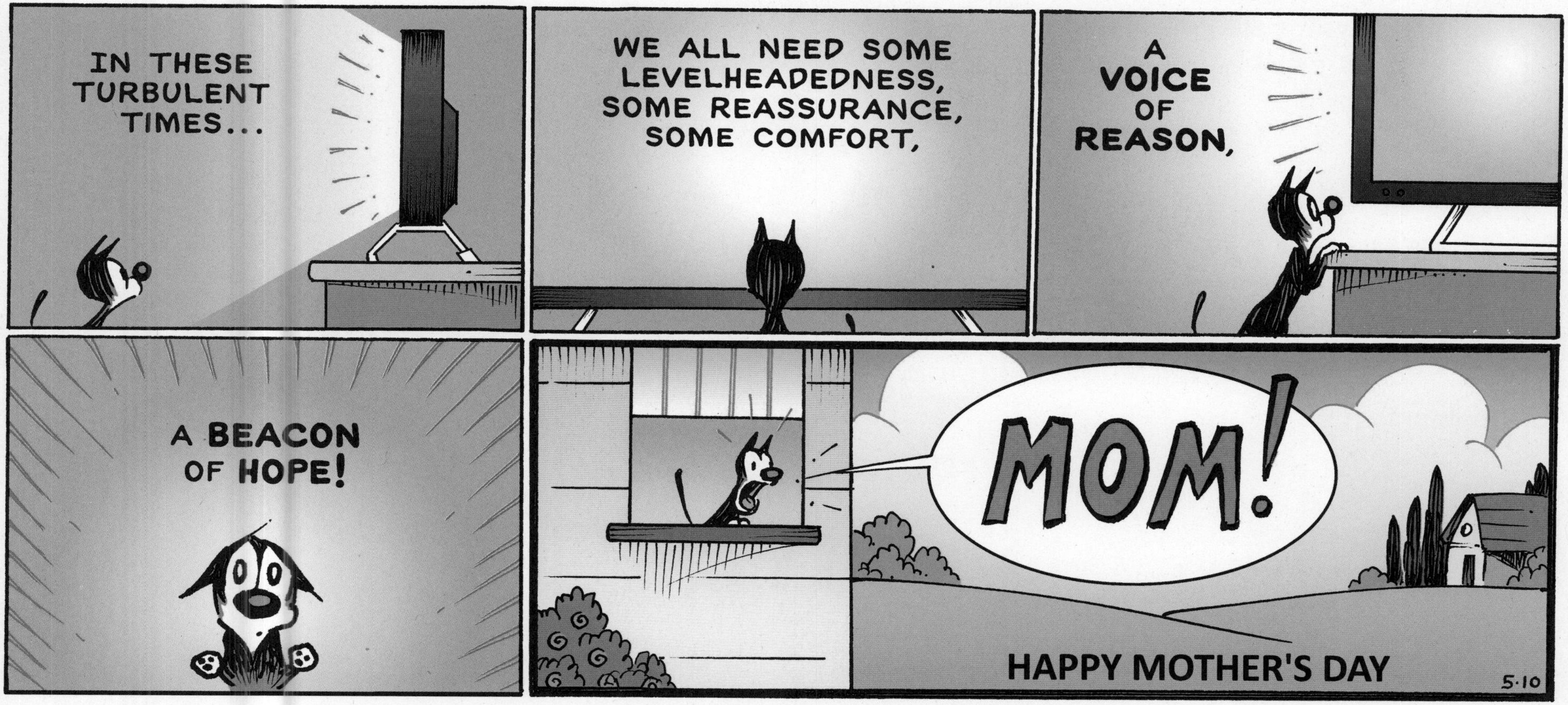
IN THESE TURBULENT TIMES...
WE ALL NEED SOME LEVELHEADEDNESS, SOME REASSURANCE, SOME COMFORT,
A VOICE OF REASON,
A BEACON OF HOPE!
MOM!
HAPPY MOTHER'S DAY
5·10

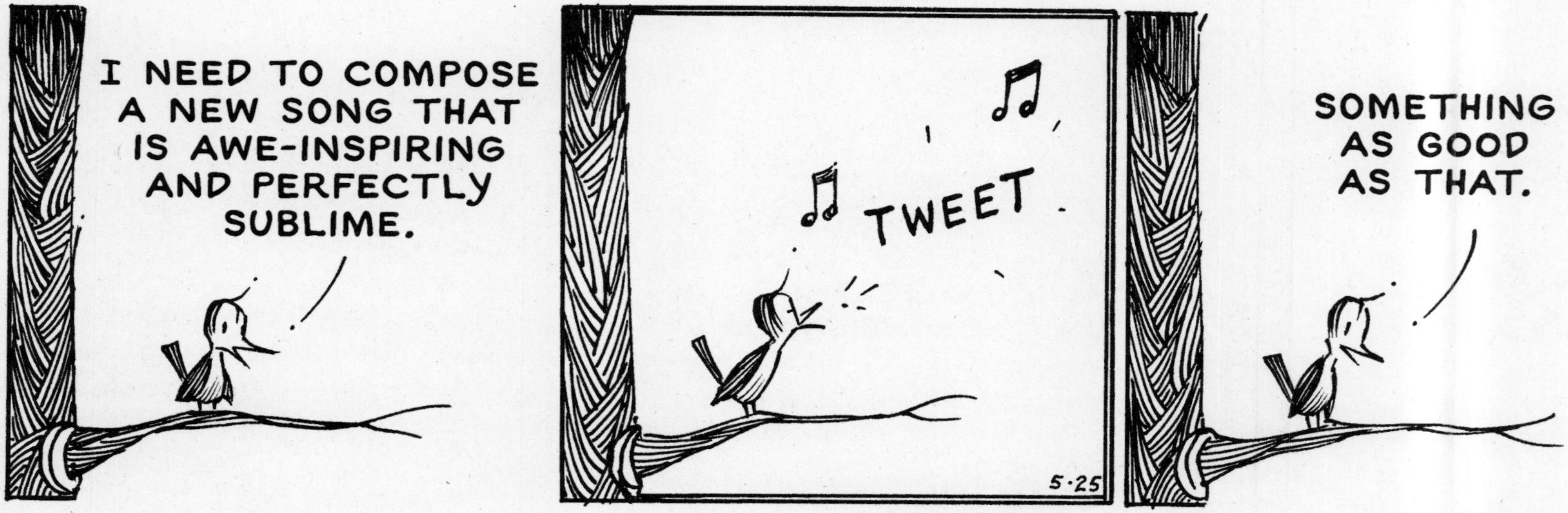
I NEED TO COMPOSE A NEW SONG THAT IS AWE-INSPIRING AND PERFECTLY SUBLIME.
TWEET
5·25
SOMETHING AS GOOD AS THAT.

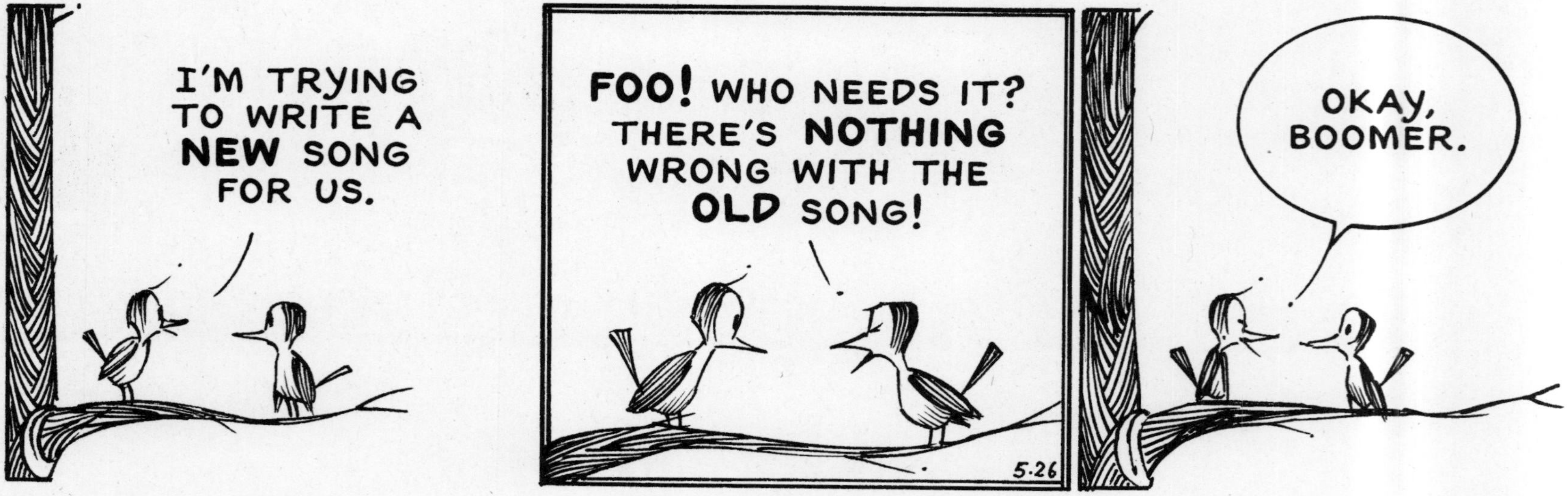
I'M TRYING TO WRITE A NEW SONG FOR US.
FOO! WHO NEEDS IT? THERE'S NOTHING WRONG WITH THE OLD SONG!
5·26
OKAY, BOOMER.

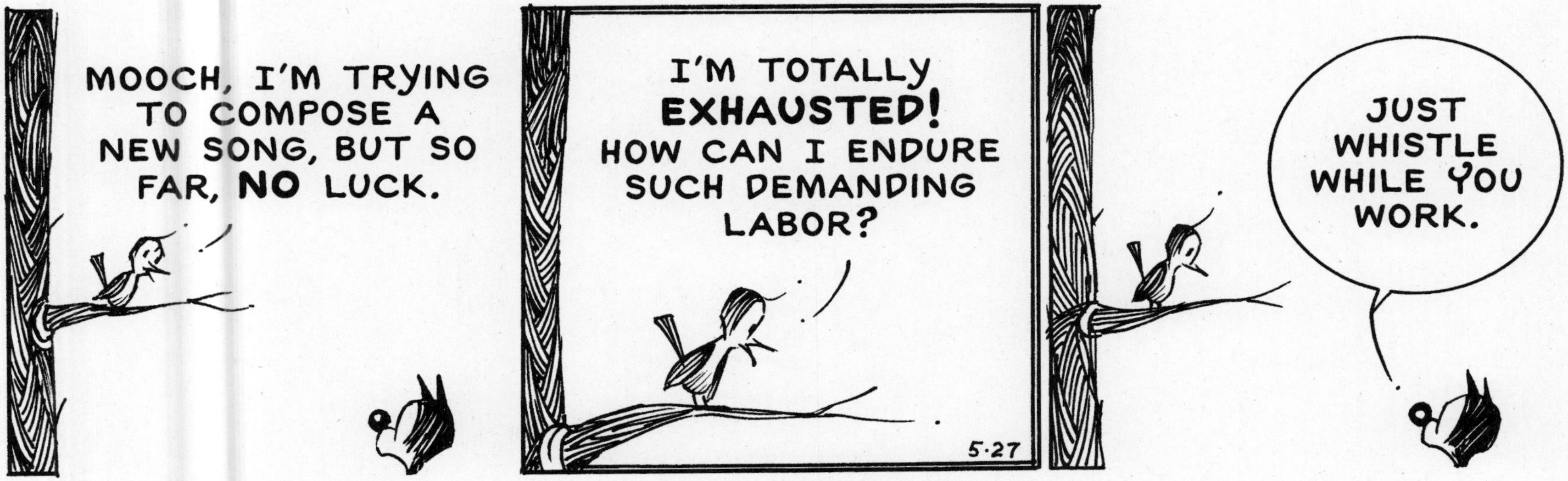
MOOCH, I'M TRYING TO COMPOSE A NEW SONG, BUT SO FAR, **NO** LUCK.
I'M TOTALLY **EXHAUSTED!** HOW CAN I ENDURE SUCH DEMANDING LABOR?
5·27
JUST WHISTLE WHILE YOU WORK.

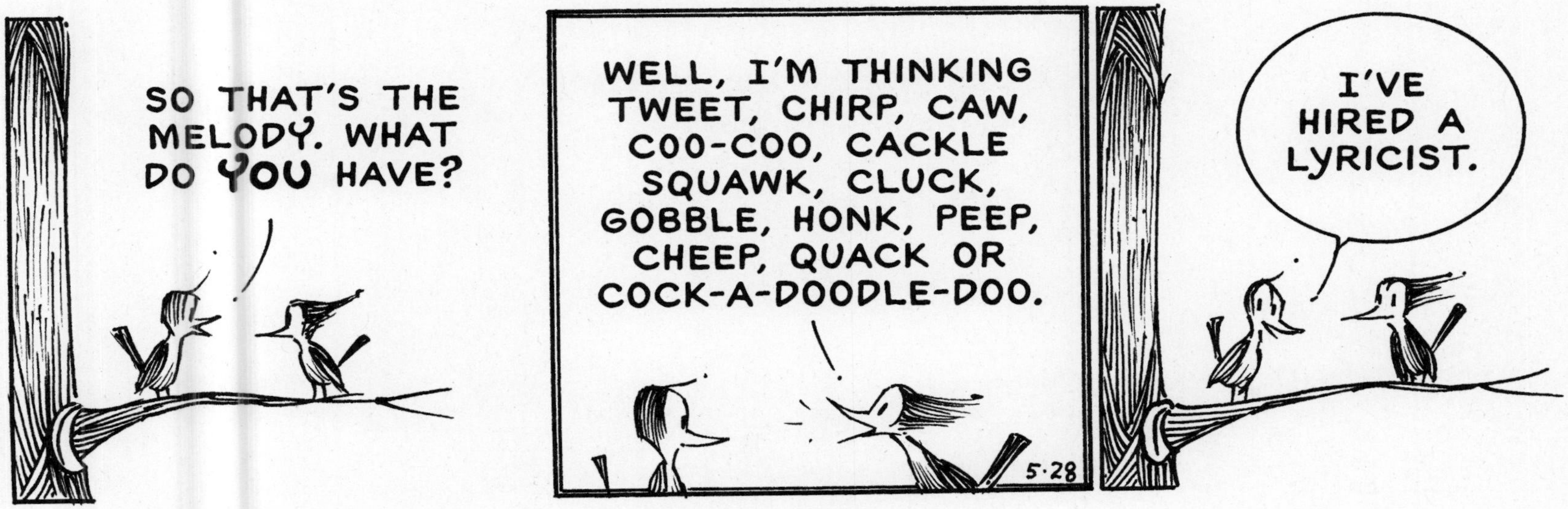
SO THAT'S THE MELODY. WHAT DO **YOU** HAVE?
WELL, I'M THINKING TWEET, CHIRP, CAW, COO-COO, CACKLE SQUAWK, CLUCK, GOBBLE, HONK, PEEP, CHEEP, QUACK OR COCK-A-DOODLE-DOO.
5·28
I'VE HIRED A LYRICIST.

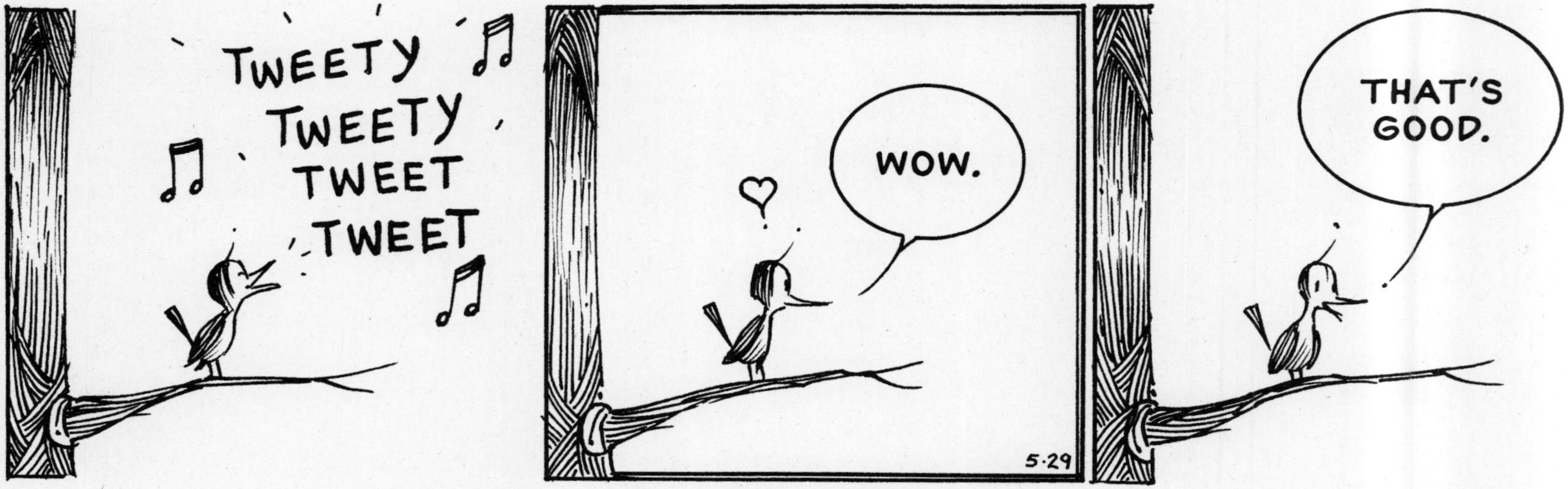
TWEETY
TWEETY
TWEET
TWEET
WOW.
THAT'S GOOD.
5·29

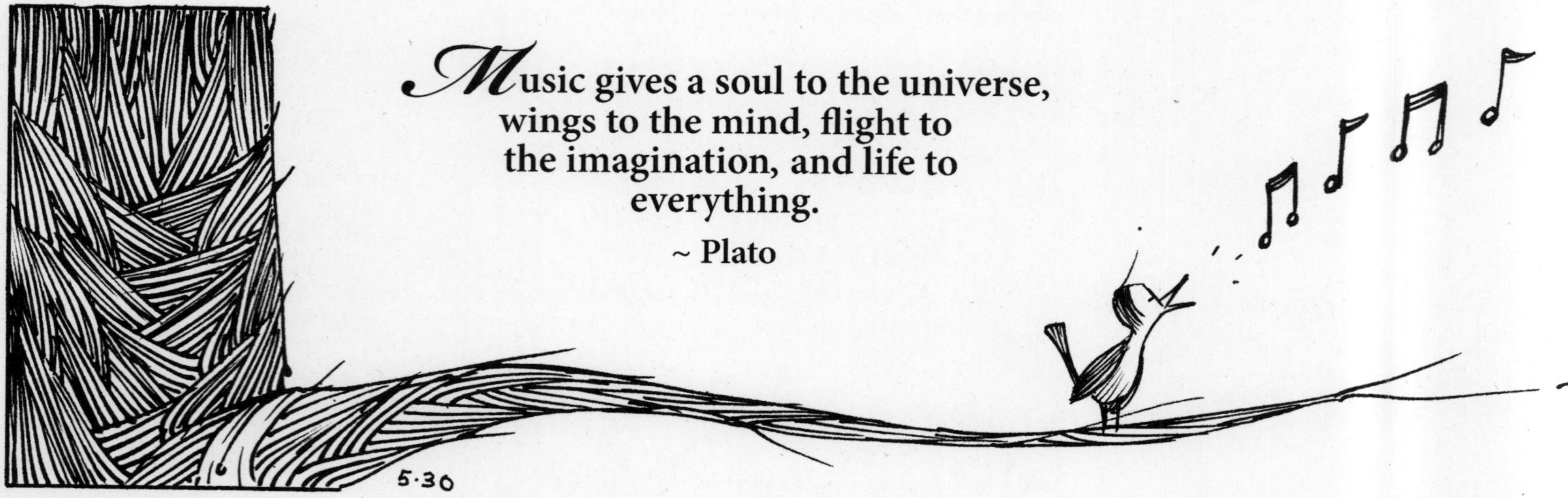
Music gives a soul to the universe, wings to the mind, flight to the imagination, and life to everything.
~ Plato
5·30

MUTTS

PATRICK McDONNELL

PLINK
PLINK
PLINK
PLINK
A PINE NUT !?!
IT'S "BE KIND TO ANIMALS WEEK."
5·3

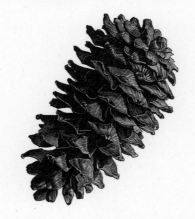

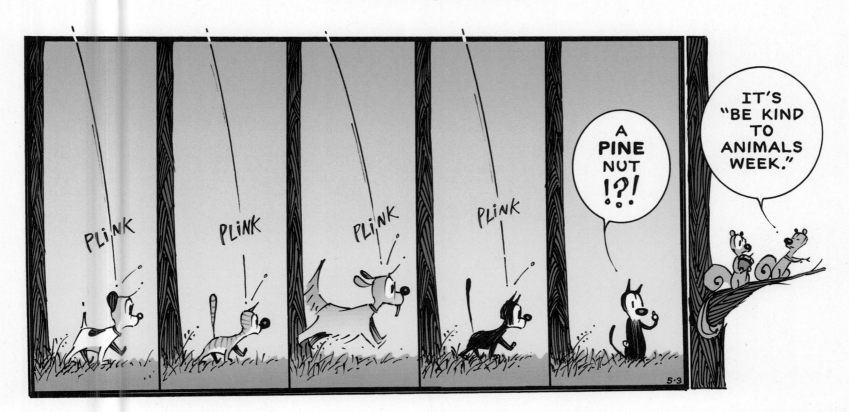

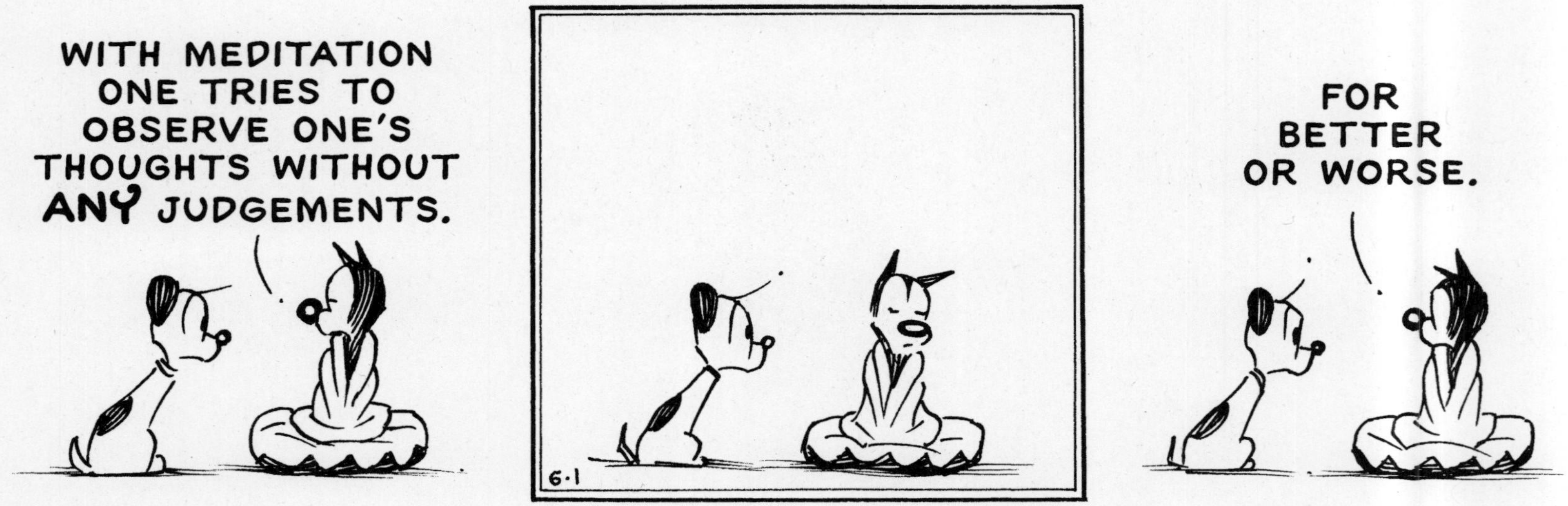
WITH MEDITATION ONE TRIES TO OBSERVE ONE'S THOUGHTS WITHOUT **ANY** JUDGEMENTS.
6·1
FOR BETTER OR WORSE.

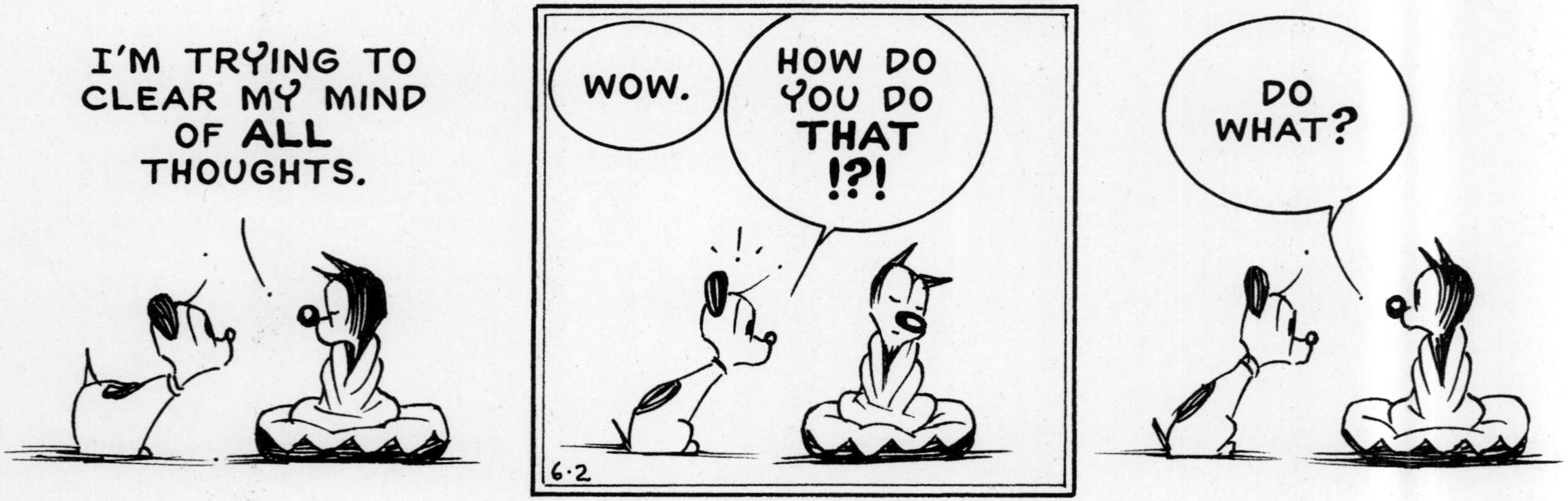
I'M TRYING TO CLEAR MY MIND OF **ALL** THOUGHTS.
WOW.
HOW DO YOU DO **THAT** !?!
6·2
DO WHAT?

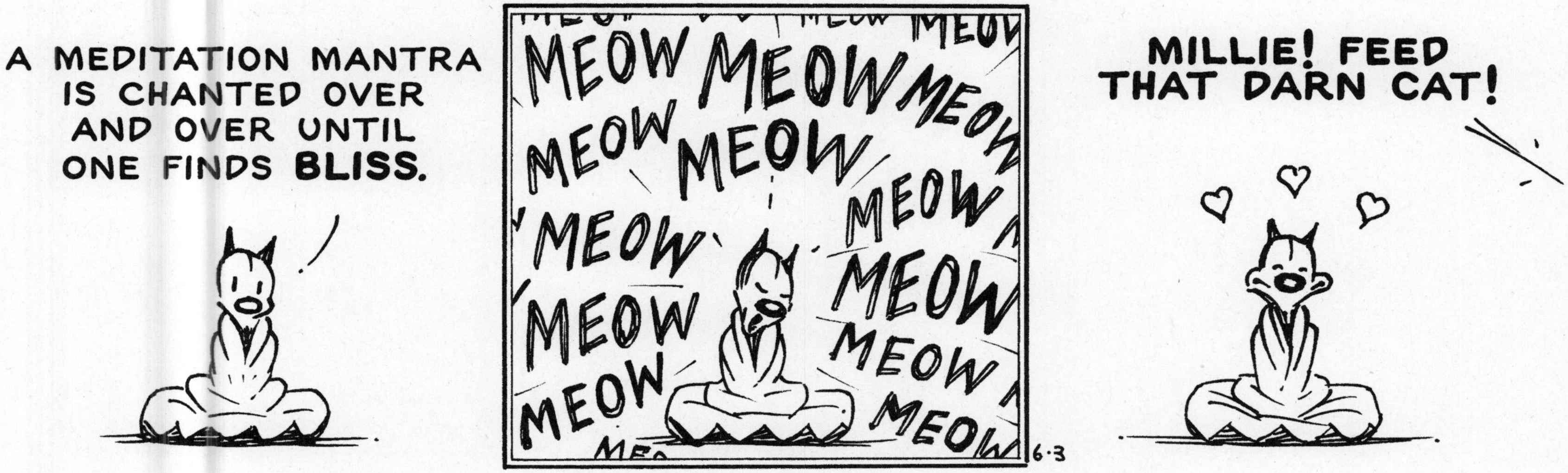
A MEDITATION MANTRA IS CHANTED OVER AND OVER UNTIL ONE FINDS **BLISS.**
MEOW MEOW MEOW MEOW MEOW MEOW MEOW MEOW MEOW MEOW MEOW MEOW MEOW
MILLIE! FEED THAT DARN CAT!
6·3

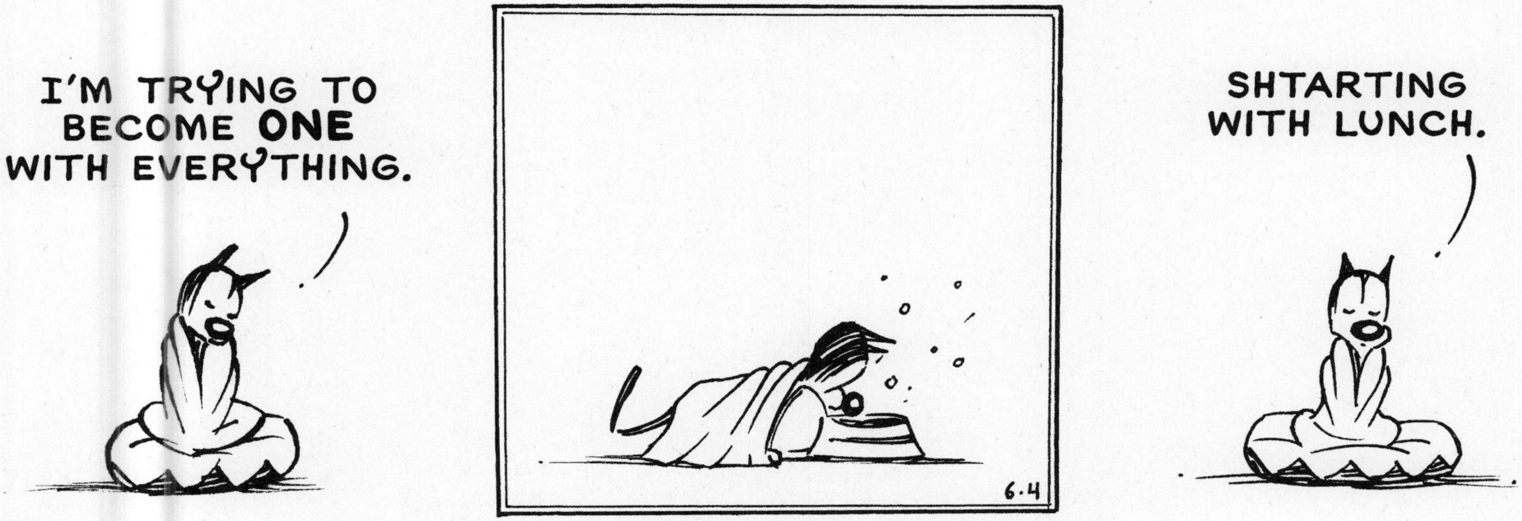
I'M TRYING TO BECOME **ONE** WITH EVERYTHING.
SHTARTING WITH LUNCH.
6·4

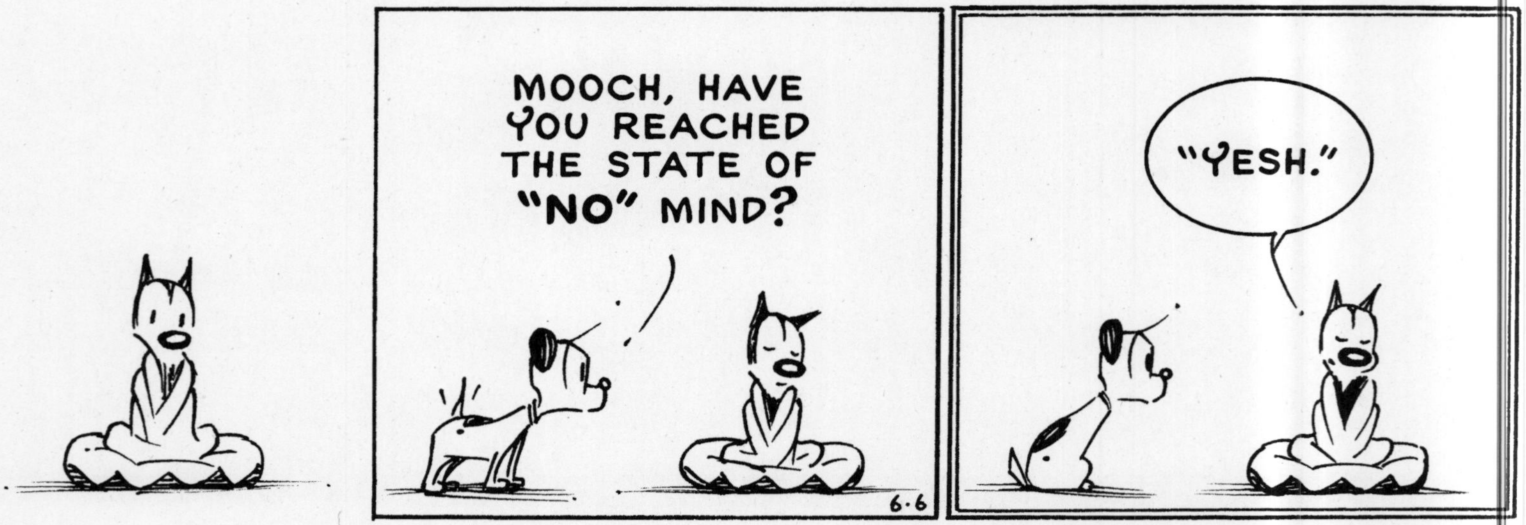
MOOCH, HAVE YOU REACHED THE STATE OF "NO" MIND?
"YESH."
6·6

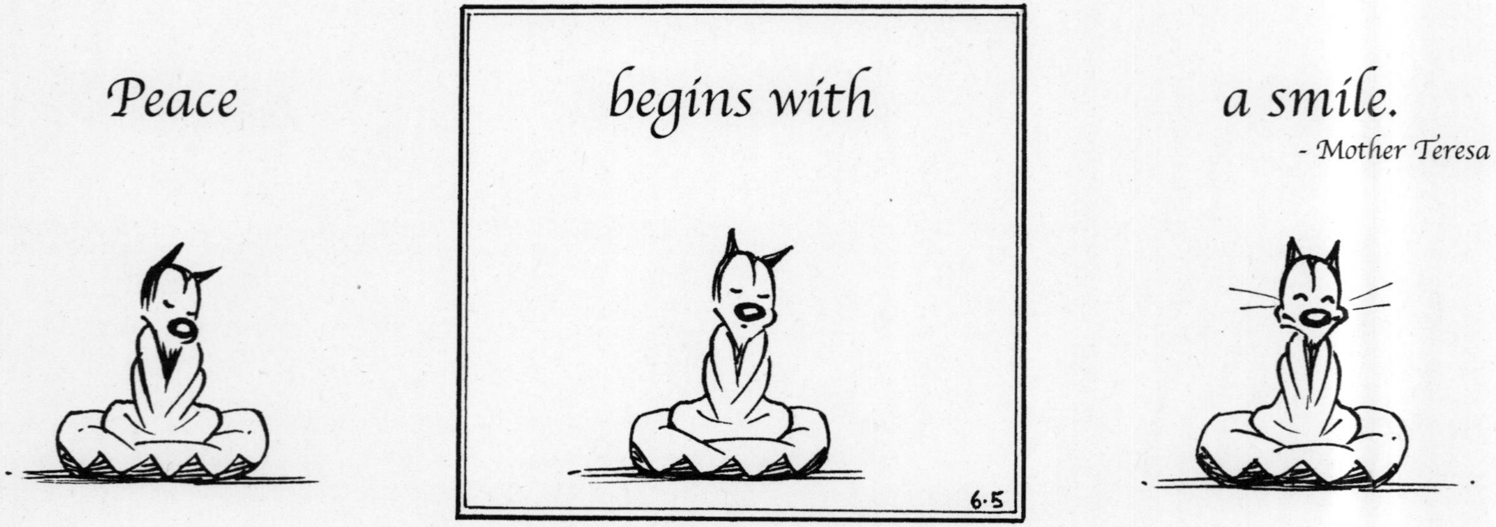
Peace
begins with
a smile.
- Mother Teresa
6·5

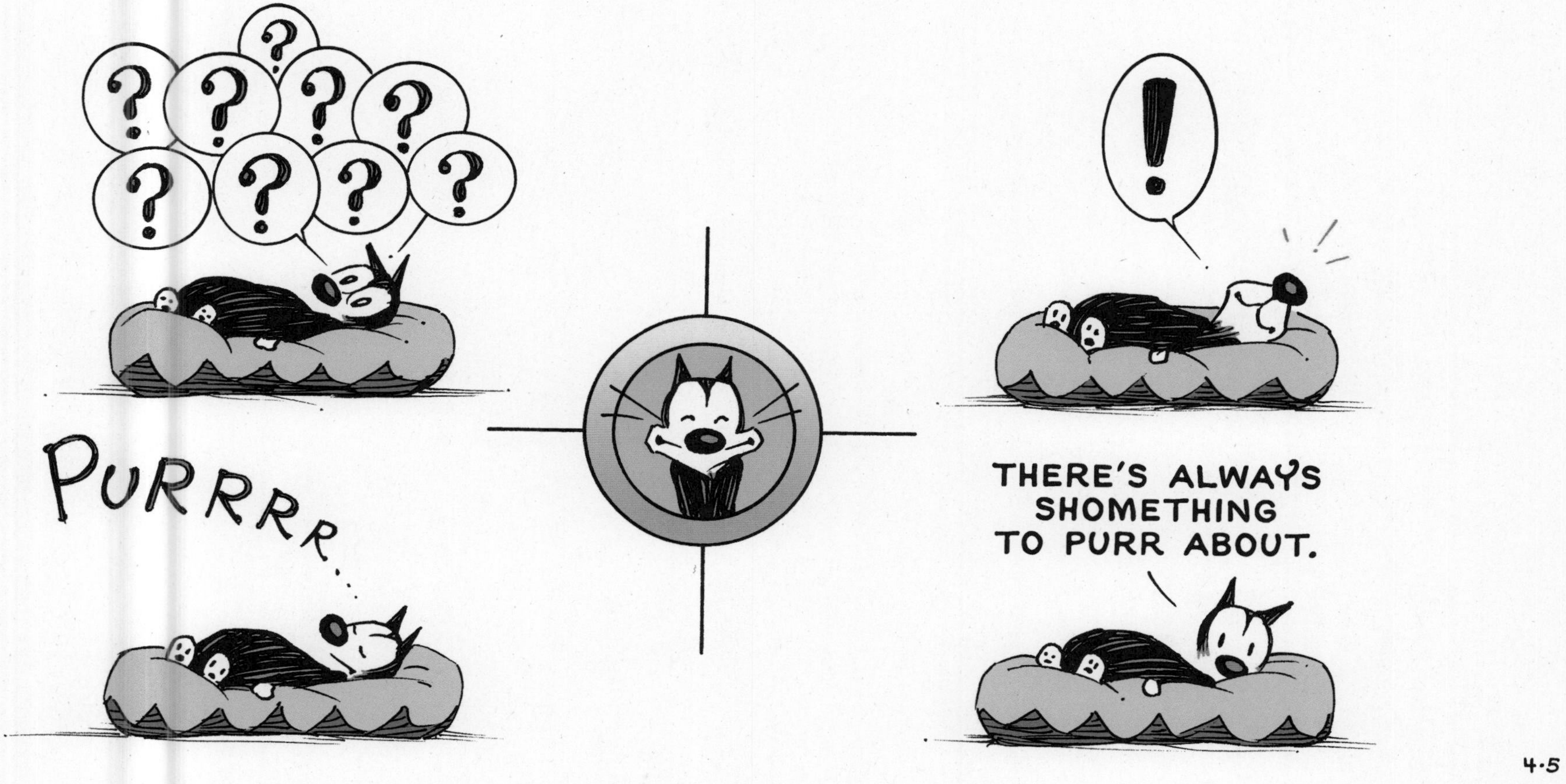
?
!
PURRRRR...
THERE'S ALWAYS SHOMETHING TO PURR ABOUT.
4·5

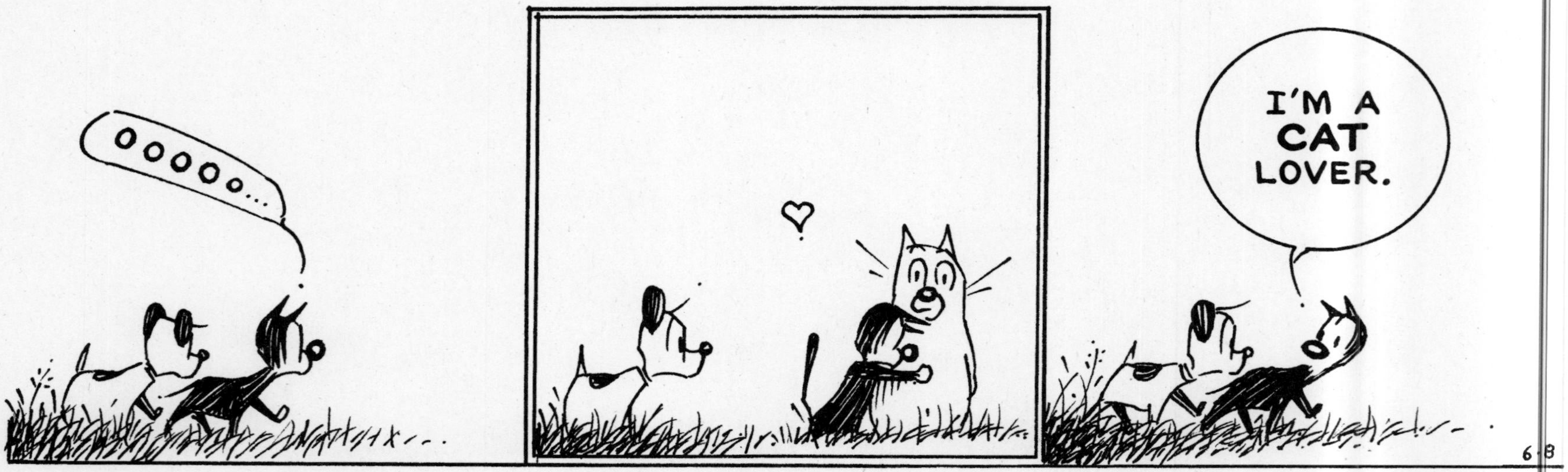
OOOOO....
I'M A CAT LOVER.
6-8

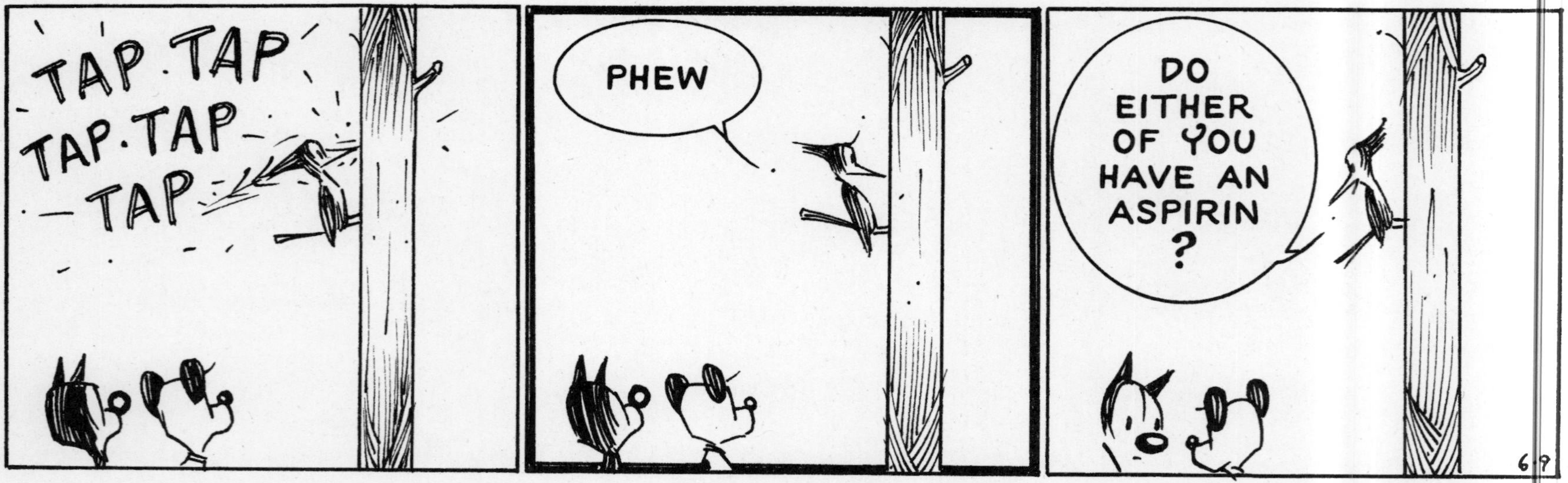
TAP TAP TAP TAP TAP
PHEW
DO EITHER OF YOU HAVE AN ASPIRIN ?
6-9

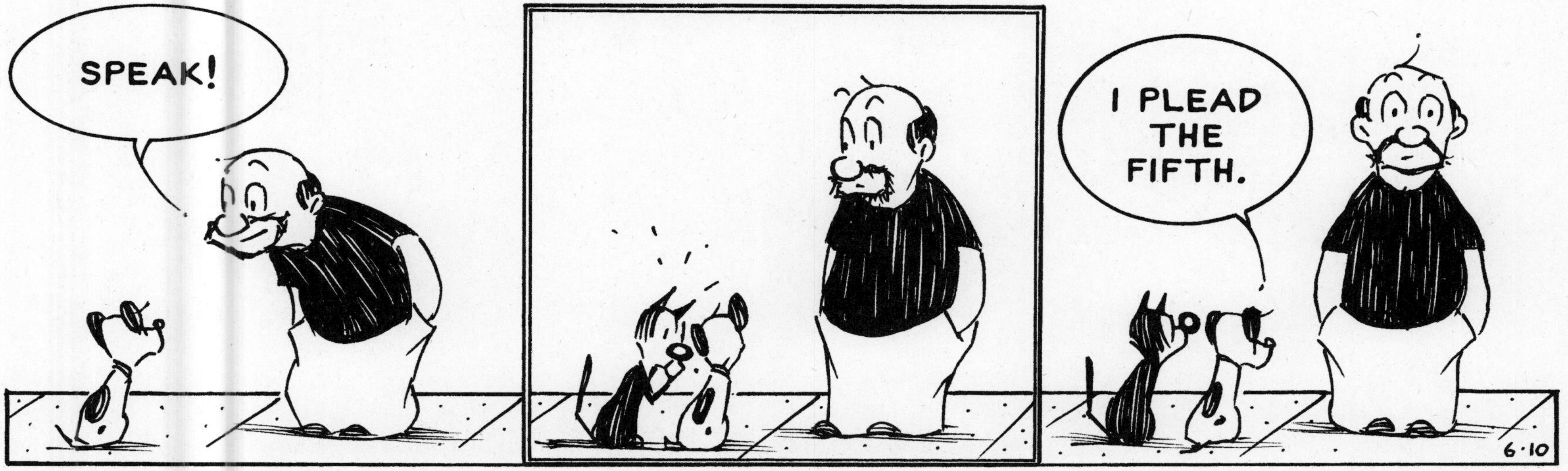
SPEAK!
I PLEAD THE FIFTH.
6·10

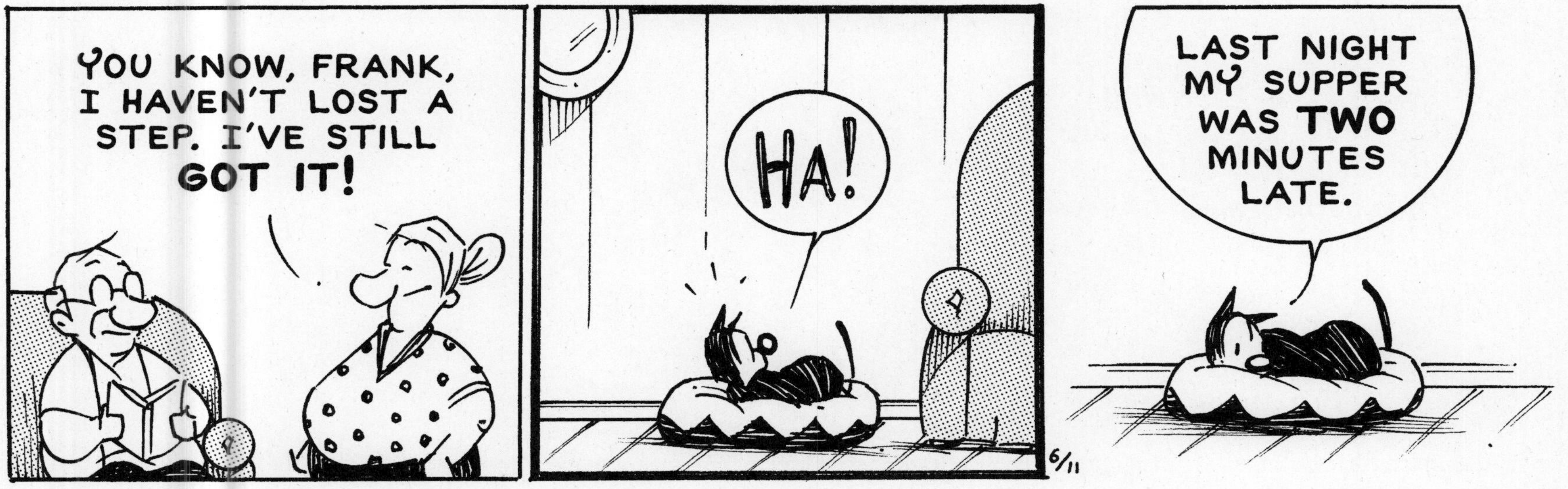
YOU KNOW, FRANK, I HAVEN'T LOST A STEP. I'VE STILL GOT IT!
HA!
LAST NIGHT MY SUPPER WAS TWO MINUTES LATE.
6/11

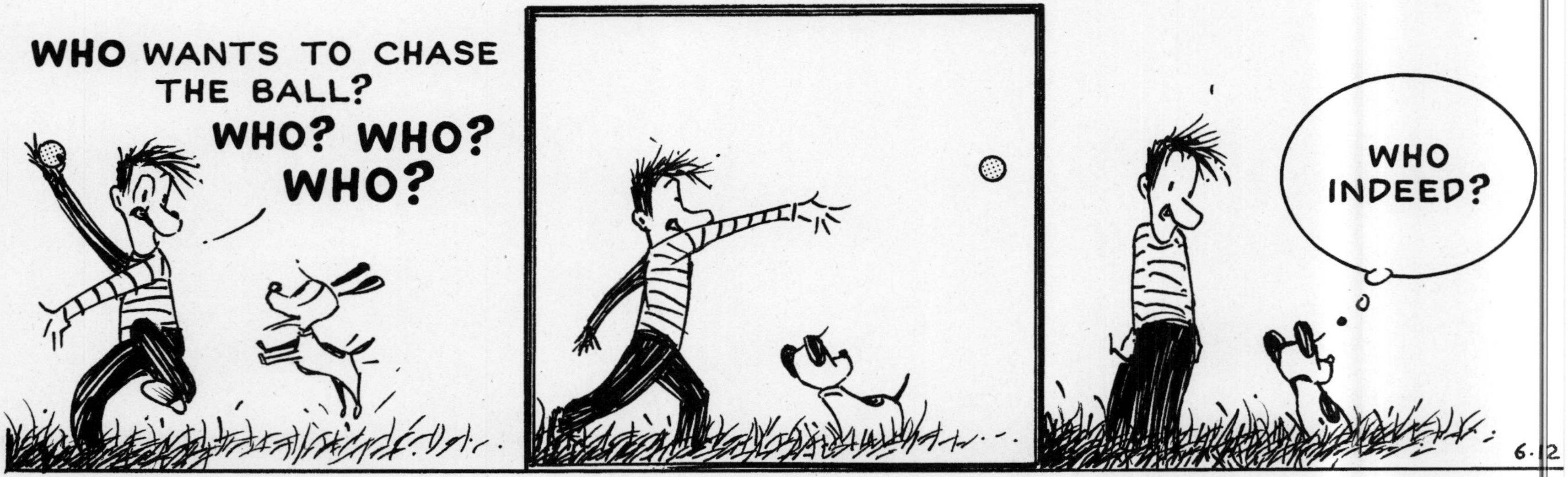
WHO WANTS TO CHASE THE BALL?
WHO? WHO? WHO?
WHO INDEED?
6.12

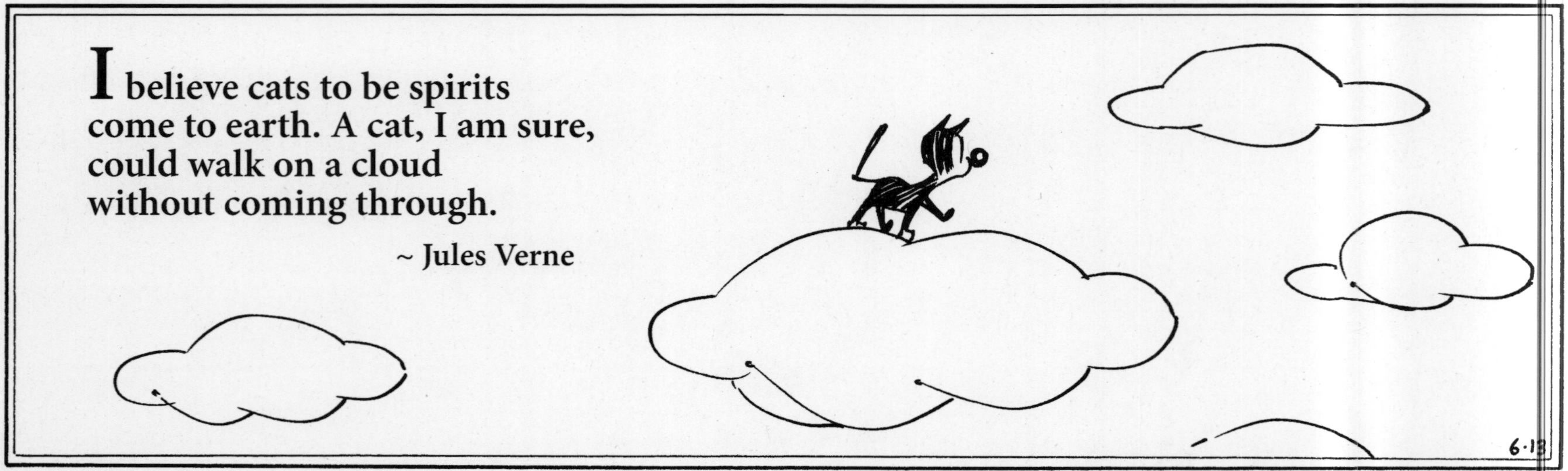
I believe cats to be spirits come to earth. A cat, I am sure, could walk on a cloud without coming through.
~ Jules Verne
6.13

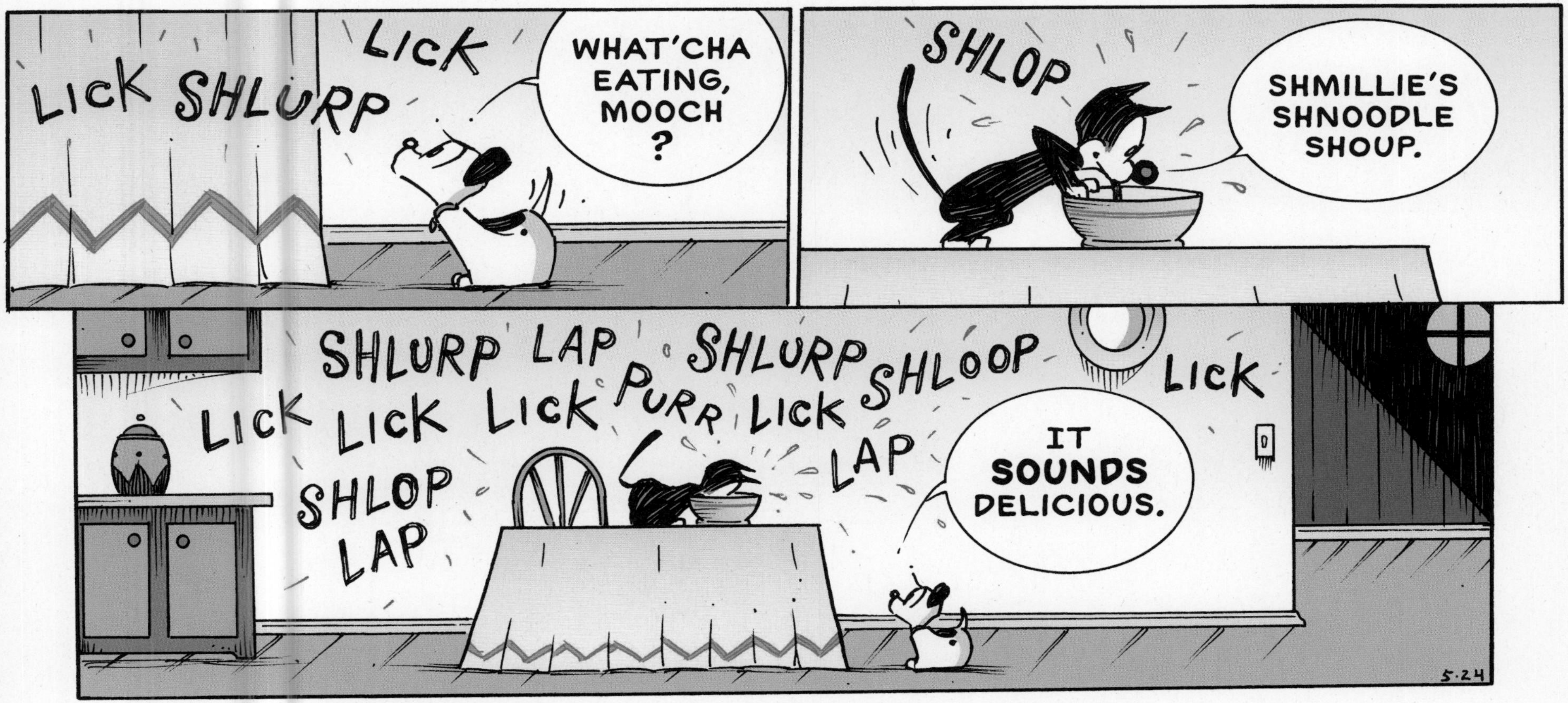
LICK SHLURP
LICK
WHAT'CHA EATING, MOOCH ?
SHLOP
SHMILLIE'S SHNOODLE SHOUP.
SHLURP LAP SHLURP SHLOOP LICK
LICK LICK LICK PURR LICK
SHLOP LAP LAP
IT SOUNDS DELICIOUS.
5.24

MUTTS.

WE'RE ALL SET!
I BROUGHT A SHCRUB BRUSH, SHOME SHOAP AND THE WATER HOSE.
?
NO, MOOCH.
I SAID- LET'S GO BIRD "WATCHING" !
5·31

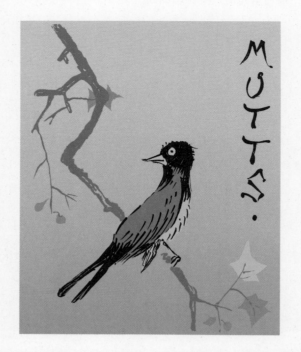

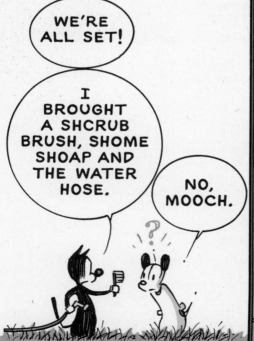

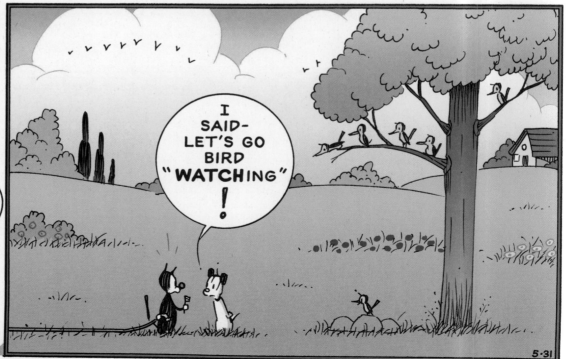

R eading gives us
someplace to go
when we have to stay
where we are.

~ Mason Cooley

98

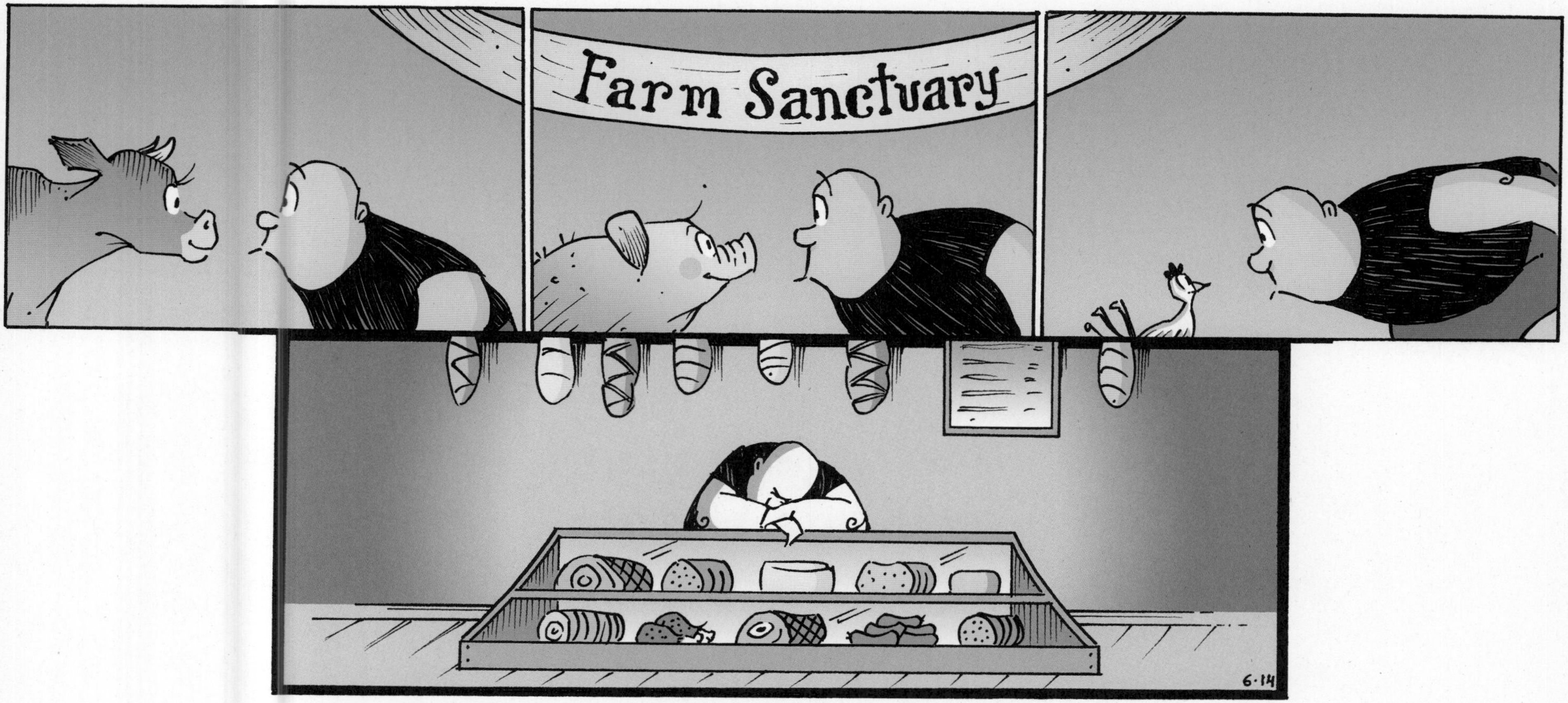
Farm Sanctuary
6·14

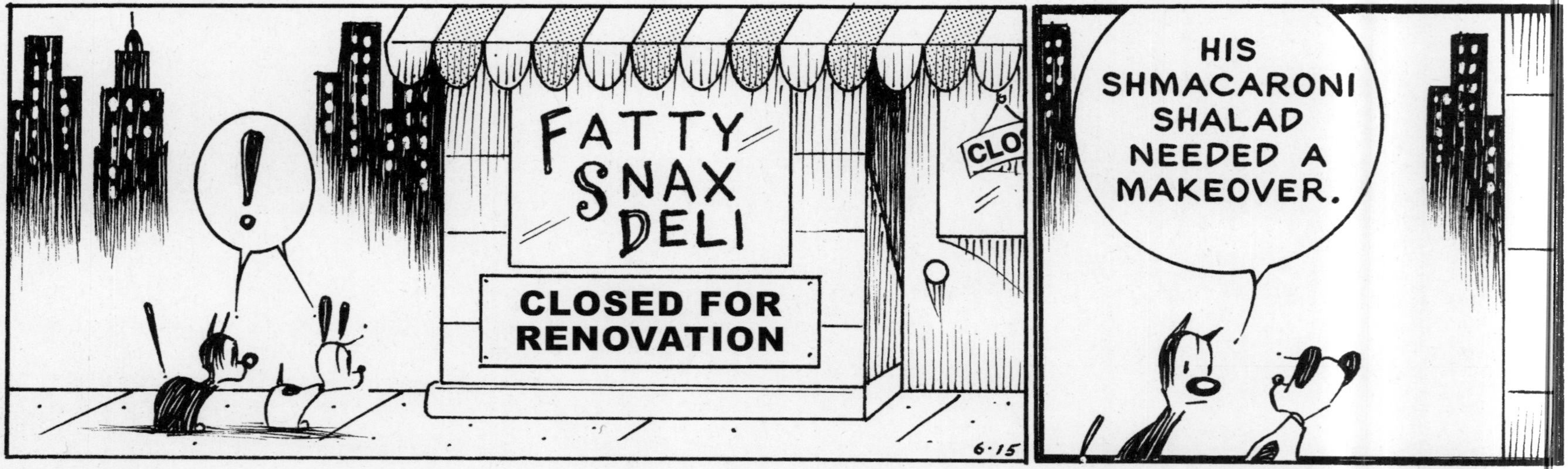
!
FATTY SNAX DELI
CLOSED FOR RENOVATION
6·15
HIS SHMACARONI SHALAD NEEDED A MAKEOVER.

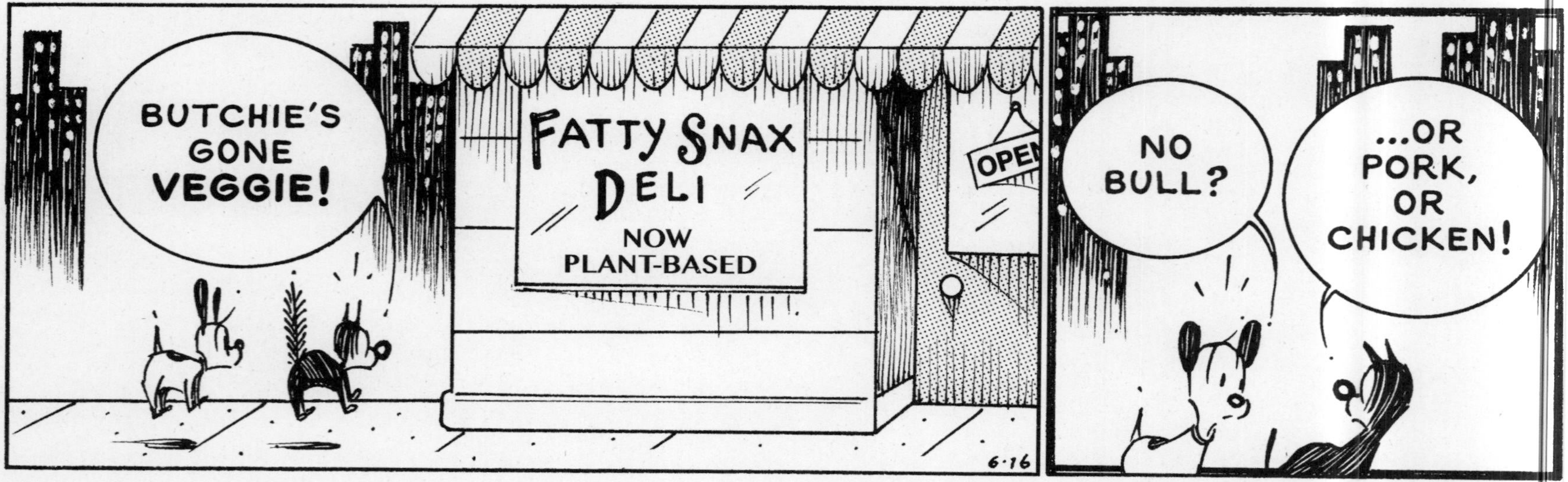
BUTCHIE'S GONE **VEGGIE!**
FATTY SNAX DELI
NOW PLANT-BASED
6·16
NO BULL?
...OR PORK, OR CHICKEN!

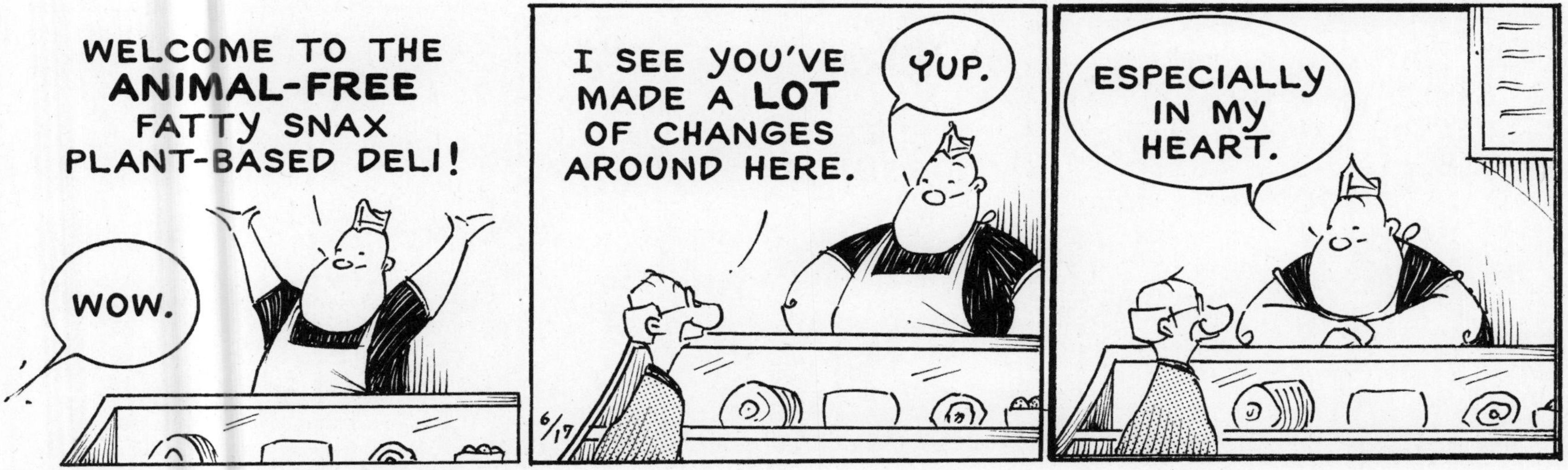
WELCOME TO THE ANIMAL-FREE FATTY SNAX PLANT-BASED DELI!
WOW.
I SEE YOU'VE MADE A LOT OF CHANGES AROUND HERE.
YUP.
ESPECIALLY IN MY HEART.
6/17

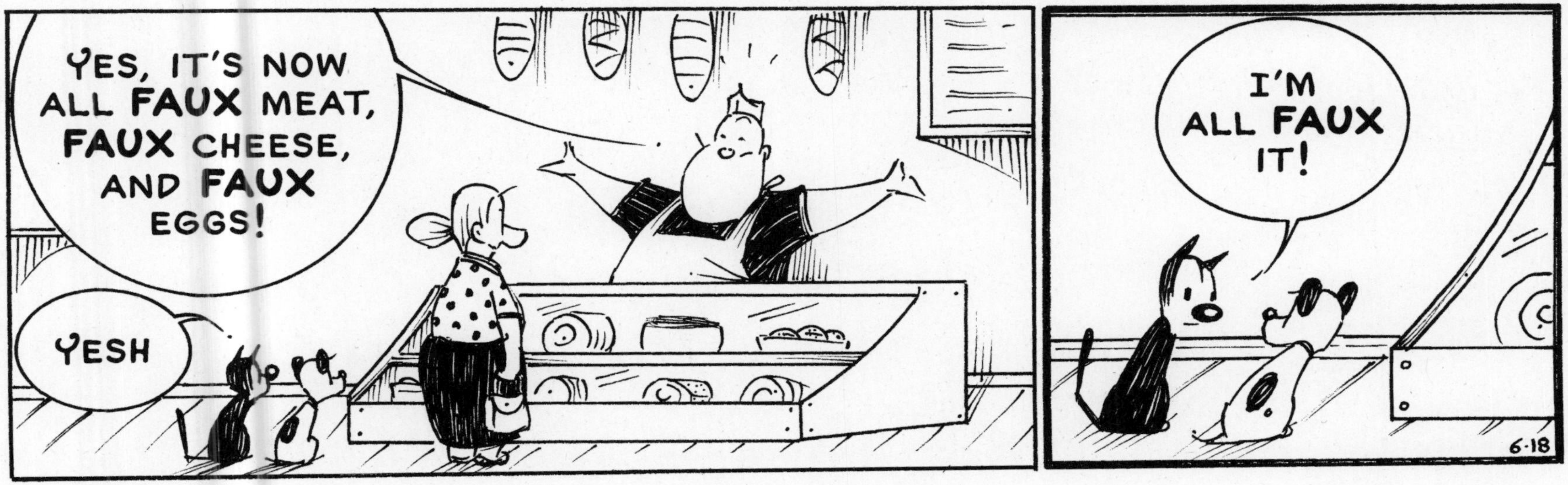
YES, IT'S NOW ALL FAUX MEAT, FAUX CHEESE, AND FAUX EGGS!
YESH
I'M ALL FAUX IT!
6·18

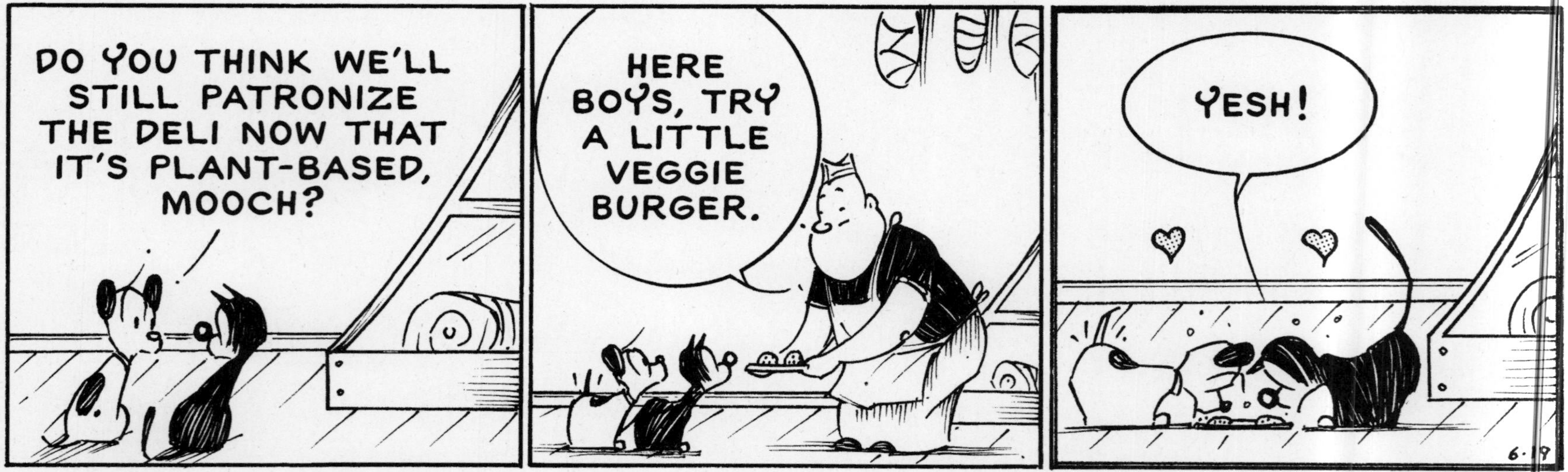
DO YOU THINK WE'LL STILL PATRONIZE THE DELI NOW THAT IT'S PLANT-BASED, MOOCH?
HERE BOYS, TRY A LITTLE VEGGIE BURGER.
YESH!
6·19

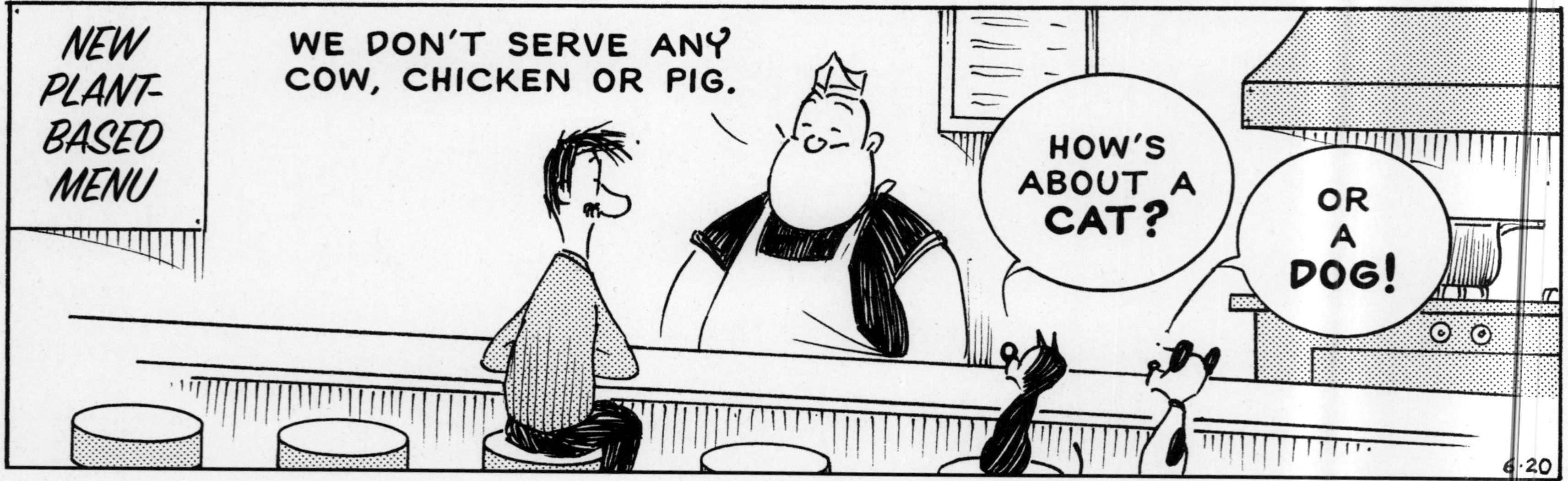
NEW PLANT-BASED MENU
WE DON'T SERVE ANY COW, CHICKEN OR PIG.
HOW'S ABOUT A CAT?
OR A DOG!
6·20

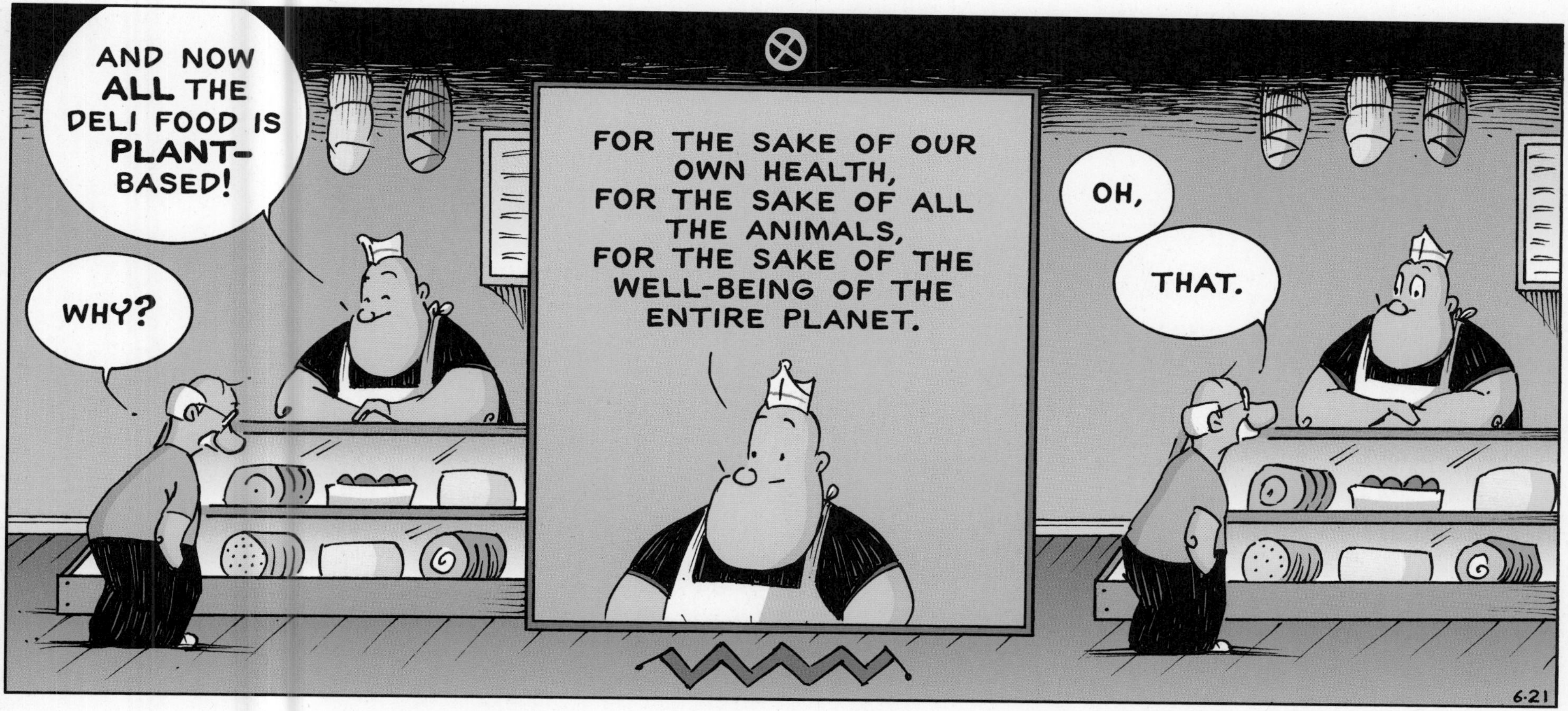
AND NOW ALL THE DELI FOOD IS PLANT-BASED!
WHY?
FOR THE SAKE OF OUR OWN HEALTH, FOR THE SAKE OF ALL THE ANIMALS, FOR THE SAKE OF THE WELL-BEING OF THE ENTIRE PLANET.
OH,
THAT.
6·21

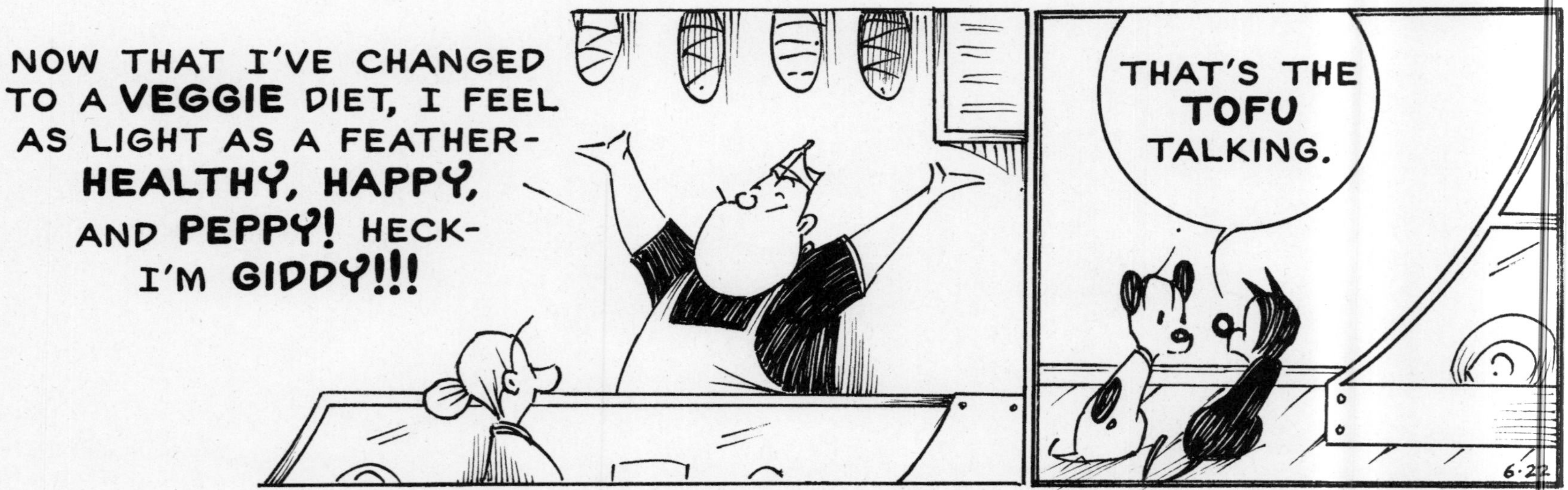
NOW THAT I'VE CHANGED TO A **VEGGIE** DIET, I FEEL AS LIGHT AS A FEATHER- **HEALTHY, HAPPY,** AND **PEPPY!** HECK- I'M **GIDDY!!!**
THAT'S THE **TOFU** TALKING.
6·22

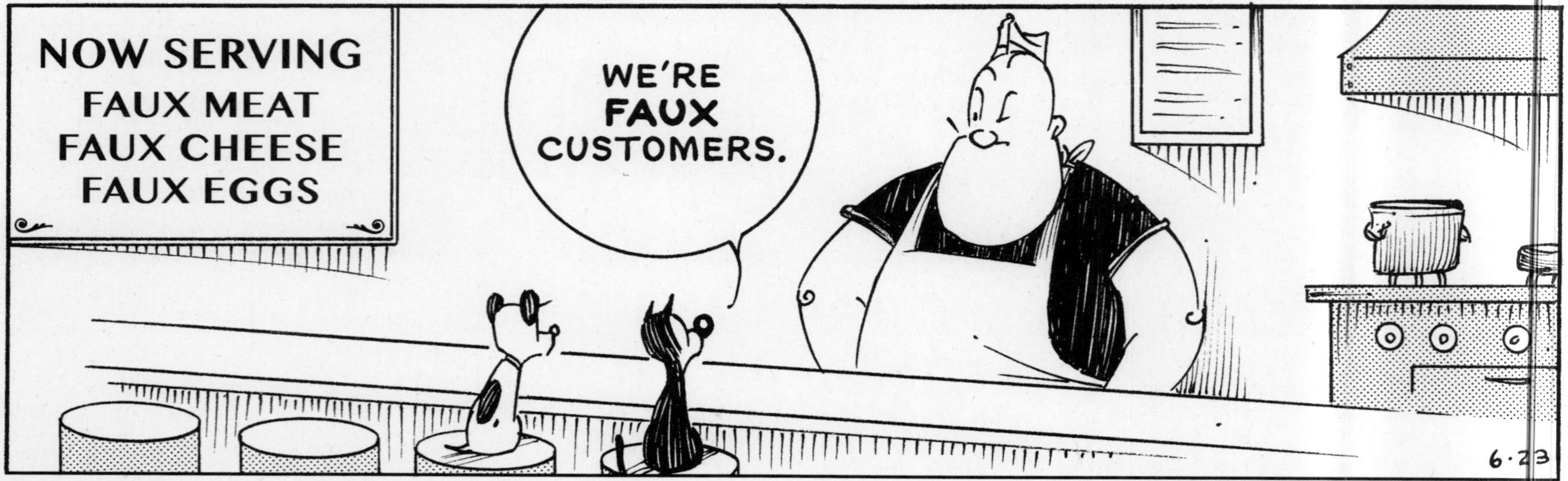
NOW SERVING
FAUX MEAT
FAUX CHEESE
FAUX EGGS
WE'RE **FAUX** CUSTOMERS.
6·23

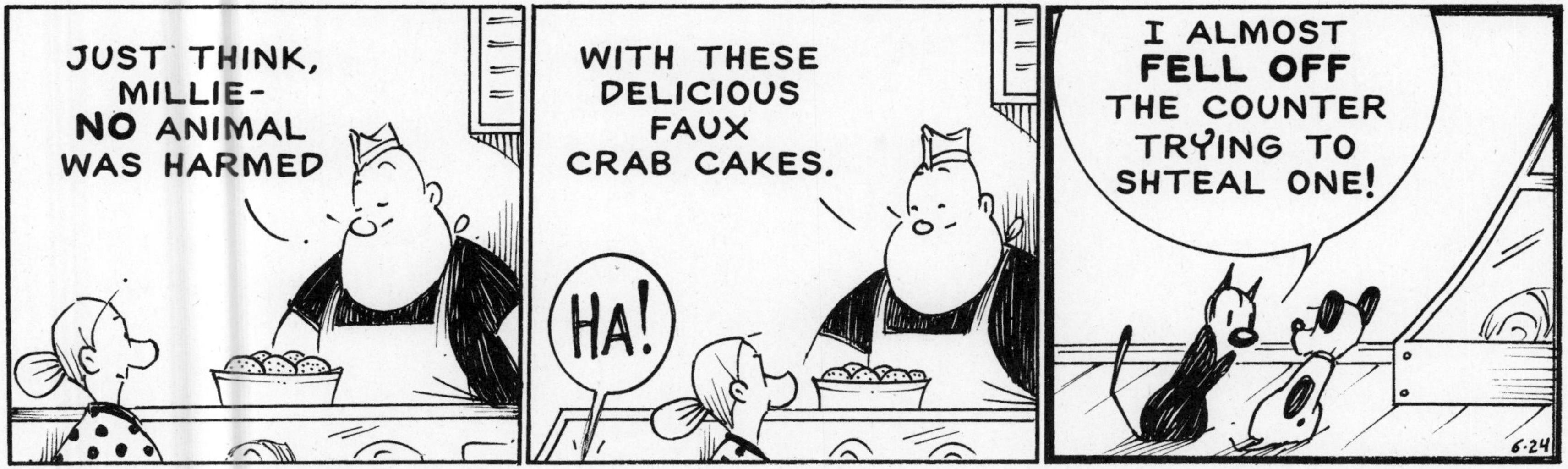
JUST THINK, MILLIE- **NO** ANIMAL WAS HARMED
WITH THESE DELICIOUS FAUX CRAB CAKES.
HA!
I ALMOST **FELL OFF** THE COUNTER TRYING TO SHTEAL ONE!
6-24

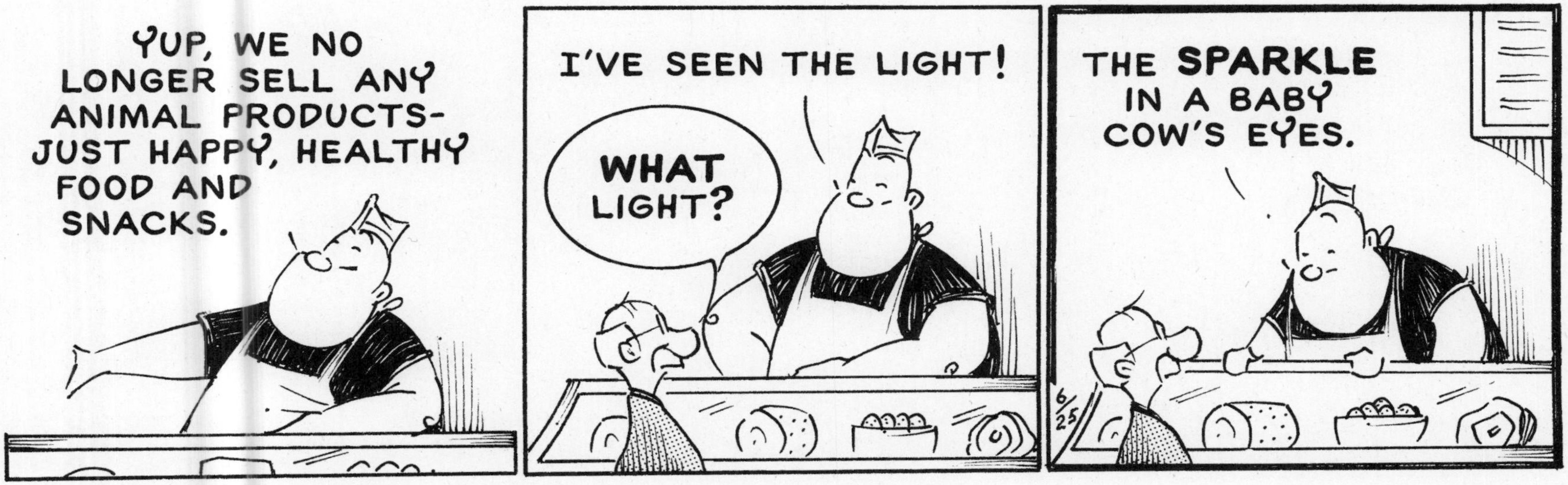
YUP, WE NO LONGER SELL ANY ANIMAL PRODUCTS- JUST HAPPY, HEALTHY FOOD AND SNACKS.
I'VE SEEN THE LIGHT!
WHAT LIGHT?
THE **SPARKLE** IN A BABY COW'S EYES.
6/25

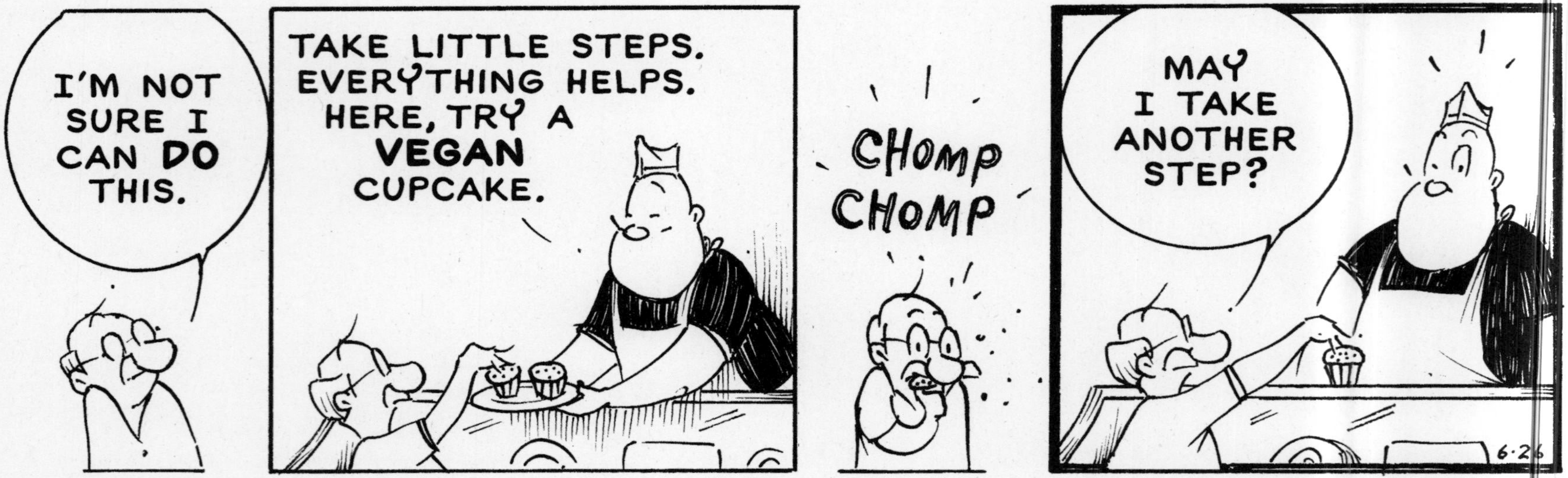
I'M NOT SURE I CAN DO THIS.
TAKE LITTLE STEPS. EVERYTHING HELPS. HERE, TRY A VEGAN CUPCAKE.
CHOMP CHOMP
MAY I TAKE ANOTHER STEP?
6·26

Nothing will benefit human health and increase the chances for survival of life on Earth as much as the evolution to a vegetarian diet.

-Albert Einstein

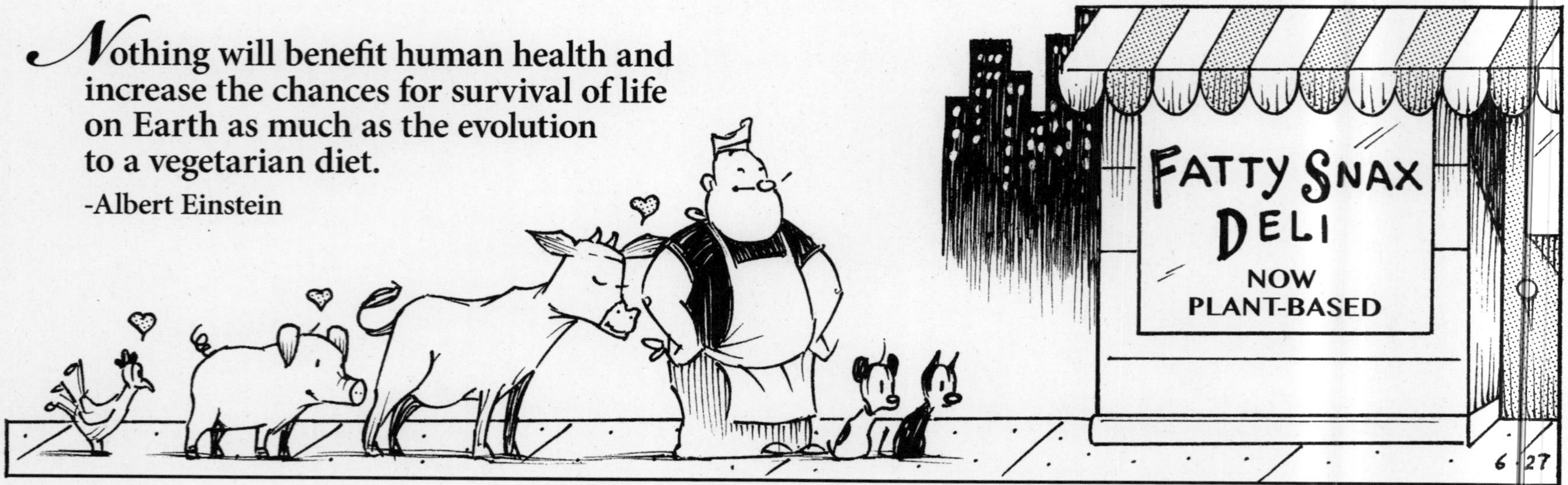
FATTY SNAX DELI
NOW PLANT-BASED
6·27

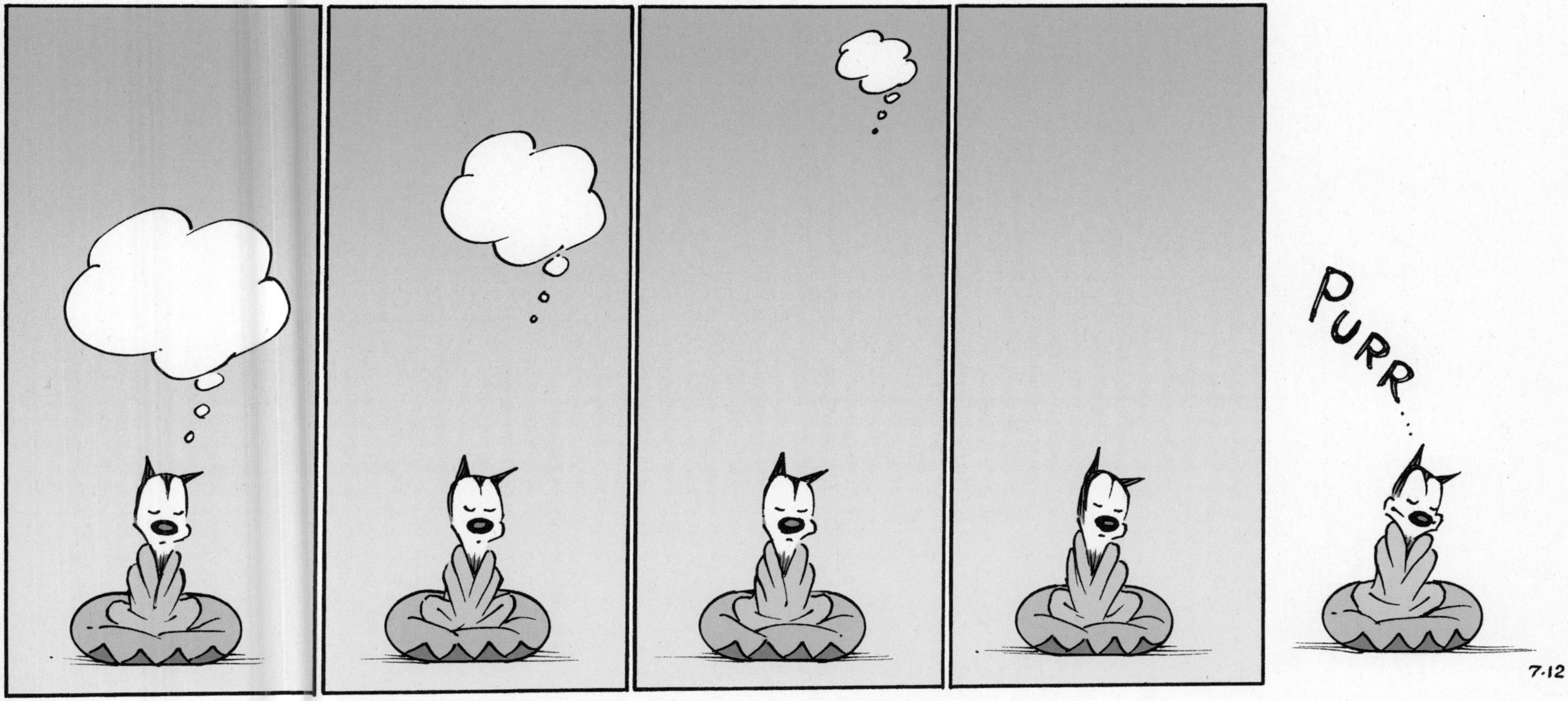
PURR...
7-12

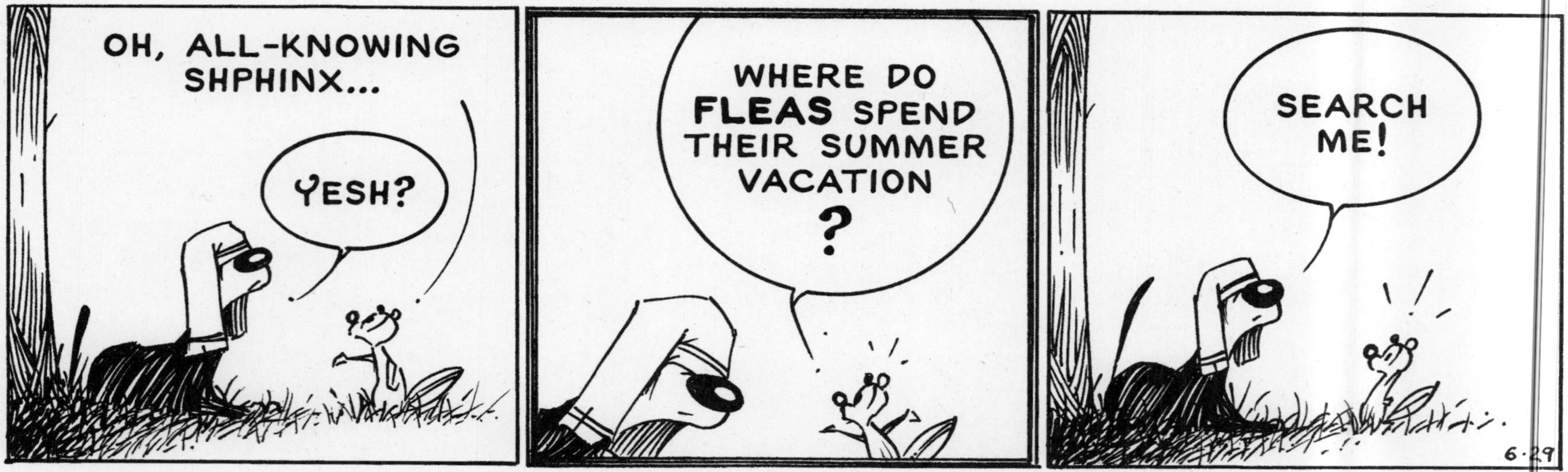
OH, ALL-KNOWING SHPHINX...
YESH?
WHERE DO FLEAS SPEND THEIR SUMMER VACATION ?
SEARCH ME!
6·29

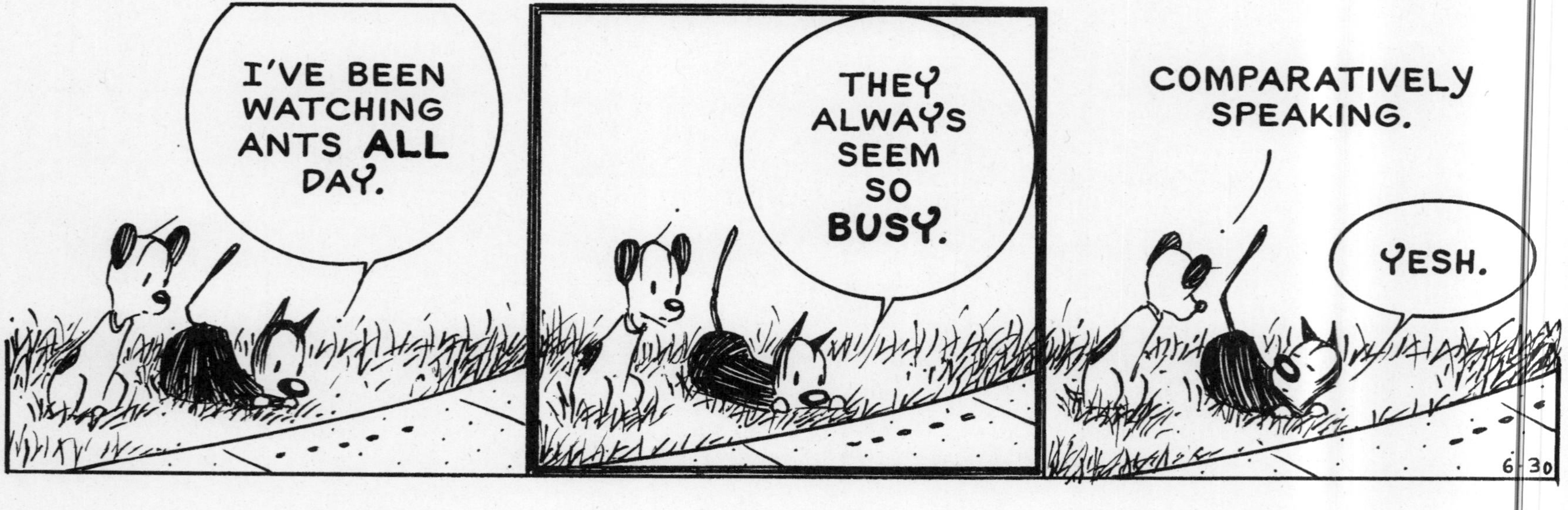
I'VE BEEN WATCHING ANTS ALL DAY.
THEY ALWAYS SEEM SO BUSY.
COMPARATIVELY SPEAKING.
YESH.
6·30

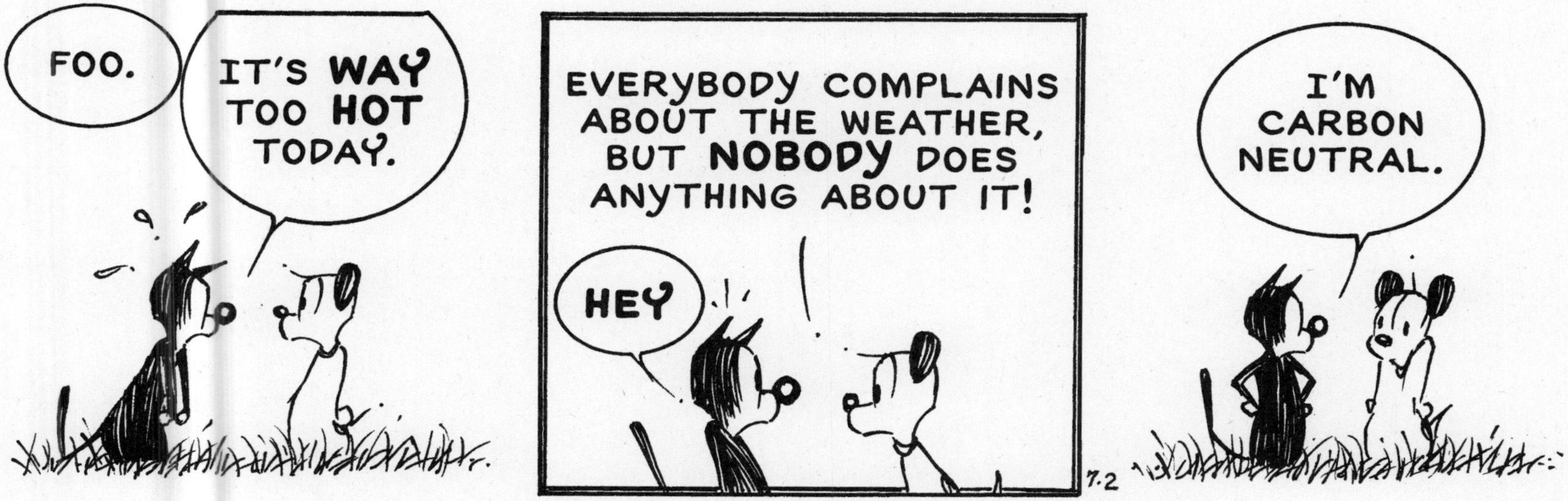
FOO.
IT'S **WAY** TOO **HOT** TODAY.
EVERYBODY COMPLAINS ABOUT THE WEATHER, BUT **NOBODY** DOES ANYTHING ABOUT IT!
HEY
I'M CARBON NEUTRAL.
7.2

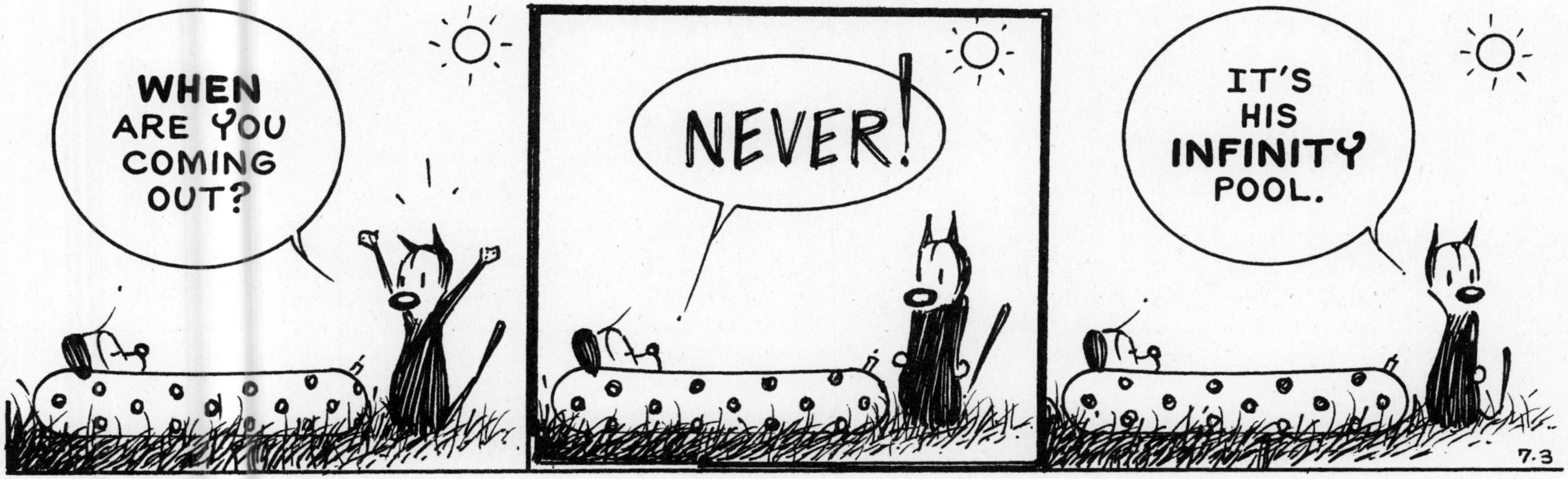
WHEN ARE YOU COMING OUT?
NEVER!
IT'S HIS **INFINITY** POOL.
7.3

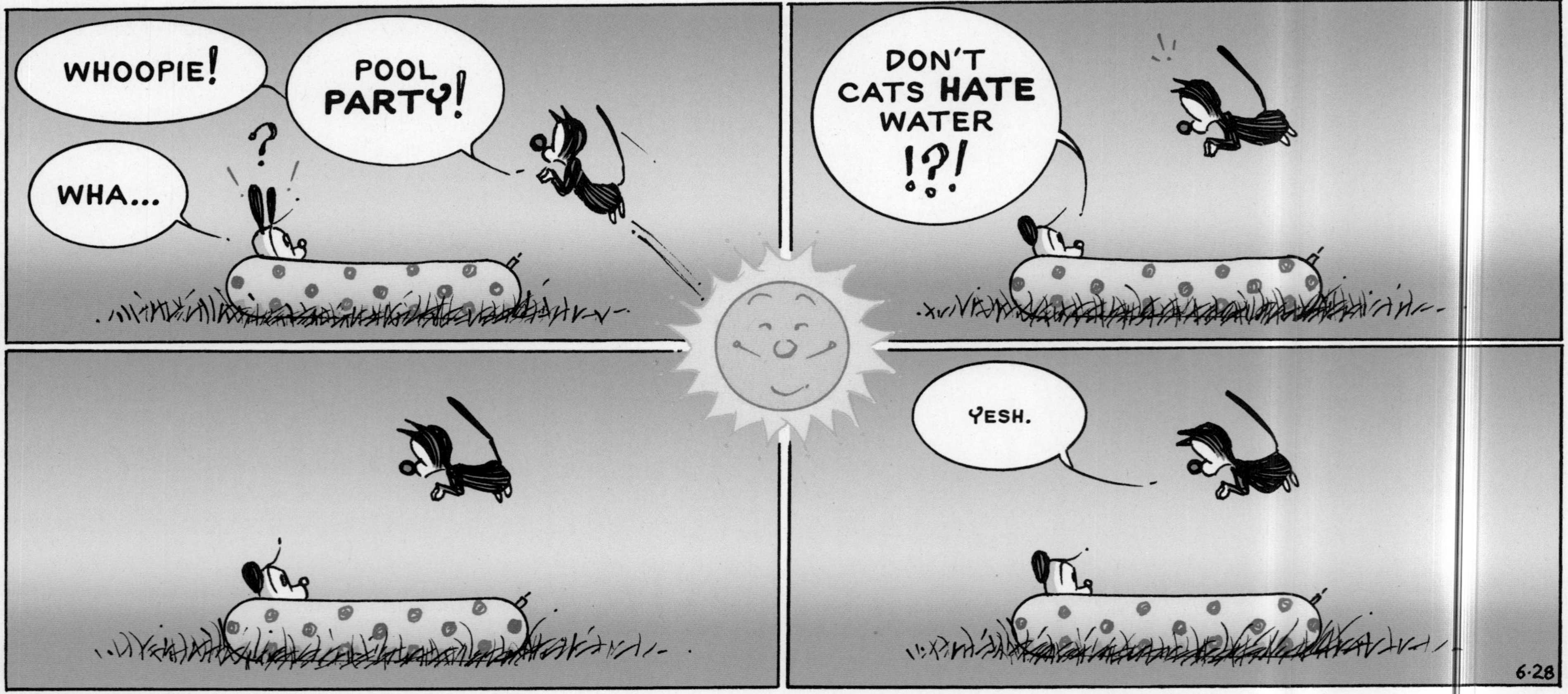
WHOOPIE!
POOL PARTY!
WHA...
DON'T CATS HATE WATER !?!
YESH.
6·28

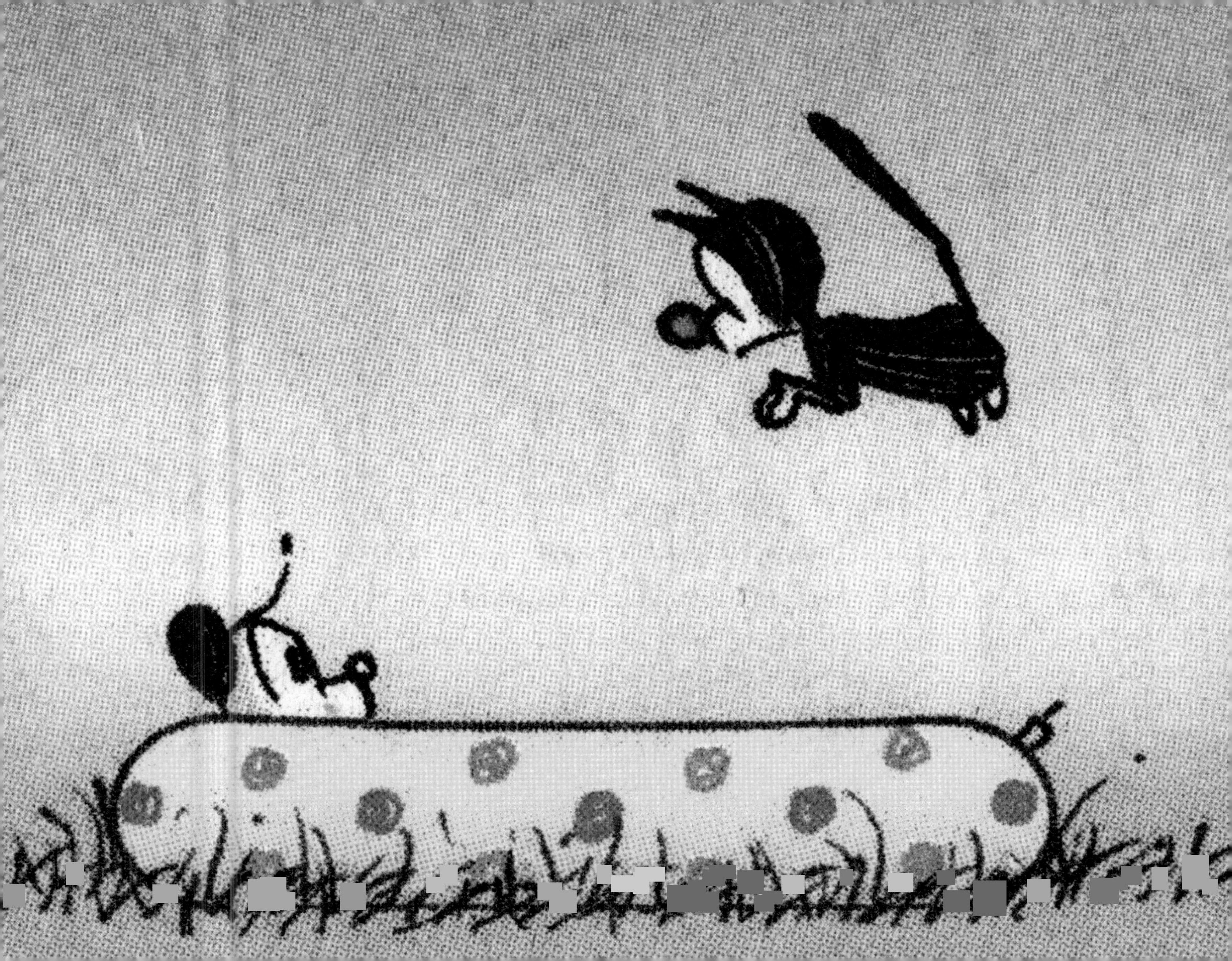

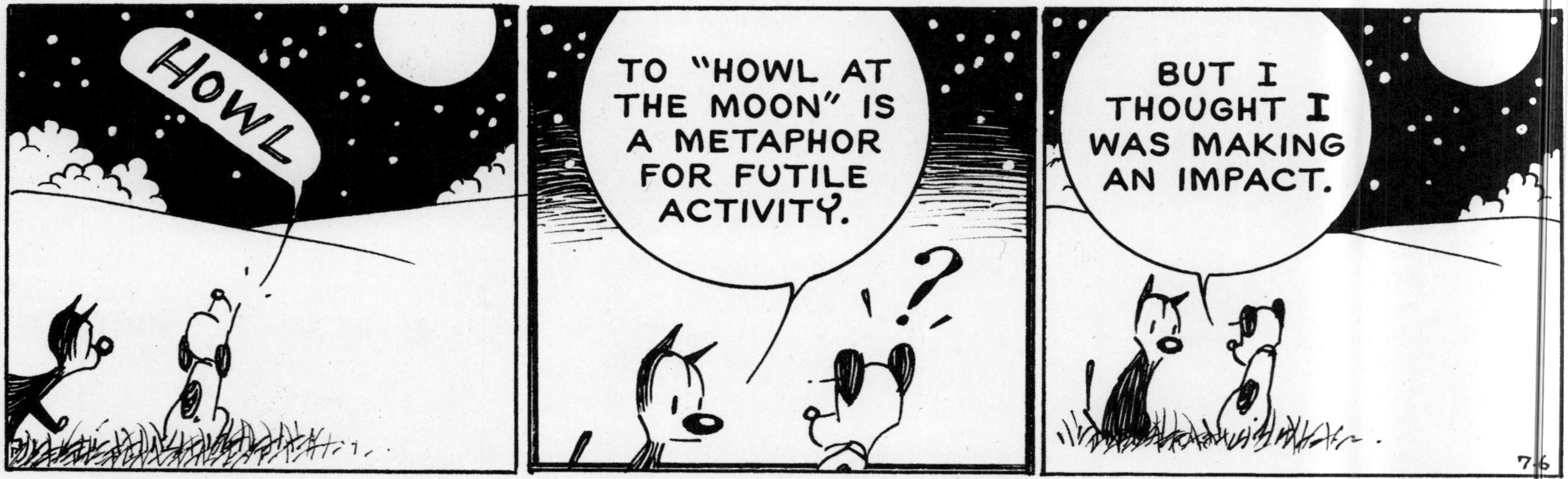
HOWL
TO "HOWL AT THE MOON" IS A METAPHOR FOR FUTILE ACTIVITY.
?
BUT I THOUGHT I WAS MAKING AN IMPACT.
7-6

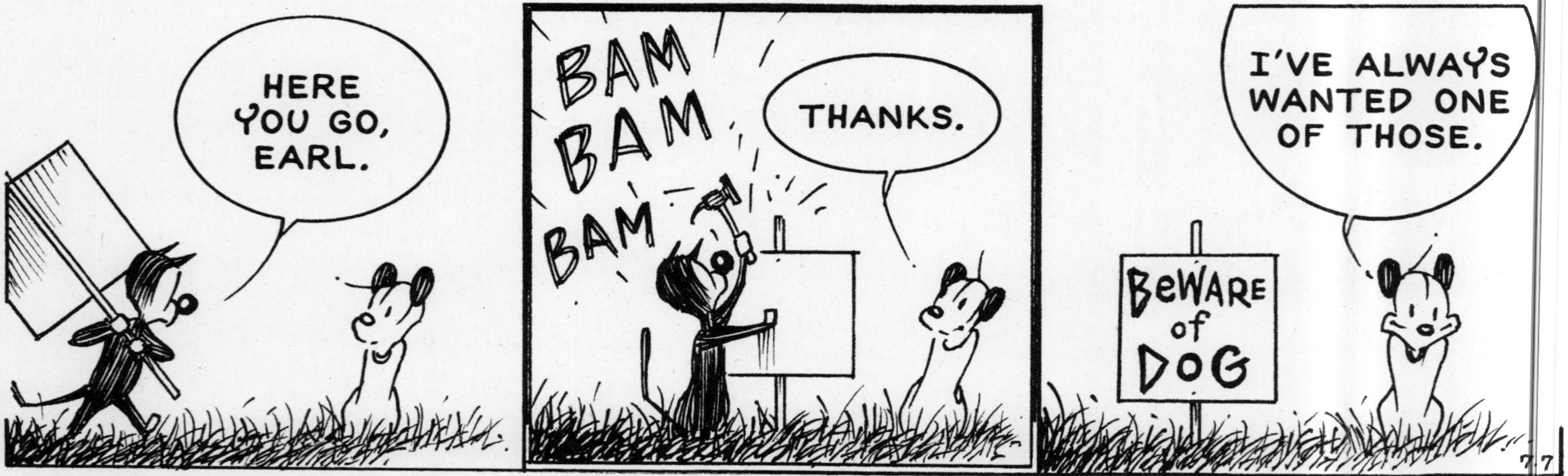
HERE YOU GO, EARL.
BAM BAM BAM
THANKS.
BEWARE of DOG
I'VE ALWAYS WANTED ONE OF THOSE.
7-7

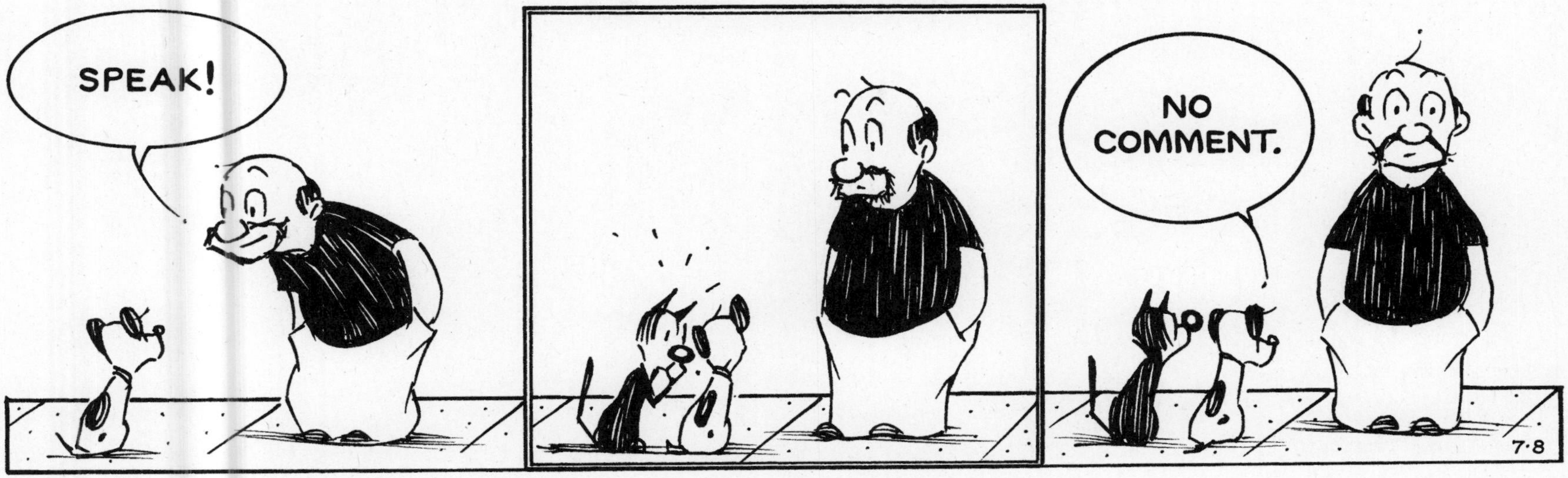
SPEAK!
NO COMMENT.
7·8

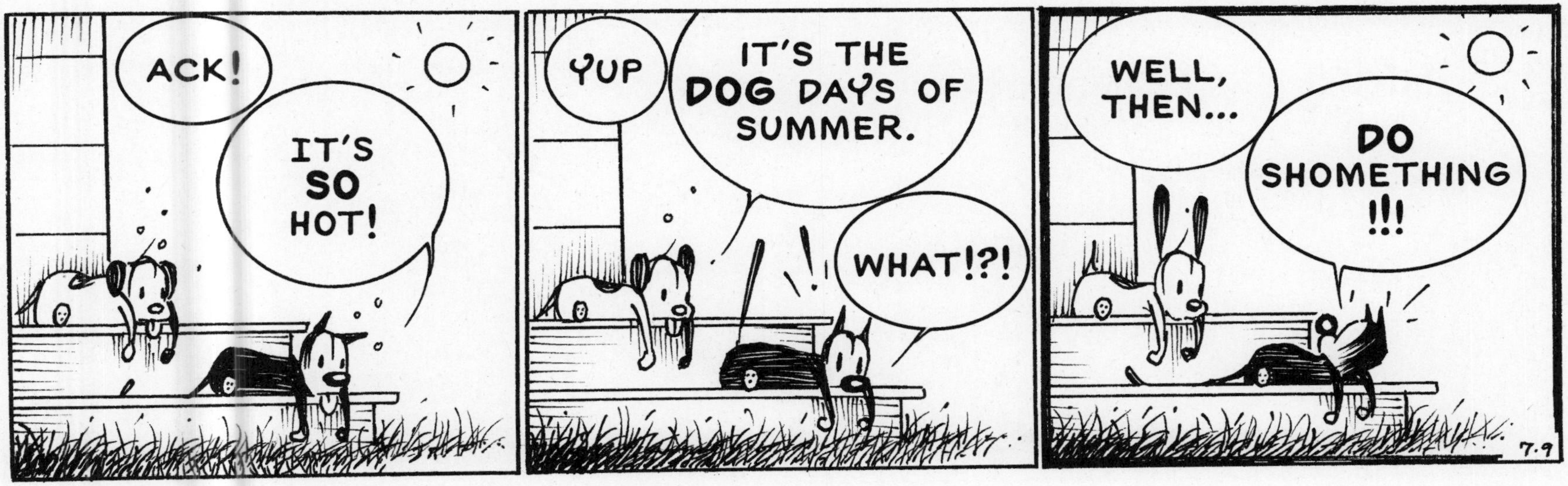
ACK!
IT'S SO HOT!
YUP
IT'S THE DOG DAYS OF SUMMER.
WHAT!?!
WELL, THEN...
DO SHOMETHING !!!
7·9

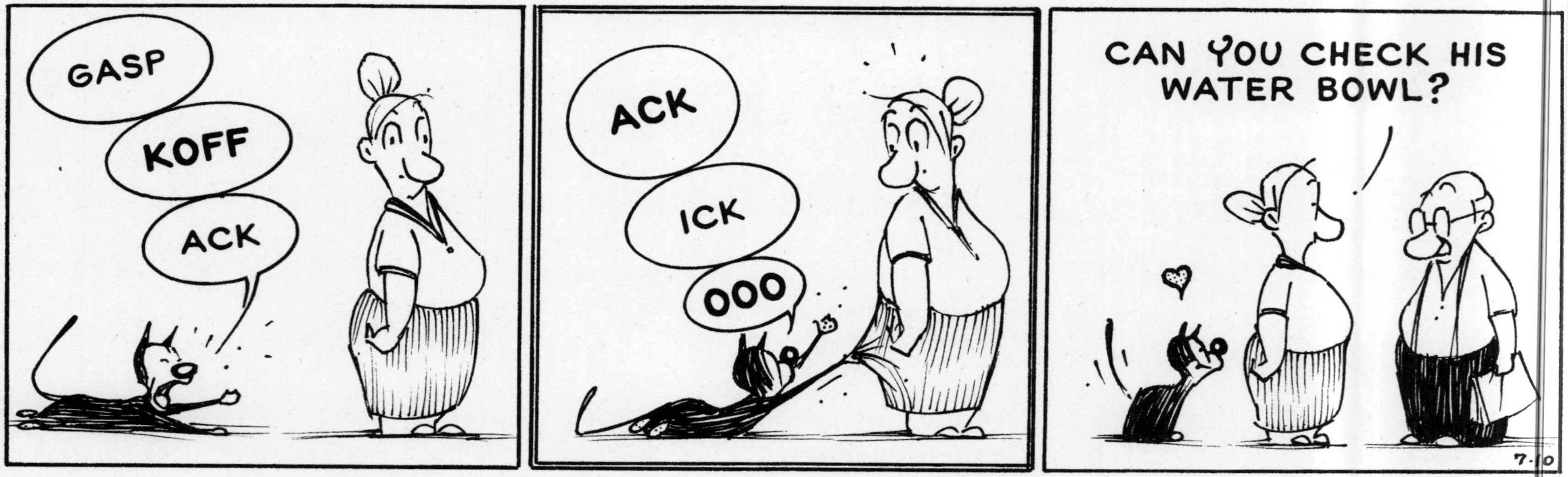
GASP
KOFF
ACK
ACK
ICK
OOO
CAN YOU CHECK HIS WATER BOWL?
7·10

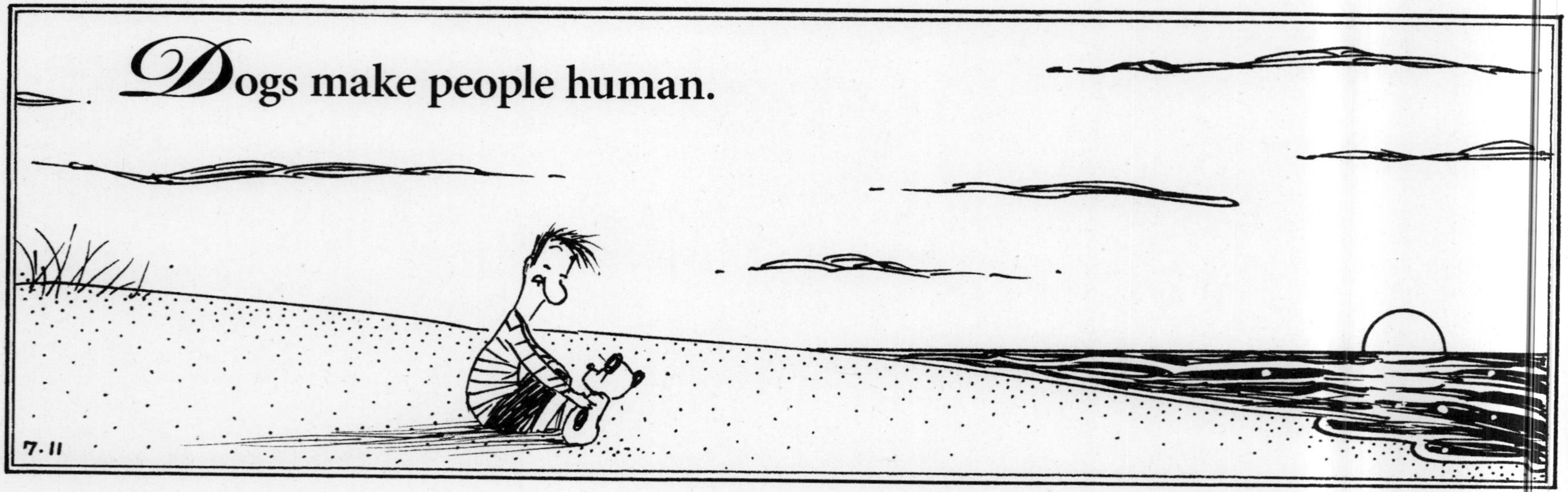
Dogs make people human.
7·11

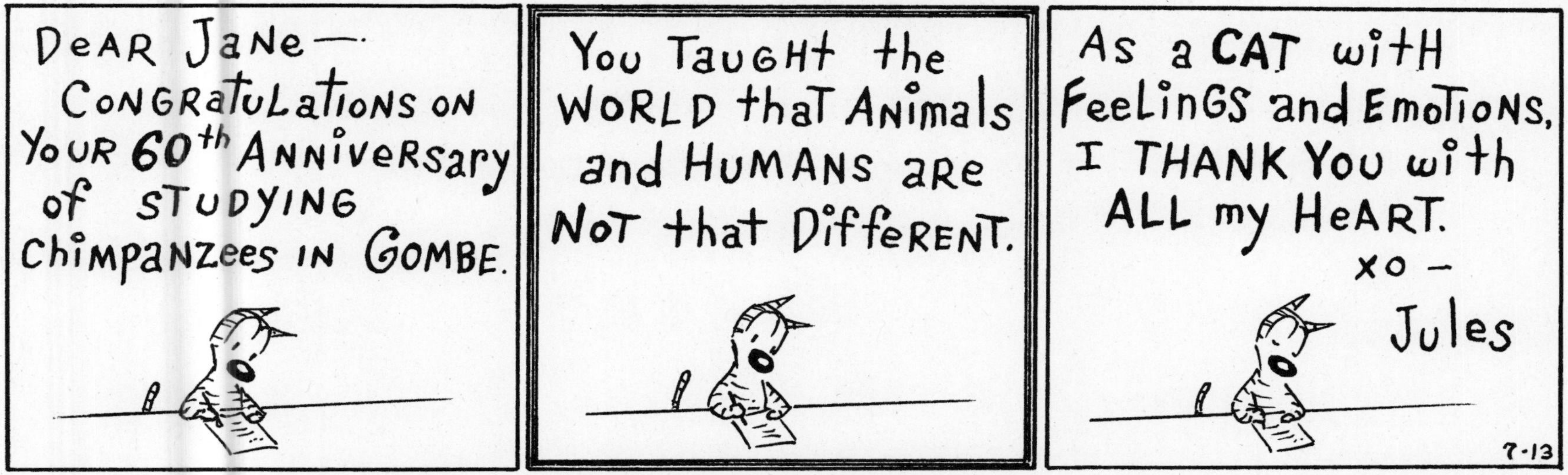
Dear Jane—
Congratulations on your 60th Anniversary of studying chimpanzees in Gombe.
You taught the WORLD that Animals and HUMANS are NOT that Different.
As a CAT with Feelings and Emotions, I THANK You with ALL my Heart.
xo —
Jules
7-13

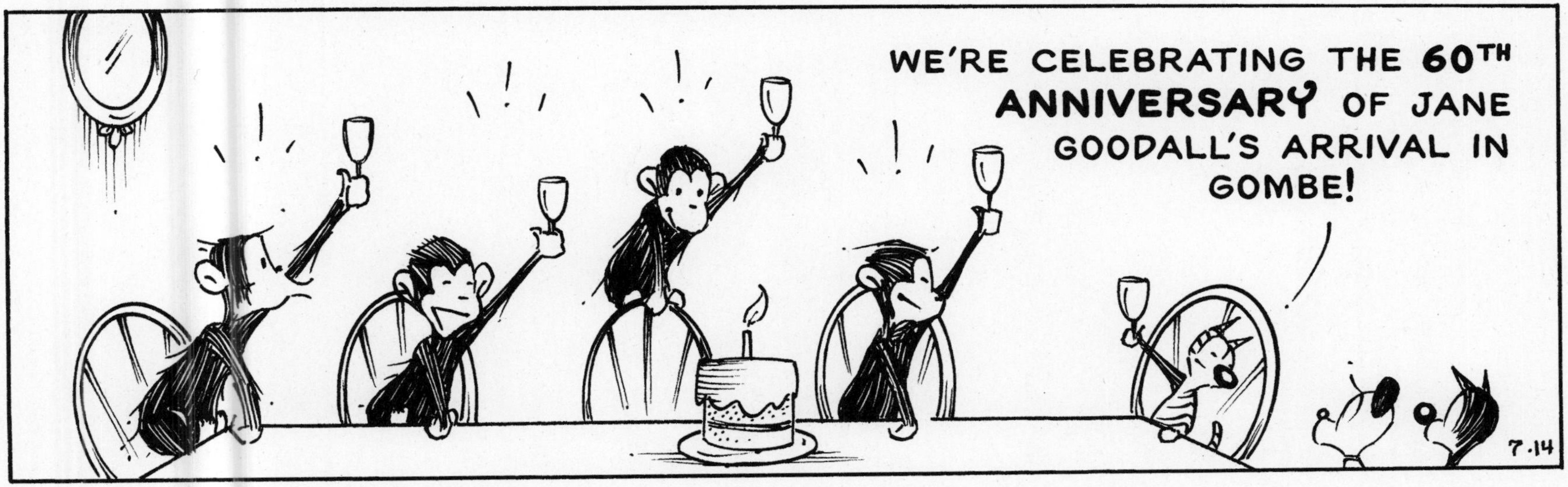
WE'RE CELEBRATING THE 60TH ANNIVERSARY OF JANE GOODALL'S ARRIVAL IN GOMBE!
7-14

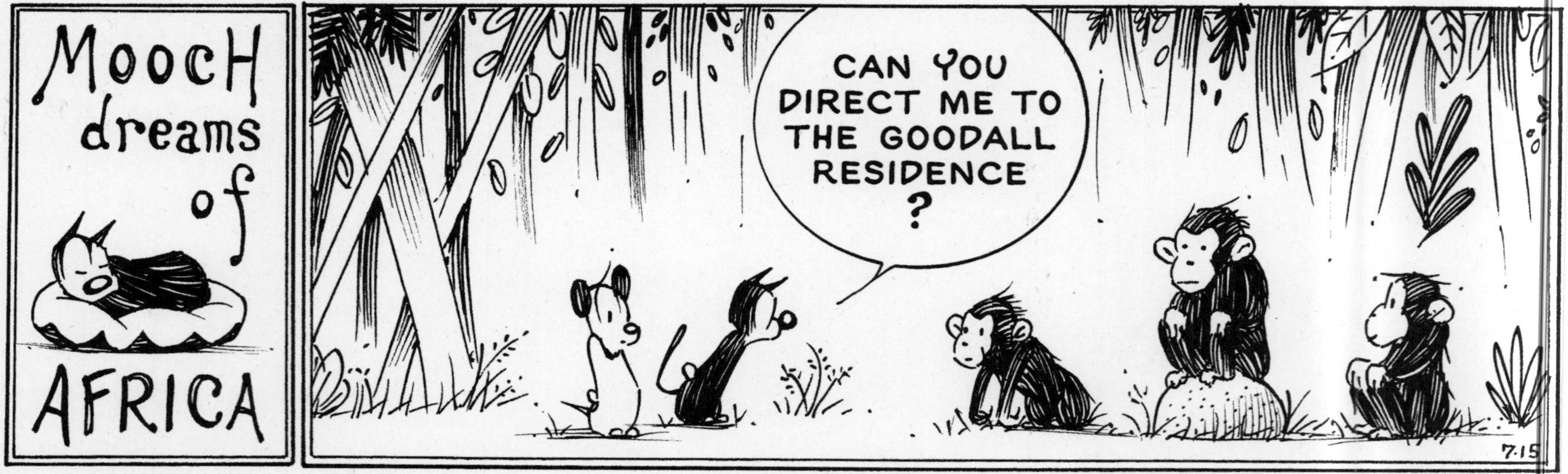
Mooch dreams of AFRICA
CAN YOU DIRECT ME TO THE GOODALL RESIDENCE ?
7.15

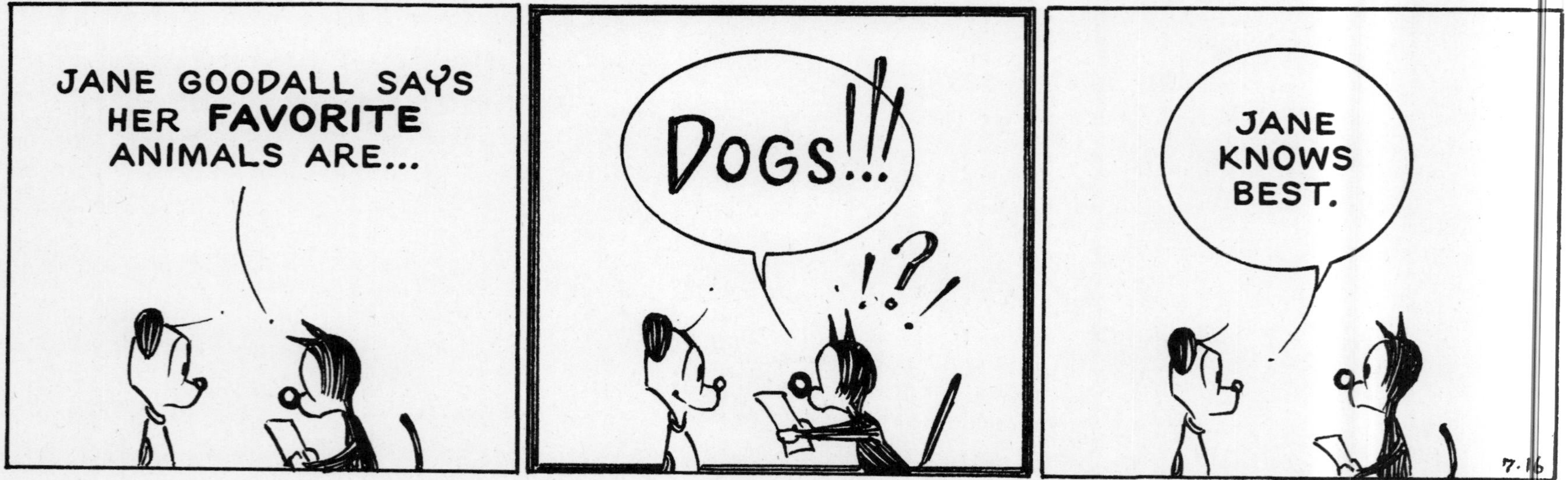
JANE GOODALL SAYS HER **FAVORITE** ANIMALS ARE...
DOGS!!!
!?!
JANE KNOWS BEST.
7.16

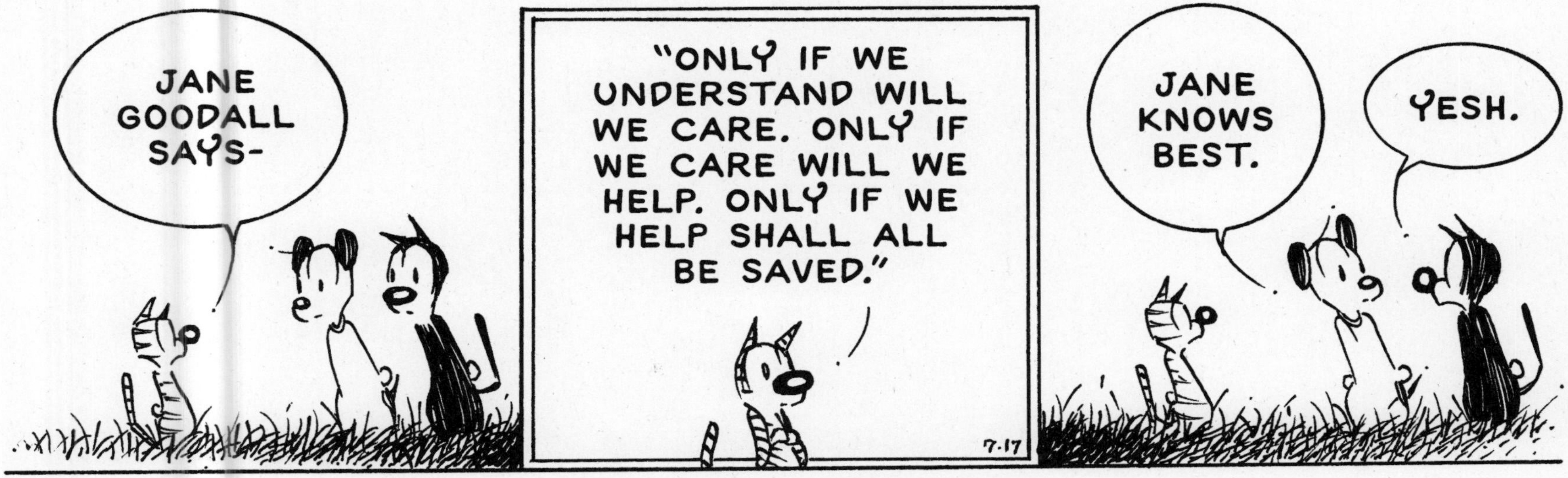
JANE GOODALL SAYS-
"ONLY IF WE UNDERSTAND WILL WE CARE. ONLY IF WE CARE WILL WE HELP. ONLY IF WE HELP SHALL ALL BE SAVED."
7.17
JANE KNOWS BEST.
YESH.

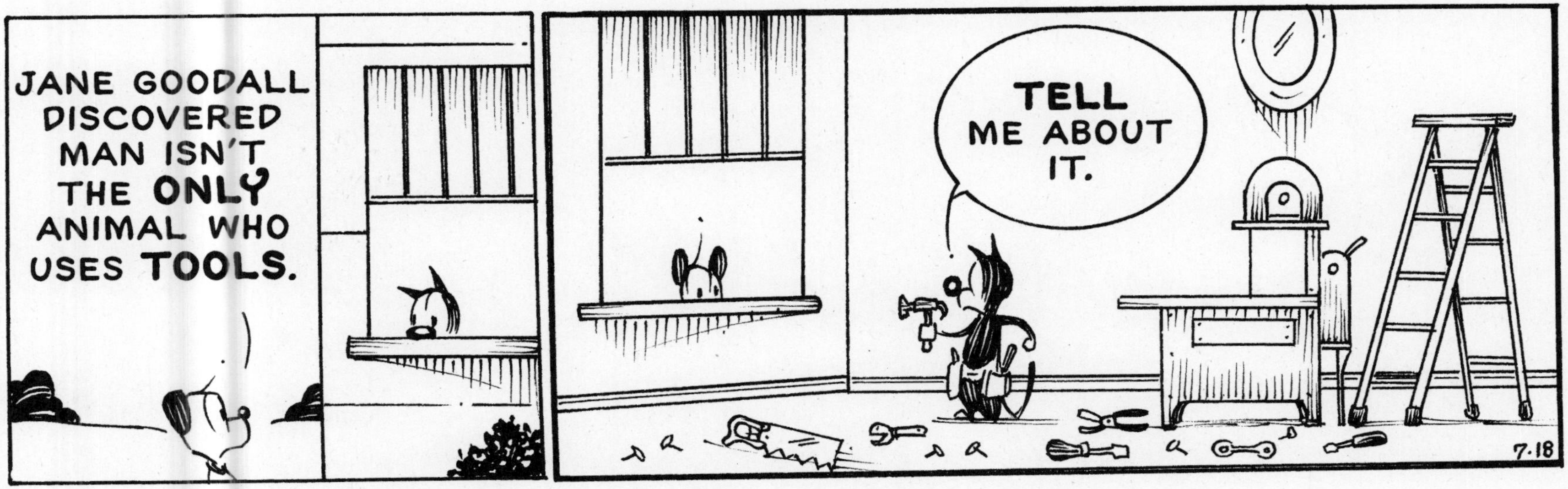
JANE GOODALL DISCOVERED MAN ISN'T THE ONLY ANIMAL WHO USES TOOLS.
TELL ME ABOUT IT.
7.18

MUTTS
Patrick McDonnell

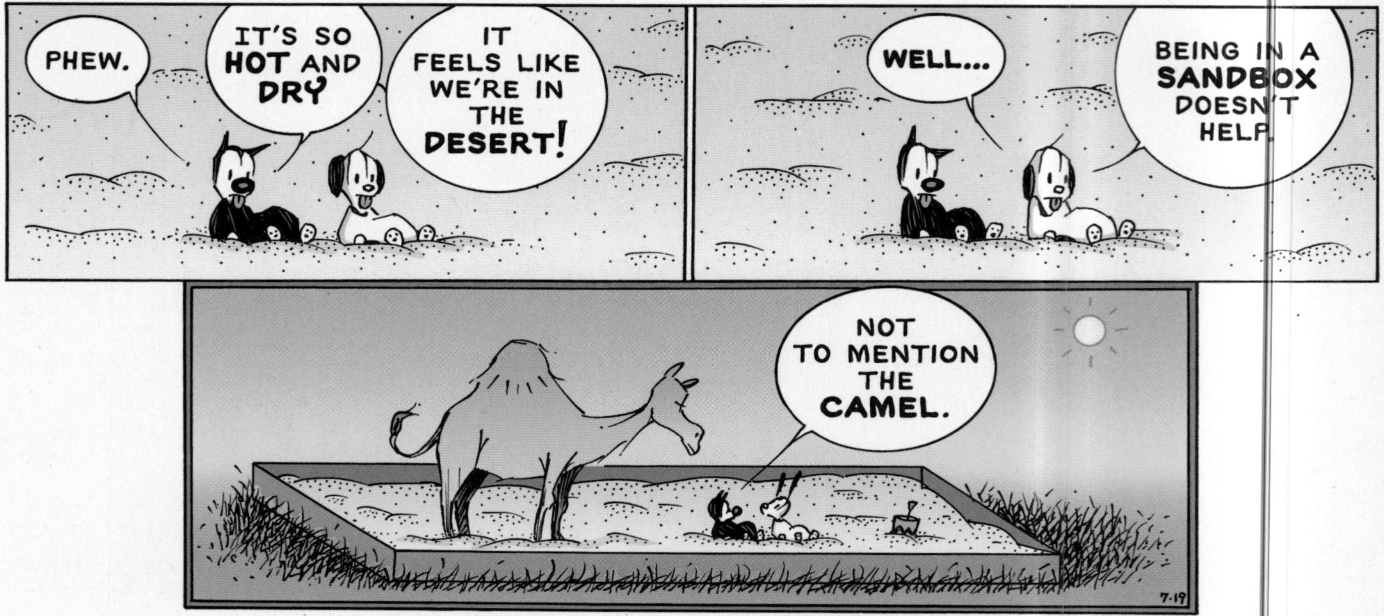
PHEW.
IT'S SO HOT AND DRY
IT FEELS LIKE WE'RE IN THE DESERT!
WELL...
BEING IN A SANDBOX DOESN'T HELP.
NOT TO MENTION THE CAMEL.
7·19

MUTTS
Patrick McDonnell

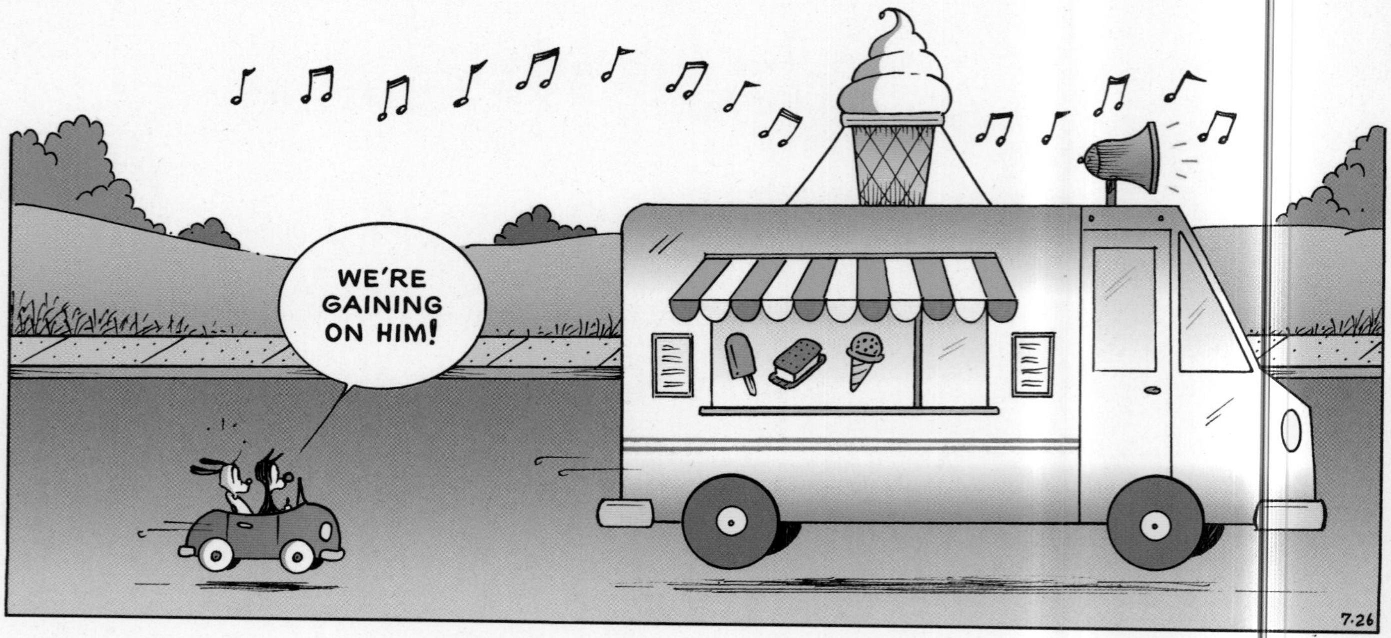
WE'RE GAINING ON HIM!
7·26

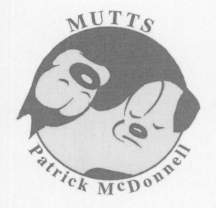

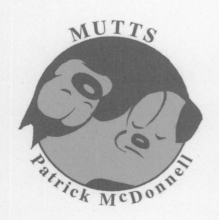

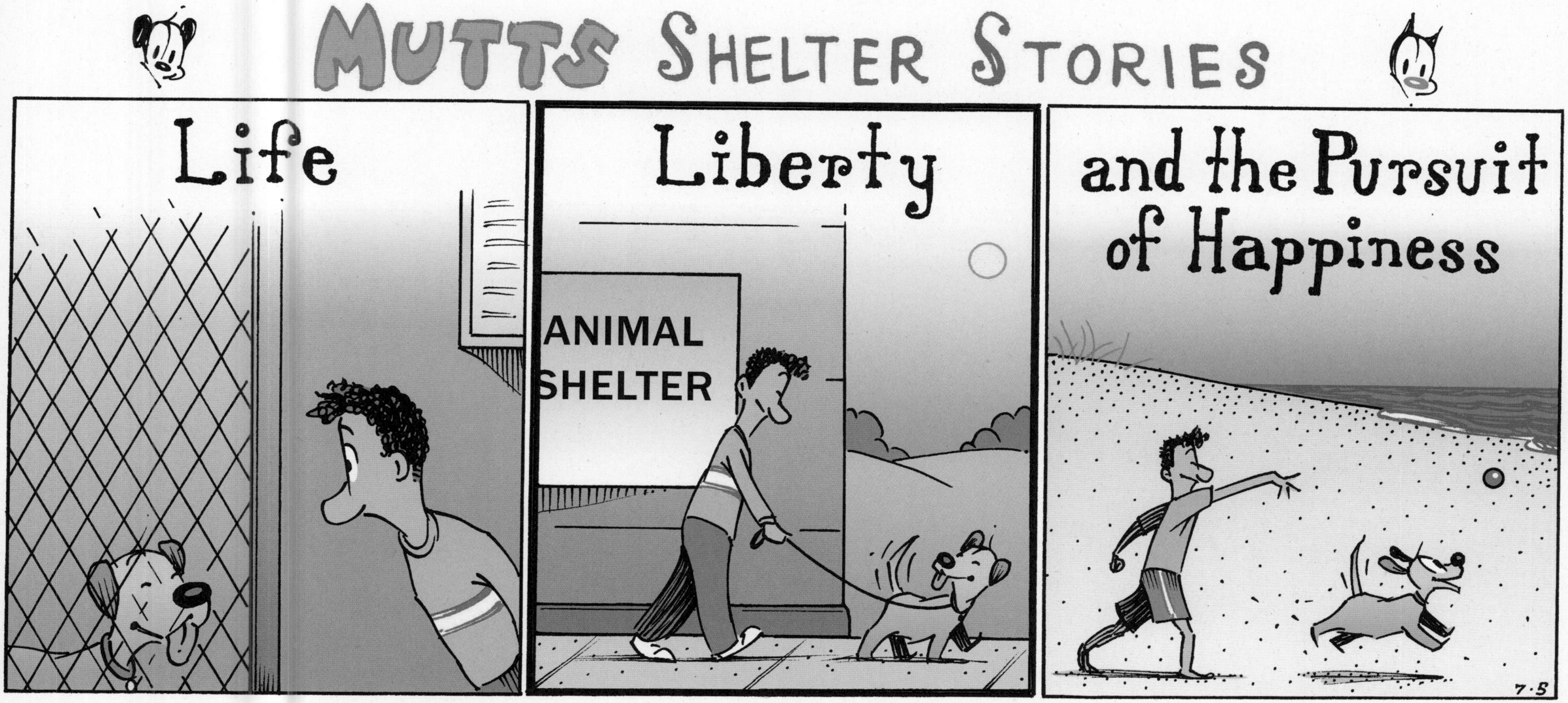
MUTTS SHELTER STORIES
Life
Liberty
ANIMAL
SHELTER
and the Pursuit of Happiness
7·5

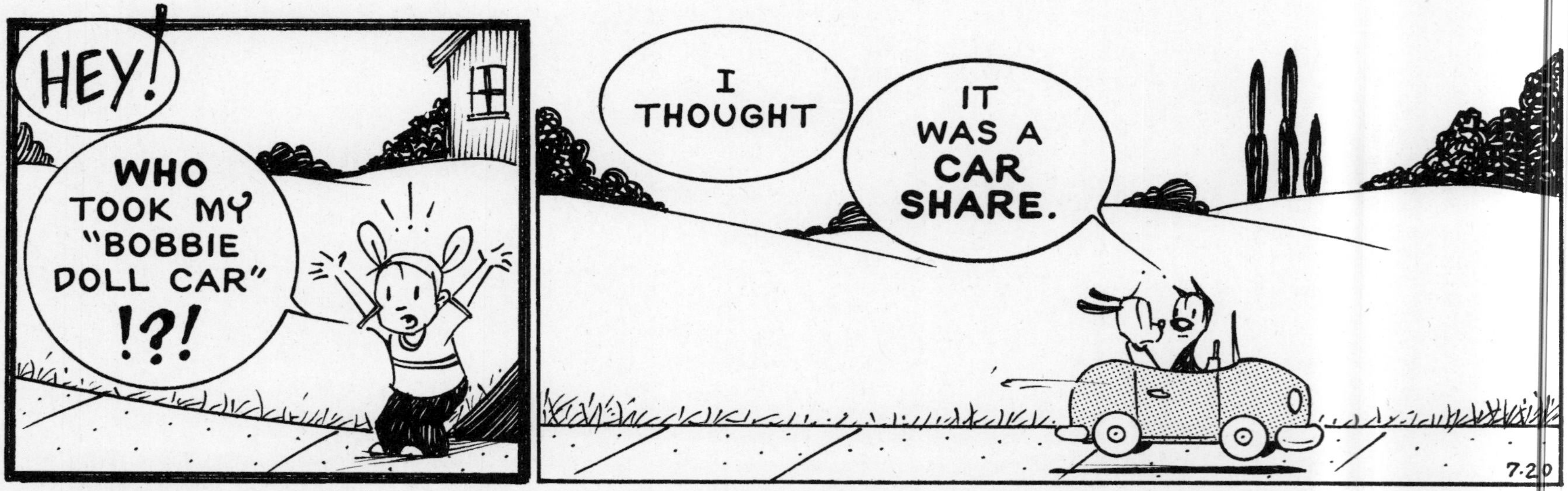
HEY!
WHO TOOK MY "BOBBIE DOLL CAR" !?!
I THOUGHT
IT WAS A CAR SHARE.
7·20

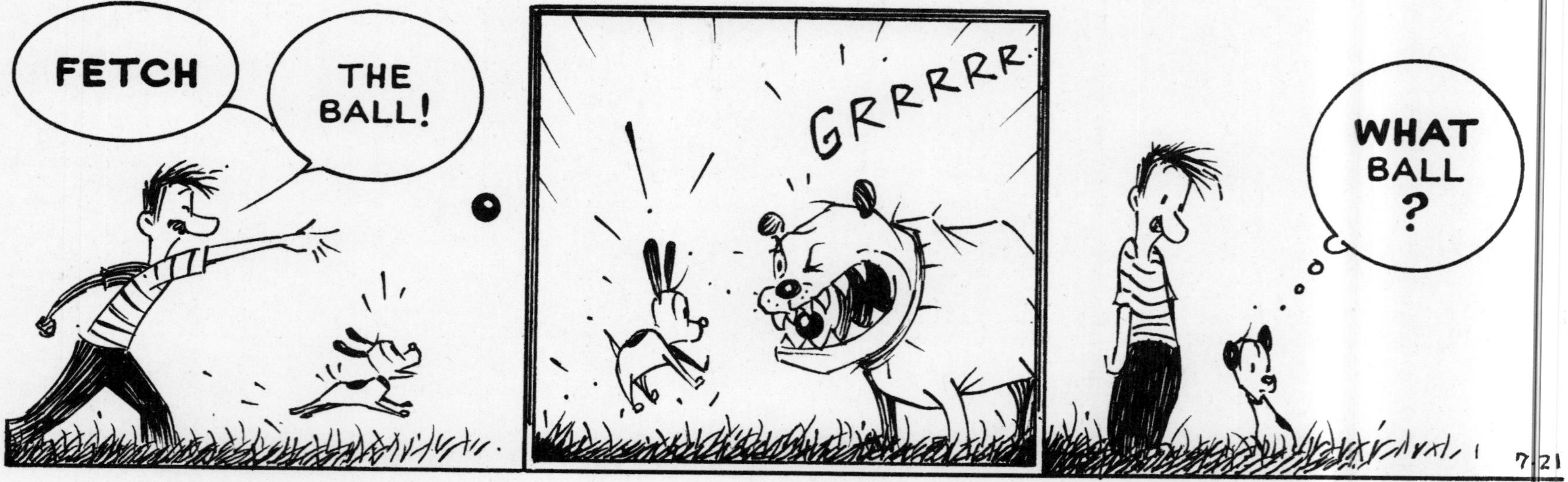
FETCH
THE BALL!
GRRRRR
WHAT BALL ?
7·21

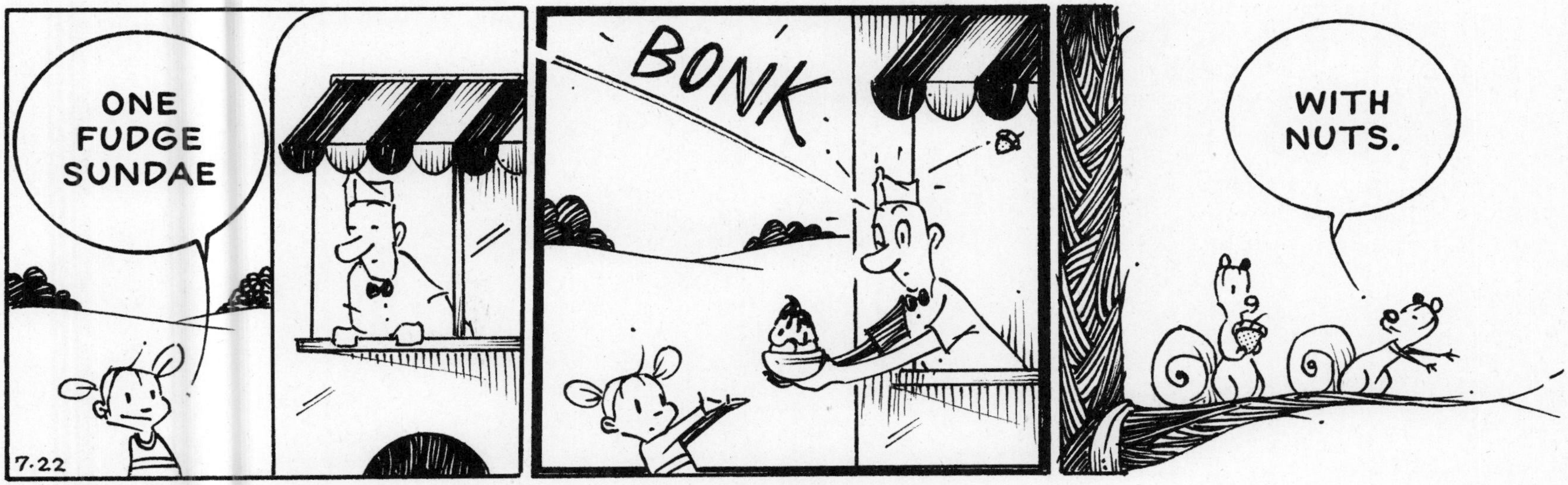
ONE FUDGE SUNDAE
BONK
WITH NUTS.
7·22

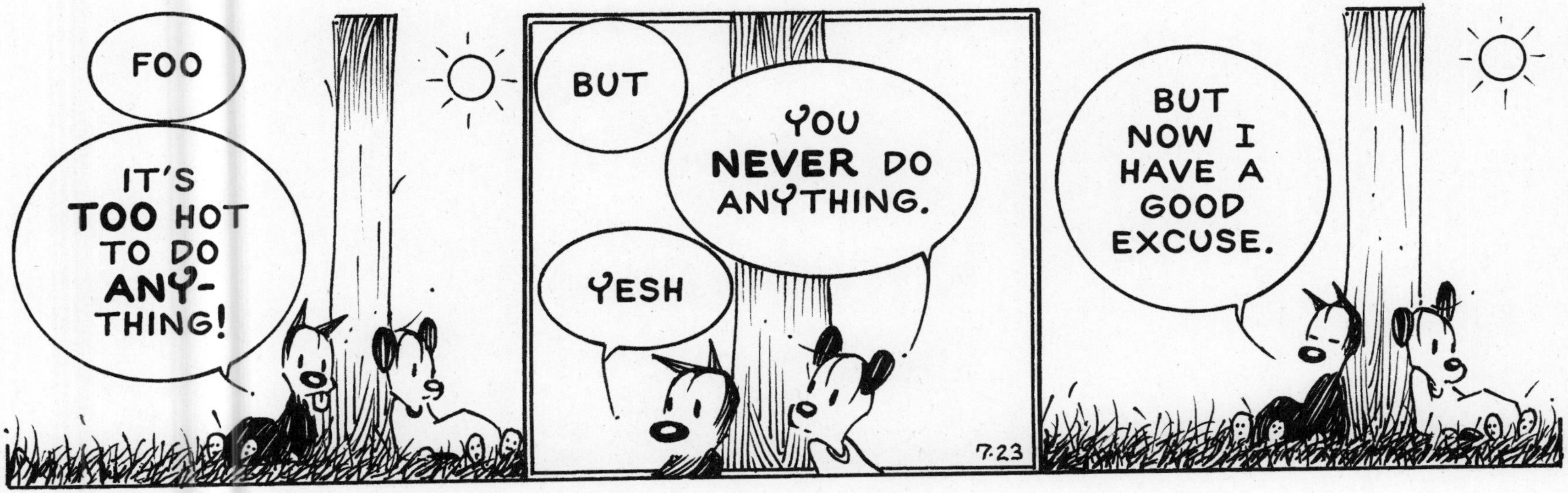
FOO
IT'S TOO HOT TO DO ANY-THING!
BUT
YOU NEVER DO ANYTHING.
YESH
7·23
BUT NOW I HAVE A GOOD EXCUSE.

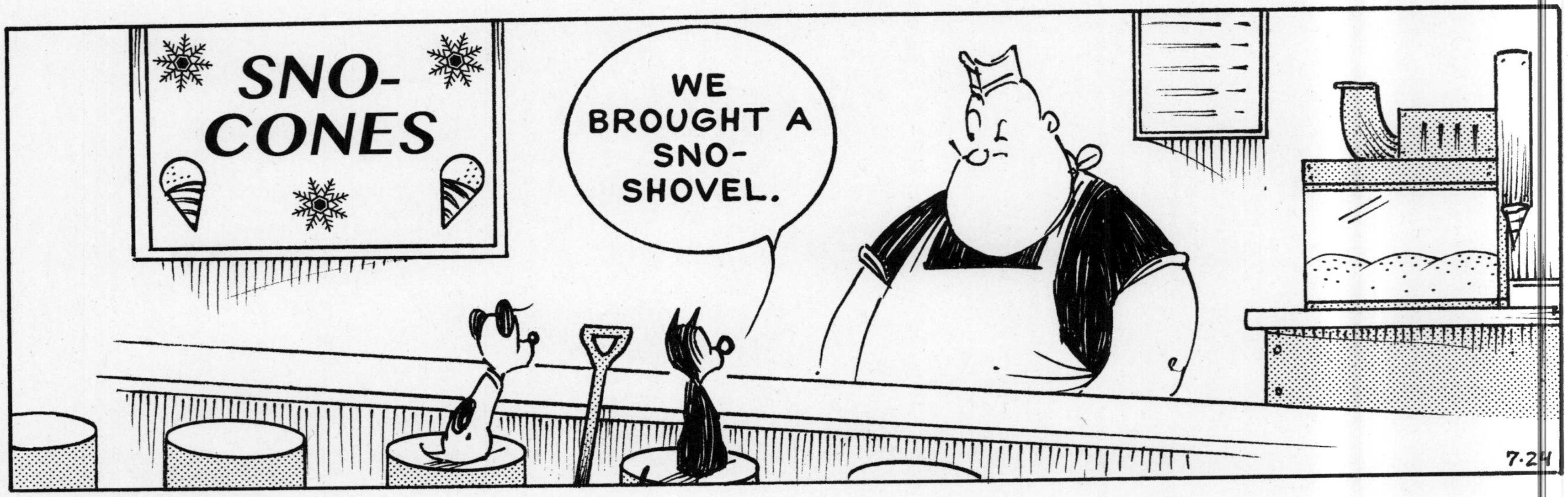
SNO-
CONES
WE BROUGHT A SNO-SHOVEL.
7·24

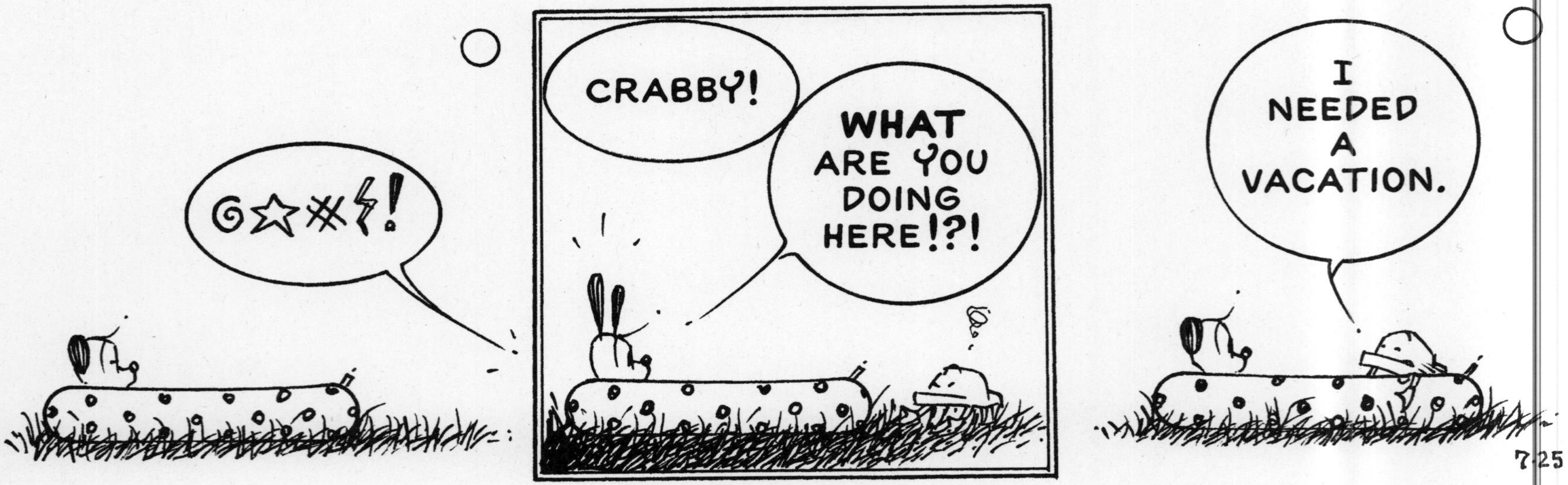
CRABBY!
WHAT ARE YOU DOING HERE!?!
I NEEDED A VACATION.
7·25

THE SUSPENSE IS UNBEARABLE.
8·16
YES!
JELLY DONUTS!

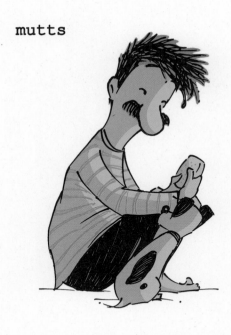

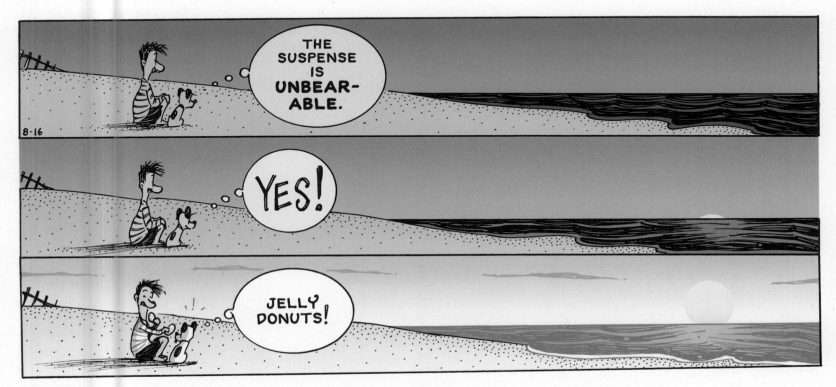

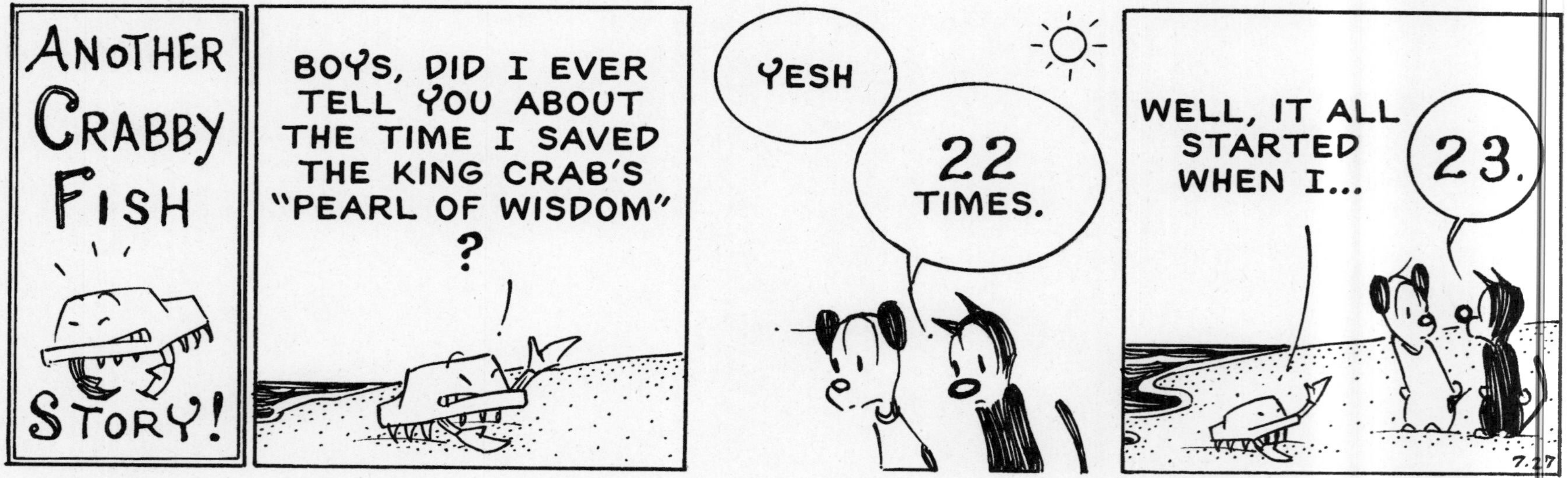
ANOTHER CRABBY FISH STORY!
BOYS, DID I EVER TELL YOU ABOUT THE TIME I SAVED THE KING CRAB'S "PEARL OF WISDOM" ?
YESH
22 TIMES.
WELL, IT ALL STARTED WHEN I...
23.
7.27

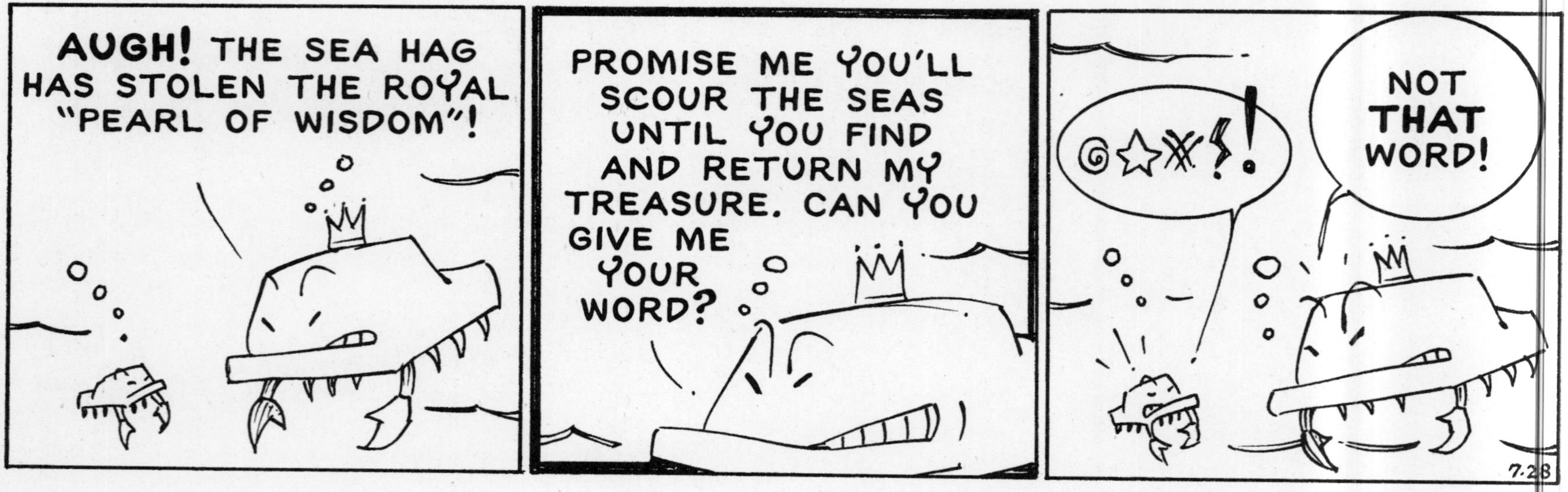
AUGH! THE SEA HAG HAS STOLEN THE ROYAL "PEARL OF WISDOM"!
PROMISE ME YOU'LL SCOUR THE SEAS UNTIL YOU FIND AND RETURN MY TREASURE. CAN YOU GIVE ME YOUR WORD?
NOT THAT WORD!
7.28

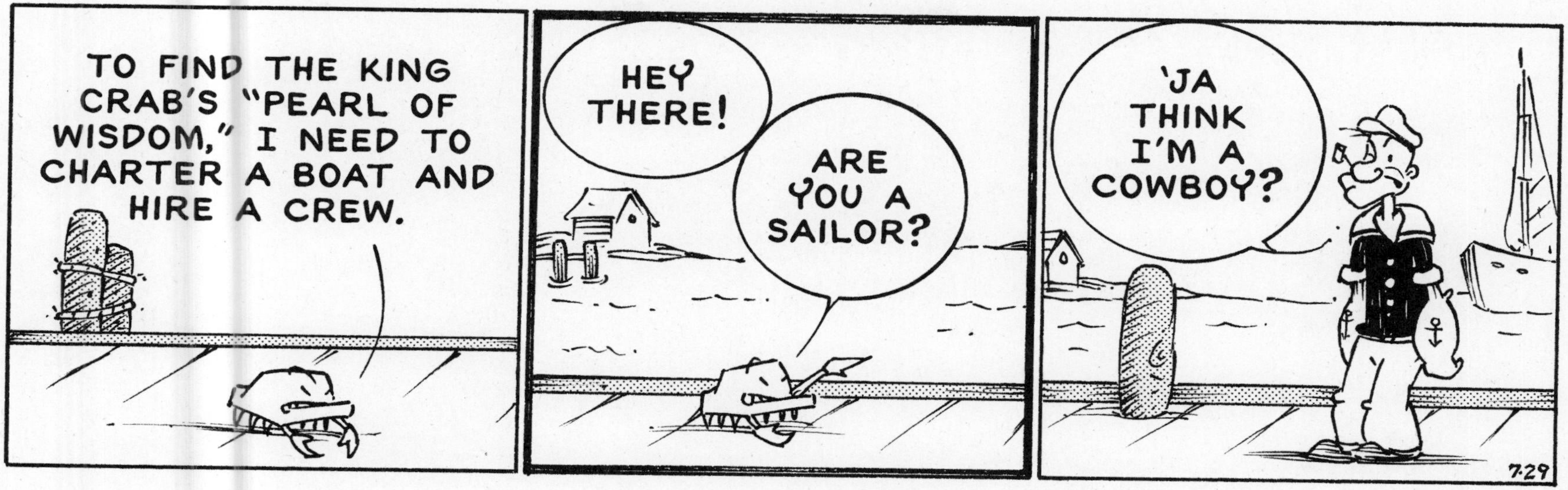
TO FIND THE KING CRAB'S "PEARL OF WISDOM," I NEED TO CHARTER A BOAT AND HIRE A CREW.
HEY THERE!
ARE YOU A SAILOR?
'JA THINK I'M A COWBOY?
7-29

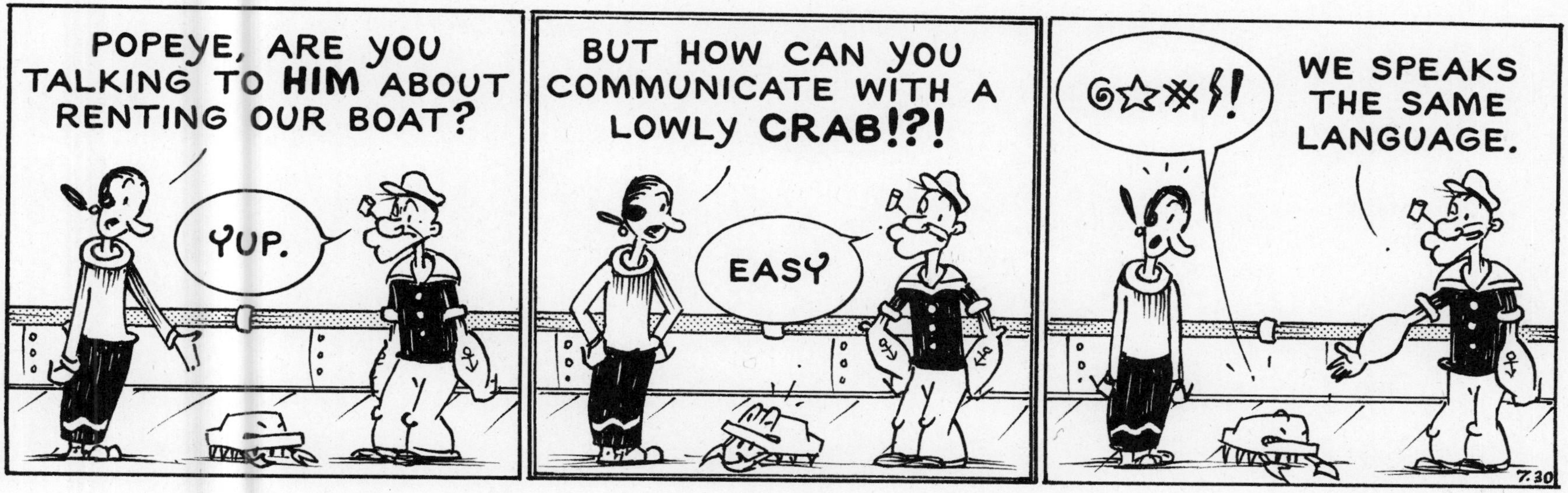
POPEYE, ARE YOU TALKING TO **HIM** ABOUT RENTING OUR BOAT?
YUP.
BUT HOW CAN YOU COMMUNICATE WITH A LOWLY **CRAB!?!**
EASY
WE SPEAKS THE SAME LANGUAGE.
7-30

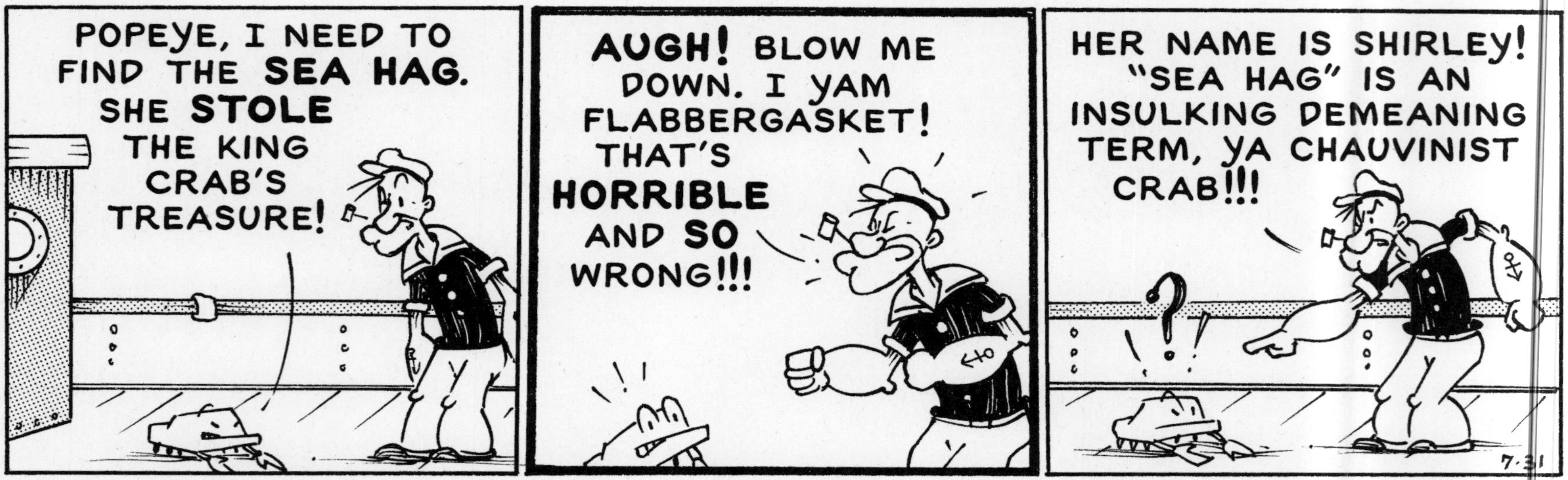
POPEYE, I NEED TO FIND THE **SEA HAG.** SHE **STOLE** THE KING CRAB'S TREASURE!
AUGH! BLOW ME DOWN. I YAM FLABBERGASKET! THAT'S **HORRIBLE** AND **SO** WRONG!!!
HER NAME IS SHIRLEY! "SEA HAG" IS AN INSULKING DEMEANING TERM, YA CHAUVINIST CRAB!!!
7·31

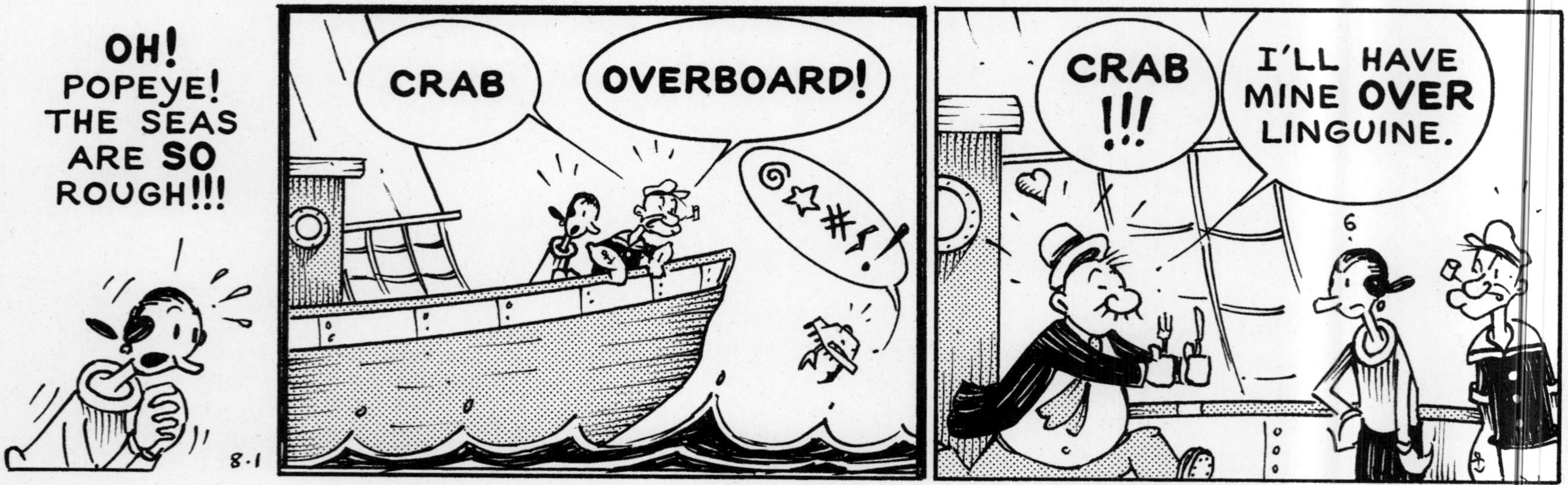
OH! POPEYE! THE SEAS ARE **SO** ROUGH!!!
8·1
CRAB
OVERBOARD!
CRAB !!!
I'LL HAVE MINE **OVER** LINGUINE.

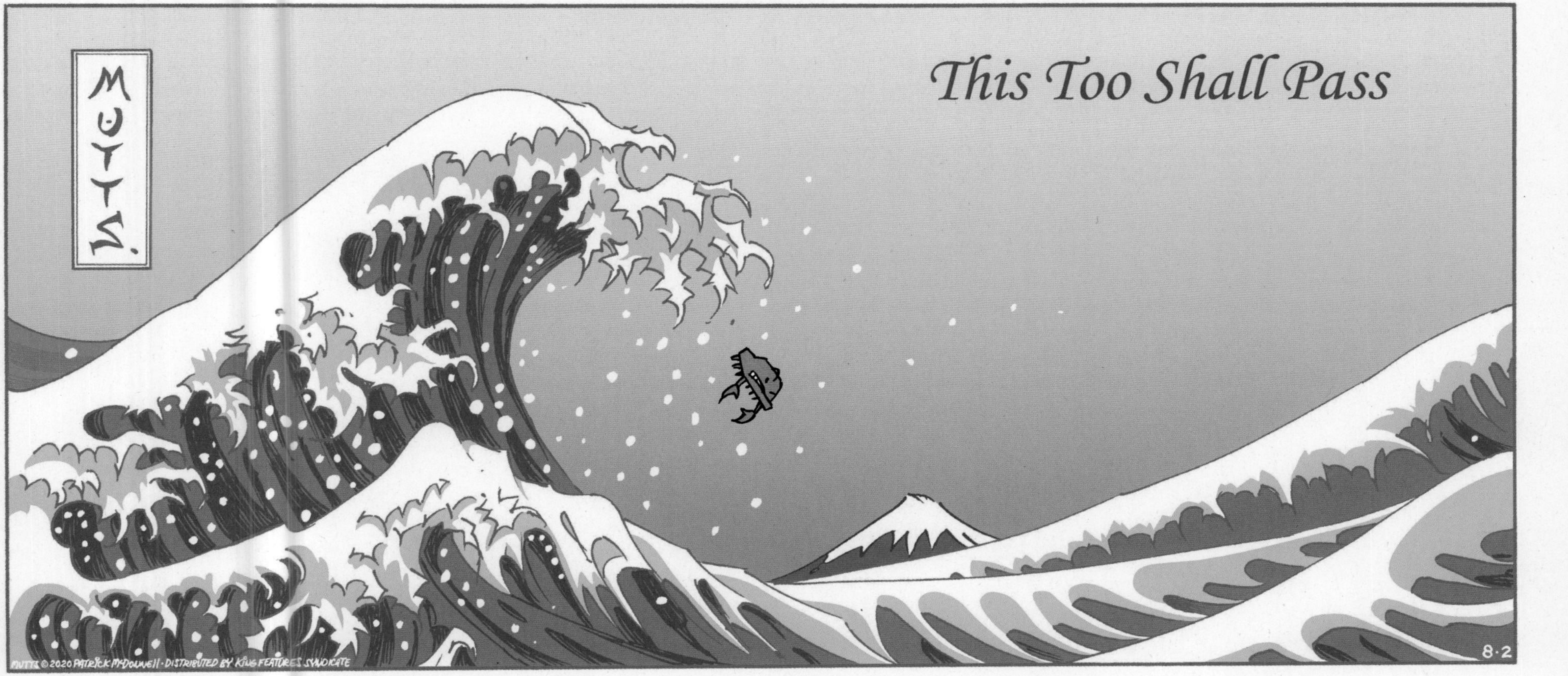
MUTTS.
This Too Shall Pass
MUTTS © 2020 PATRICK McDONNELL · DISTRIBUTED BY KING FEATURES SYNDICATE
8·2

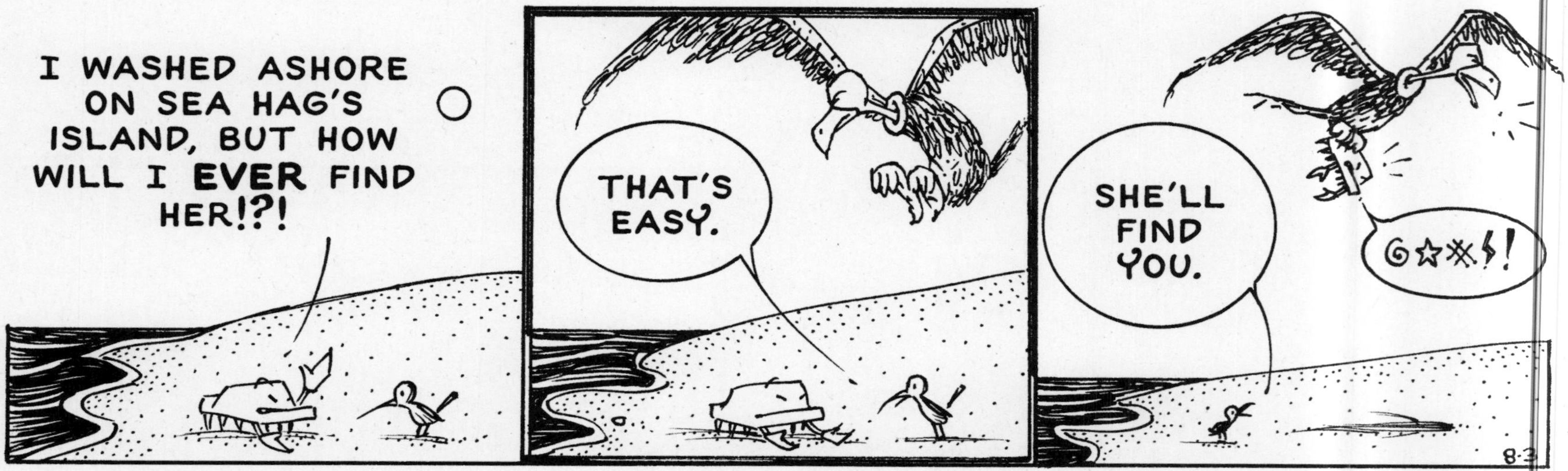
I WASHED ASHORE ON SEA HAG'S ISLAND, BUT HOW WILL I EVER FIND HER!?!
THAT'S EASY.
SHE'LL FIND YOU.
8-3

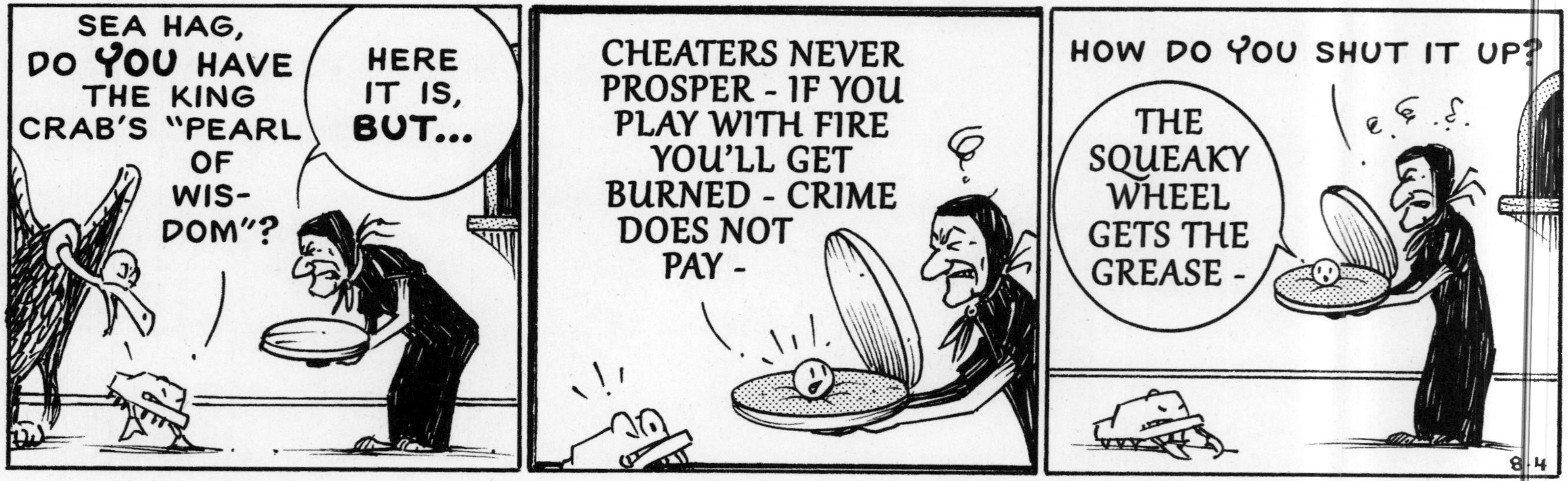
SEA HAG, DO YOU HAVE THE KING CRAB'S "PEARL OF WIS-DOM"?
HERE IT IS, BUT...
CHEATERS NEVER PROSPER - IF YOU PLAY WITH FIRE YOU'LL GET BURNED - CRIME DOES NOT PAY -
HOW DO YOU SHUT IT UP?
THE SQUEAKY WHEEL GETS THE GREASE -
8-4

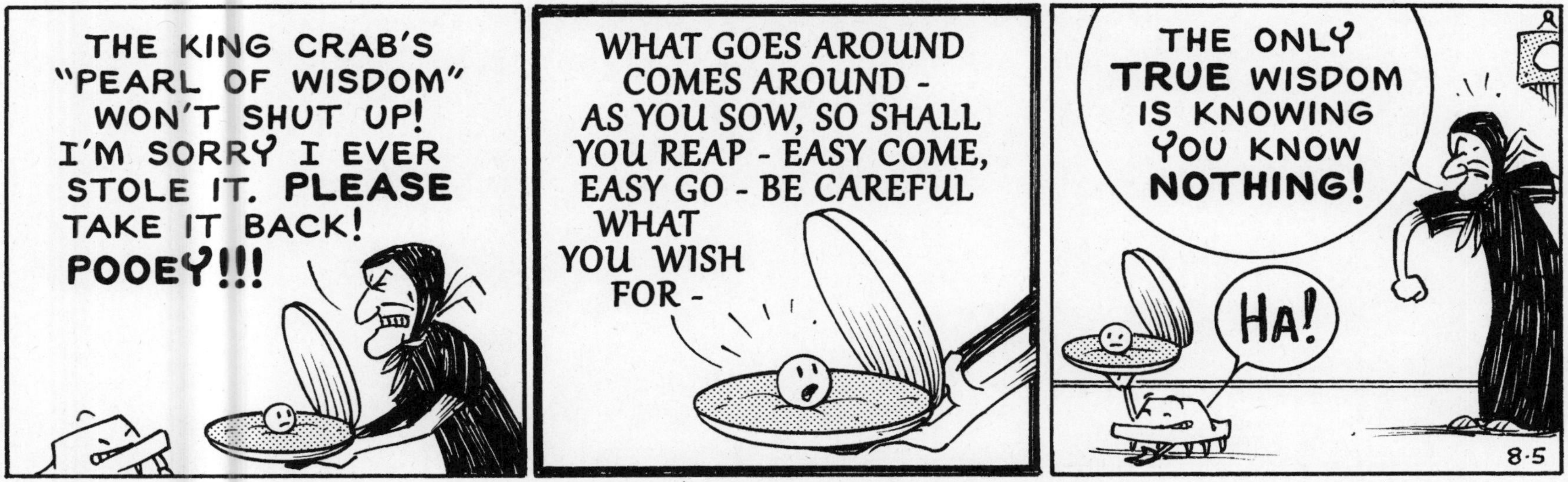
THE KING CRAB'S "PEARL OF WISDOM" WON'T SHUT UP! I'M SORRY I EVER STOLE IT. PLEASE TAKE IT BACK! POOEY!!!
WHAT GOES AROUND COMES AROUND - AS YOU SOW, SO SHALL YOU REAP - EASY COME, EASY GO - BE CAREFUL WHAT YOU WISH FOR -
THE ONLY TRUE WISDOM IS KNOWING YOU KNOW NOTHING!
HA!
8·5

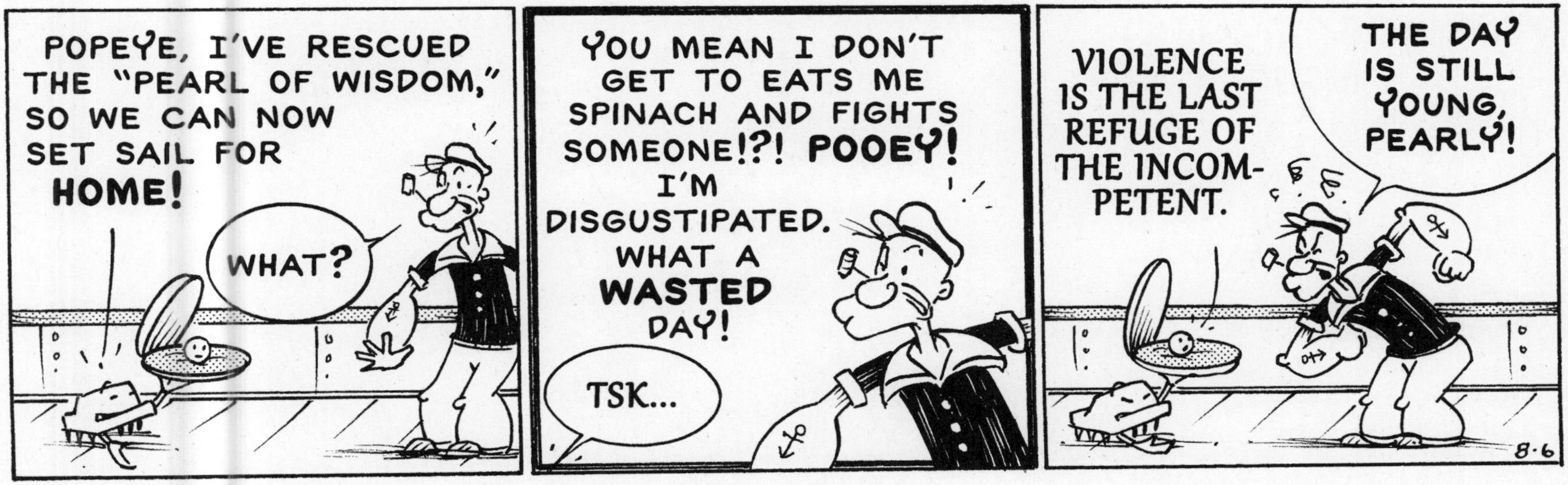
POPEYE, I'VE RESCUED THE "PEARL OF WISDOM," SO WE CAN NOW SET SAIL FOR HOME!
WHAT?
YOU MEAN I DON'T GET TO EATS ME SPINACH AND FIGHTS SOMEONE!?! POOEY! I'M DISGUSTIPATED. WHAT A WASTED DAY!
TSK...
VIOLENCE IS THE LAST REFUGE OF THE INCOM-PETENT.
THE DAY IS STILL YOUNG, PEARLY!
8·6

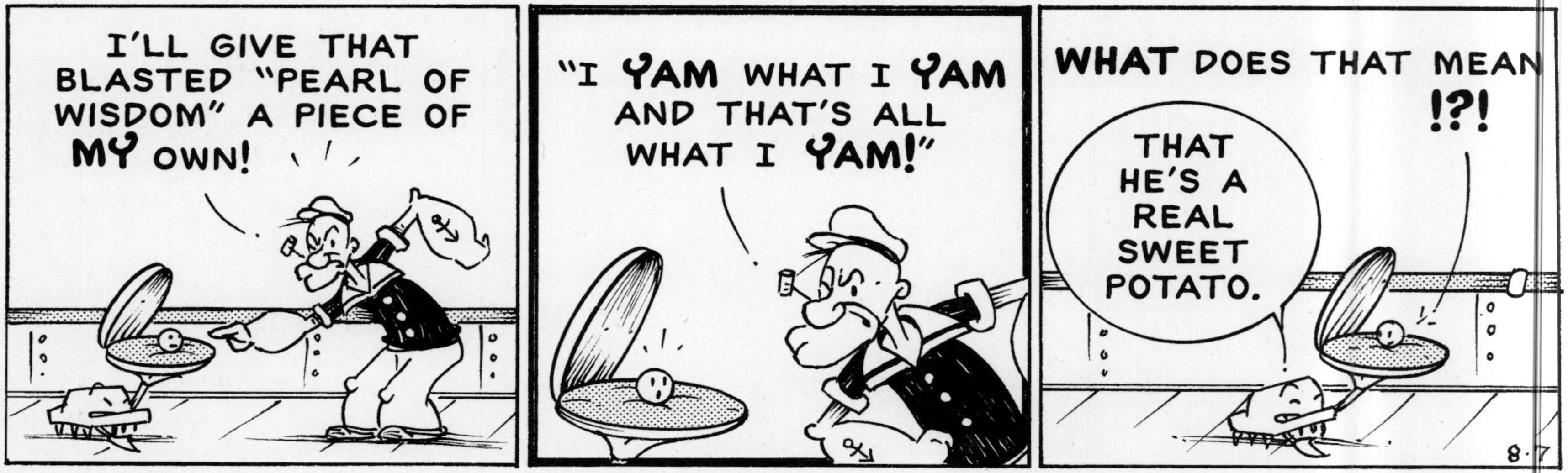
I'LL GIVE THAT BLASTED "PEARL OF WISDOM" A PIECE OF MY OWN!
"I YAM WHAT I YAM AND THAT'S ALL WHAT I YAM!"
WHAT DOES THAT MEAN !?!
THAT HE'S A REAL SWEET POTATO.
8·7

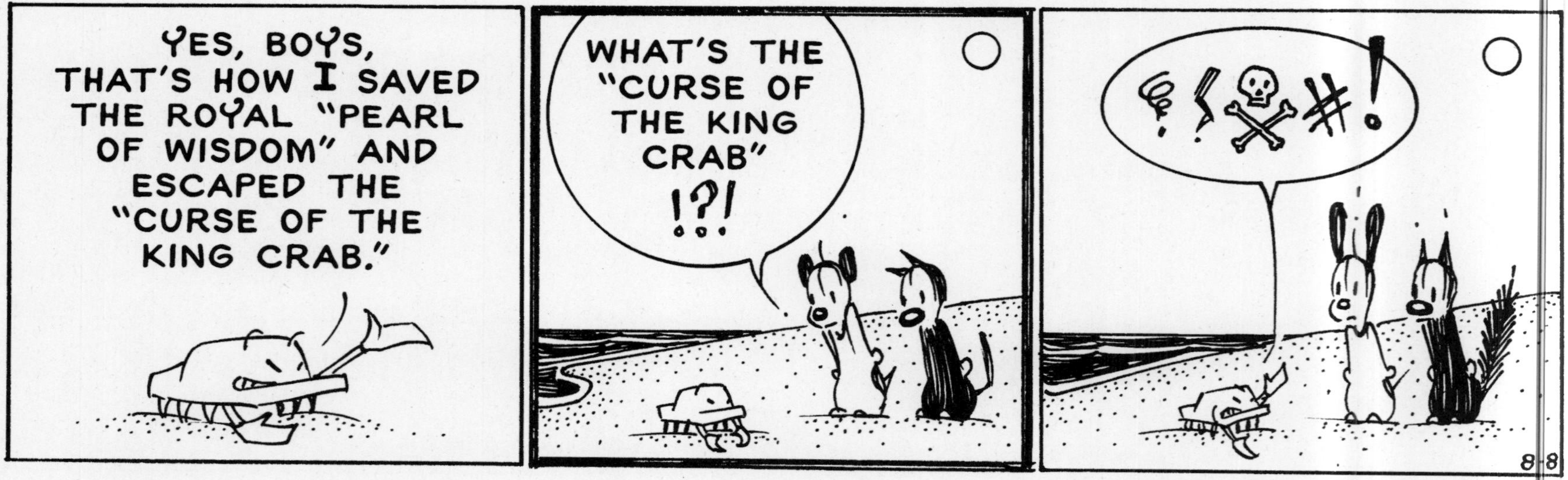
YES, BOYS, THAT'S HOW I SAVED THE ROYAL "PEARL OF WISDOM" AND ESCAPED THE "CURSE OF THE KING CRAB."
WHAT'S THE "CURSE OF THE KING CRAB" !?!
8·8

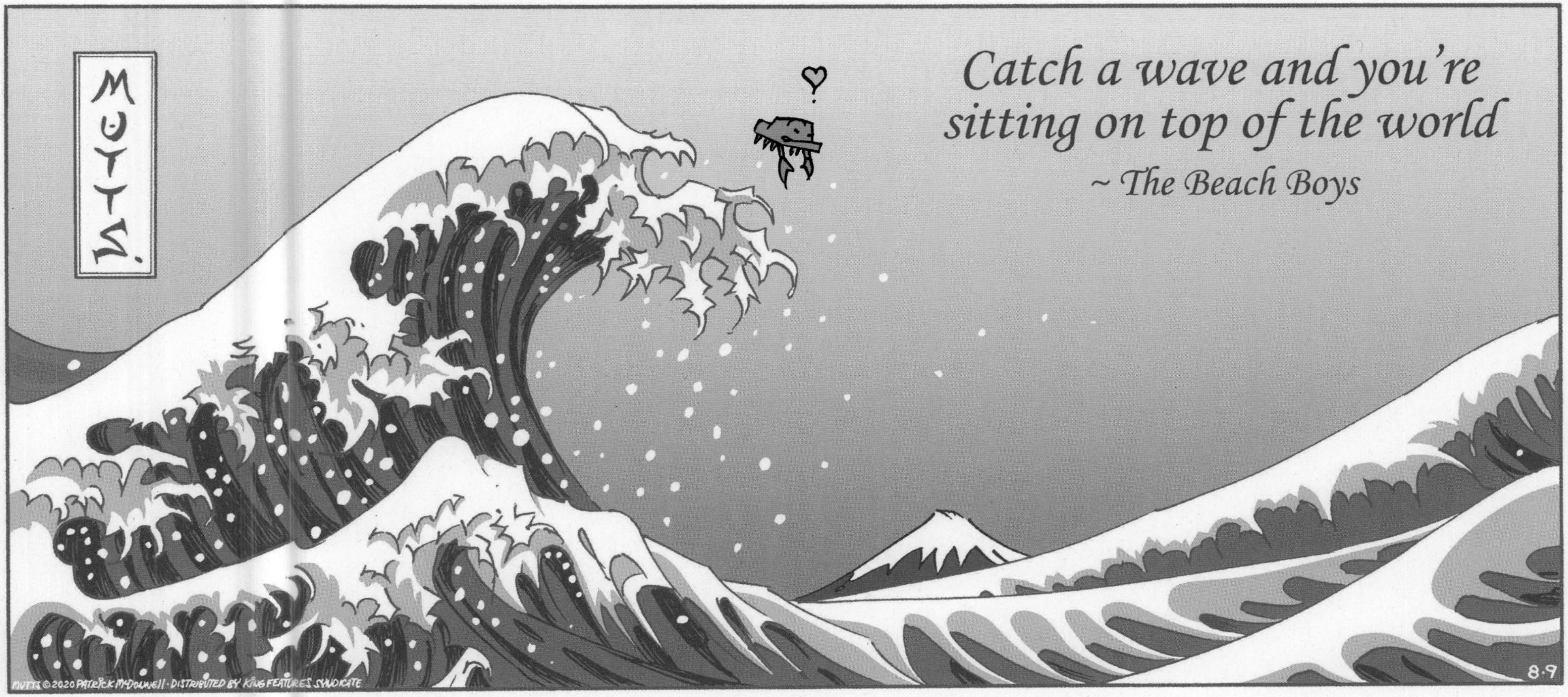
MUTTS.
Catch a wave and you're sitting on top of the world
~ The Beach Boys
MUTTS © 2020 PATRICK McDONNELL · DISTRIBUTED BY KING FEATURES SYNDICATE
8·9

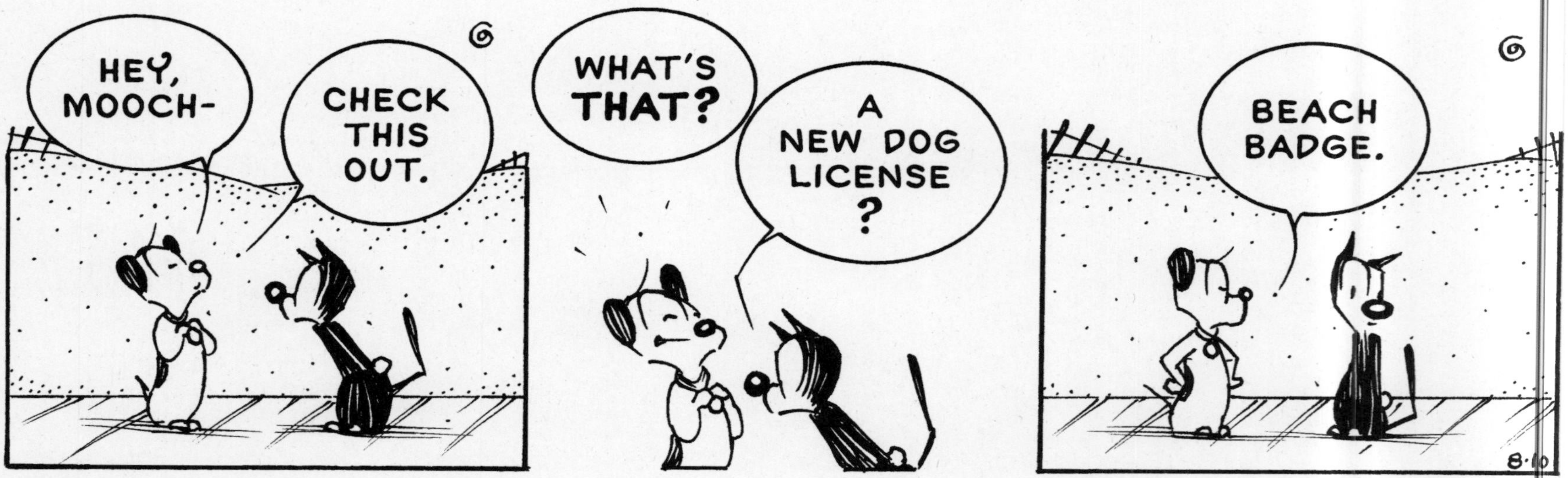
HEY, MOOCH-
CHECK THIS OUT.
WHAT'S THAT?
A NEW DOG LICENSE ?
BEACH BADGE.
8·10

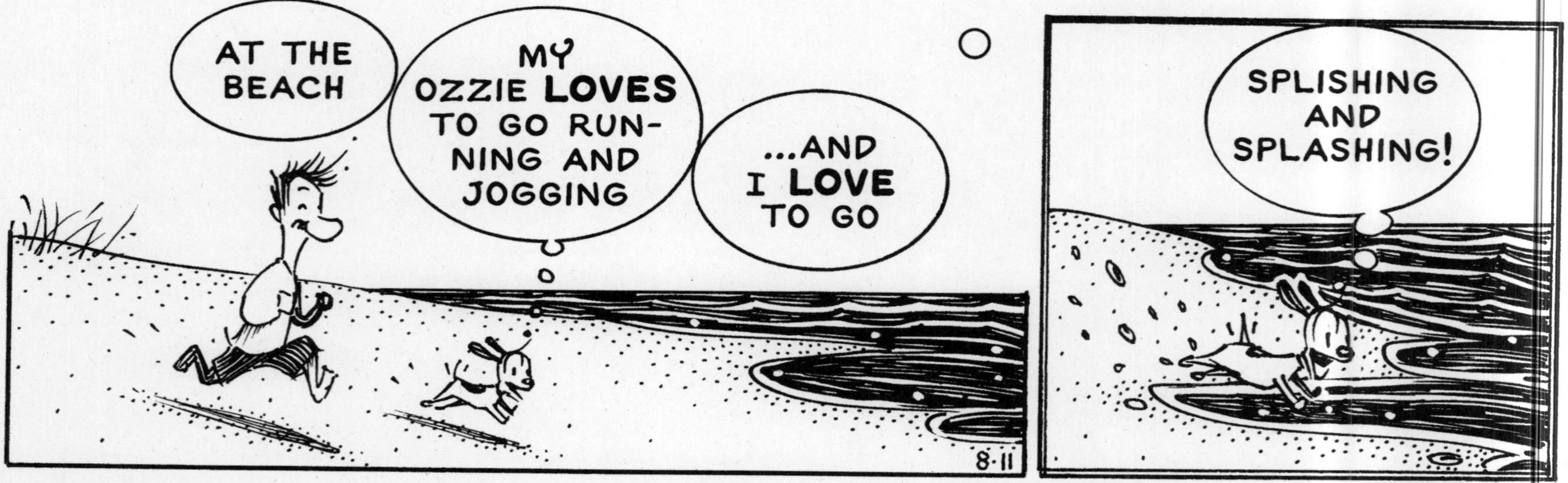
AT THE BEACH
MY OZZIE LOVES TO GO RUN-NING AND JOGGING
...AND I LOVE TO GO
SPLISHING AND SPLASHING!
8·11

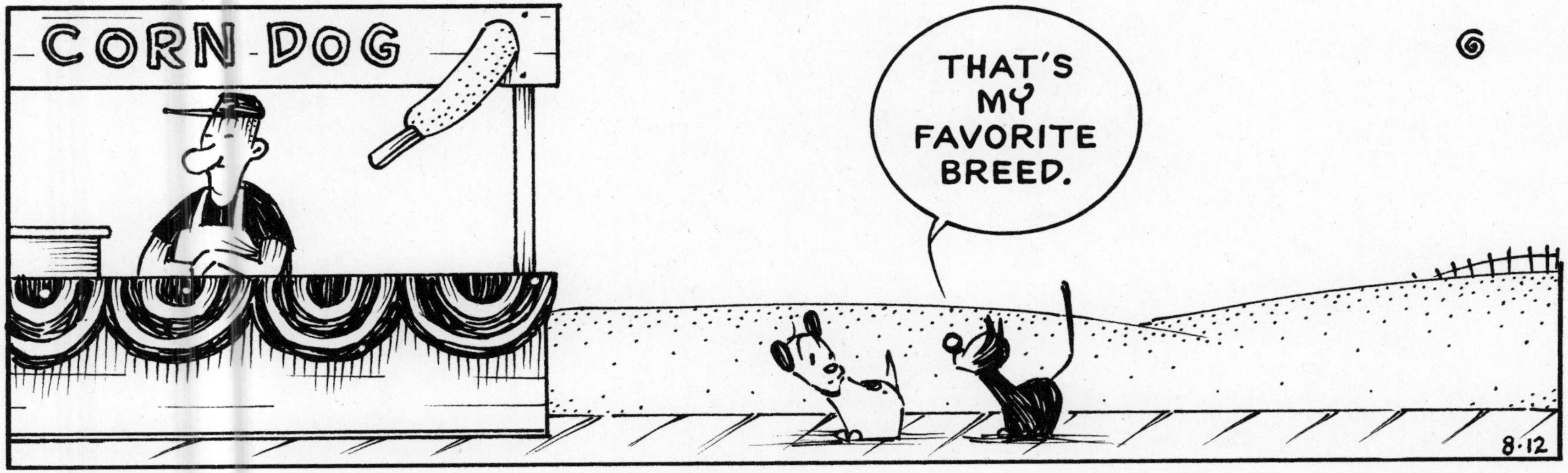
CORN DOG
THAT'S MY FAVORITE BREED.
8·12

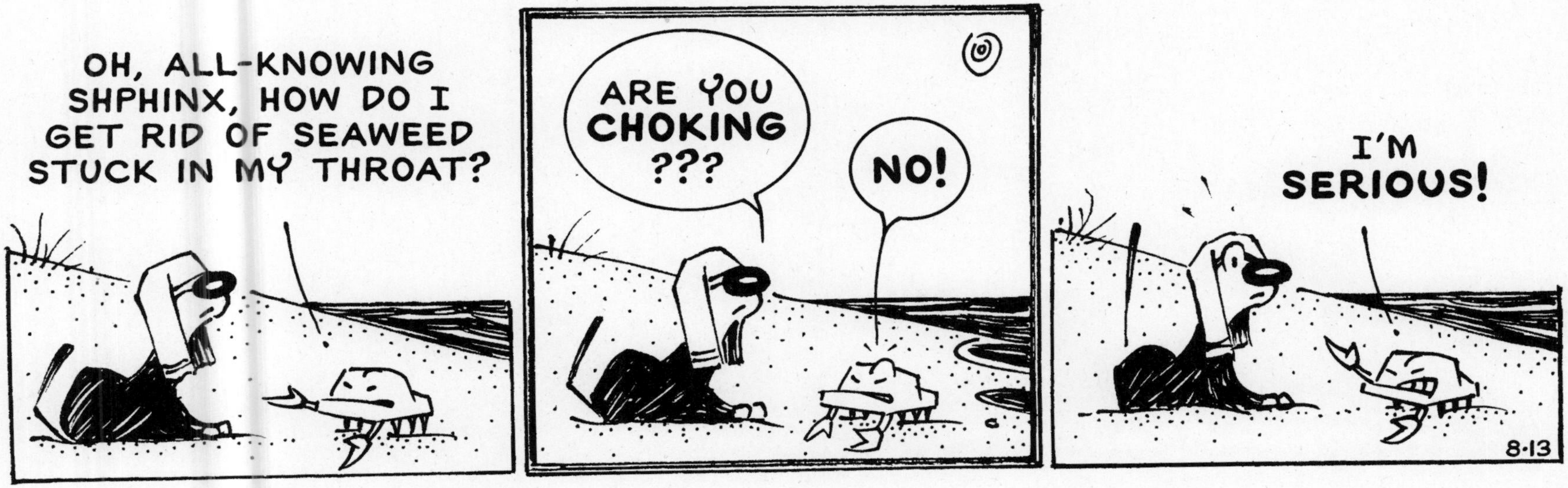
OH, ALL-KNOWING SHPHINX, HOW DO I GET RID OF SEAWEED STUCK IN MY THROAT?
ARE YOU CHOKING ???
NO!
I'M SERIOUS!
8·13

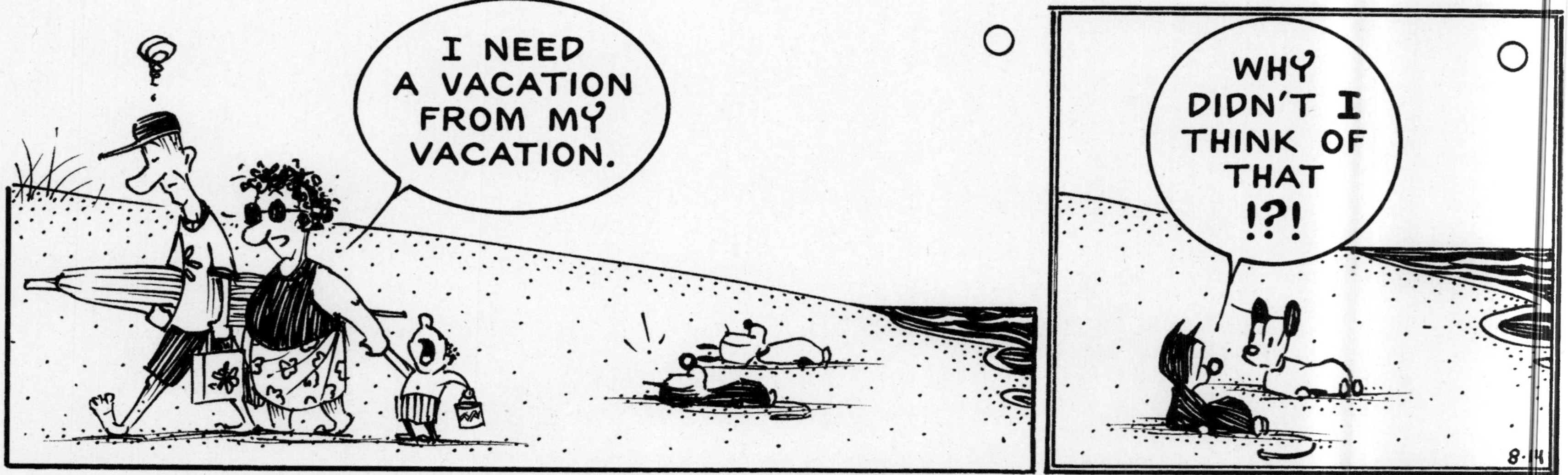
I NEED A VACATION FROM MY VACATION.
WHY DIDN'T I THINK OF THAT !?!
8·14

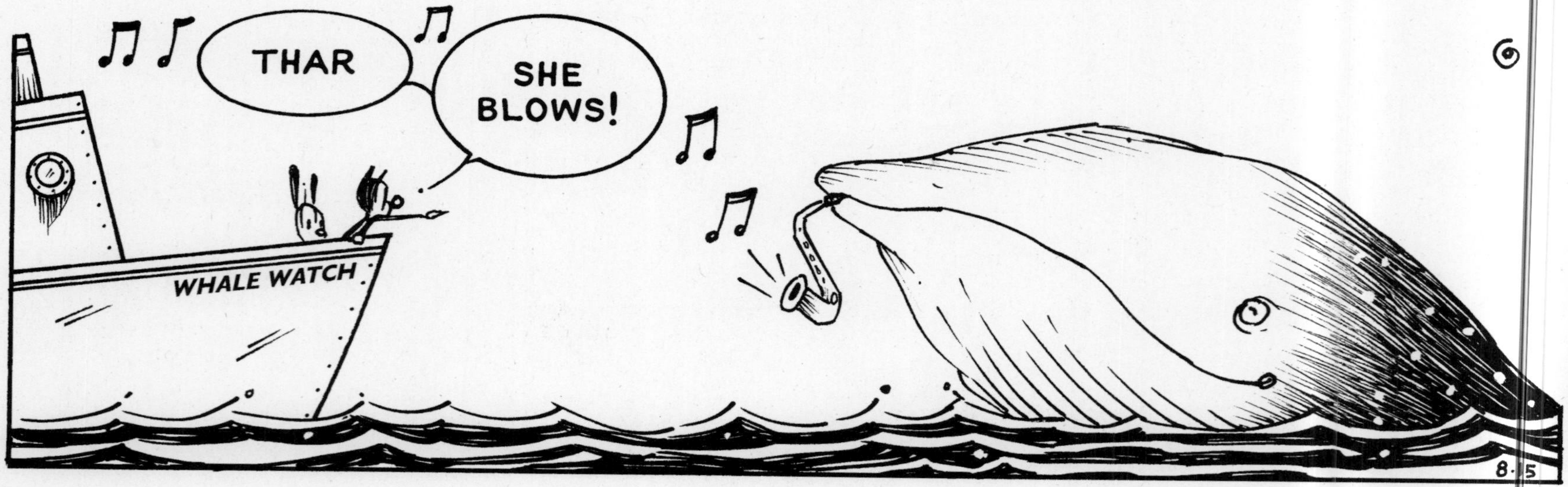
THAR
SHE BLOWS!
WHALE WATCH
8·15

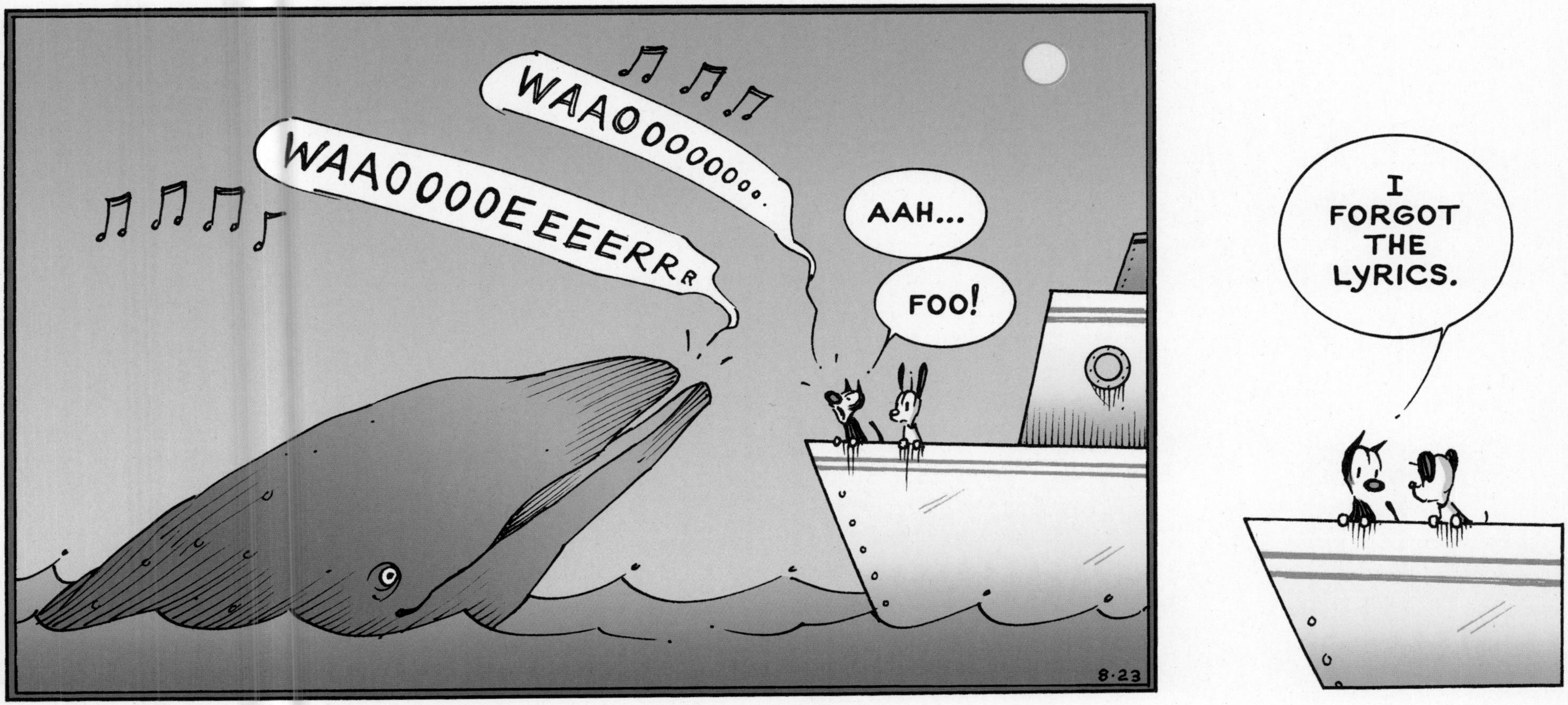
WAAOOOOEEEERRRR
WAAOOOOOOOO.
AAH...
FOO!
8·23
I FORGOT THE LYRICS.

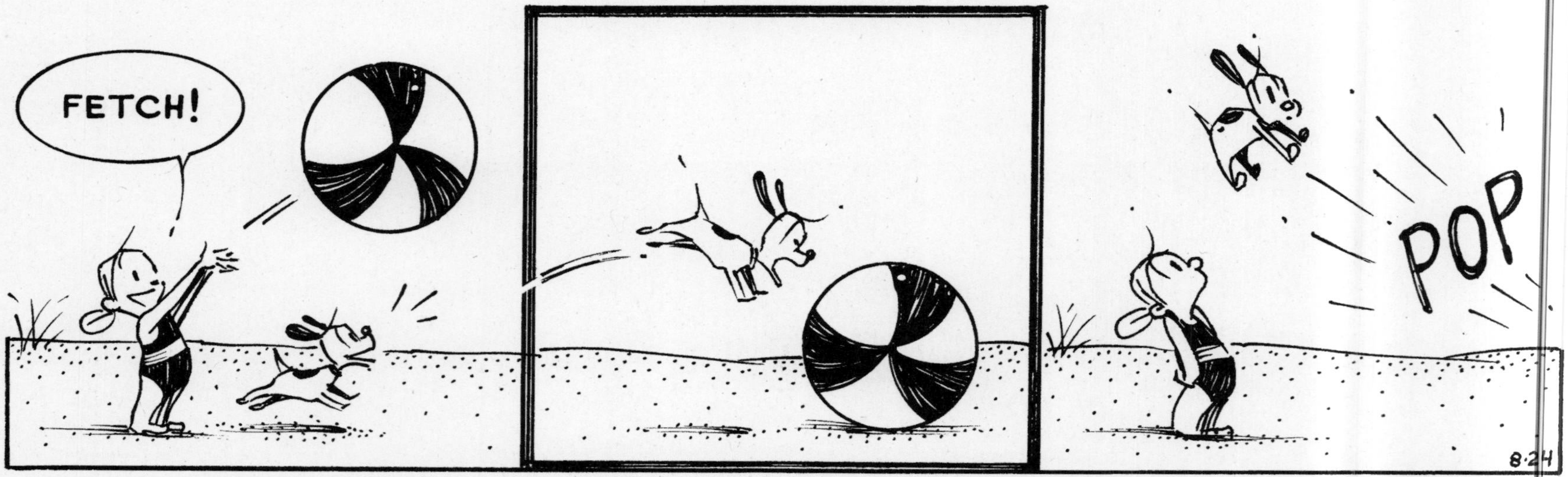
FETCH!
POP
8·24

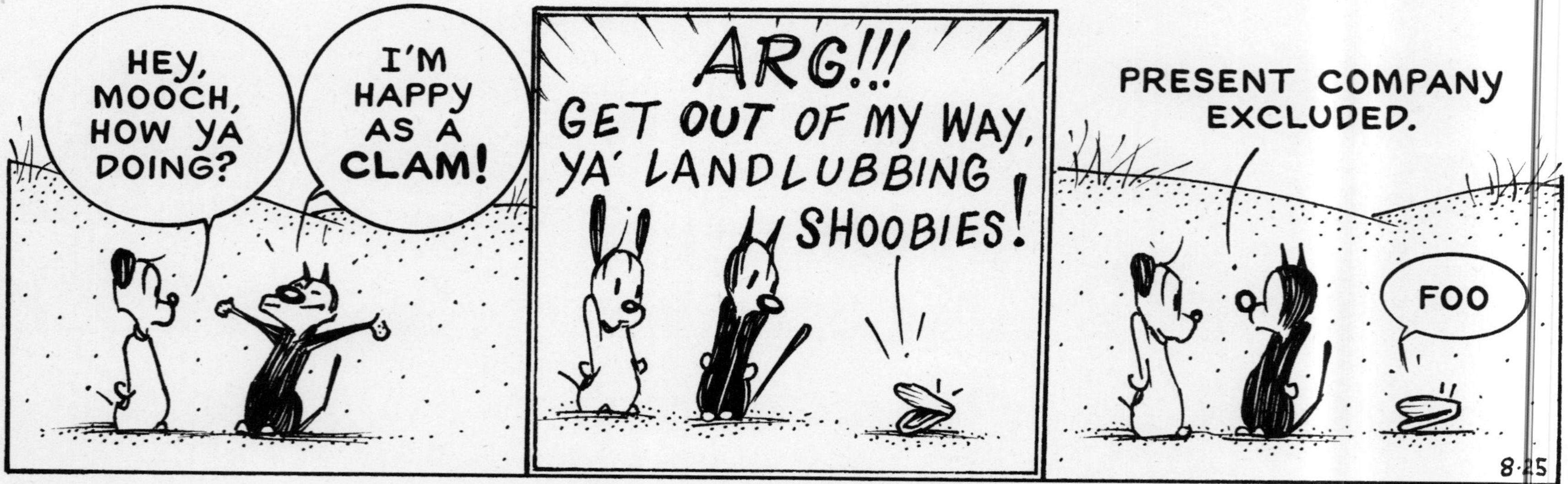
HEY, MOOCH, HOW YA DOING?
I'M HAPPY AS A CLAM!
ARG!!! GET OUT OF MY WAY, YA' LANDLUBBING SHOOBIES!
PRESENT COMPANY EXCLUDED.
FOO
8·25

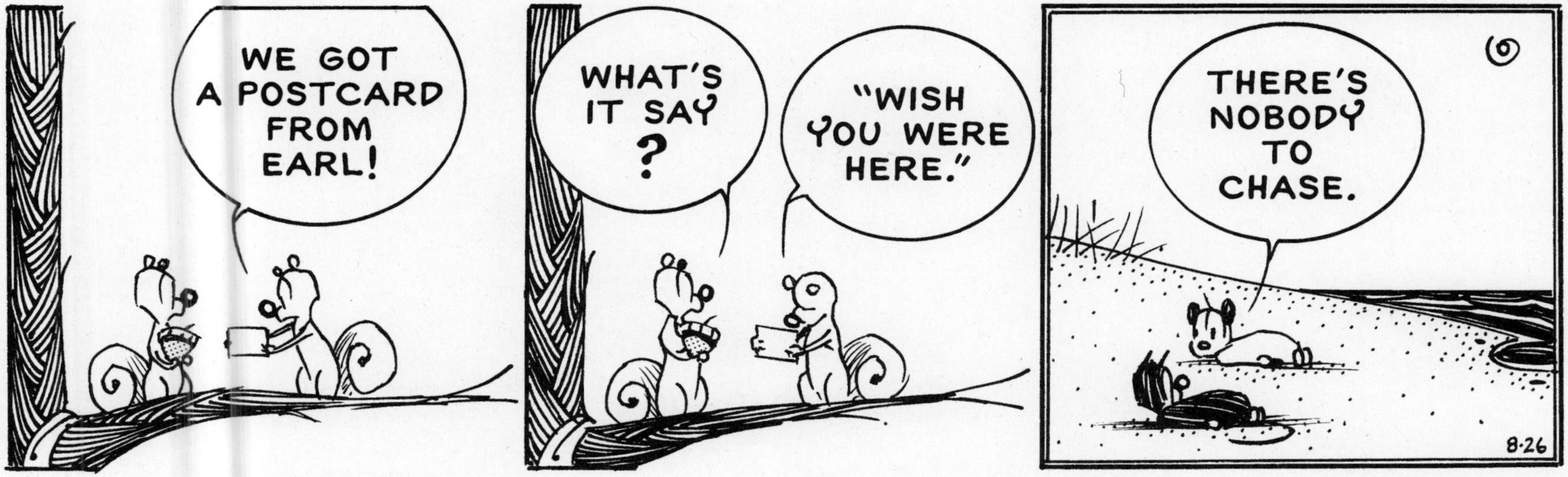
WE GOT A POSTCARD FROM EARL!
WHAT'S IT SAY ?
"WISH YOU WERE HERE."
THERE'S NOBODY TO CHASE.
8·26

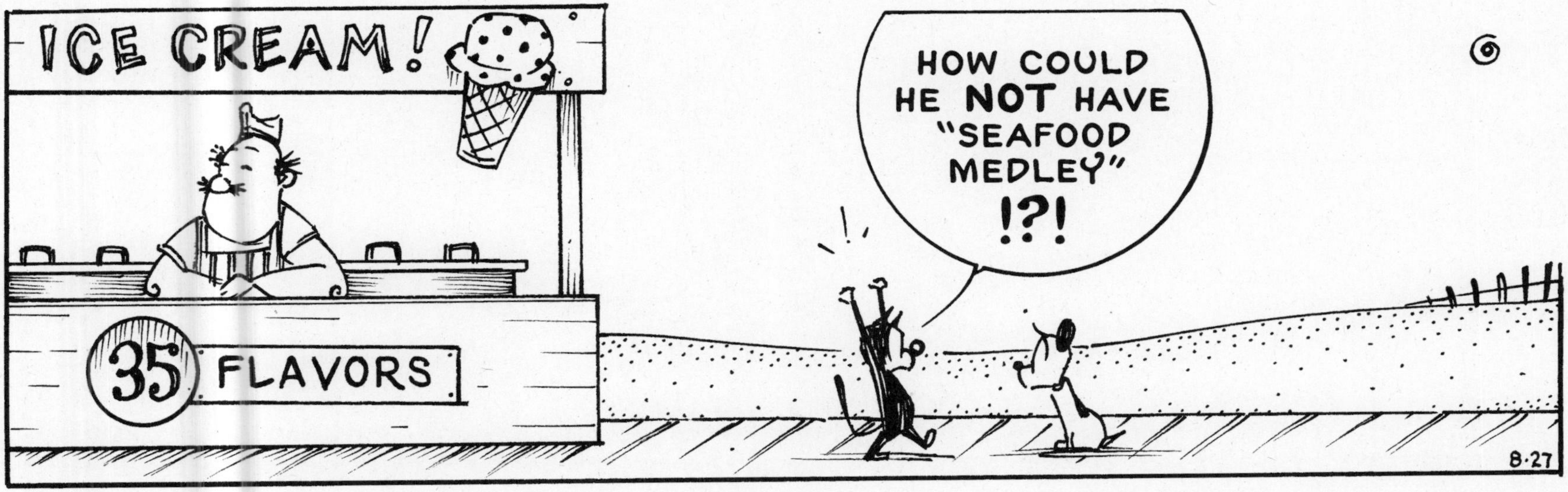
ICE CREAM!
35 FLAVORS
HOW COULD HE NOT HAVE "SEAFOOD MEDLEY" !?!
8·27

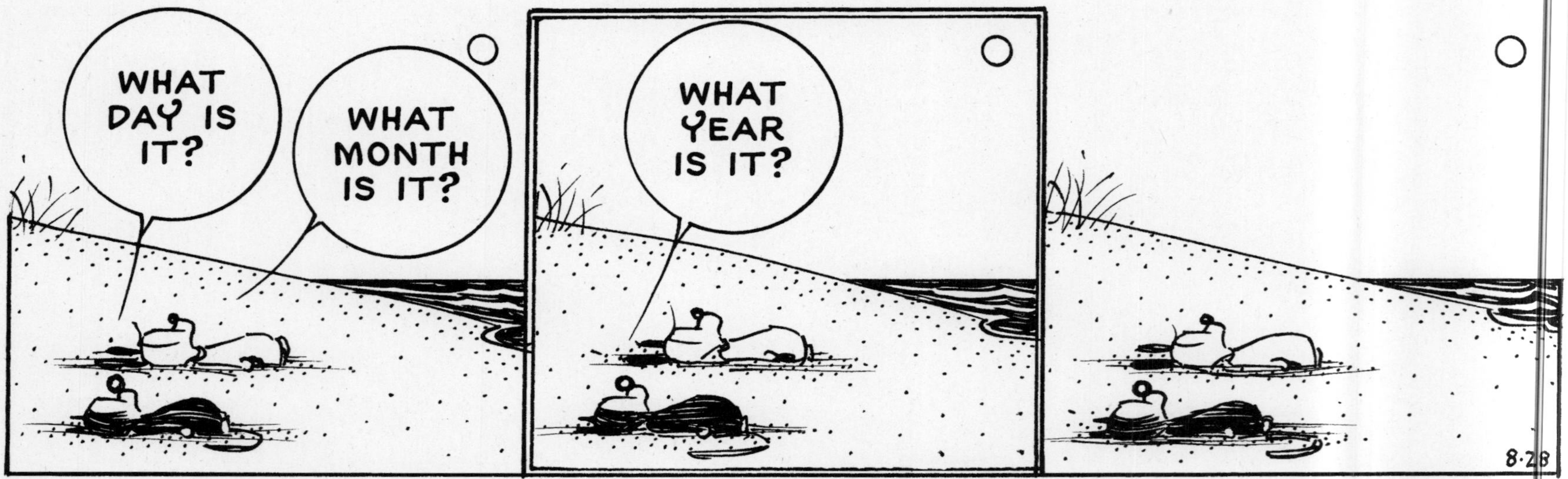
WHAT DAY IS IT?
WHAT MONTH IS IT?
WHAT YEAR IS IT?
8·28

The cure for anything is salt water:
sweat, tears, or the sea.

~ Isak Dinesen

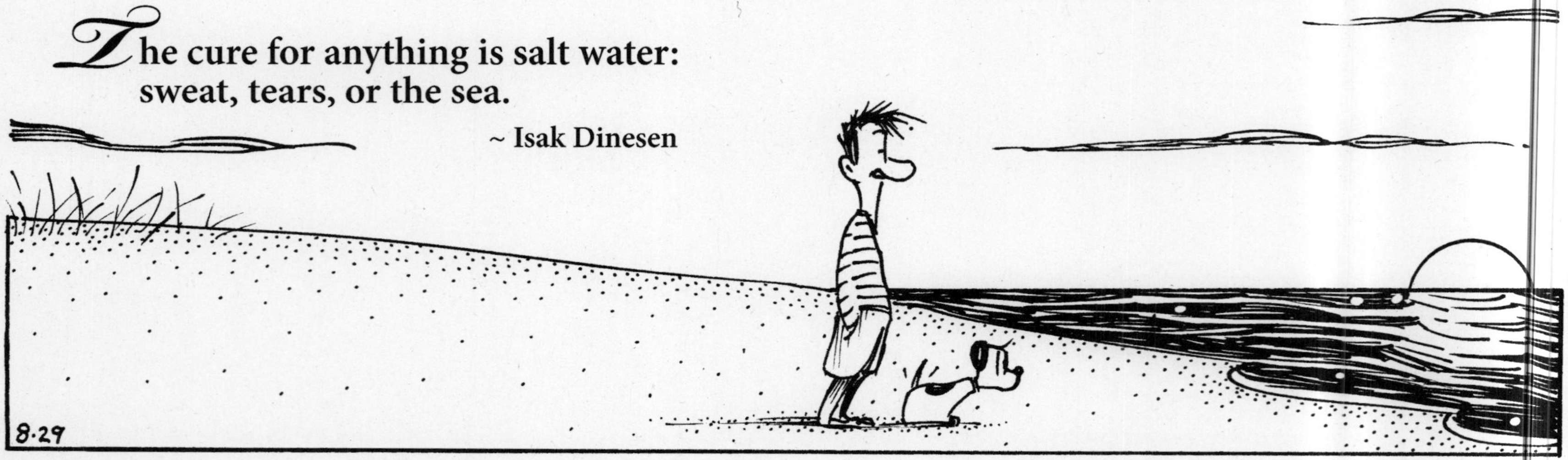
8·29

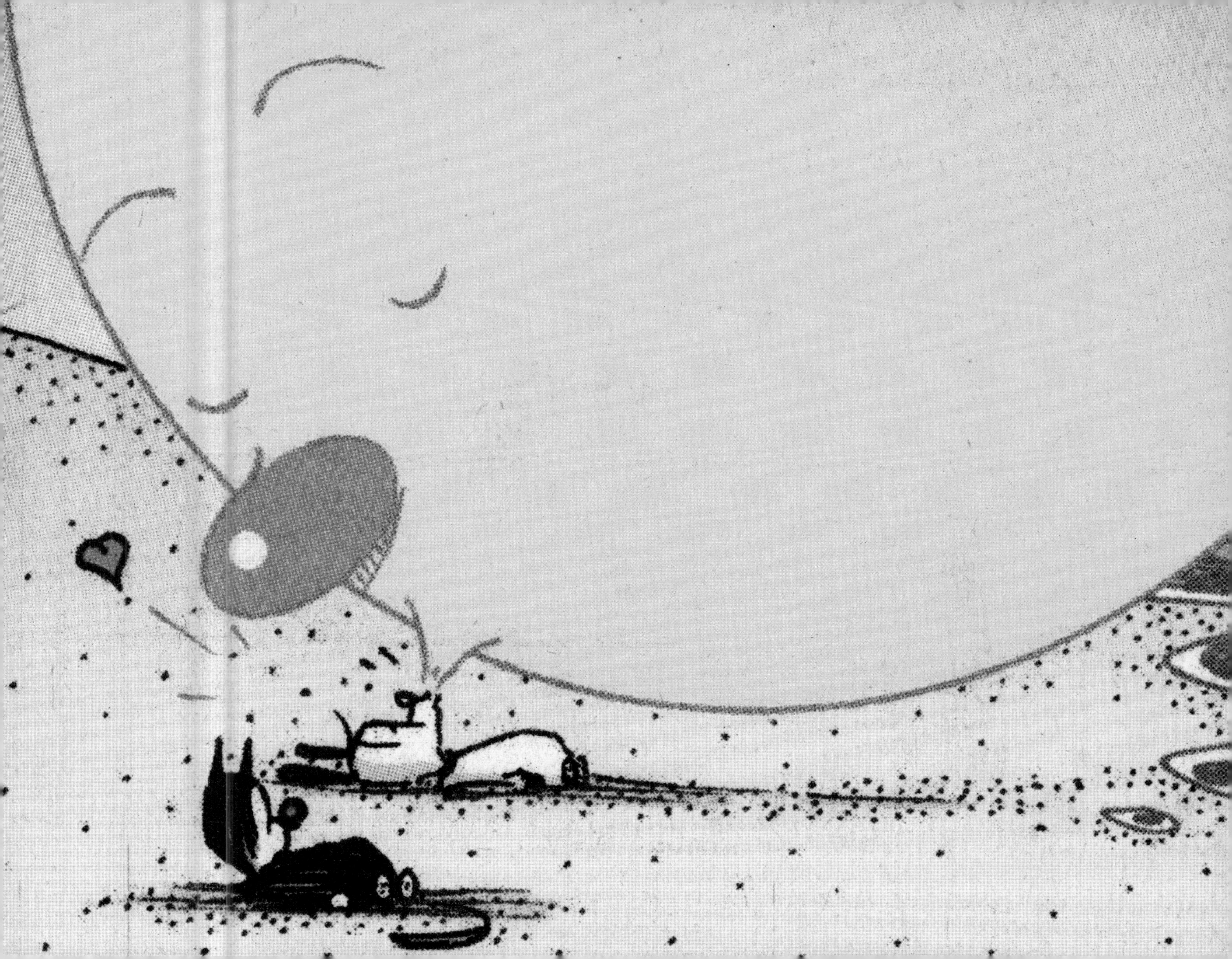

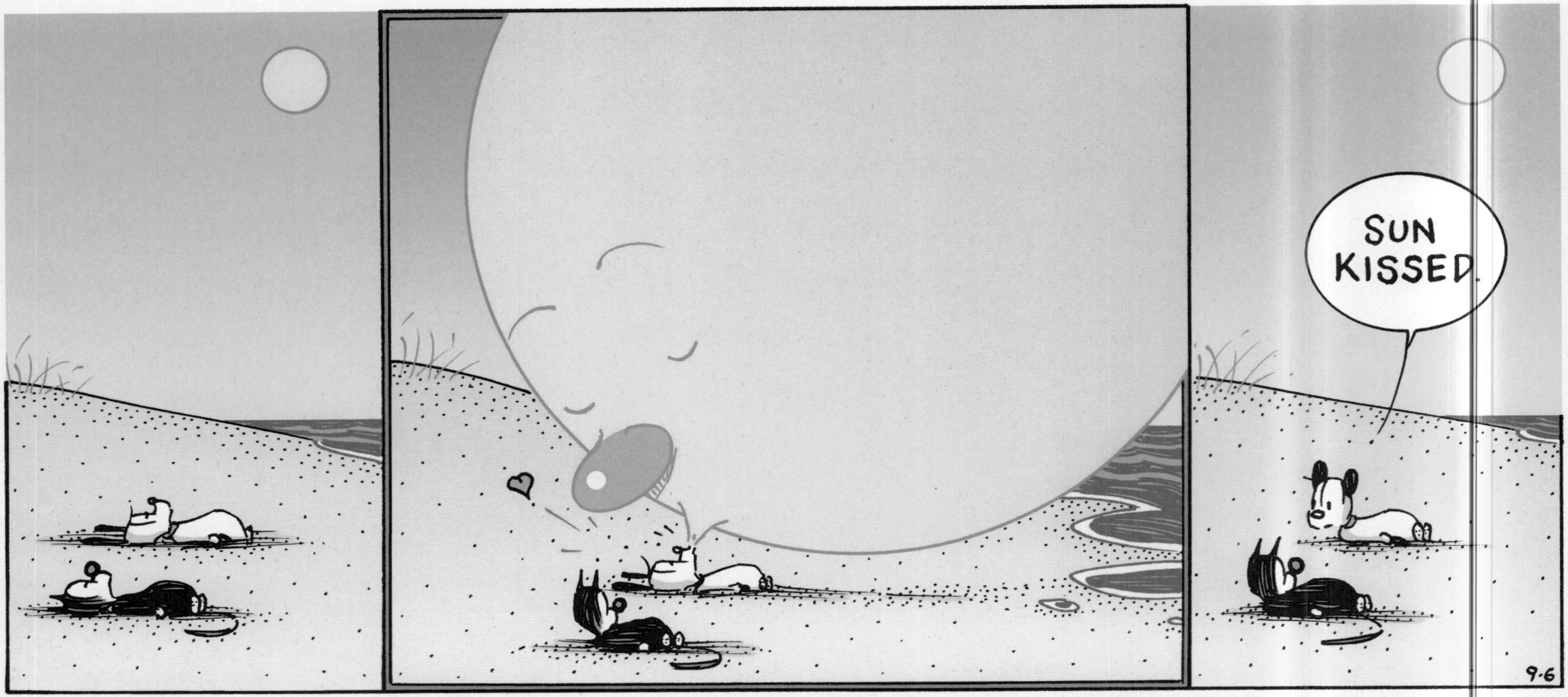
SUN KISSED.
9·6

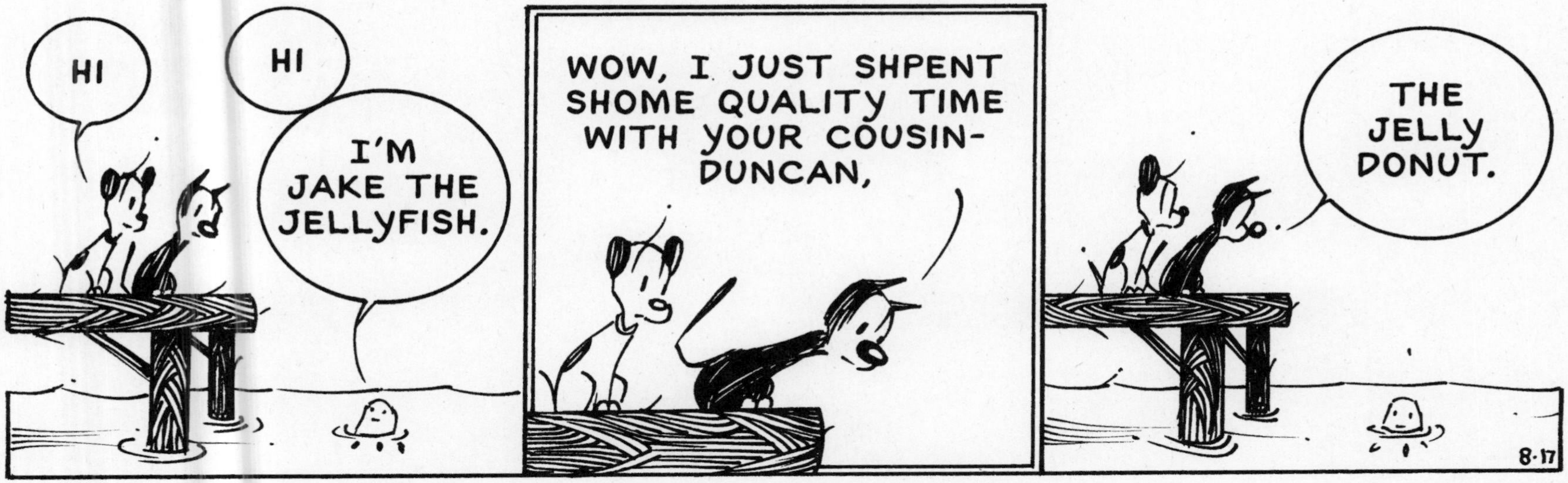
HI
HI
I'M JAKE THE JELLYFISH.
WOW, I JUST SHPENT SHOME QUALITY TIME WITH YOUR COUSIN- DUNCAN,
THE JELLY DONUT.
8·17

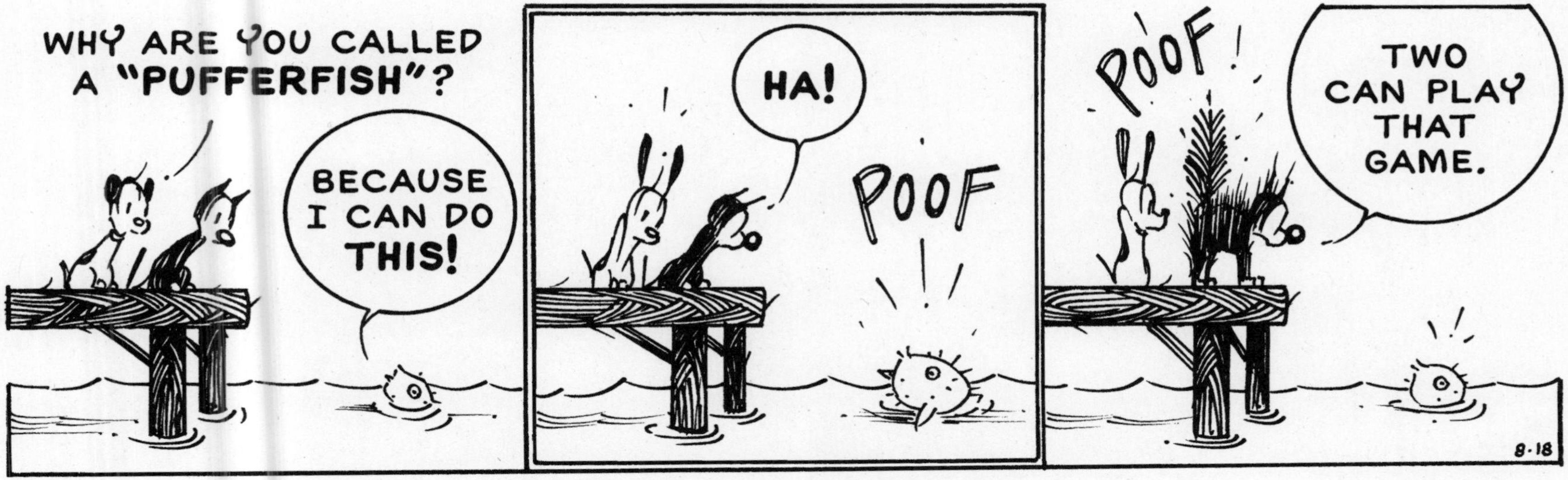
WHY ARE YOU CALLED A "PUFFERFISH"?
BECAUSE I CAN DO THIS!
HA!
POOF
POOF!
TWO CAN PLAY THAT GAME.
8·18

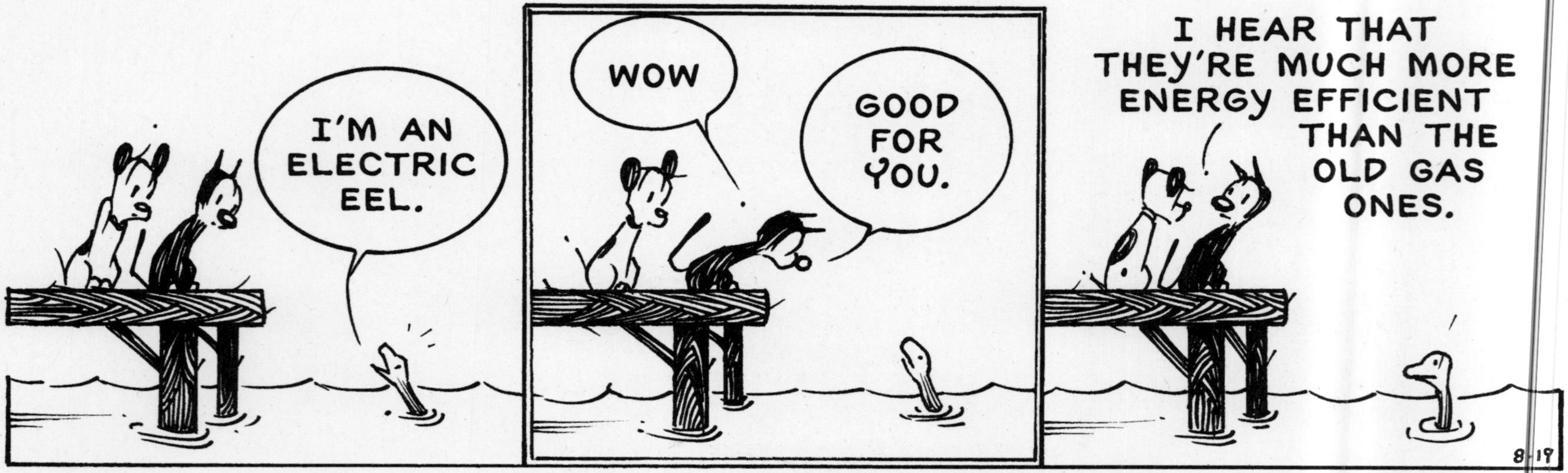
I'M AN ELECTRIC EEL.
WOW
GOOD FOR YOU.
I HEAR THAT THEY'RE MUCH MORE ENERGY EFFICIENT THAN THE OLD GAS ONES.
8-19

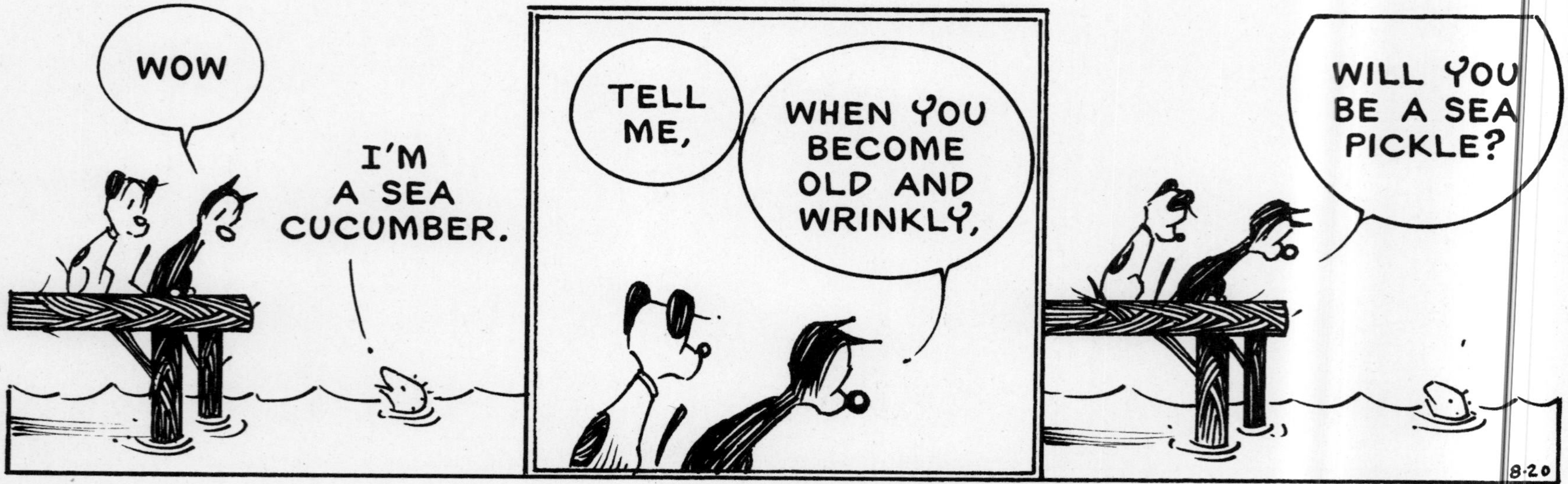
WOW
I'M A SEA CUCUMBER.
TELL ME,
WHEN YOU BECOME OLD AND WRINKLY,
WILL YOU BE A SEA PICKLE?
8-20

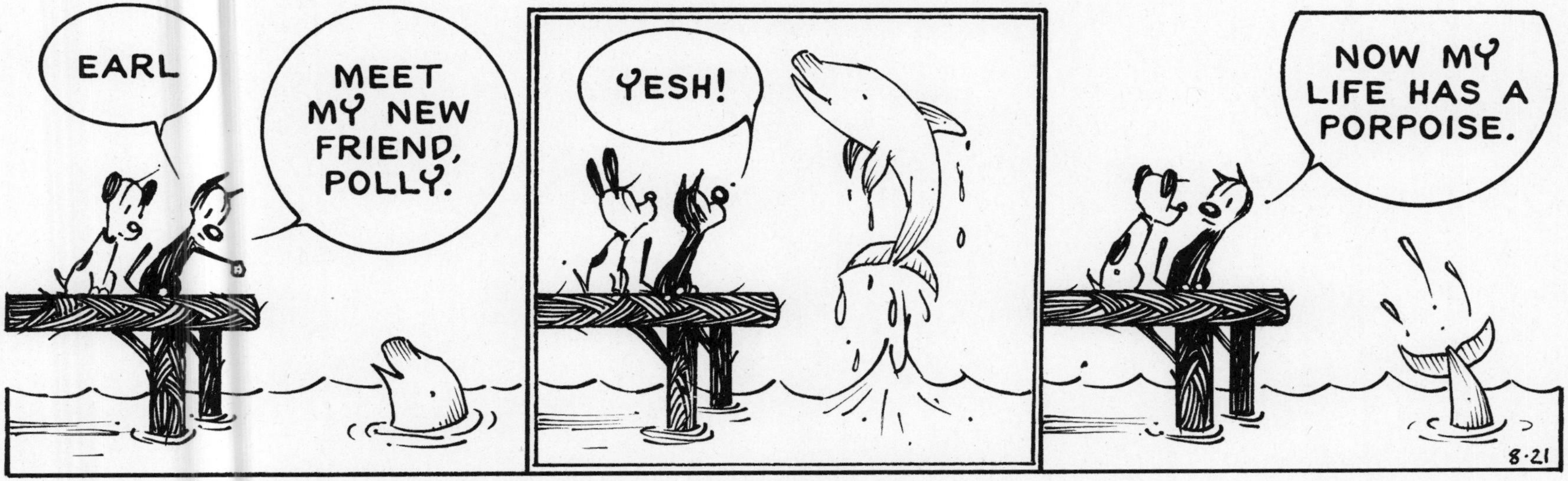
EARL
MEET MY NEW FRIEND, POLLY.
YESH!
NOW MY LIFE HAS A PORPOISE.
8·21

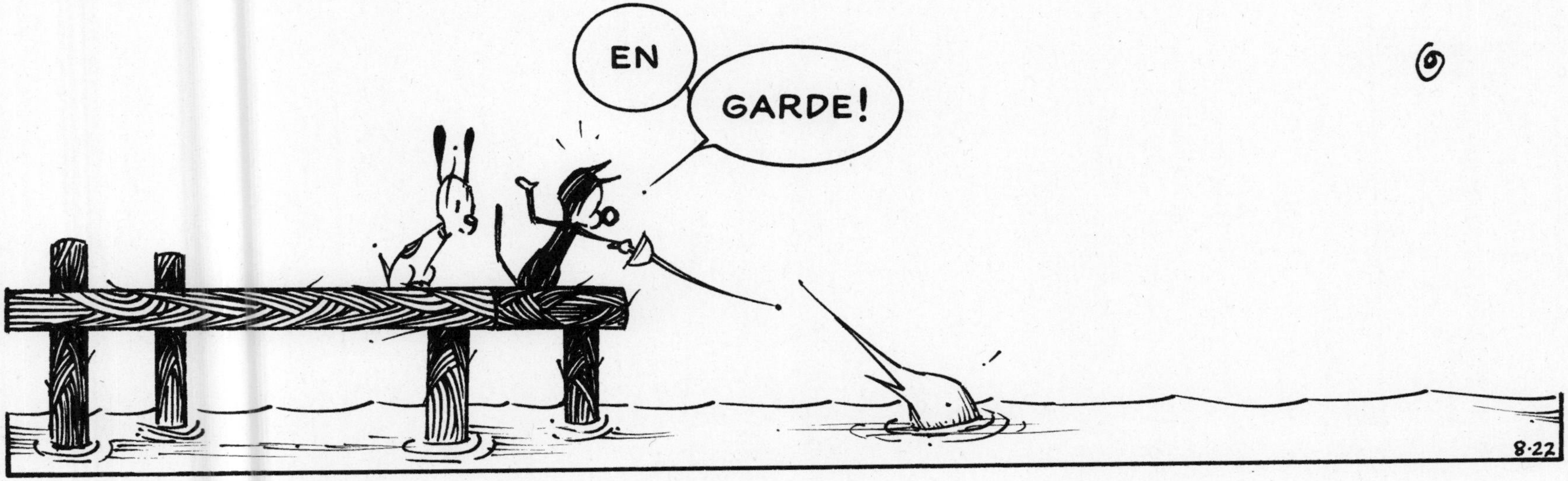
EN
GARDE!
8·22

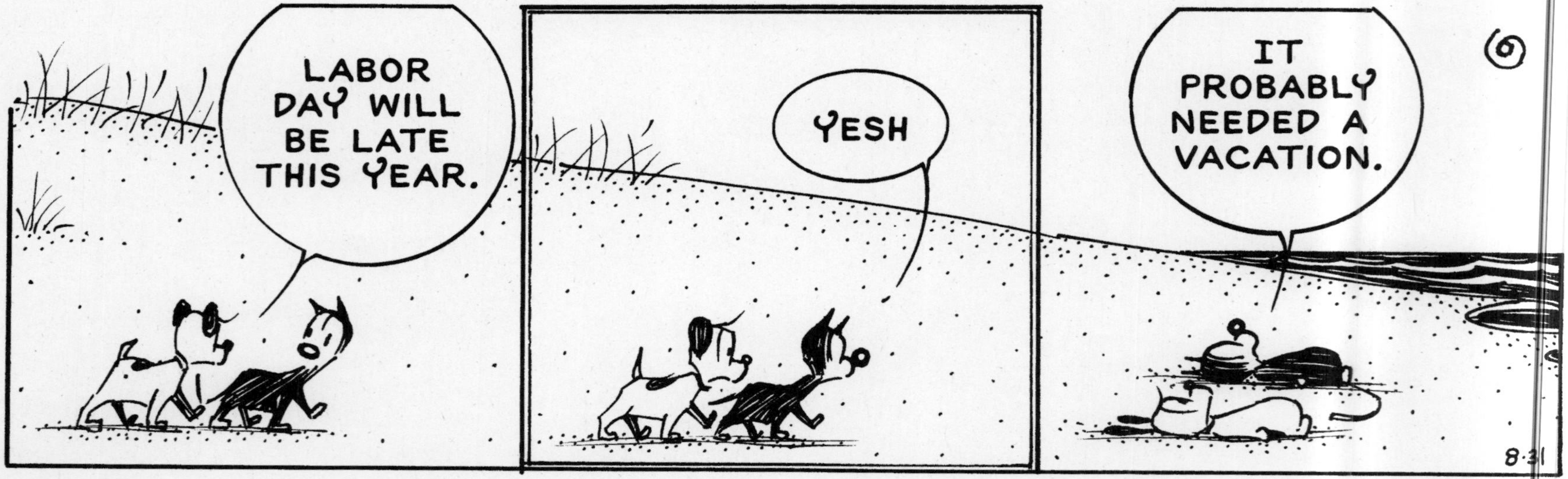
LABOR DAY WILL BE LATE THIS YEAR.
YESH
IT PROBABLY NEEDED A VACATION.
8·31

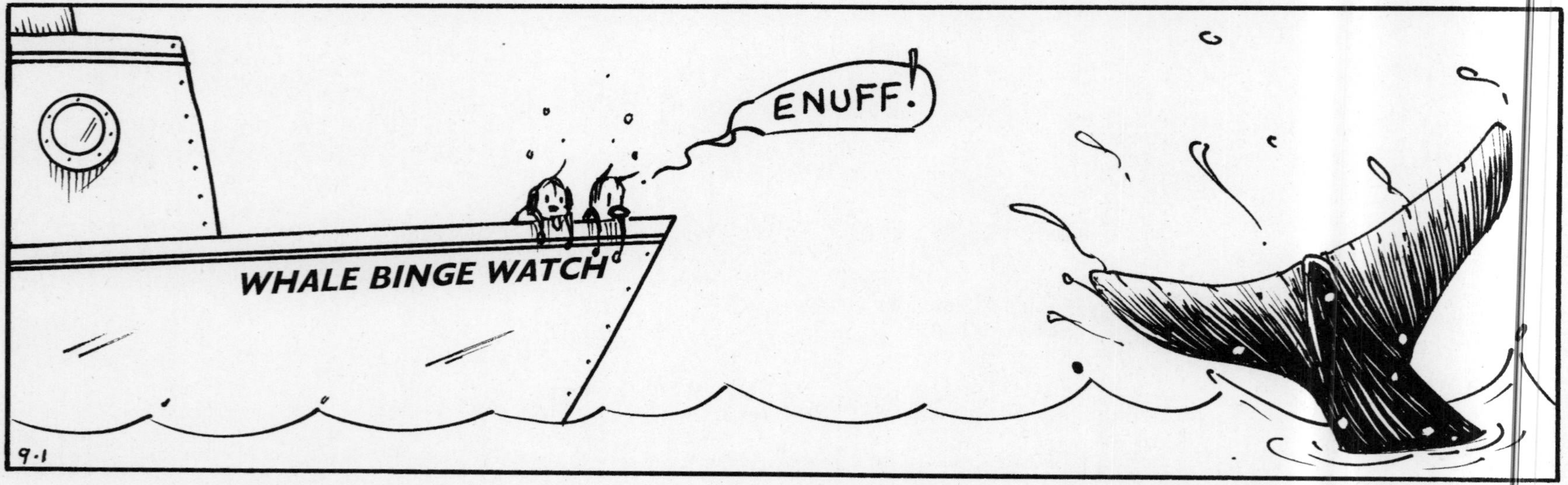
ENUFF!
WHALE BINGE WATCH
9·1

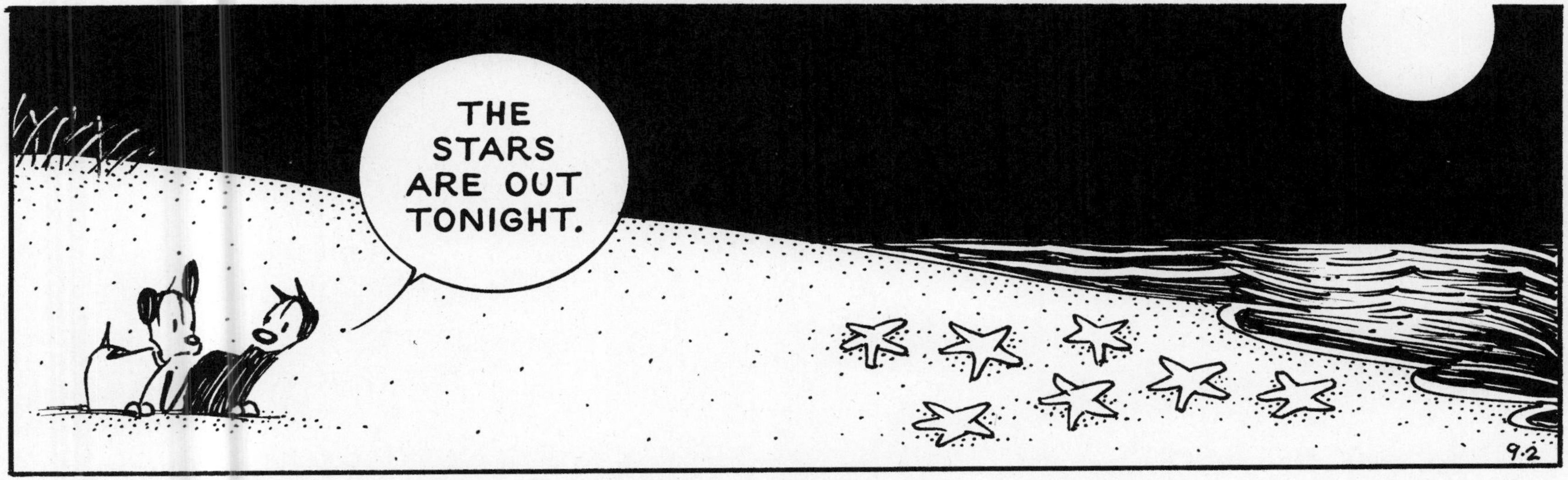
THE STARS ARE OUT TONIGHT.
9·2

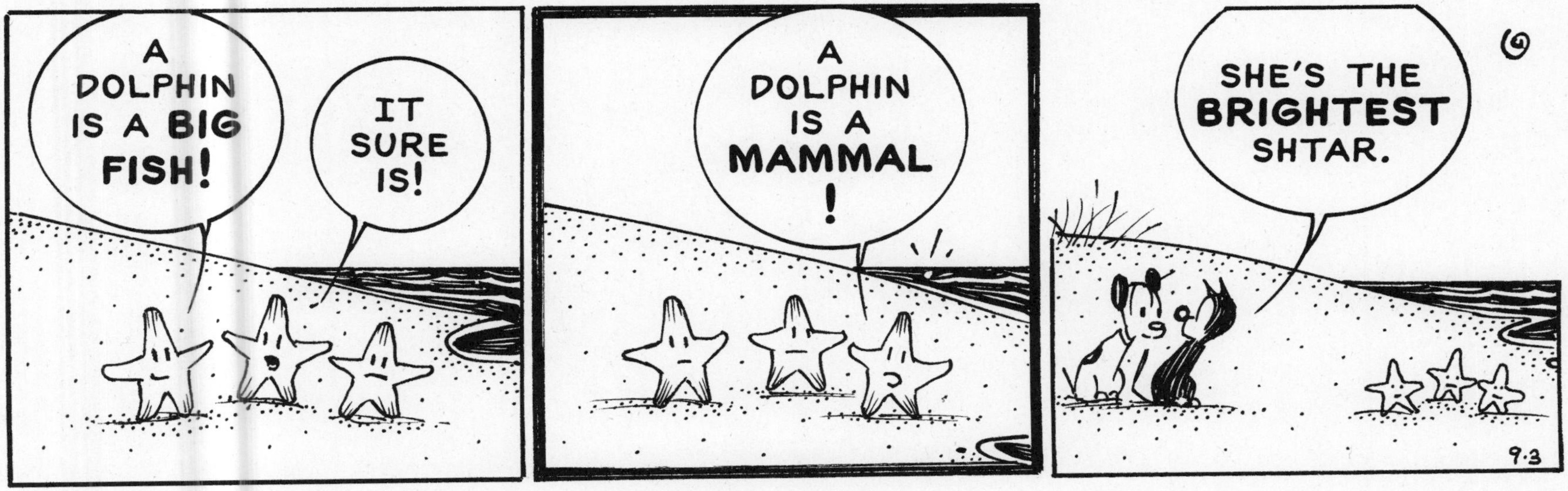
A DOLPHIN IS A BIG FISH!
IT SURE IS!
A DOLPHIN IS A MAMMAL !
SHE'S THE BRIGHTEST SHTAR.
9·3

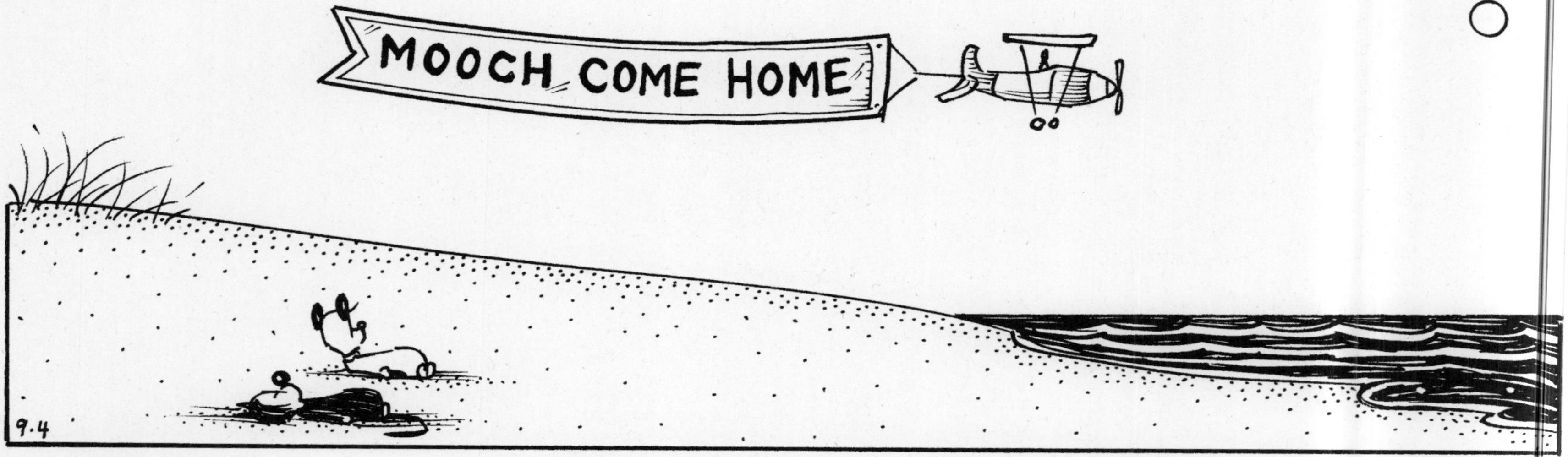
MOOCH COME HOME
9.4

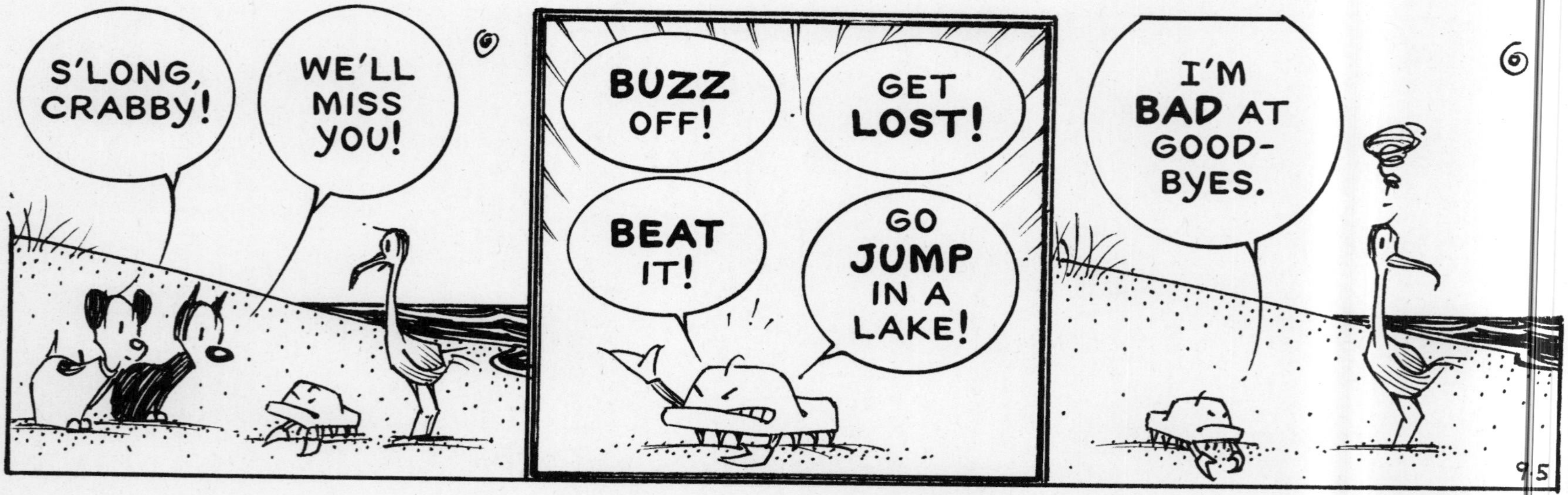
S'LONG, CRABBY!
WE'LL MISS YOU!
BUZZ OFF!
GET LOST!
BEAT IT!
GO JUMP IN A LAKE!
I'M BAD AT GOOD-BYES.
9.5

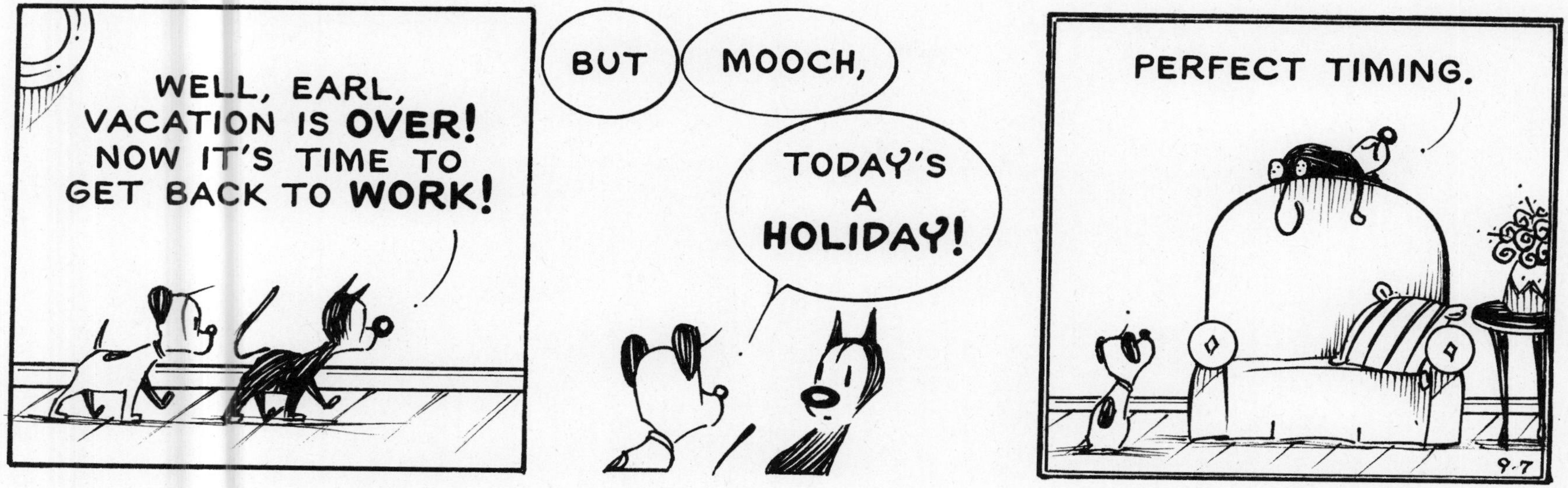
WELL, EARL, VACATION IS OVER! NOW IT'S TIME TO GET BACK TO WORK!
BUT
MOOCH,
TODAY'S A HOLIDAY!
PERFECT TIMING.
9-7

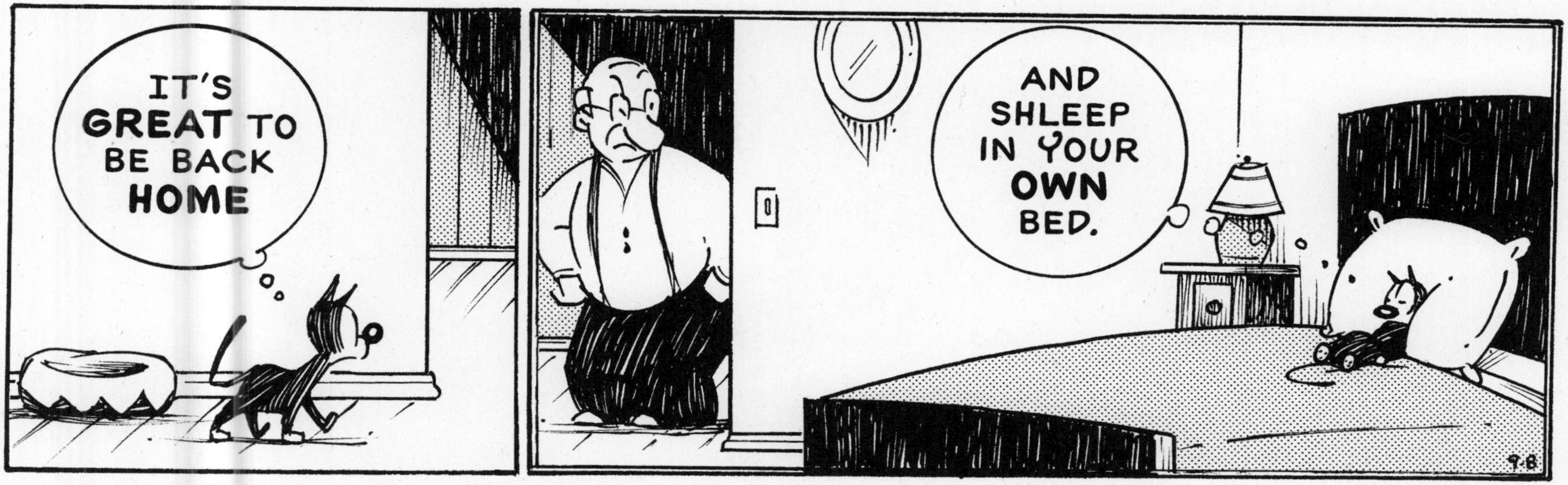
IT'S GREAT TO BE BACK HOME
AND SHLEEP IN YOUR OWN BED.
9-8

♪ LITTLE
PINK ♪
SOCKS
LI'L
PINK
SOCKS
♥

KITTY
SELF-CARE.

148

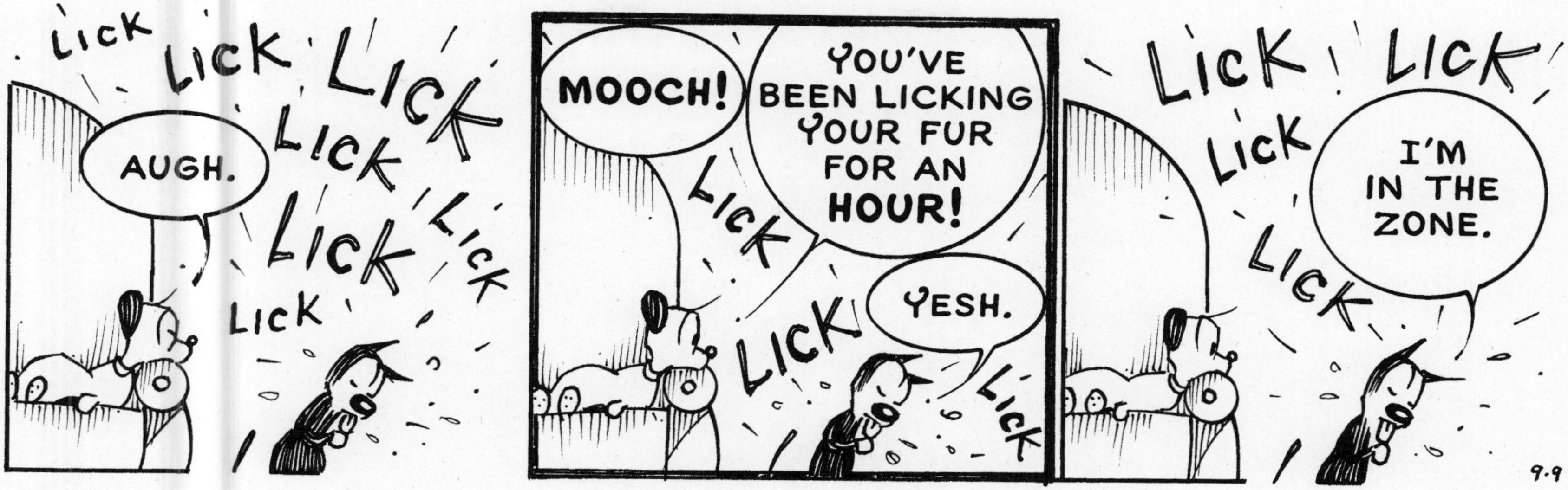
LICK
LICK
LICK
LICK
LICK
LICK
LICK
AUGH.
MOOCH!
YOU'VE BEEN LICKING YOUR FUR FOR AN **HOUR!**
LICK
LICK
YESH.
LICK
LICK
LICK
LICK
LICK
I'M IN THE ZONE.
9.9

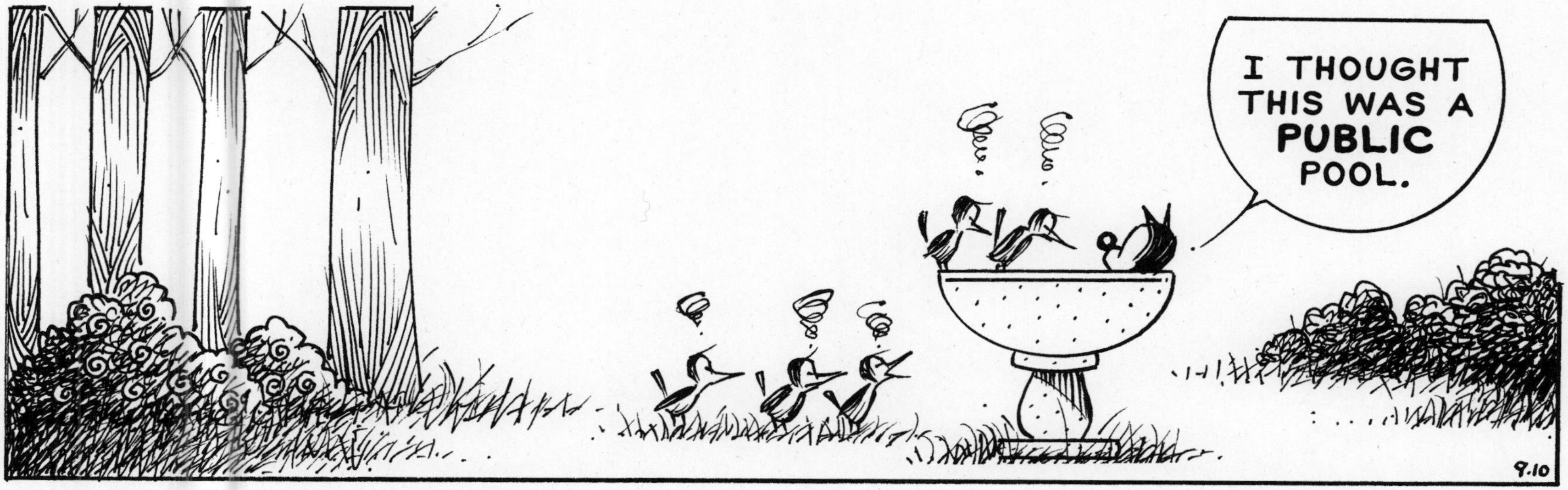
I THOUGHT THIS WAS A **PUBLIC** POOL.
9.10

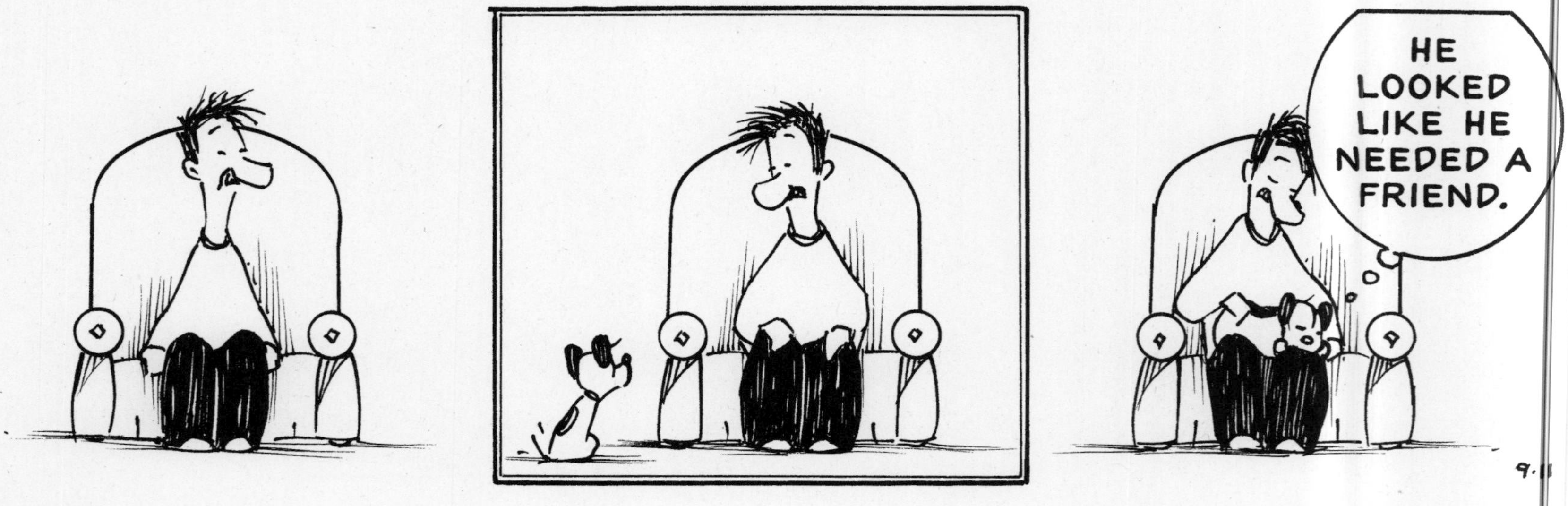
HE LOOKED LIKE HE NEEDED A FRIEND.
9.11

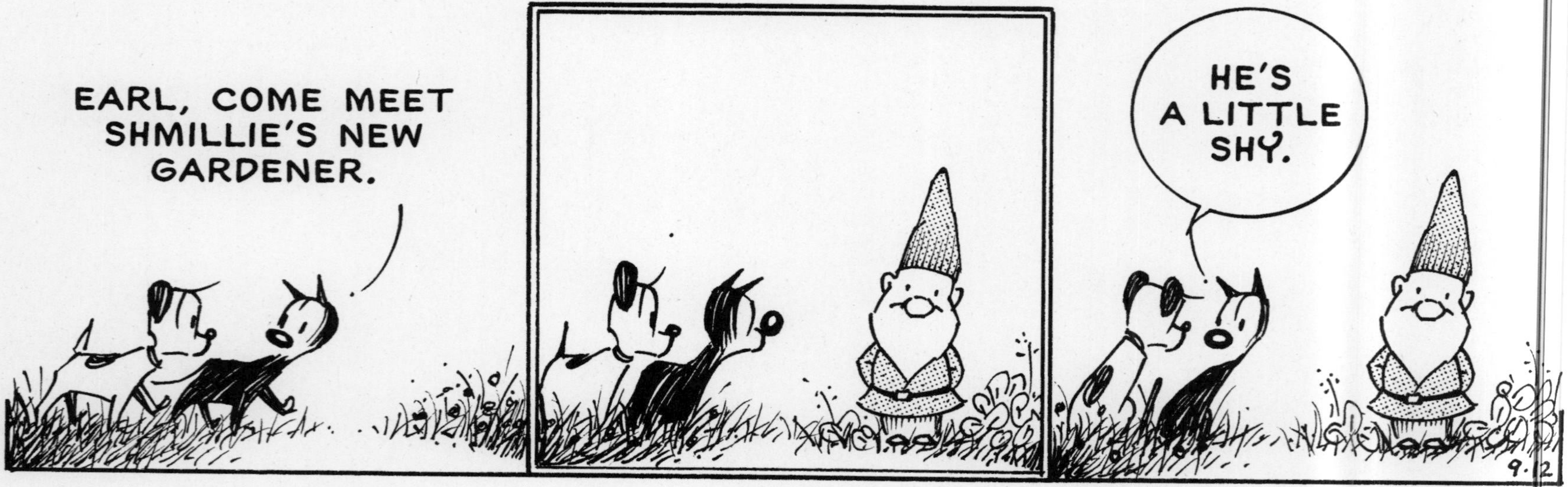
EARL, COME MEET SHMILLIE'S NEW GARDENER.
HE'S A LITTLE SHY.
9.12

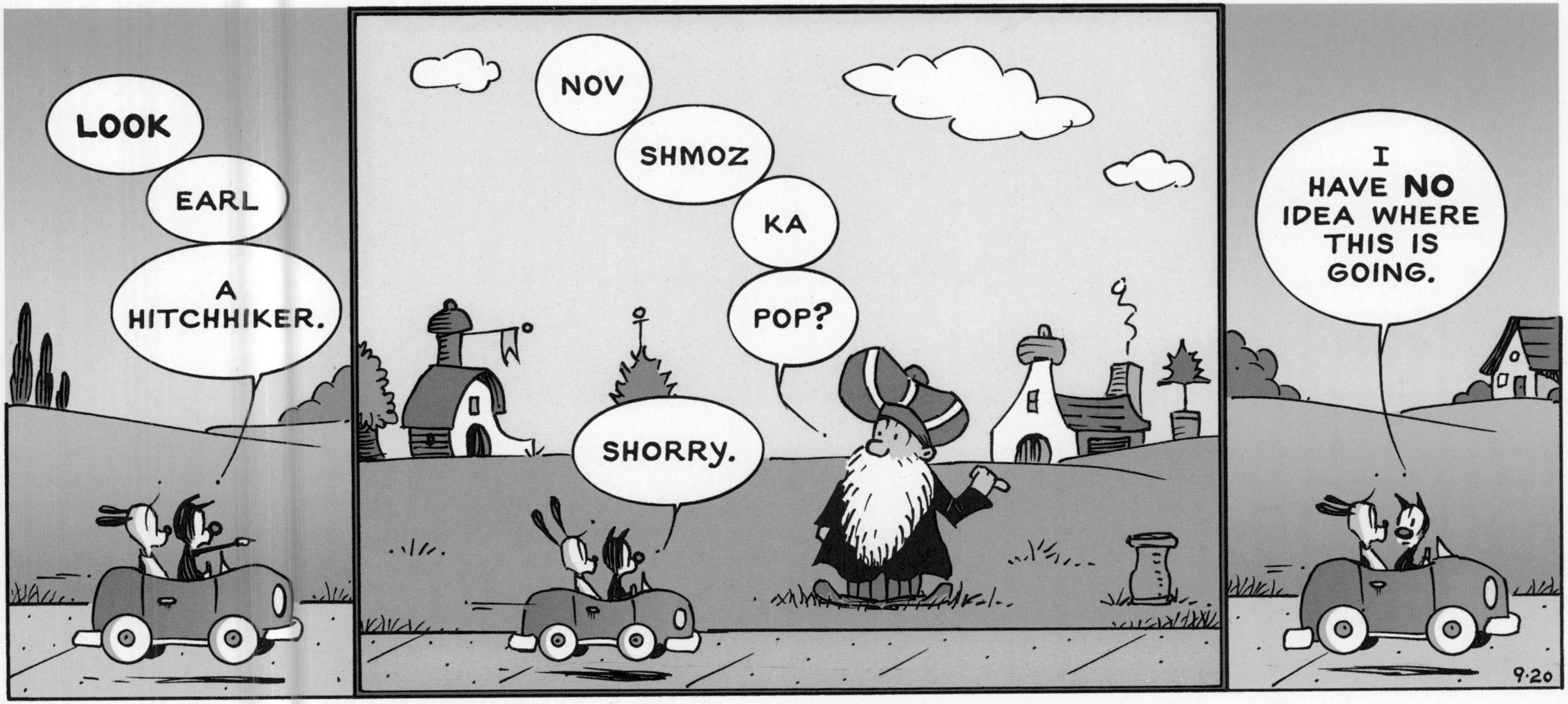
LOOK
EARL
A HITCHHIKER.
NOV
SHMOZ
KA
POP?
SHORRY.
I HAVE NO IDEA WHERE THIS IS GOING.
9·20

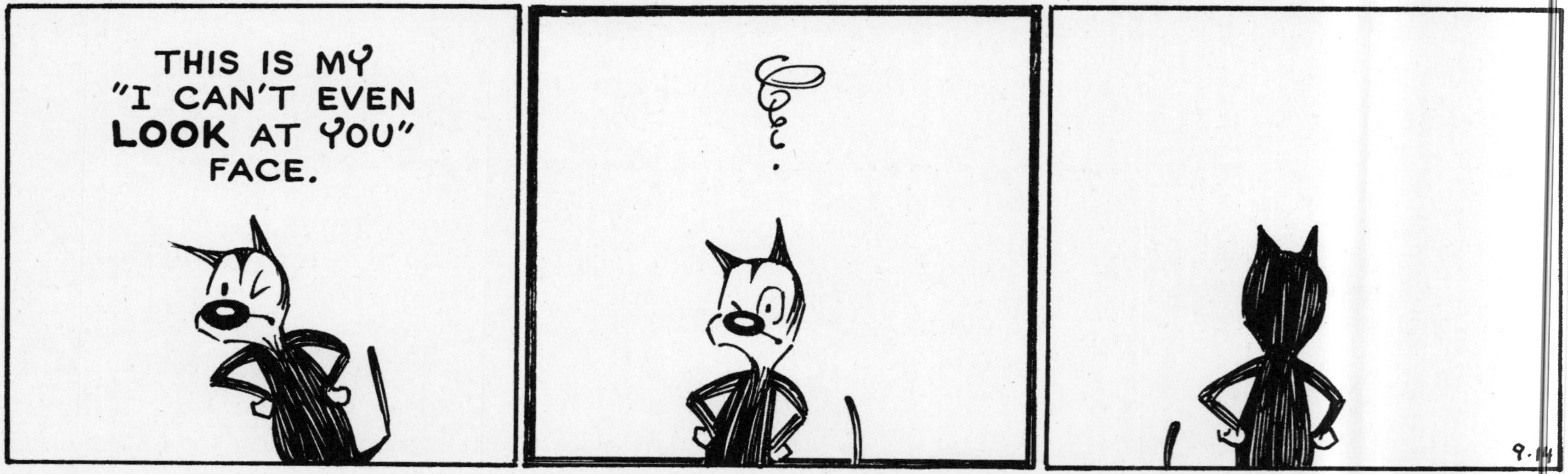
THIS IS MY "I CAN'T EVEN **LOOK** AT YOU" FACE.
9.14

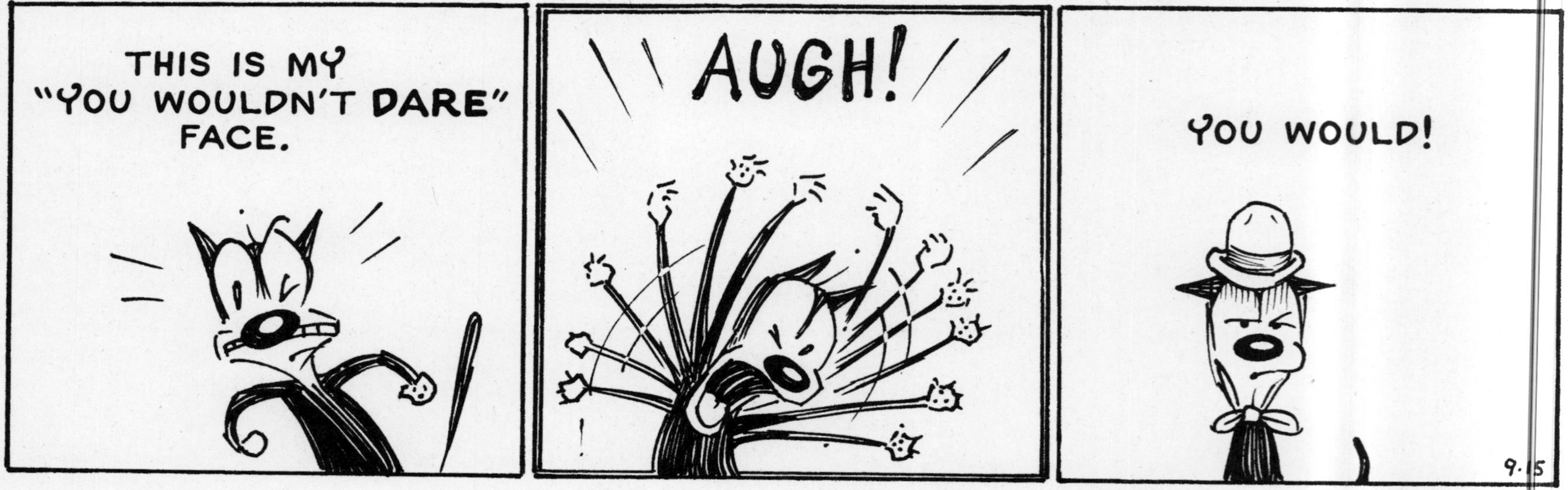
THIS IS MY "YOU WOULDN'T **DARE**" FACE.
AUGH!
YOU WOULD!
9.15

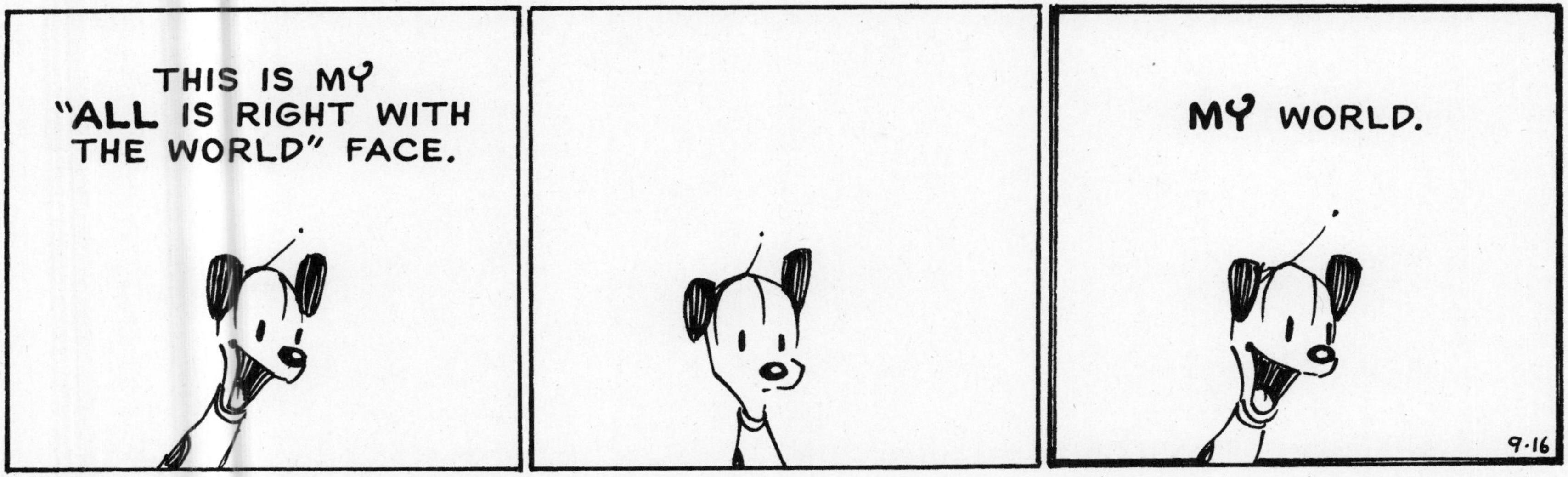
THIS IS MY "ALL IS RIGHT WITH THE WORLD" FACE.
MY WORLD.
9·16

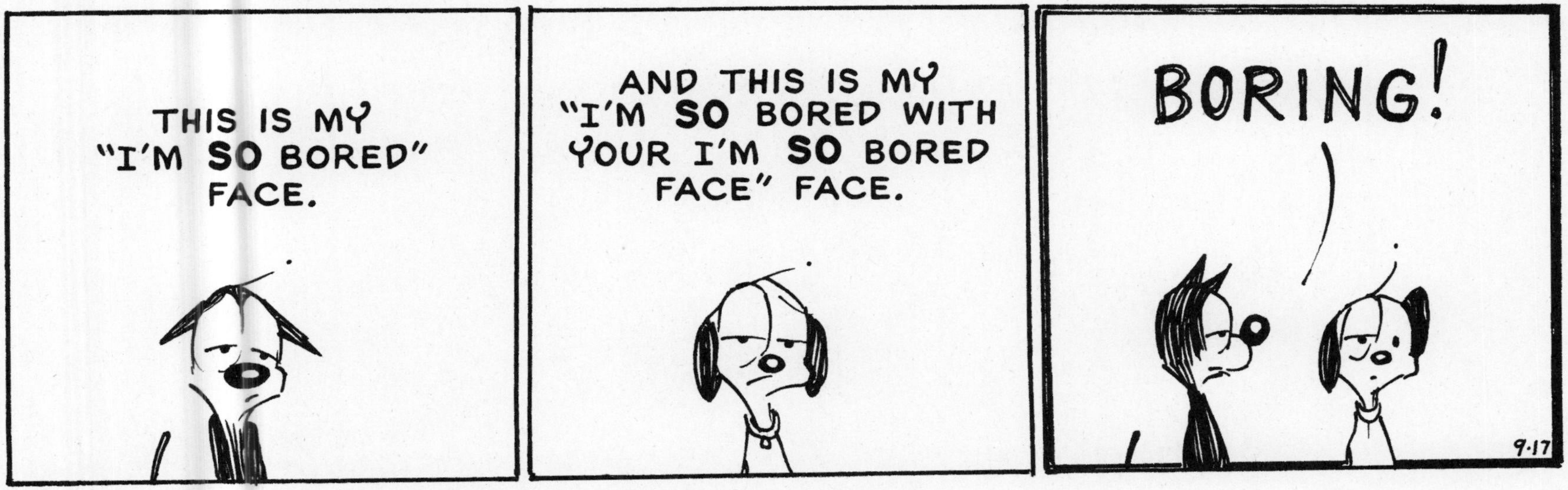
THIS IS MY "I'M SO BORED" FACE.
AND THIS IS MY "I'M SO BORED WITH YOUR I'M SO BORED FACE" FACE.
BORING!
9·17

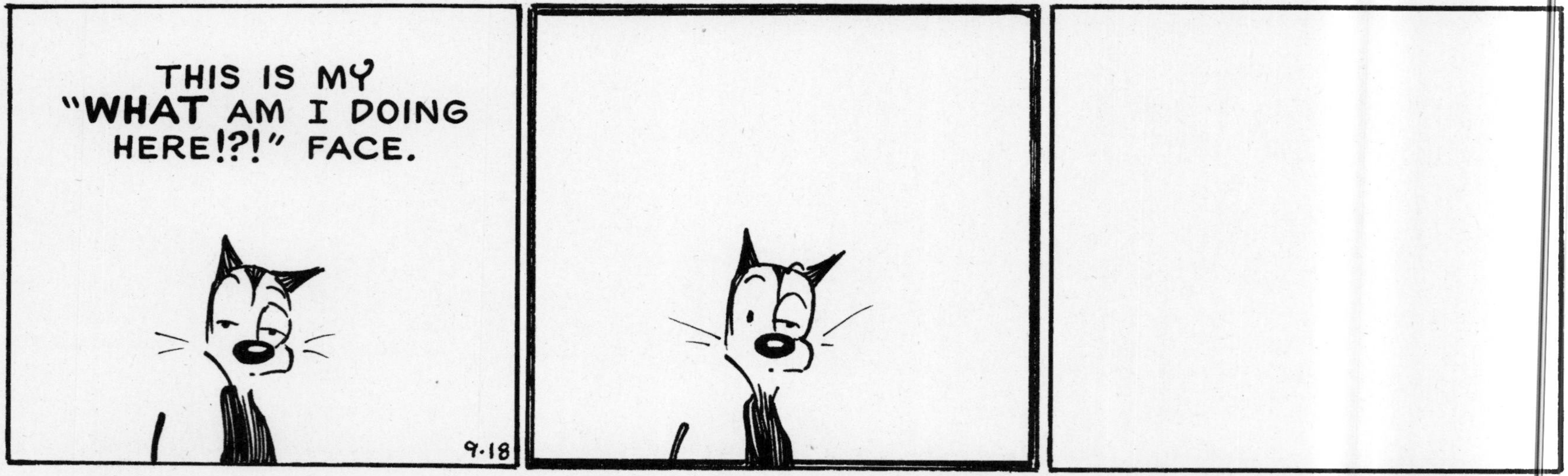
THIS IS MY
"WHAT AM I DOING
HERE!?!" FACE.
9.18

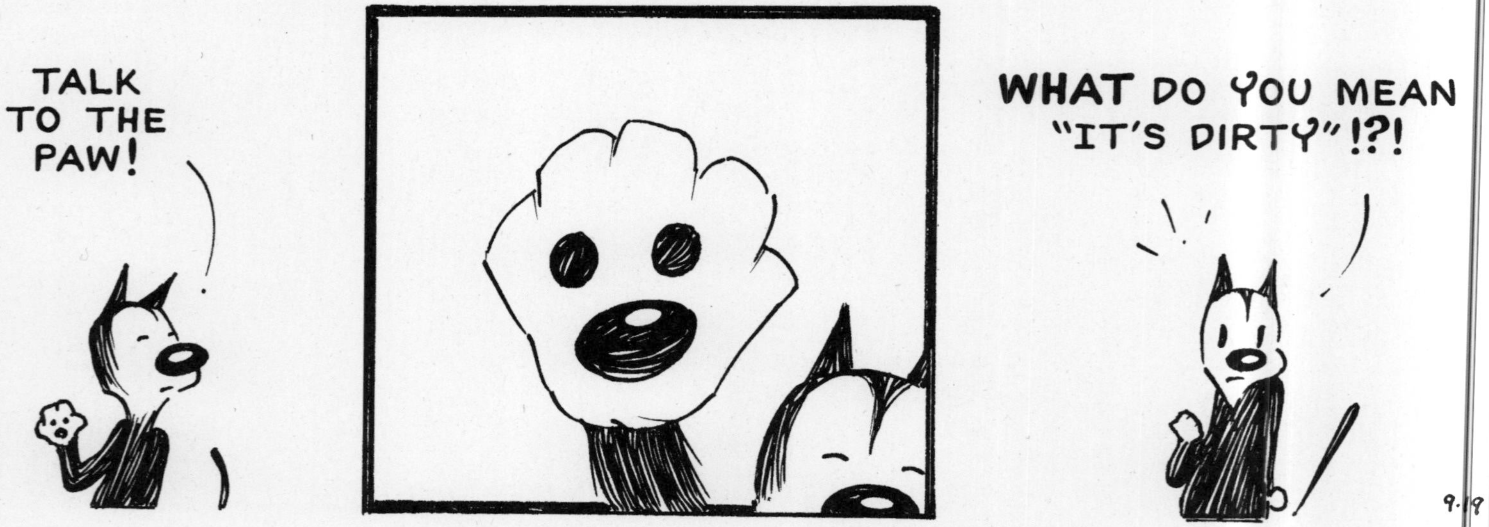
TALK
TO THE
PAW!
WHAT DO YOU MEAN
"IT'S DIRTY"!?!
9.19

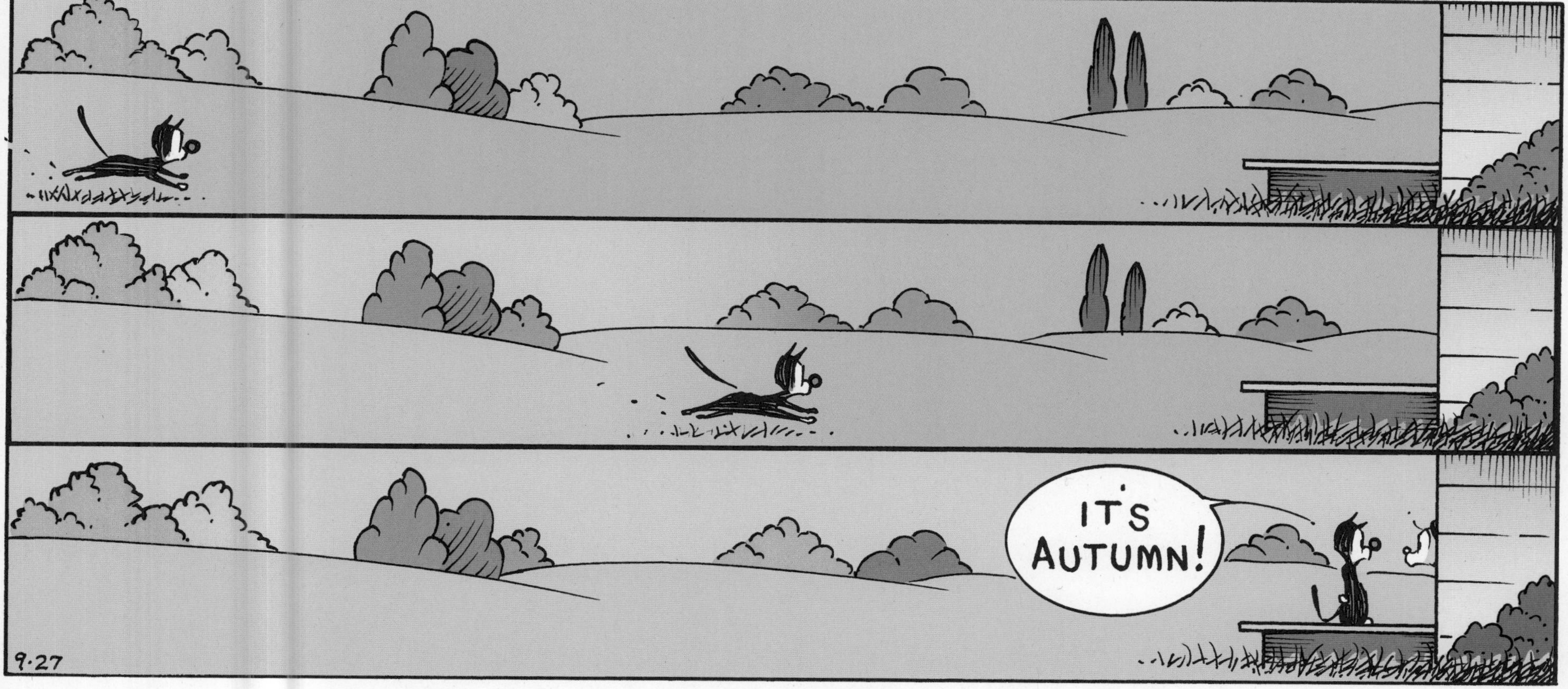
IT'S AUTUMN!
9·27

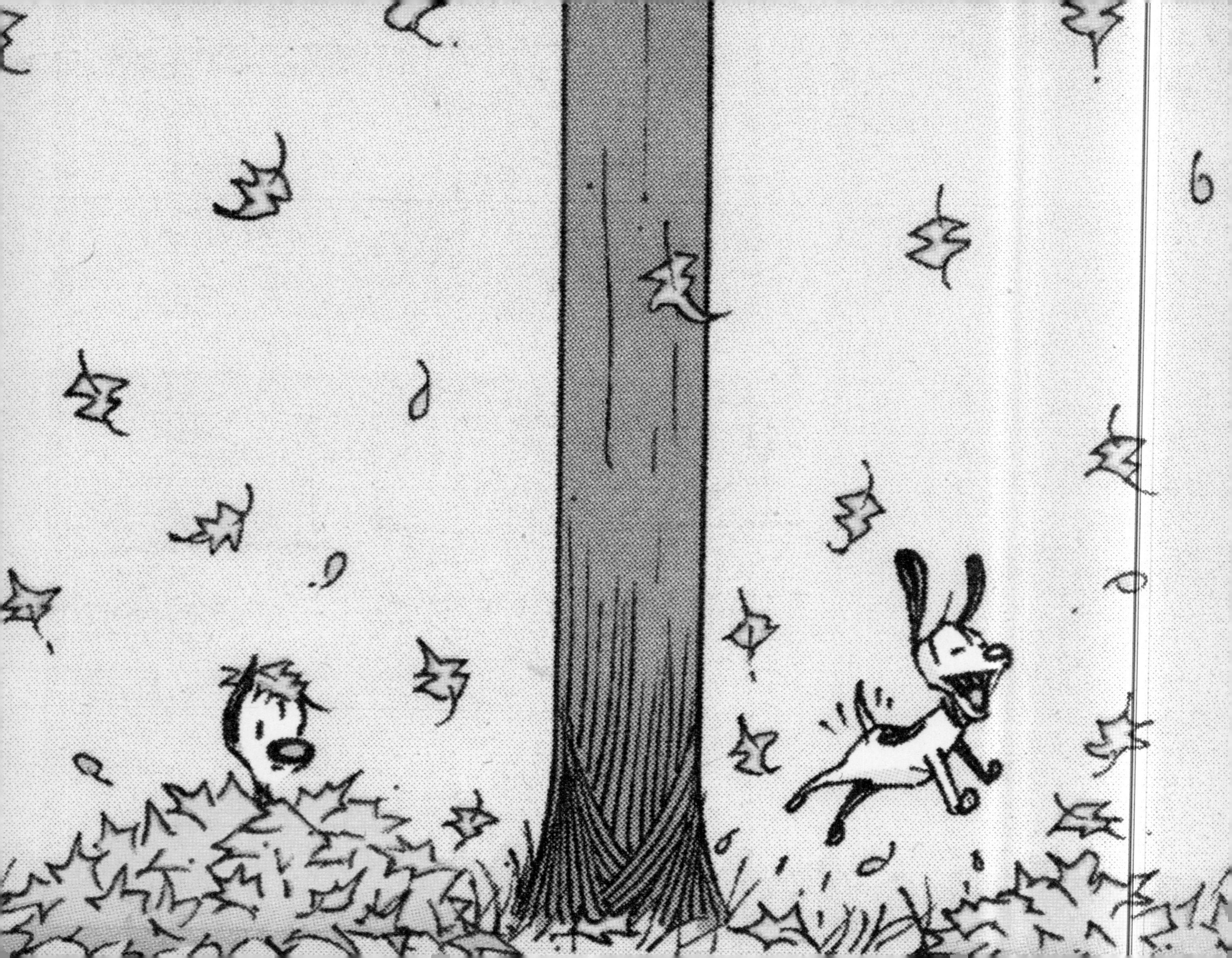

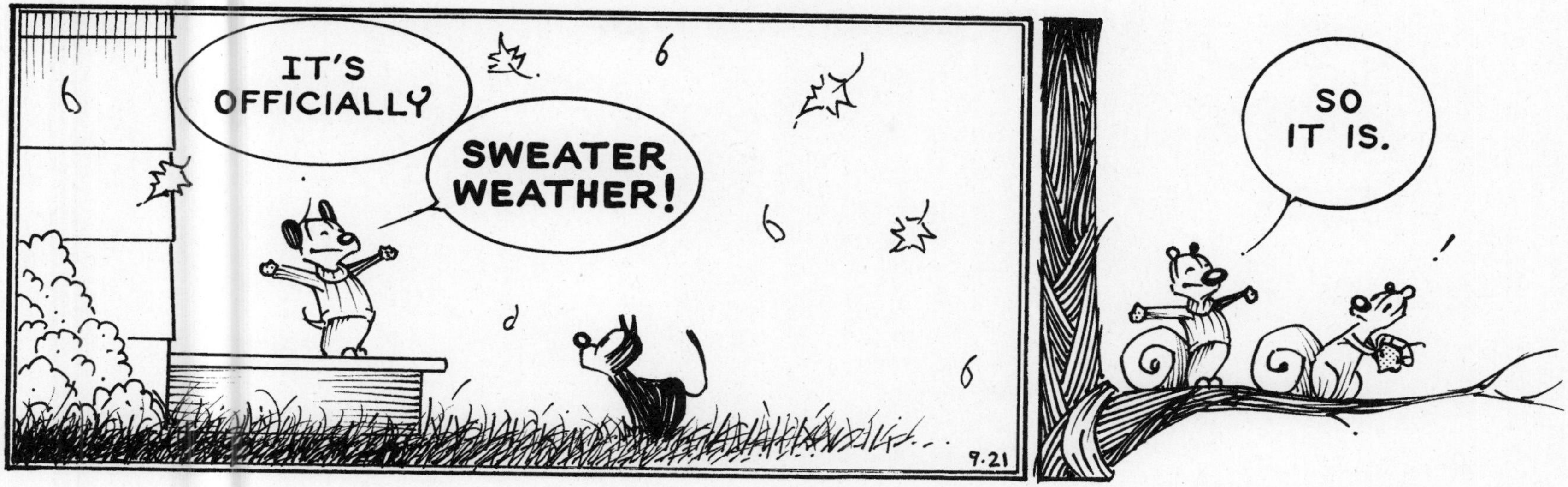
IT'S OFFICIALLY
SWEATER WEATHER!
SO IT IS.
!
9.21

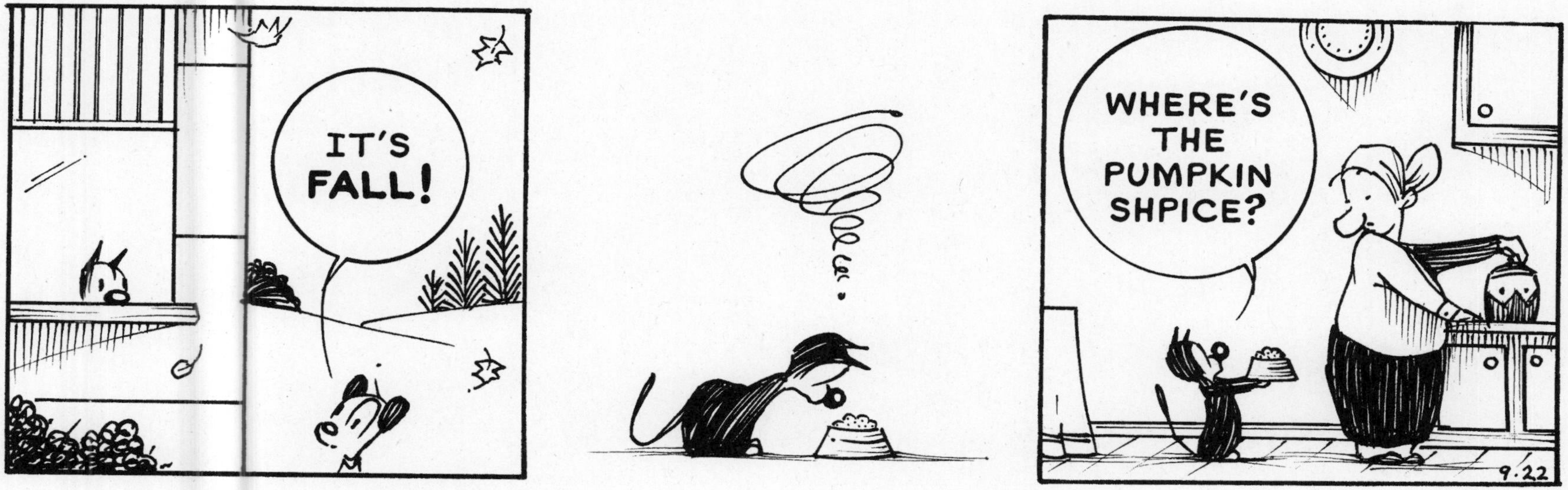
IT'S FALL!
WHERE'S THE PUMPKIN SHPICE?
9.22

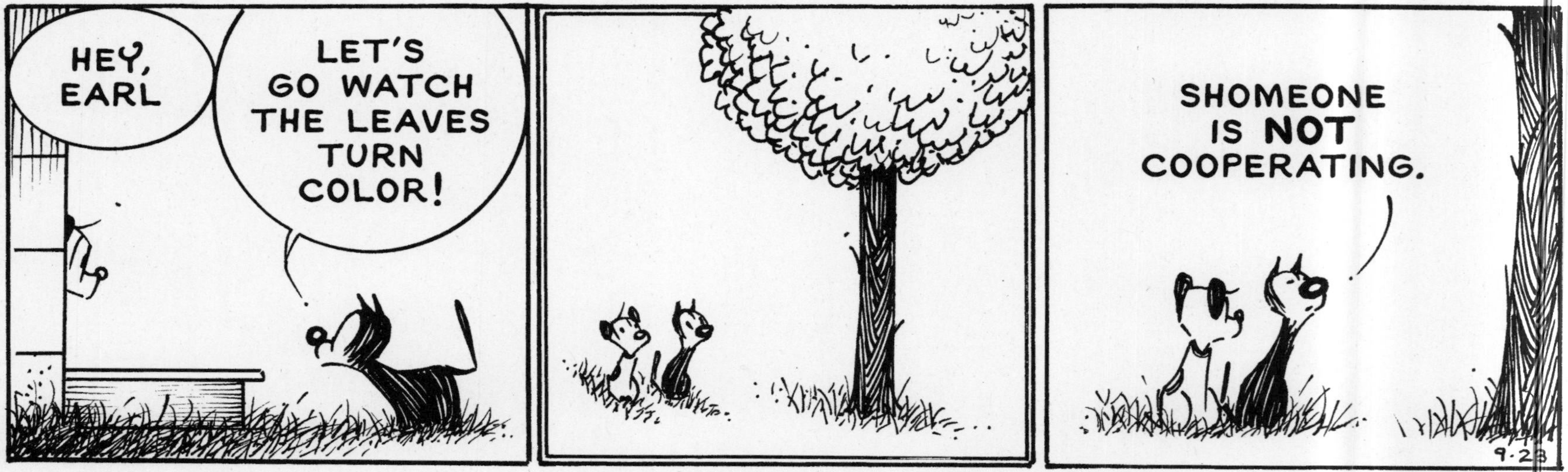
HEY, EARL
LET'S GO WATCH THE LEAVES TURN COLOR!
SHOMEONE IS **NOT** COOPERATING.
9·23

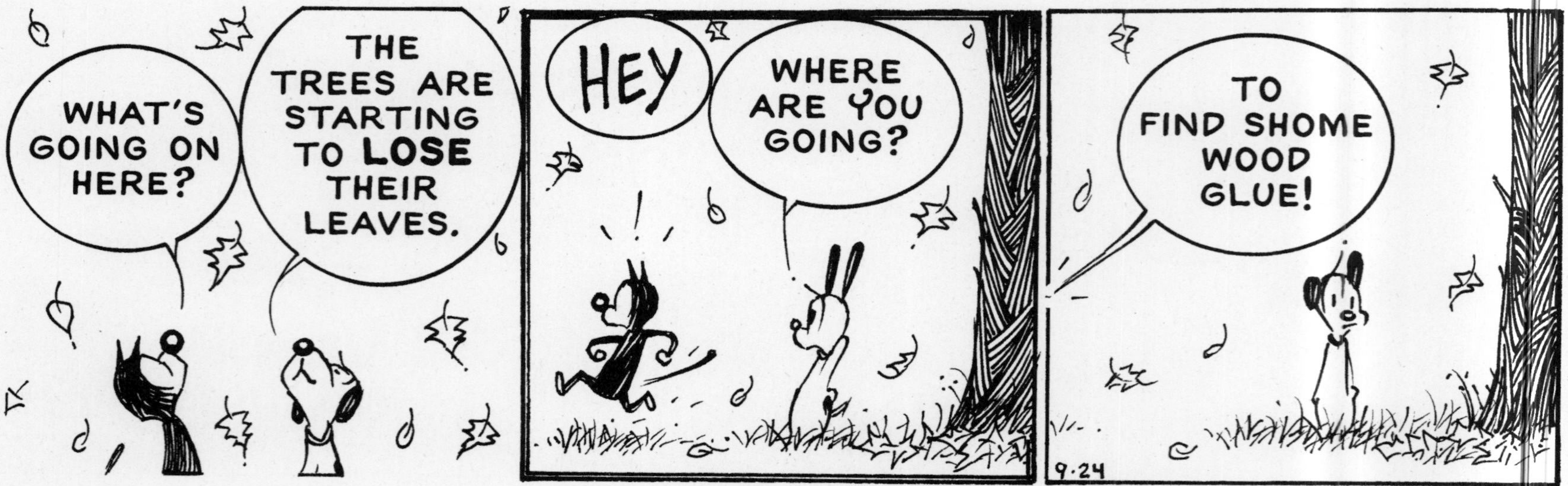
WHAT'S GOING ON HERE?
THE TREES ARE STARTING TO **LOSE** THEIR LEAVES.
HEY
WHERE ARE YOU GOING?
TO FIND SHOME WOOD GLUE!
9·24

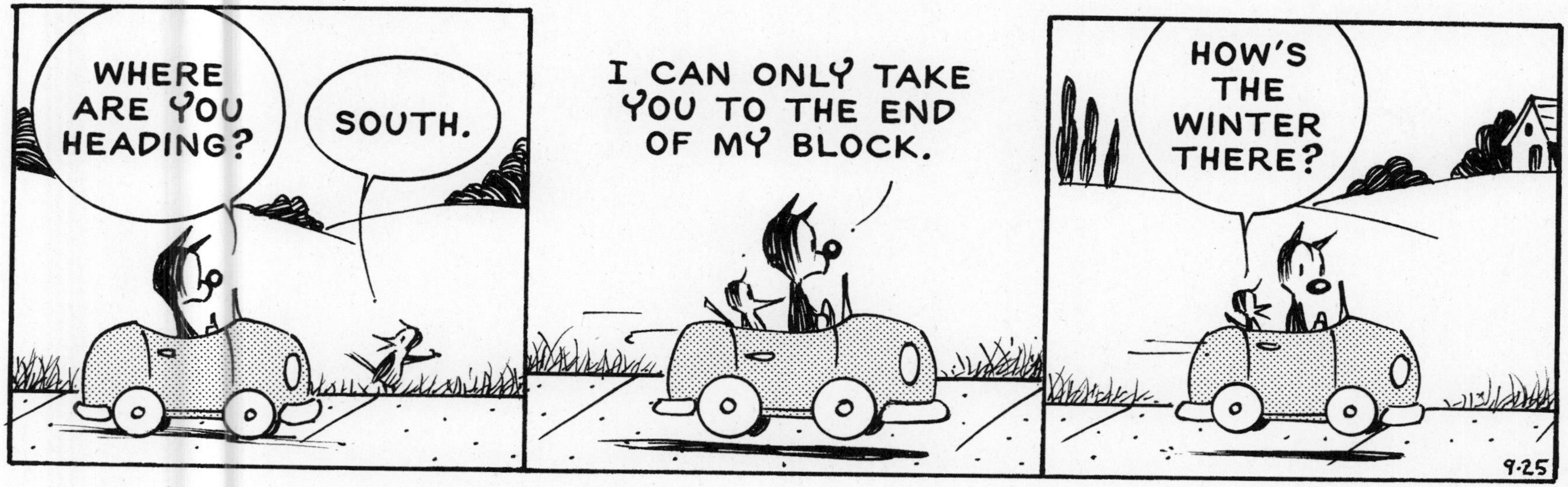
WHERE ARE YOU HEADING?
SOUTH.
I CAN ONLY TAKE YOU TO THE END OF MY BLOCK.
HOW'S THE WINTER THERE?
9·25

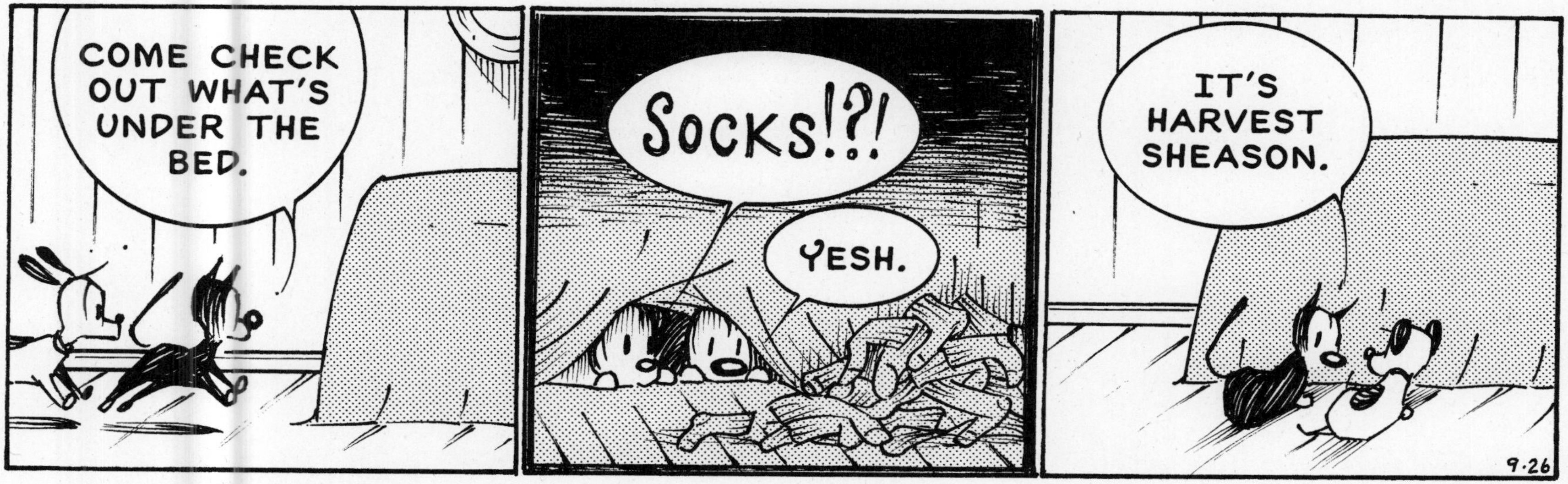
COME CHECK OUT WHAT'S UNDER THE BED.
SOCKS!?!
YESH.
IT'S HARVEST SHEASON.
9·26

MUTTS
PATRICK MC DONNELL

BONK
HEY
WHAT DID YOU DO THAT FOR?
I WAS JUST TRYING
TO GET YOUR ATTENTION.
THAT'S RIDICULOUS!!! AND A POOR EXCUSE FOR A DESHPICABLE, BAD HABIT!
NOT THAT MUCH ATTENTION.
10·4

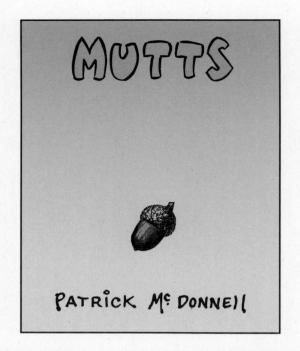

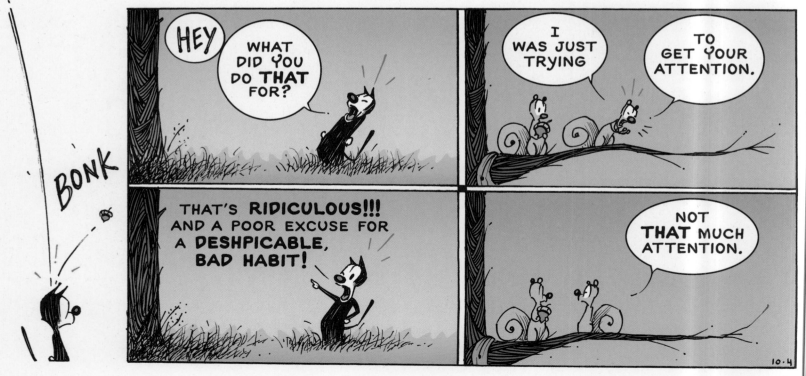

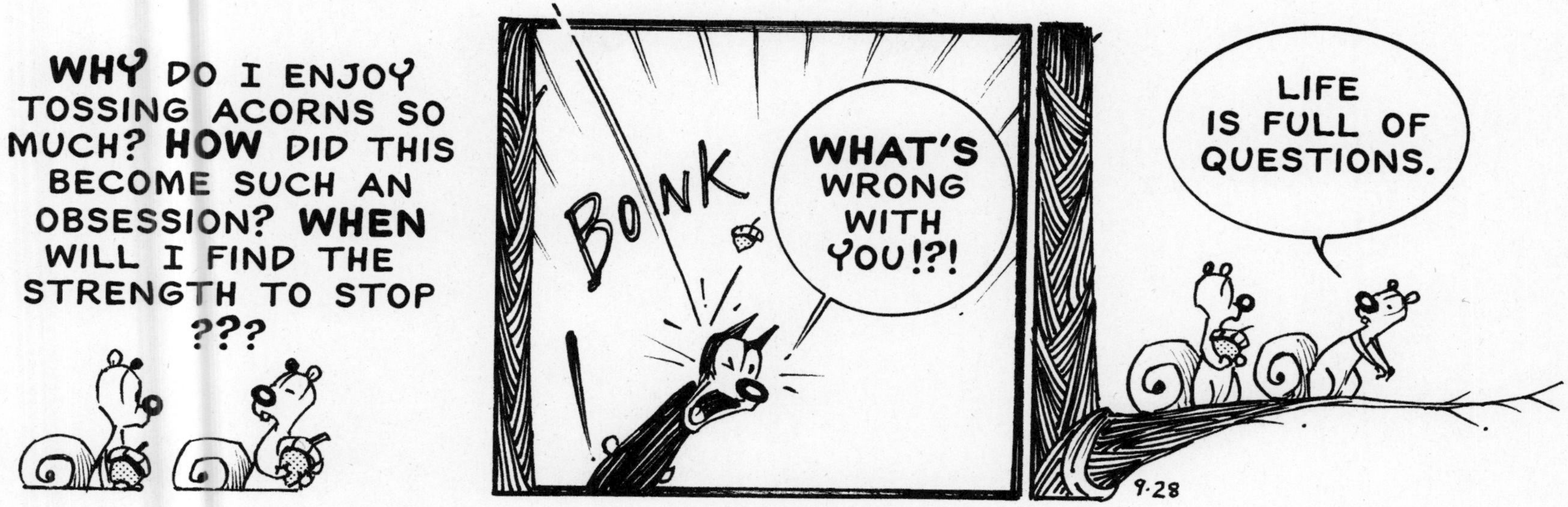
WHY DO I ENJOY TOSSING ACORNS SO MUCH? HOW DID THIS BECOME SUCH AN OBSESSION? WHEN WILL I FIND THE STRENGTH TO STOP ???
BONK
WHAT'S WRONG WITH YOU!?!
LIFE IS FULL OF QUESTIONS.
9·28

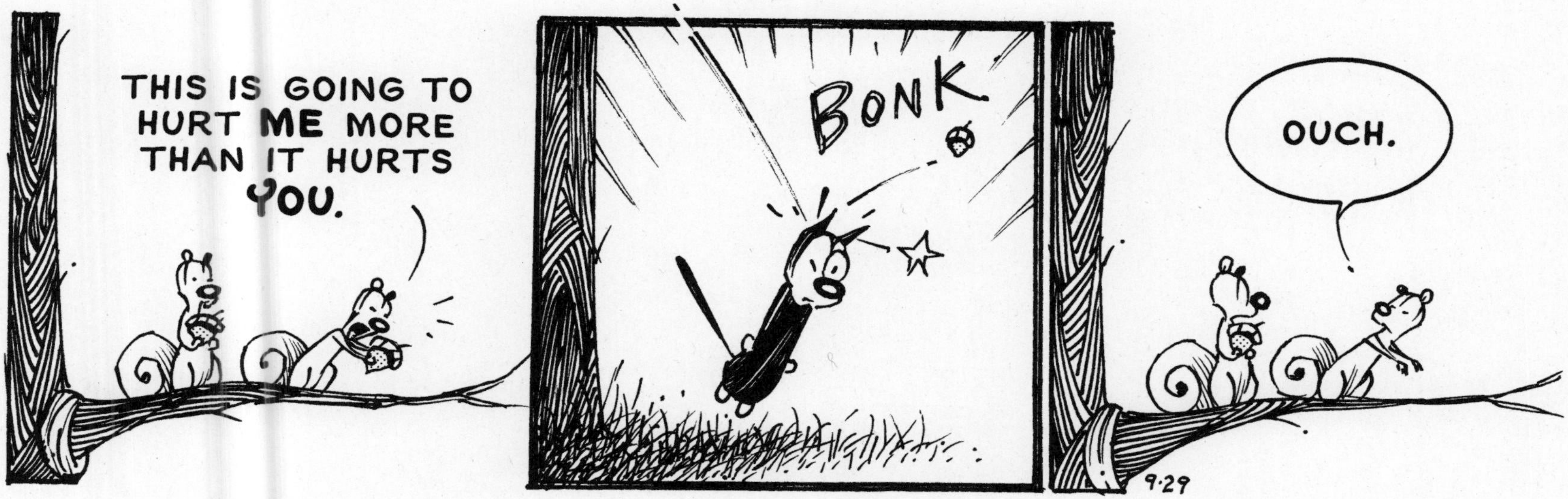
THIS IS GOING TO HURT ME MORE THAN IT HURTS YOU.
BONK
OUCH.
9·29

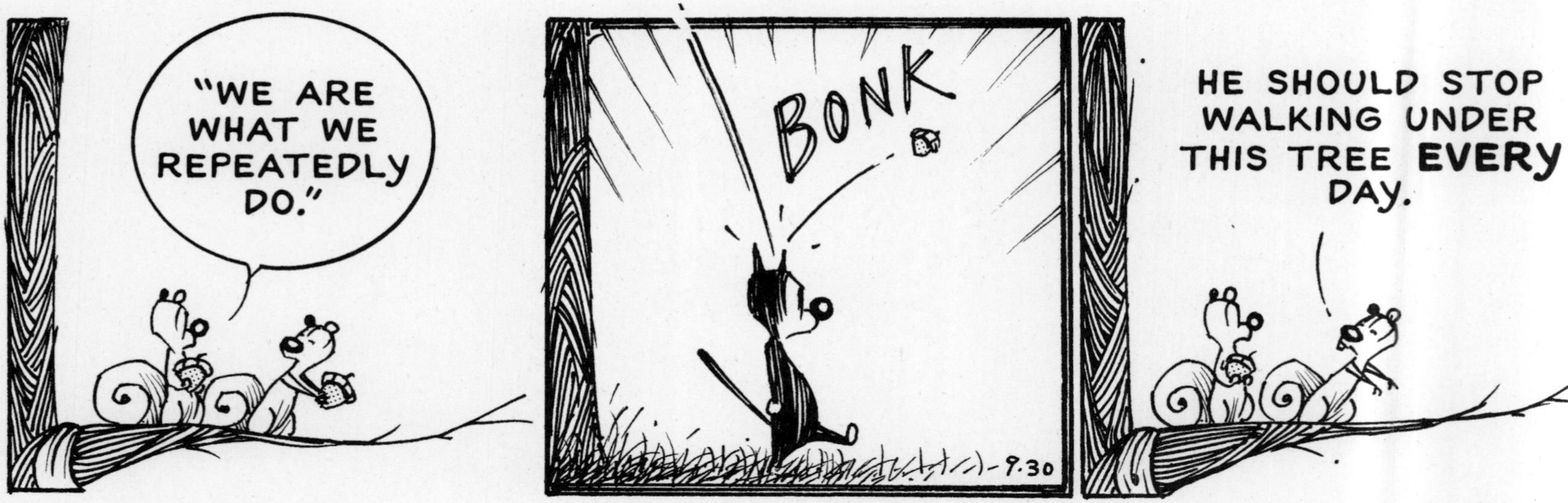
"WE ARE WHAT WE REPEATEDLY DO."
BONK
9.30
HE SHOULD STOP WALKING UNDER THIS TREE EVERY DAY.

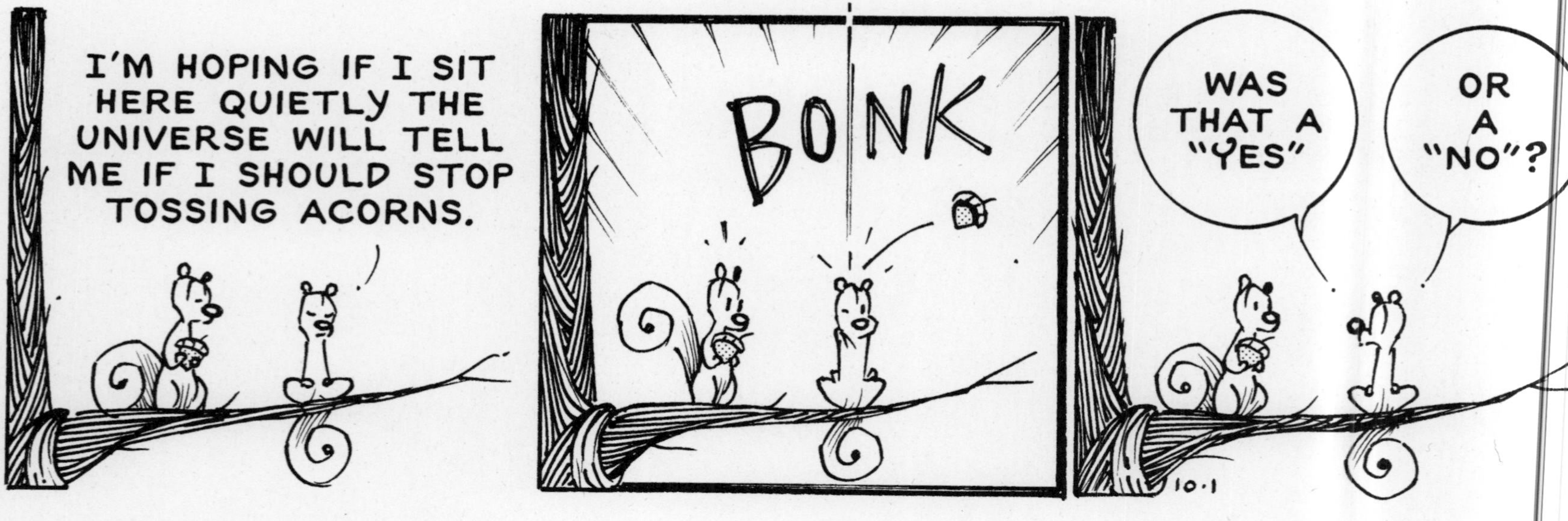
I'M HOPING IF I SIT HERE QUIETLY THE UNIVERSE WILL TELL ME IF I SHOULD STOP TOSSING ACORNS.
BONK
WAS THAT A "YES"
OR A "NO"?
10.1

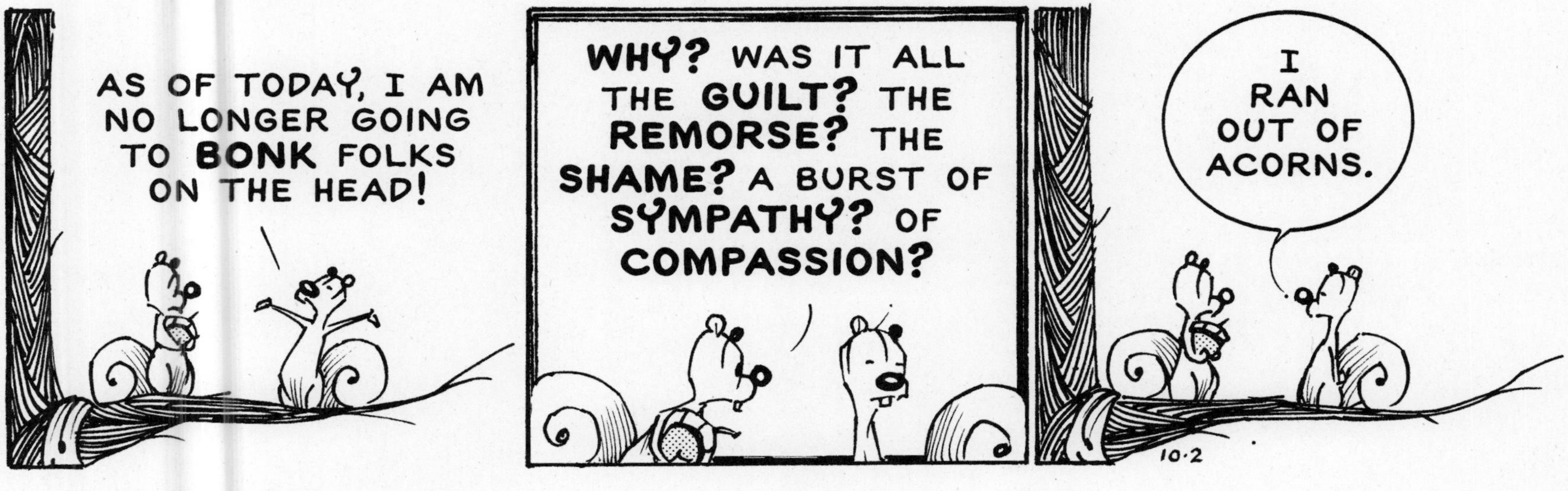
AS OF TODAY, I AM NO LONGER GOING TO **BONK** FOLKS ON THE HEAD!
WHY? WAS IT ALL THE **GUILT?** THE **REMORSE?** THE **SHAME?** A BURST OF **SYMPATHY?** OF **COMPASSION?**
I RAN OUT OF ACORNS.
10·2

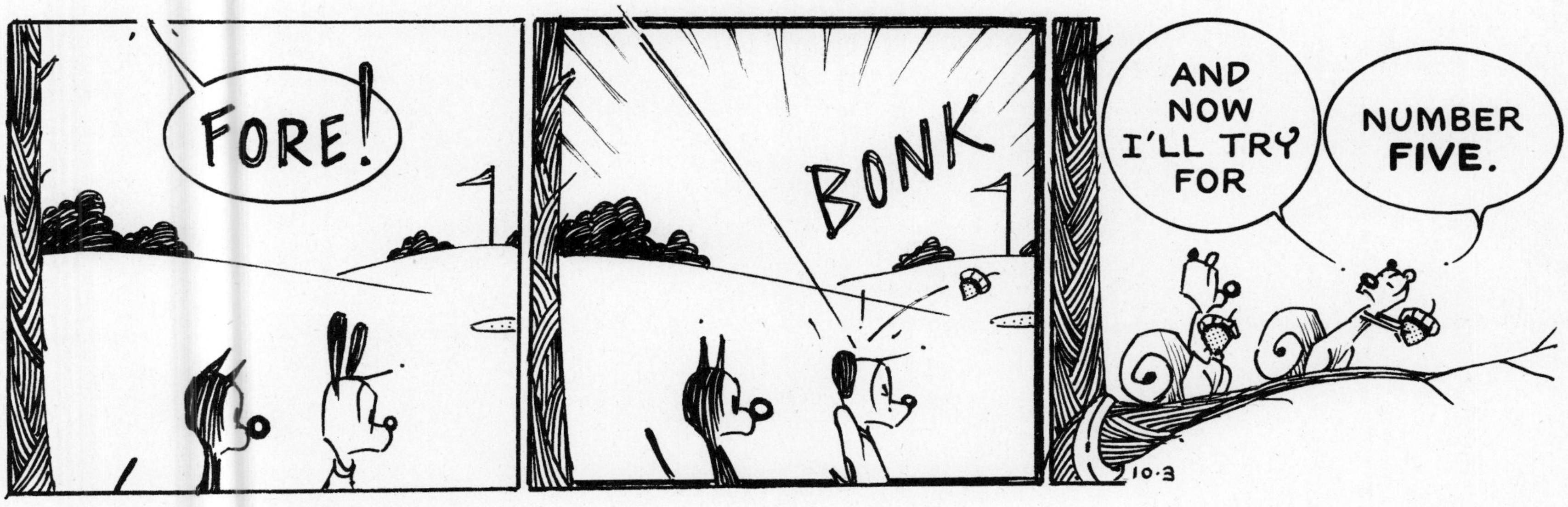
FORE!
BONK
AND NOW I'LL TRY FOR
NUMBER **FIVE.**
10·3

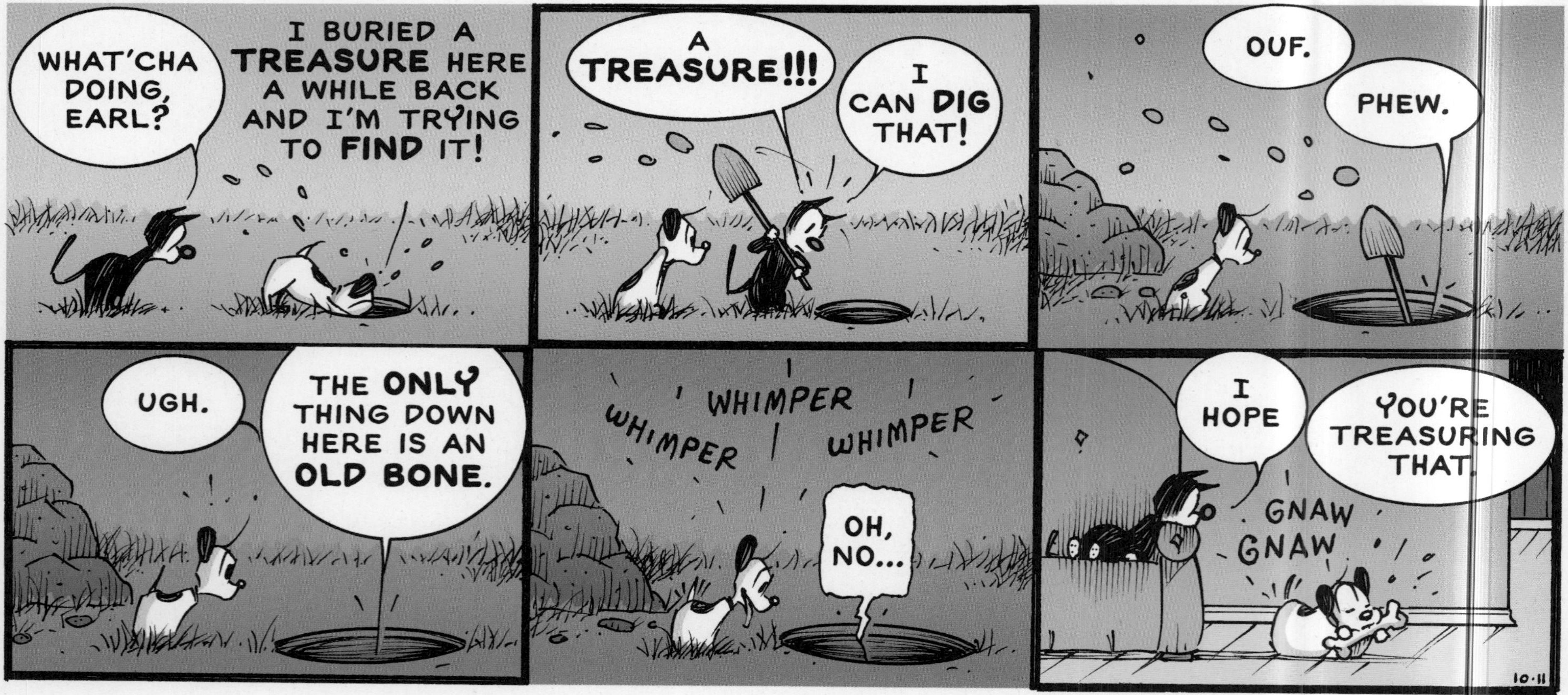
WHAT'CHA DOING, EARL?
I BURIED A TREASURE HERE A WHILE BACK AND I'M TRYING TO FIND IT!
A TREASURE!!!
I CAN DIG THAT!
OUF.
PHEW.
UGH.
THE ONLY THING DOWN HERE IS AN OLD BONE.
WHIMPER
WHIMPER
WHIMPER
OH, NO...
I HOPE
YOU'RE TREASURING THAT.
GNAW GNAW
10·11

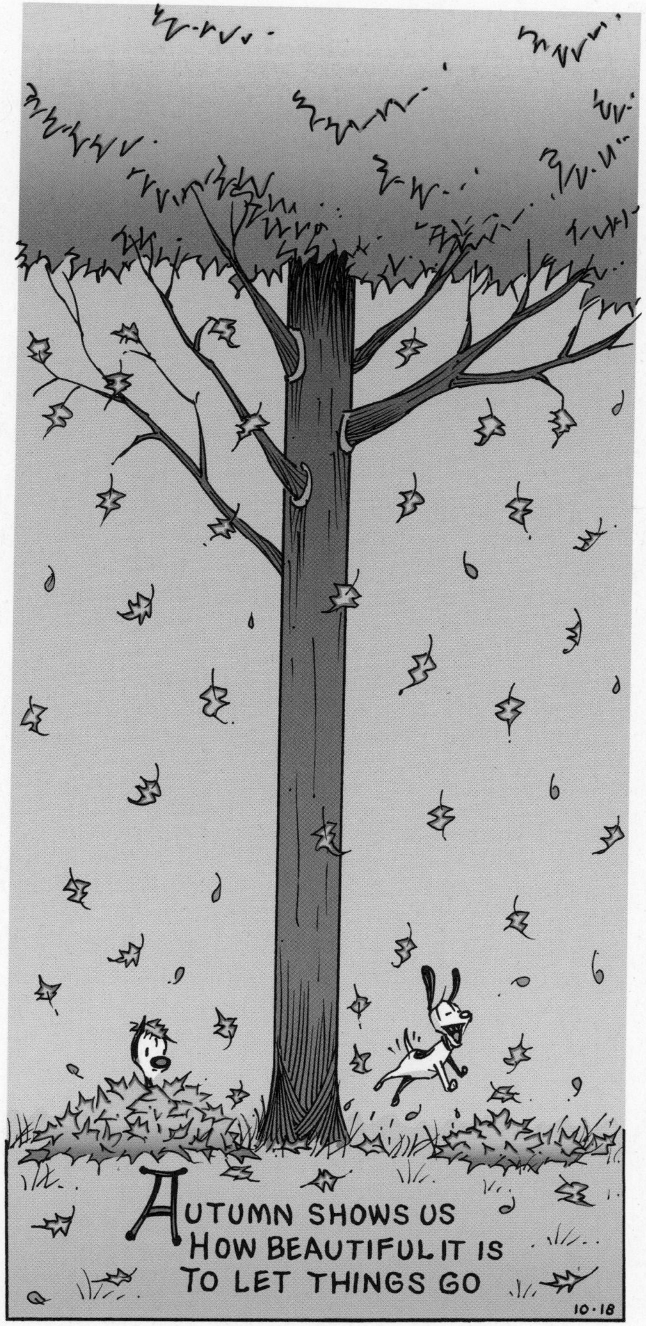
AUTUMN SHOWS US
HOW BEAUTIFUL IT IS
TO LET THINGS GO
10·18

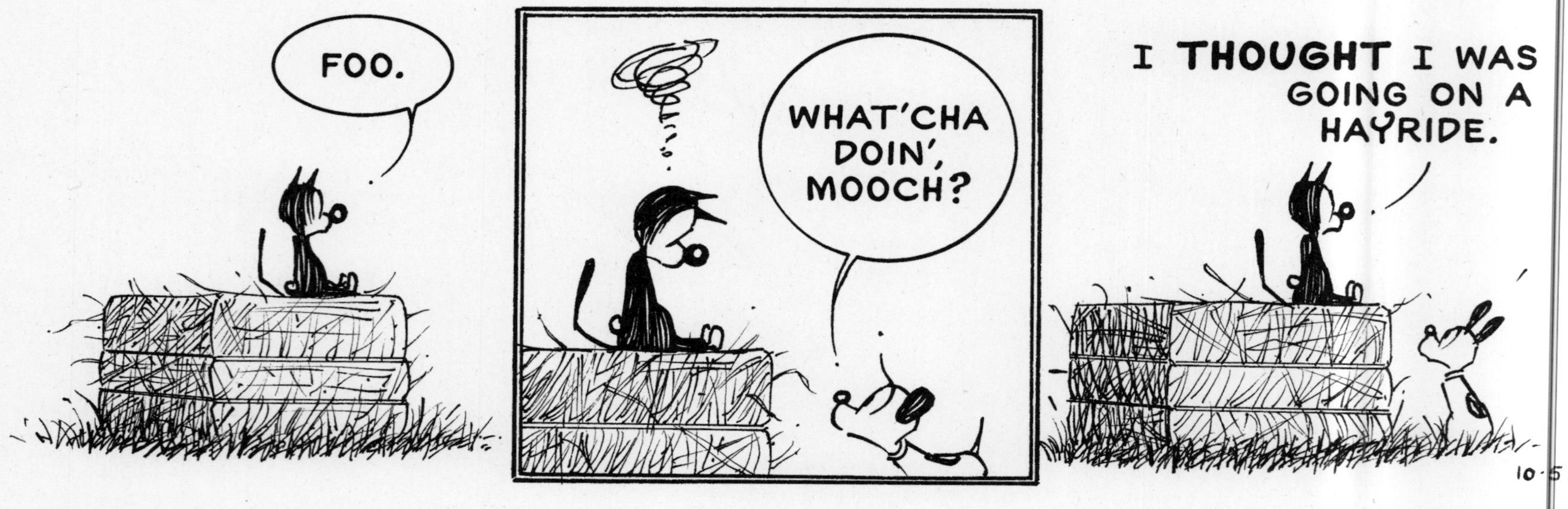
FOO.
WHAT'CHA DOIN', MOOCH?
I THOUGHT I WAS GOING ON A HAYRIDE.
10·5

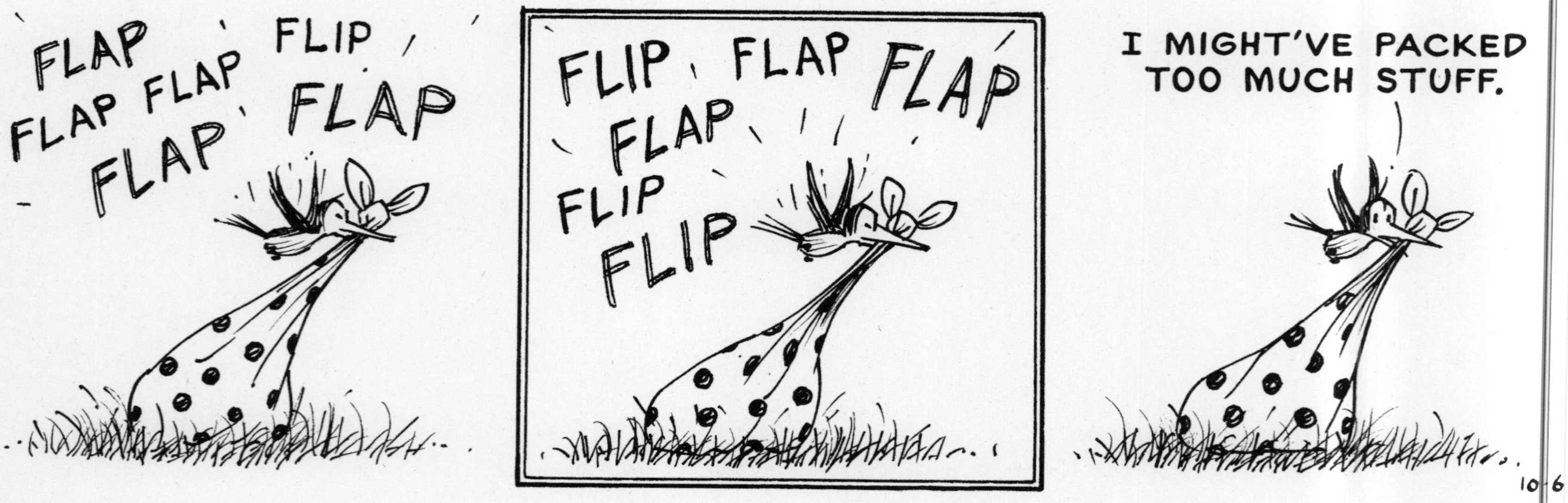
FLAP FLIP FLAP FLAP FLAP FLAP
FLIP FLAP FLAP FLAP FLIP FLIP
I MIGHT'VE PACKED TOO MUCH STUFF.
10·6

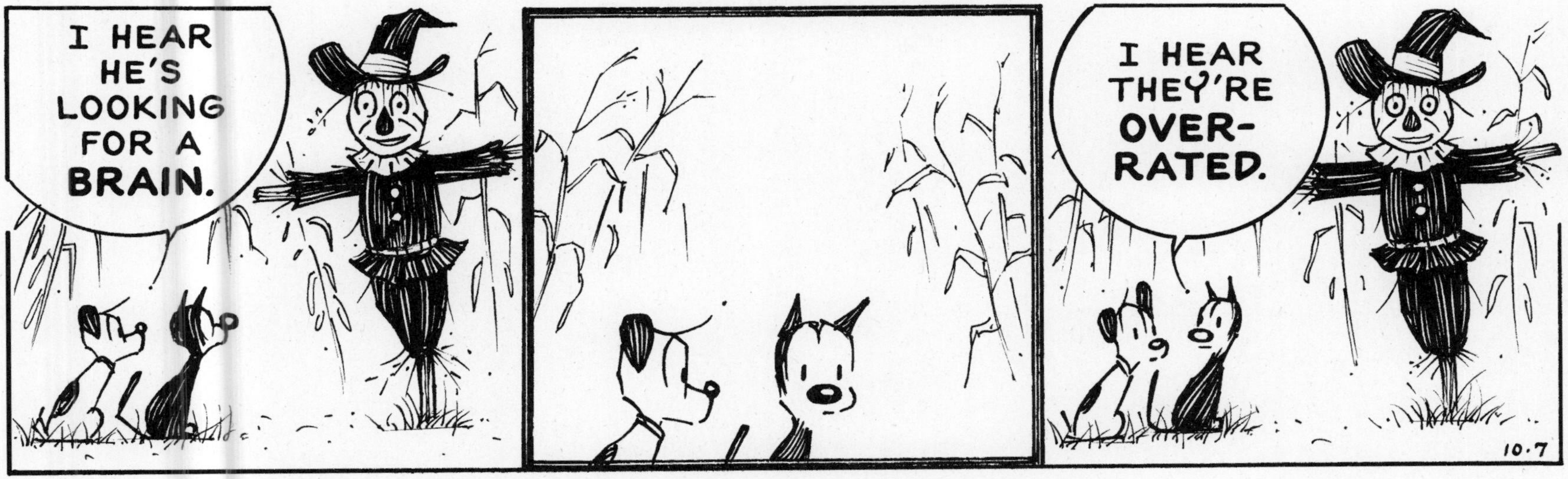
I HEAR HE'S LOOKING FOR A BRAIN.
I HEAR THEY'RE OVER-RATED.
10·7

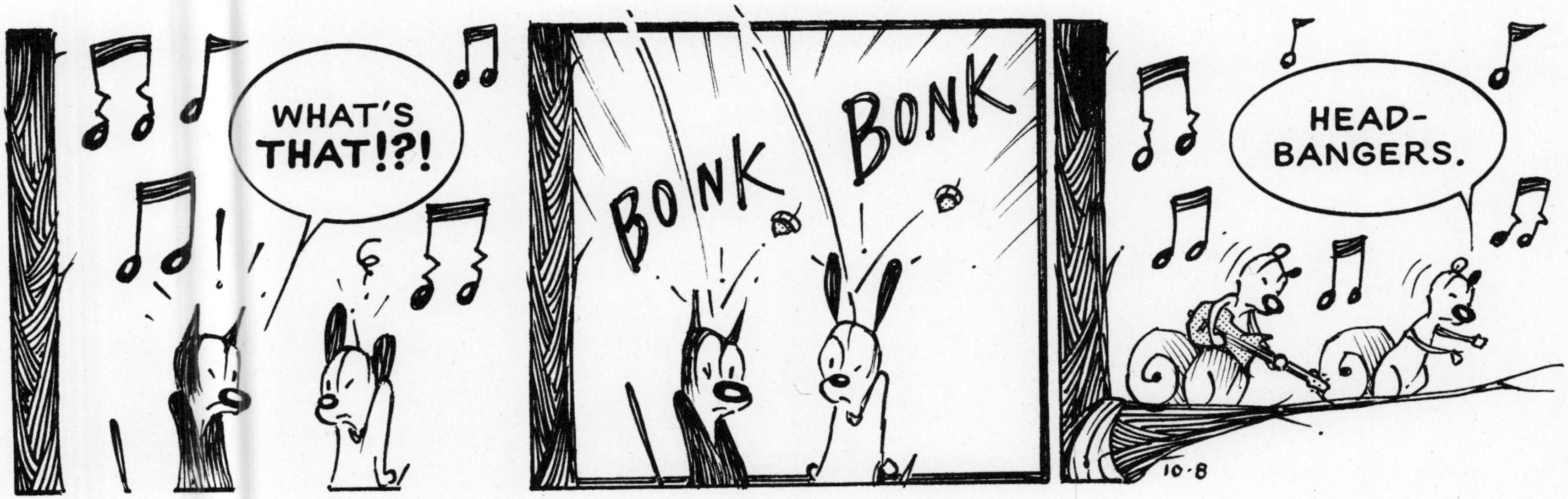
WHAT'S THAT!?!
BONK
BONK
HEAD-BANGERS.
10·8

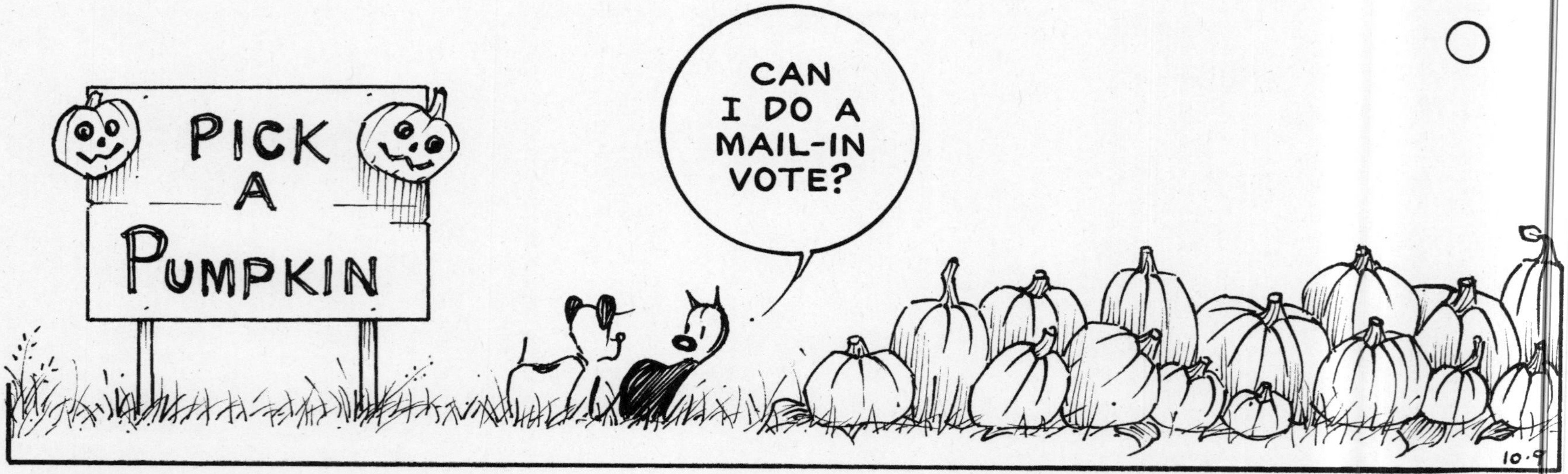
PICK A PUMPKIN
CAN I DO A MAIL-IN VOTE?
10·9

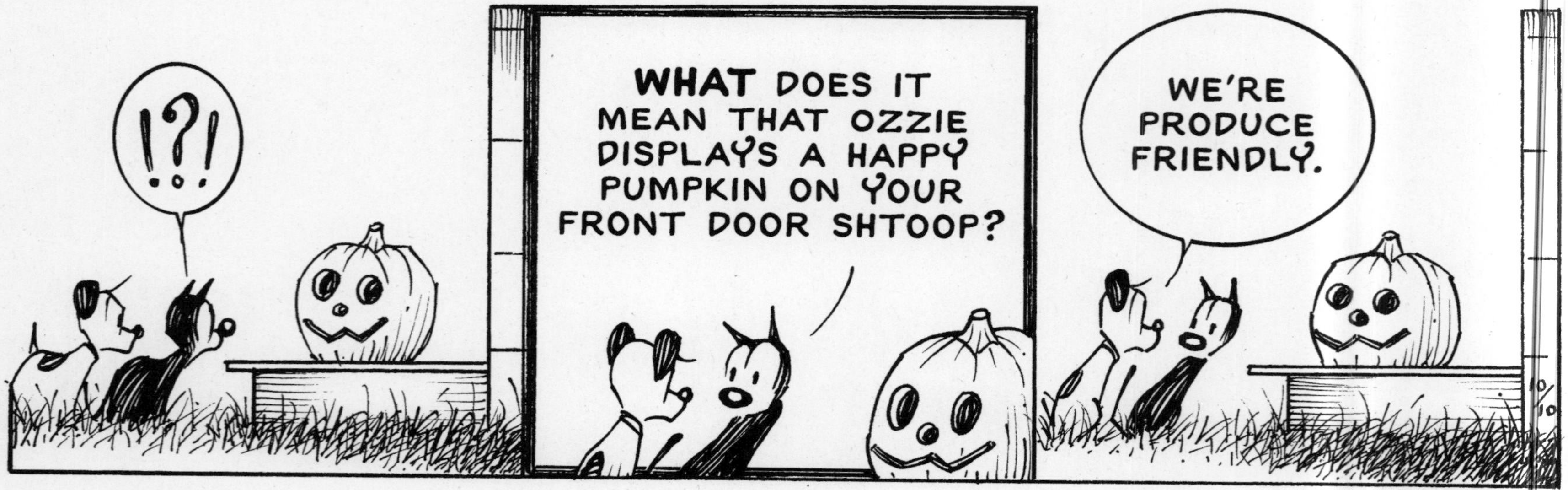
!?!
WHAT DOES IT MEAN THAT OZZIE DISPLAYS A HAPPY PUMPKIN ON YOUR FRONT DOOR SHTOOP?
WE'RE PRODUCE FRIENDLY.
10/10

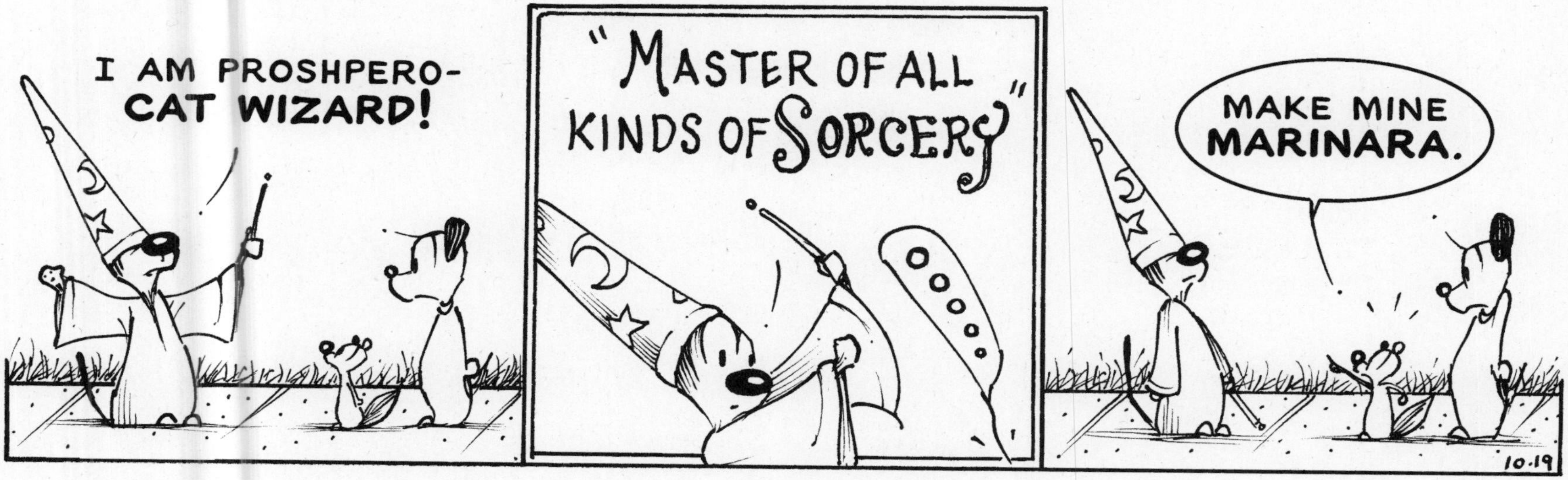
I AM PROSHPERO-
CAT WIZARD!
"MASTER OF ALL
KINDS OF SORCERY"
OOOOO
MAKE MINE
MARINARA.
10·19

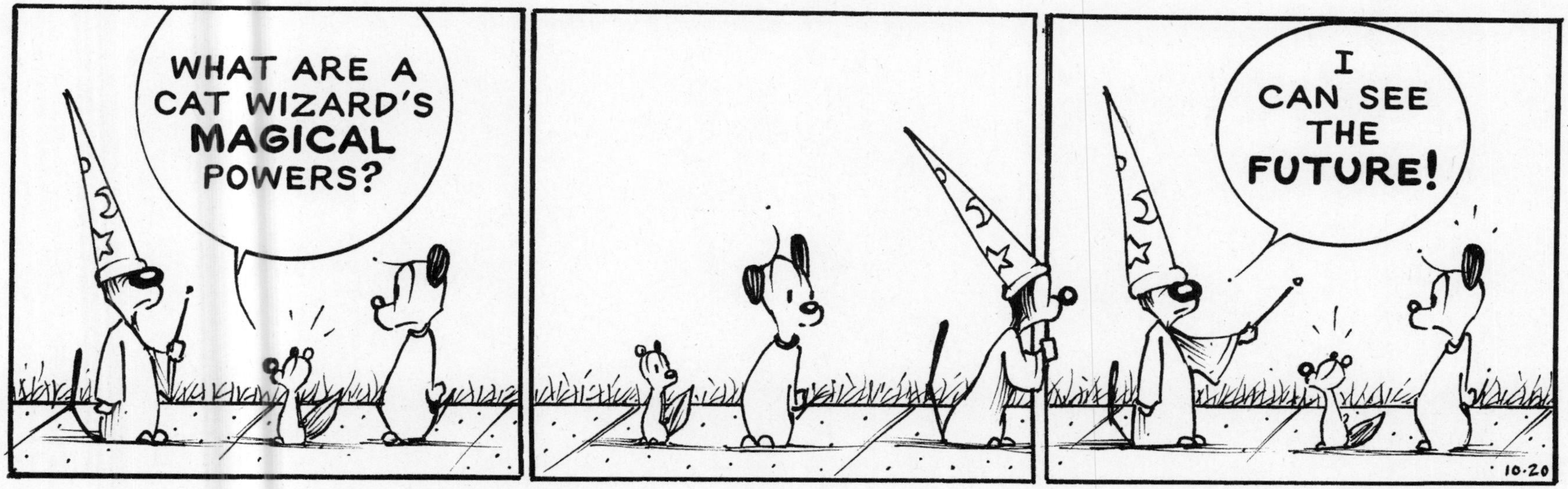
WHAT ARE A
CAT WIZARD'S
MAGICAL
POWERS?
I
CAN SEE
THE
FUTURE!
10·20

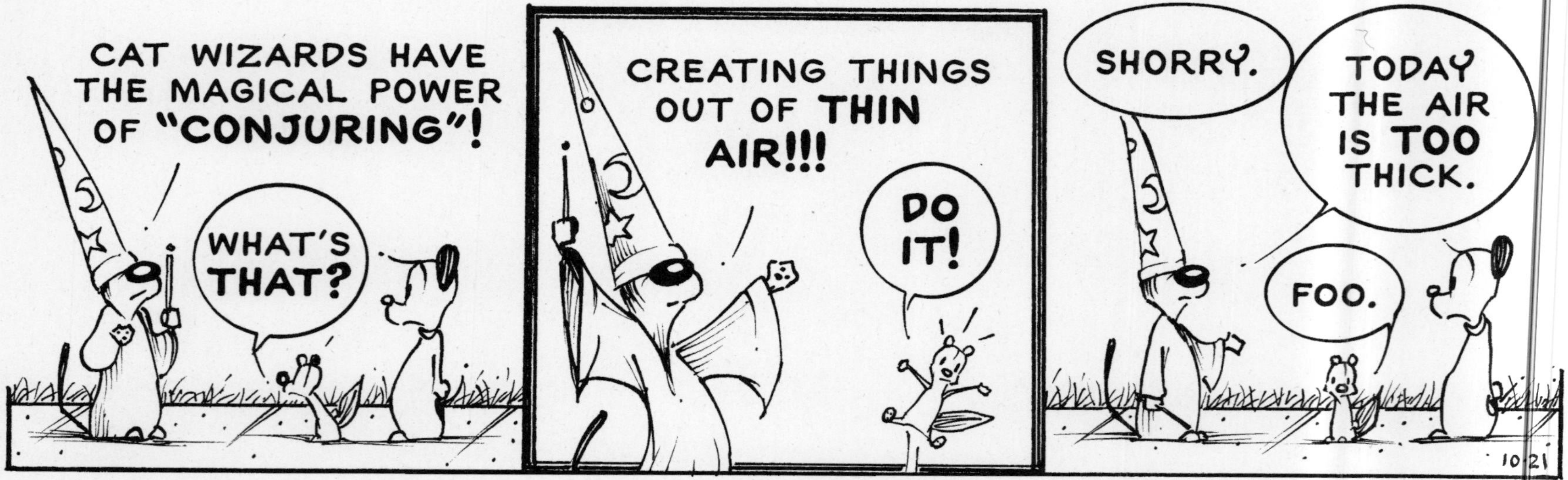
CAT WIZARDS HAVE THE MAGICAL POWER OF "CONJURING"!
WHAT'S THAT?
CREATING THINGS OUT OF THIN AIR!!!
DO IT!
SHORRY.
TODAY THE AIR IS TOO THICK.
FOO.
10·21

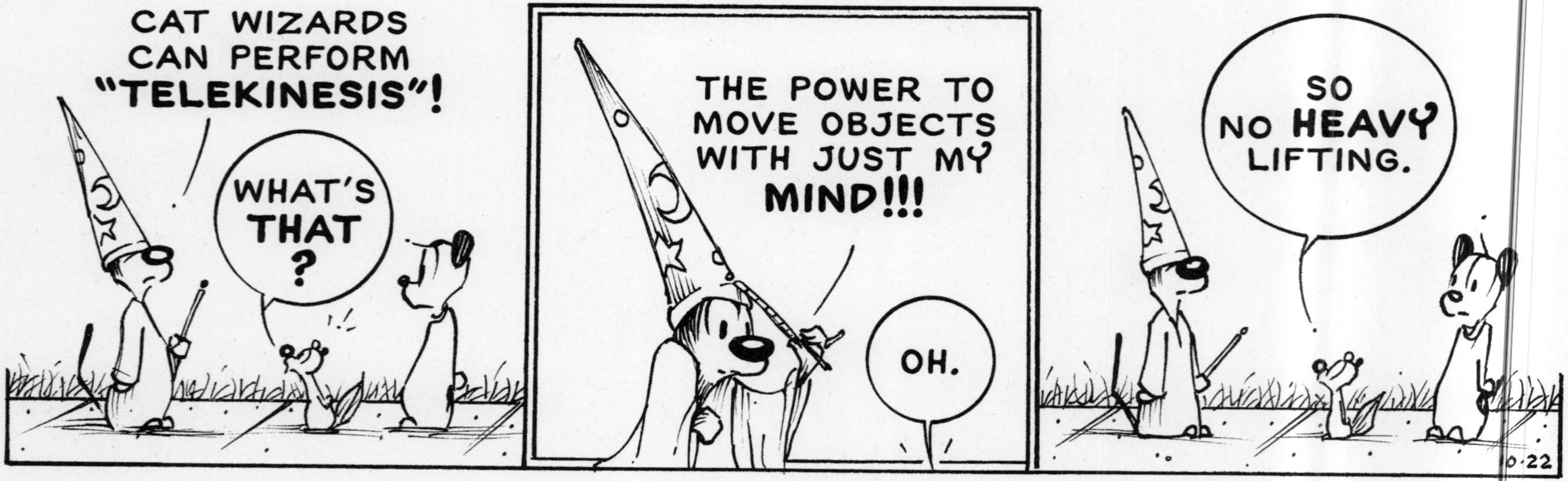
CAT WIZARDS CAN PERFORM "TELEKINESIS"!
WHAT'S THAT ?
THE POWER TO MOVE OBJECTS WITH JUST MY MIND!!!
OH.
SO NO HEAVY LIFTING.
10·22

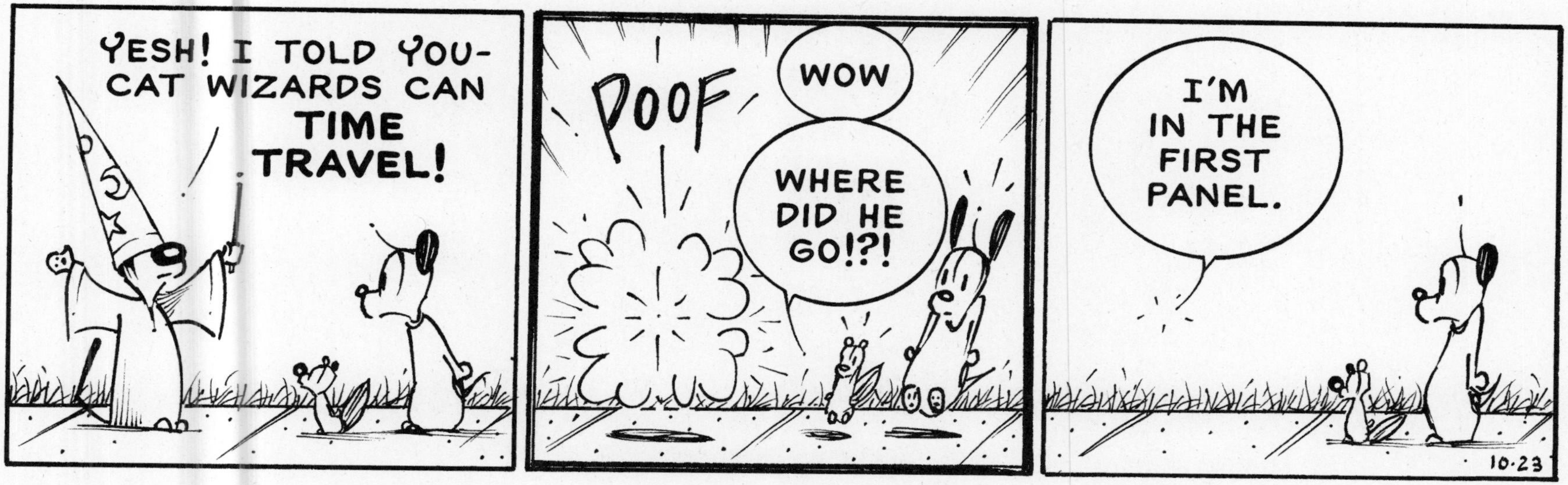
YESH! I TOLD YOU-
CAT WIZARDS CAN TIME TRAVEL!
POOF
WOW
WHERE DID HE GO!?!
I'M IN THE FIRST PANEL.
10·23

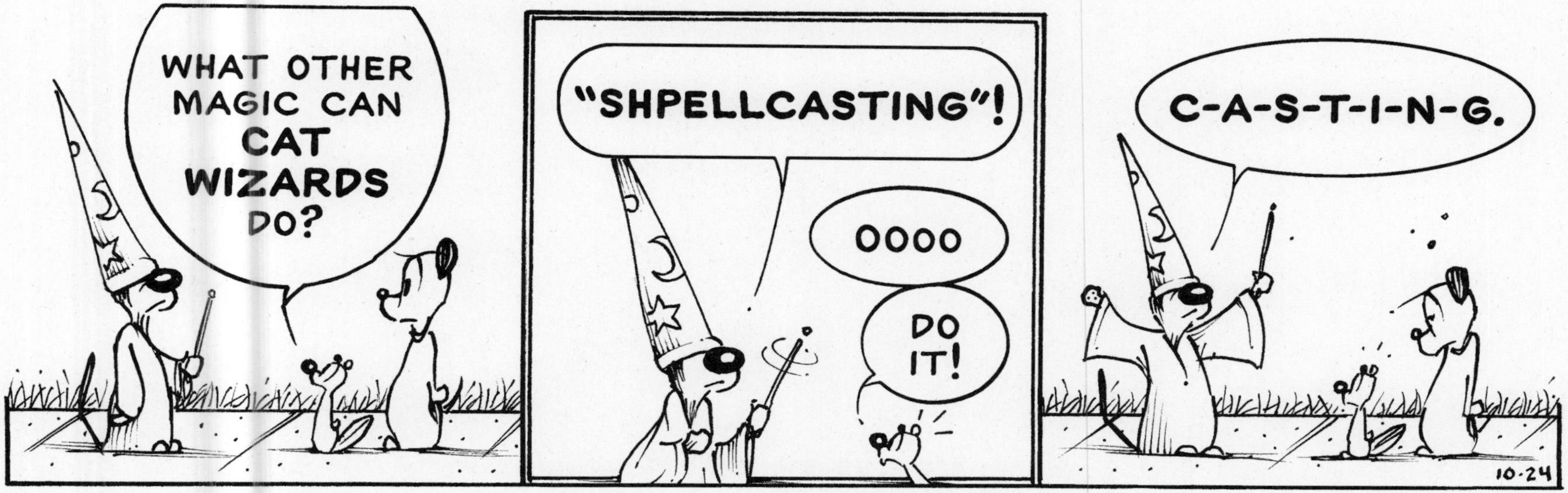
WHAT OTHER MAGIC CAN CAT WIZARDS DO?
"SHPELLCASTING"!
OOOO
DO IT!
C-A-S-T-I-N-G.
10·24

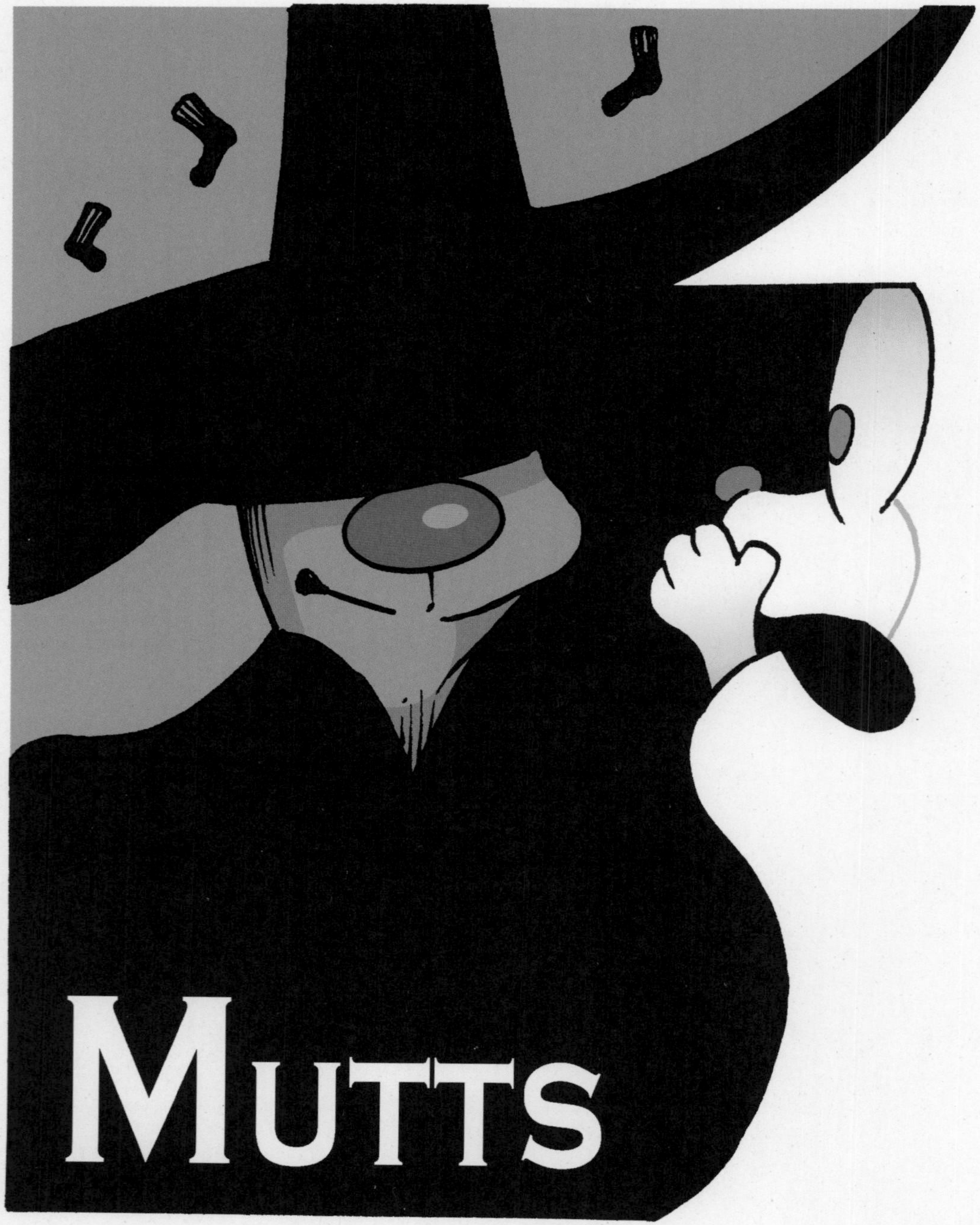
MUTTS

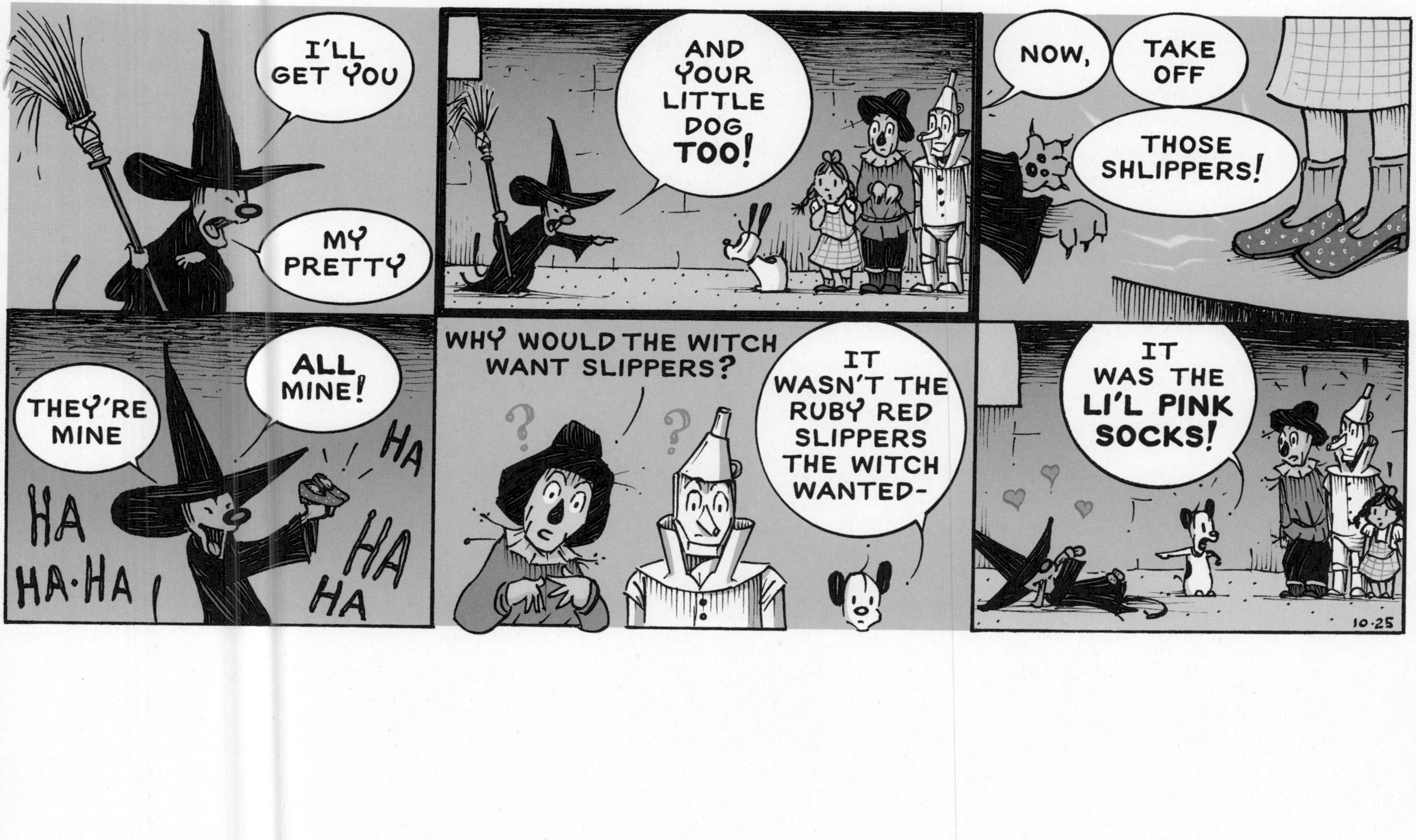
I'LL GET YOU
MY PRETTY
AND YOUR LITTLE DOG TOO!
NOW,
TAKE OFF
THOSE SHLIPPERS!
THEY'RE MINE
ALL MINE!
HA HA HA HA·HA HA HA HA
WHY WOULD THE WITCH WANT SLIPPERS?
IT WASN'T THE RUBY RED SLIPPERS THE WITCH WANTED-
IT WAS THE LI'L PINK SOCKS!
10·25

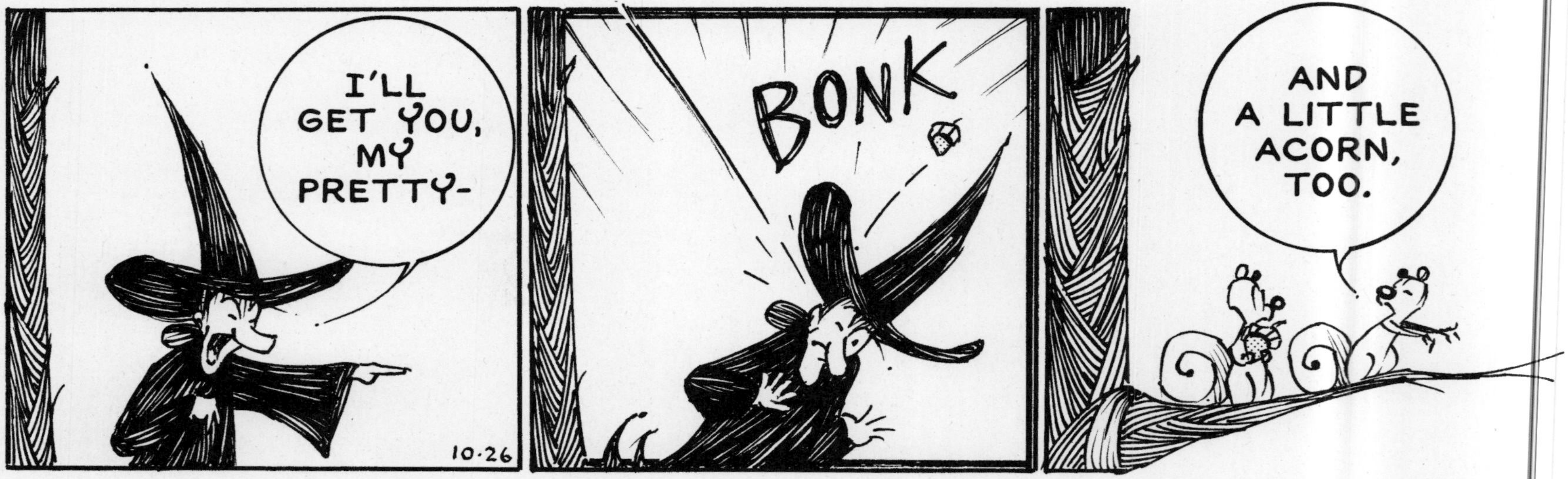
I'LL GET YOU, MY PRETTY-
10·26
BONK
AND A LITTLE ACORN, TOO.

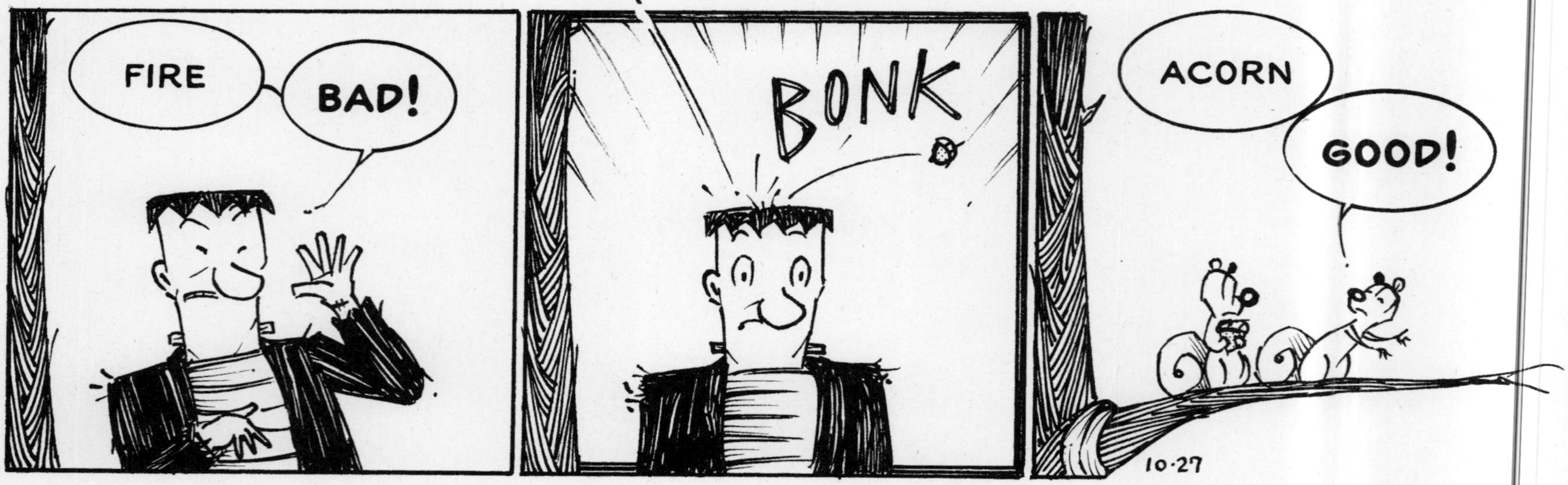
FIRE
BAD!
BONK
ACORN
GOOD!
10·27

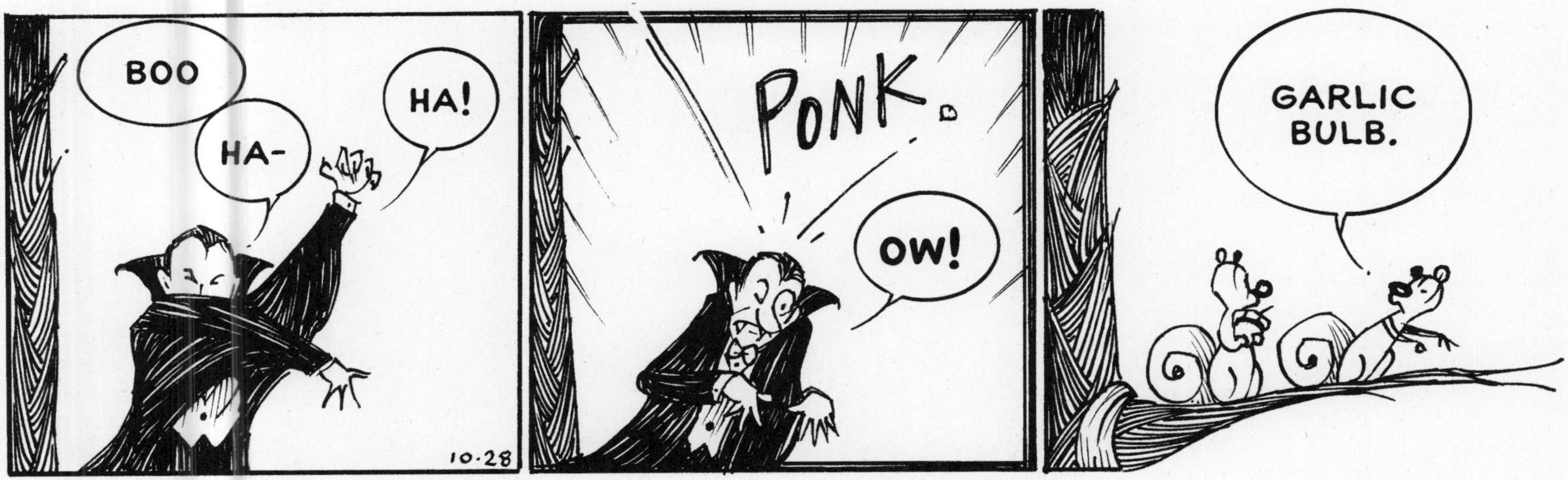
BOO
HA-
HA!
10·28
PONK
OW!
GARLIC BULB.

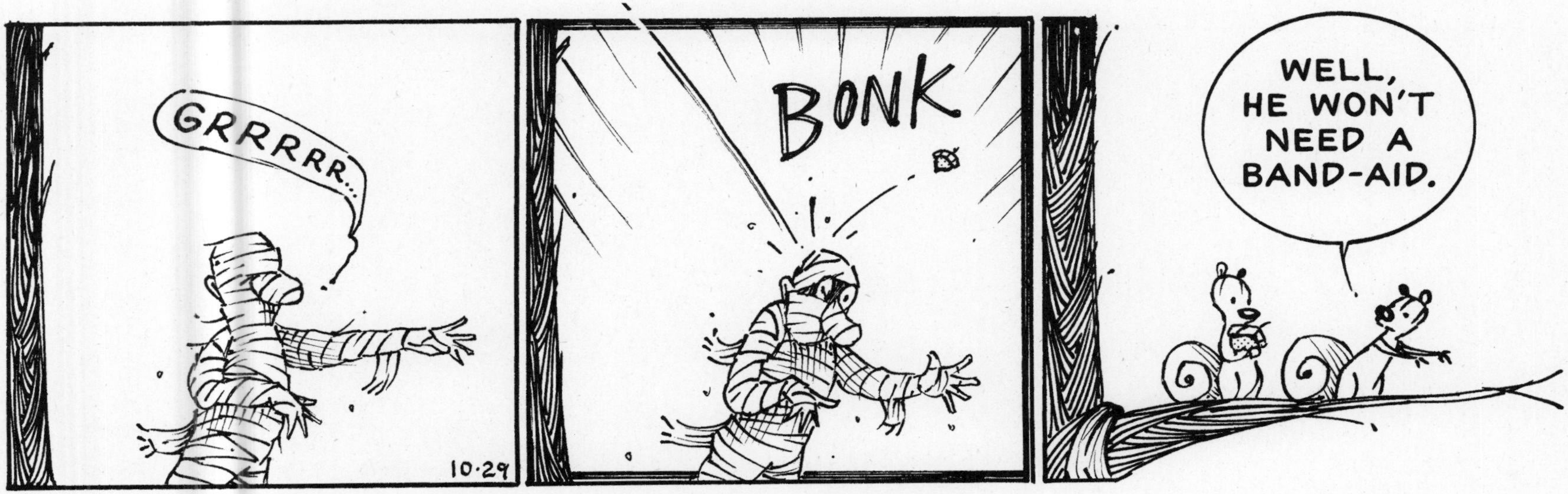
GRRRRRR...
10·29
BONK
WELL, HE WON'T NEED A BAND-AID.

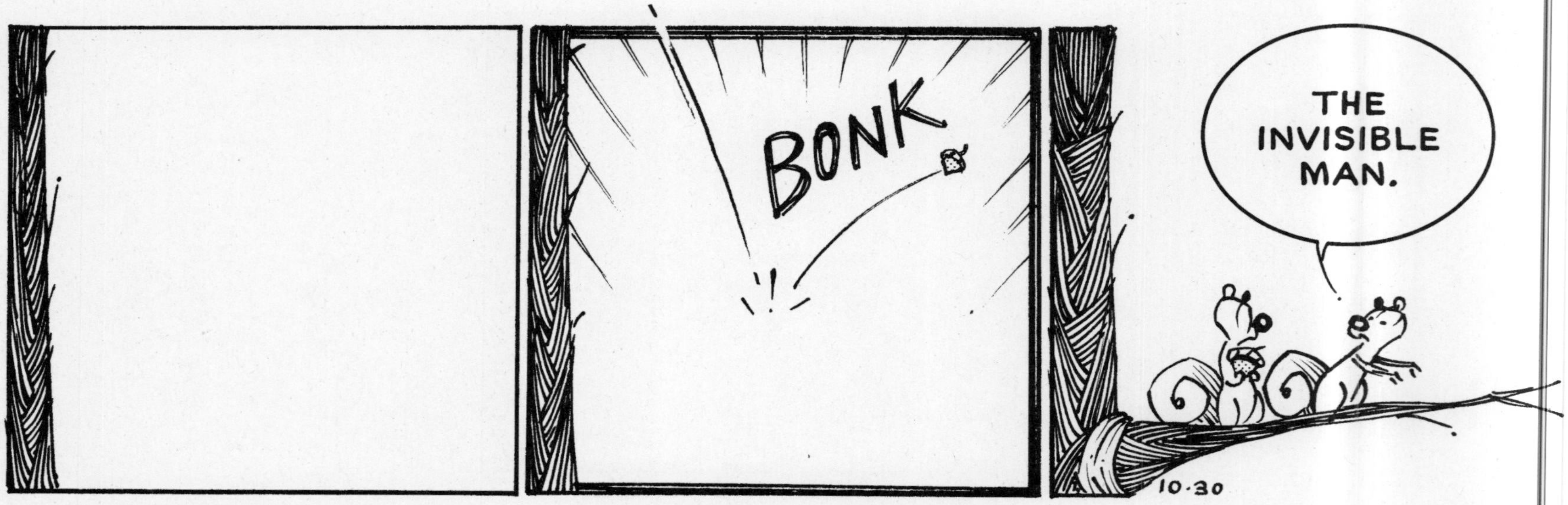
BONK
THE INVISIBLE MAN.
10·30

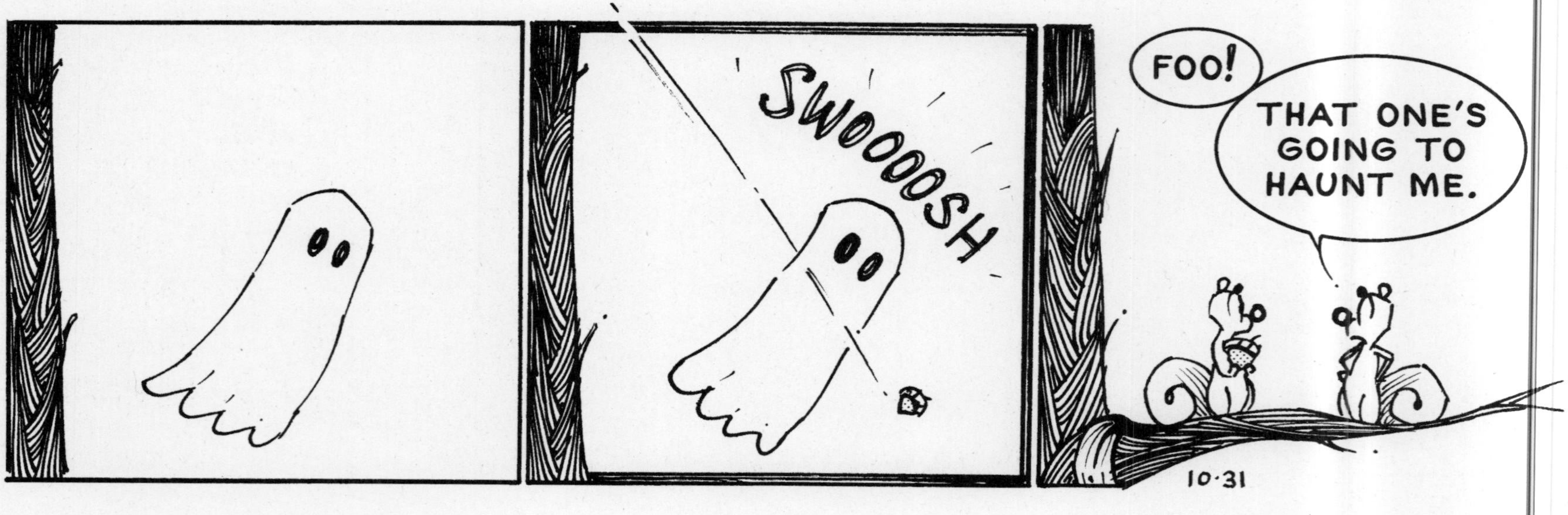
SWOOOOOSH
FOO!
THAT ONE'S GOING TO HAUNT ME.
10·31

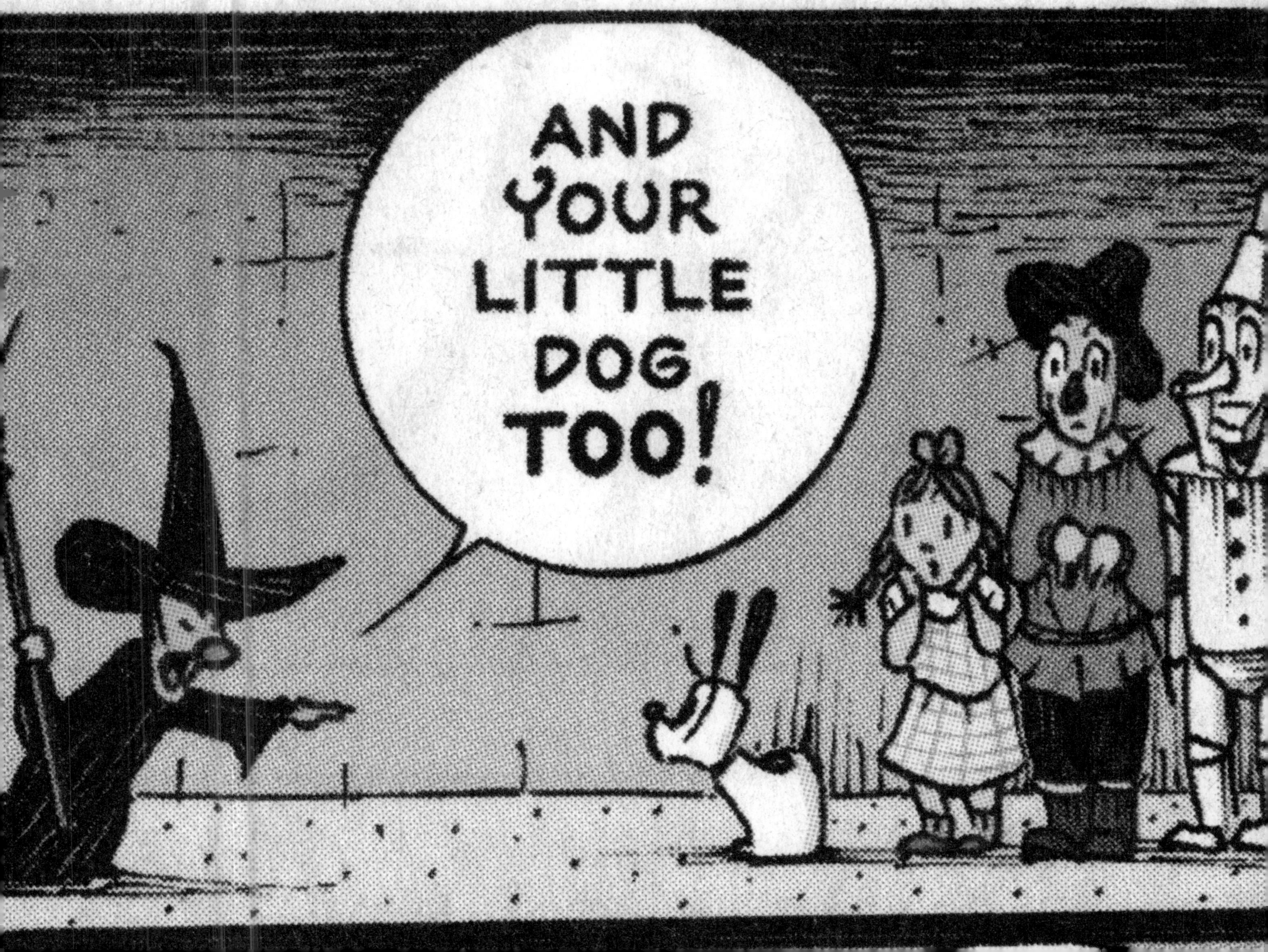
AND YOUR LITTLE DOG TOO!

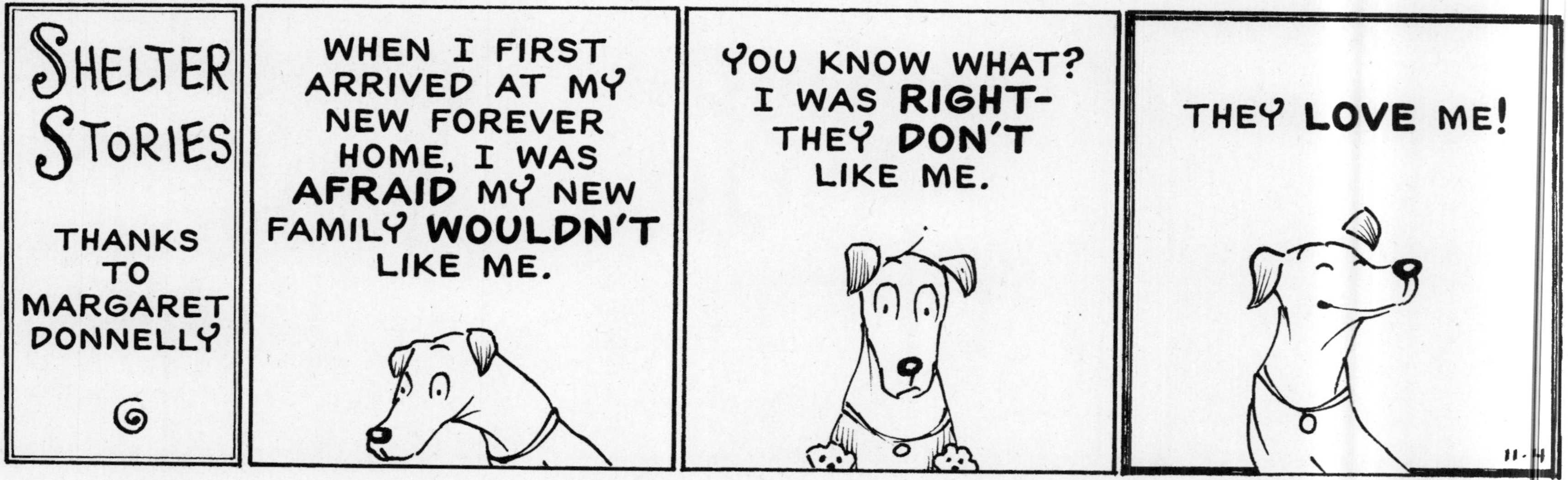
SHELTER STORIES
THANKS TO MARGARET DONNELLY
WHEN I FIRST ARRIVED AT MY NEW FOREVER HOME, I WAS AFRAID MY NEW FAMILY WOULDN'T LIKE ME.
YOU KNOW WHAT? I WAS RIGHT- THEY DON'T LIKE ME.
THEY LOVE ME!
11-4

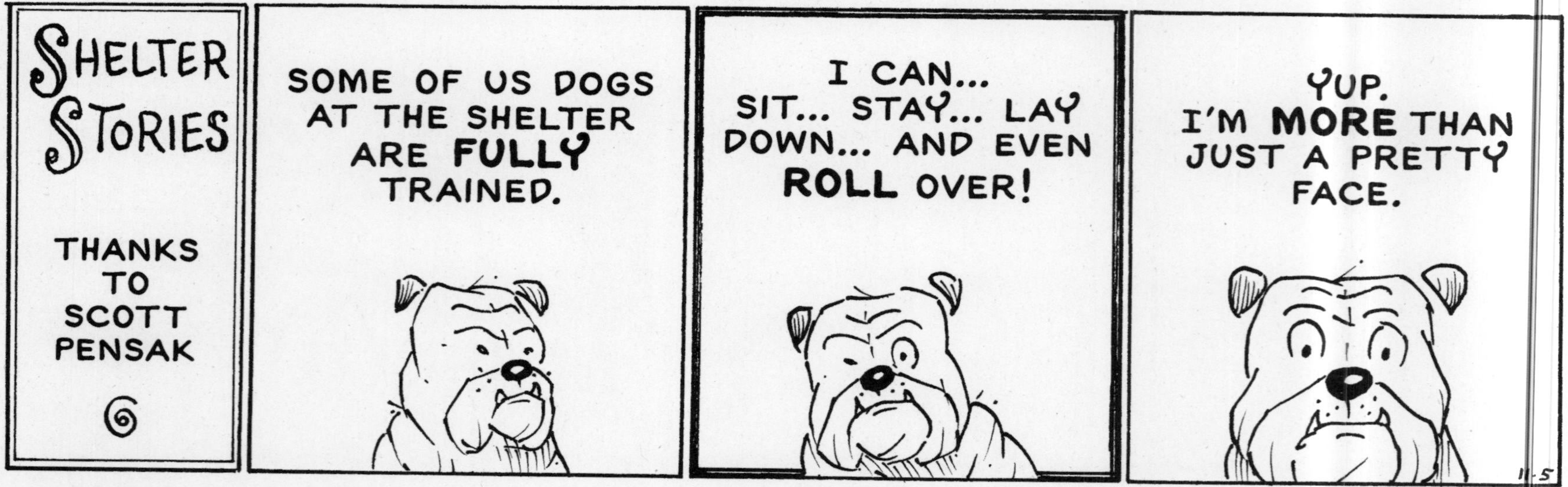
SHELTER STORIES
THANKS TO SCOTT PENSAK
SOME OF US DOGS AT THE SHELTER ARE FULLY TRAINED.
I CAN... SIT... STAY... LAY DOWN... AND EVEN ROLL OVER!
YUP. I'M MORE THAN JUST A PRETTY FACE.
11-5

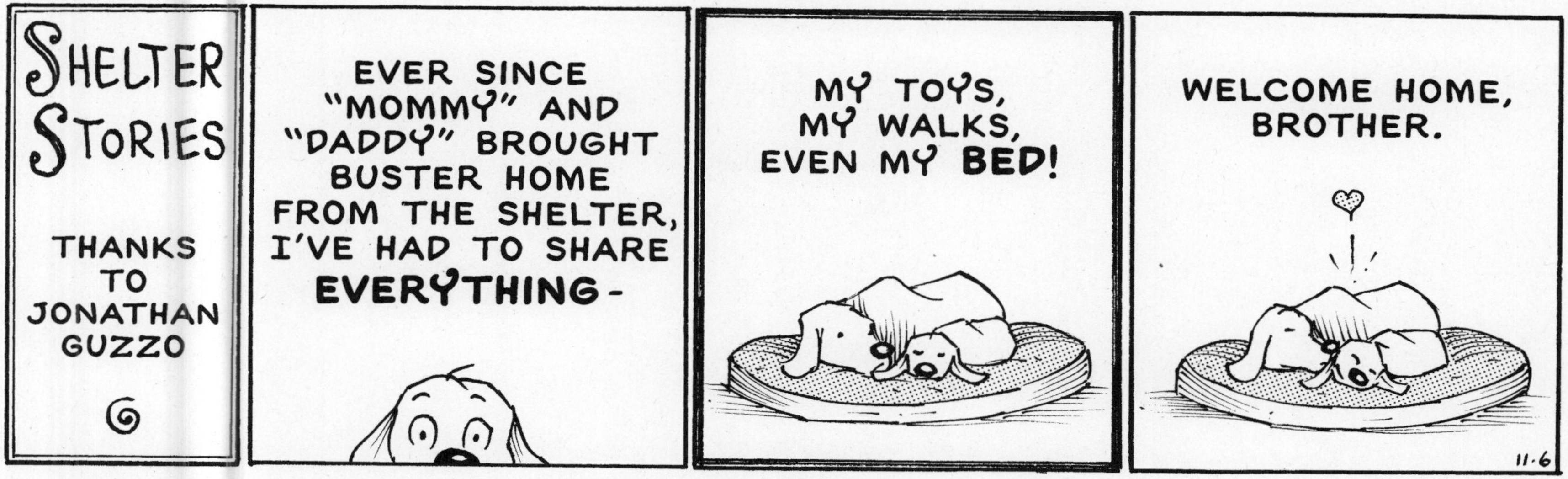
SHELTER STORIES
THANKS TO JONATHAN GUZZO
EVER SINCE "MOMMY" AND "DADDY" BROUGHT BUSTER HOME FROM THE SHELTER, I'VE HAD TO SHARE EVERYTHING-
MY TOYS, MY WALKS, EVEN MY BED!
WELCOME HOME, BROTHER.
11·6

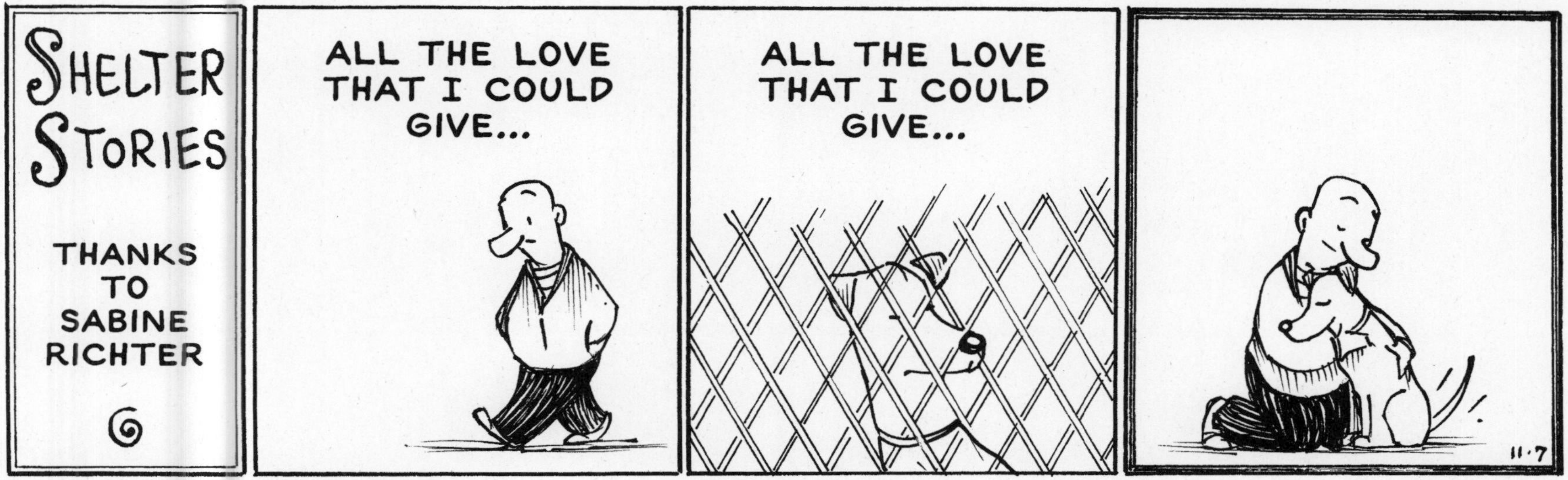
SHELTER STORIES
THANKS TO SABINE RICHTER
ALL THE LOVE THAT I COULD GIVE...
ALL THE LOVE THAT I COULD GIVE...
11·7

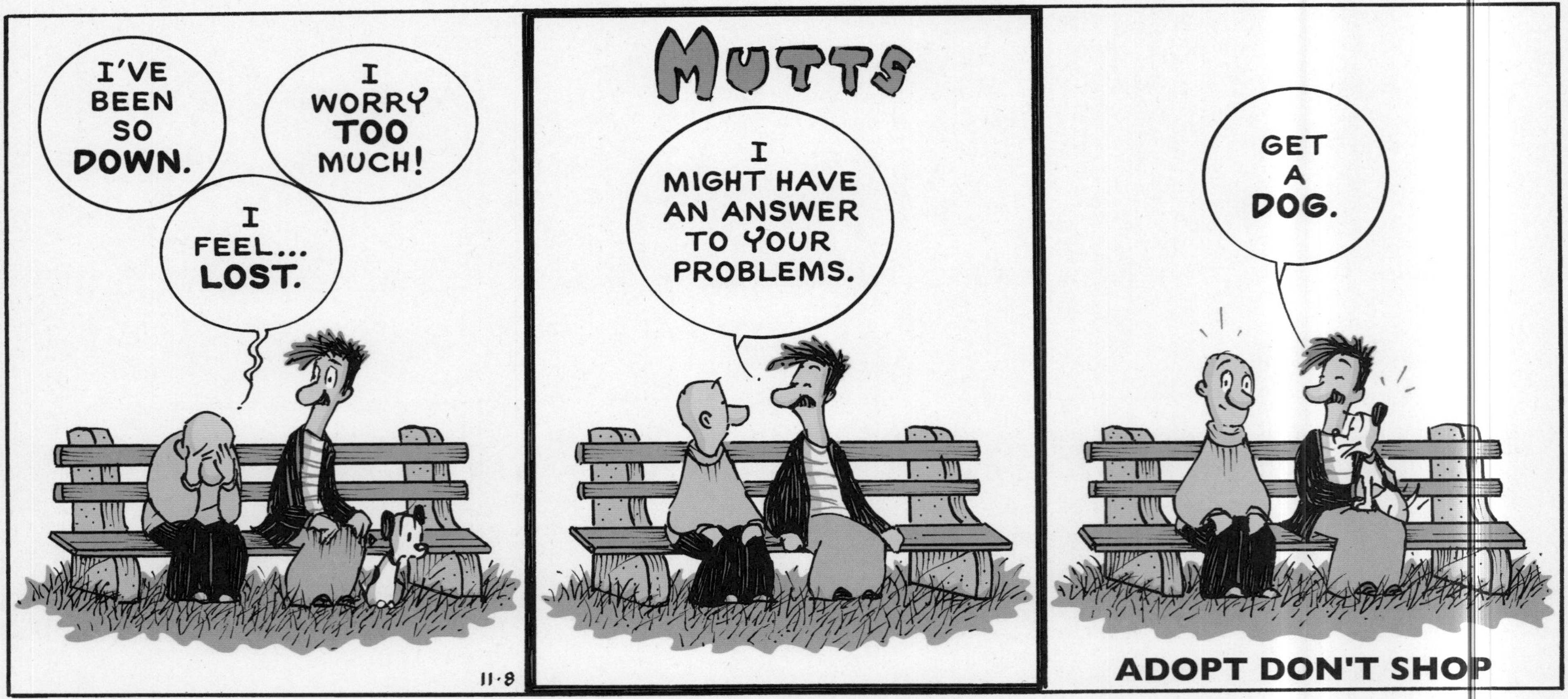
I'VE BEEN SO DOWN.
I WORRY TOO MUCH!
I FEEL... LOST.
11·8
MUTTS
I MIGHT HAVE AN ANSWER TO YOUR PROBLEMS.
GET A DOG.
ADOPT DON'T SHOP

MUTTS

Patrick McDonnell

WHAT'CHA
DOING,
EARL?
OH,
JUST ENJOYING THE FALL.
11/15

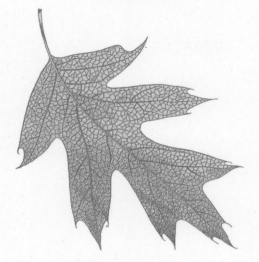

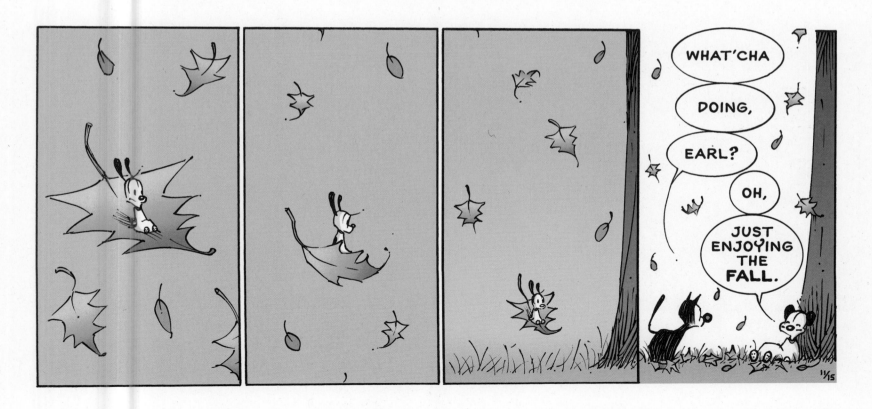

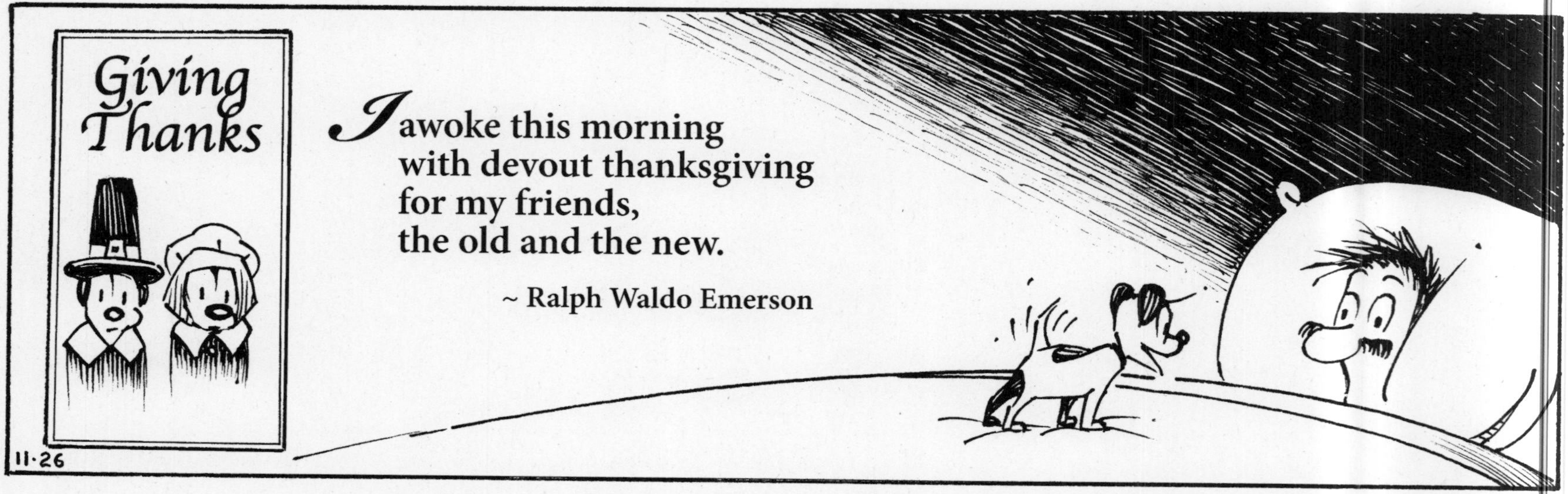
Giving Thanks
I awoke this morning with devout thanksgiving for my friends, the old and the new.
~ Ralph Waldo Emerson
11·26

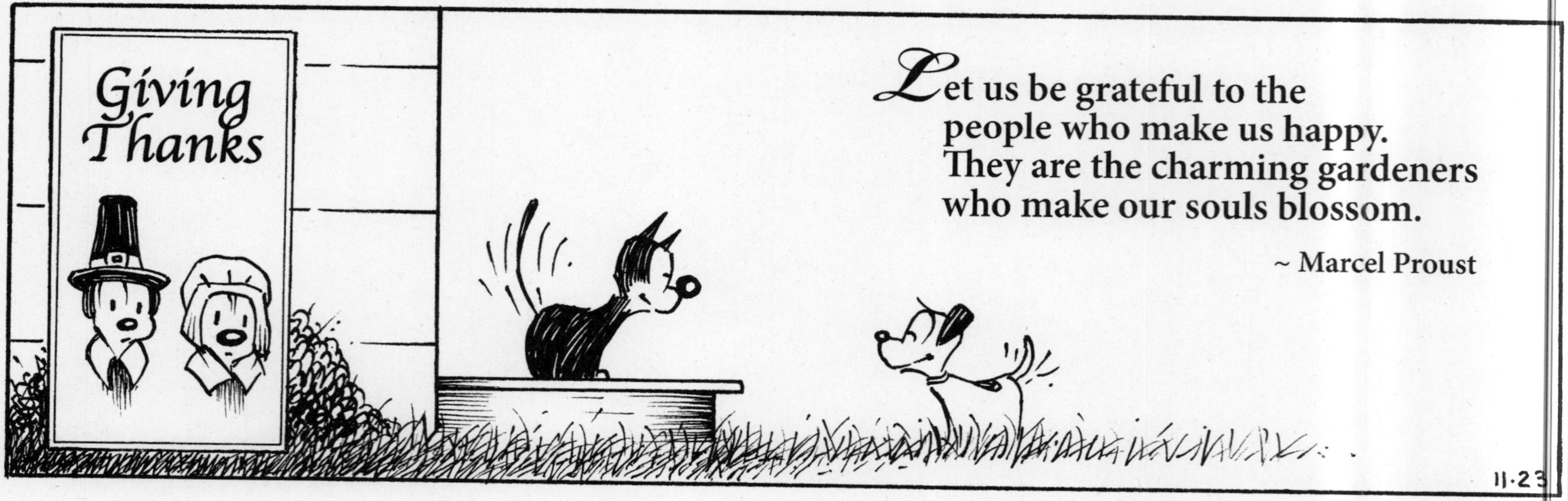
Giving Thanks
Let us be grateful to the people who make us happy. They are the charming gardeners who make our souls blossom.
~ Marcel Proust
11·23

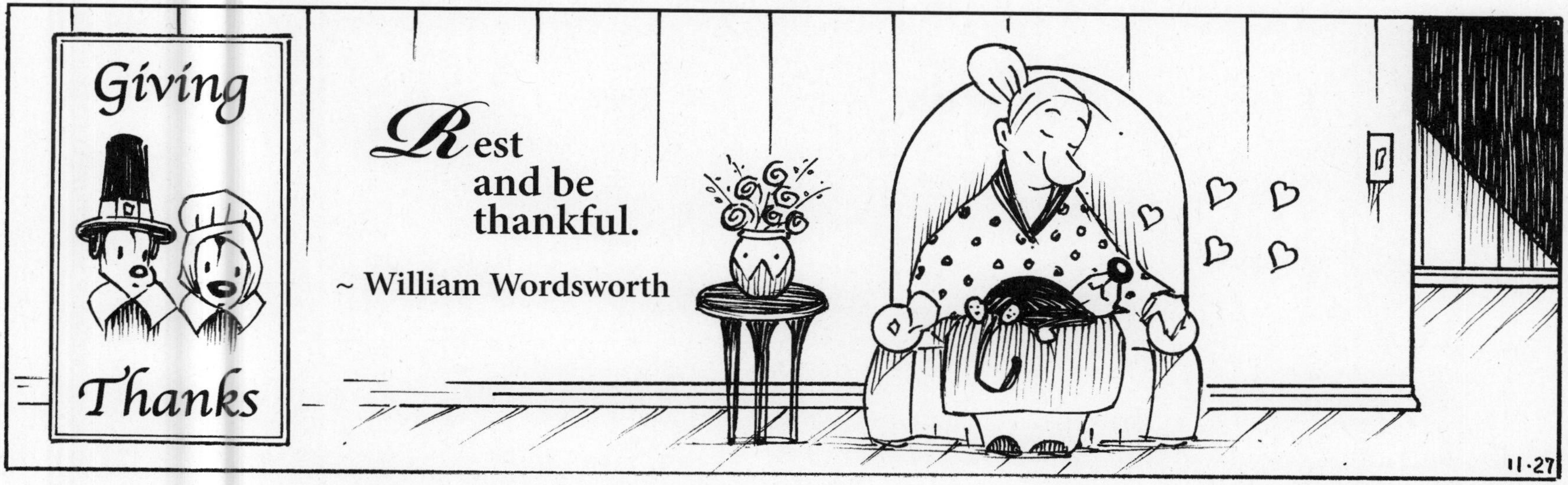
Giving
Thanks
Rest and be thankful.
~ William Wordsworth
11·27

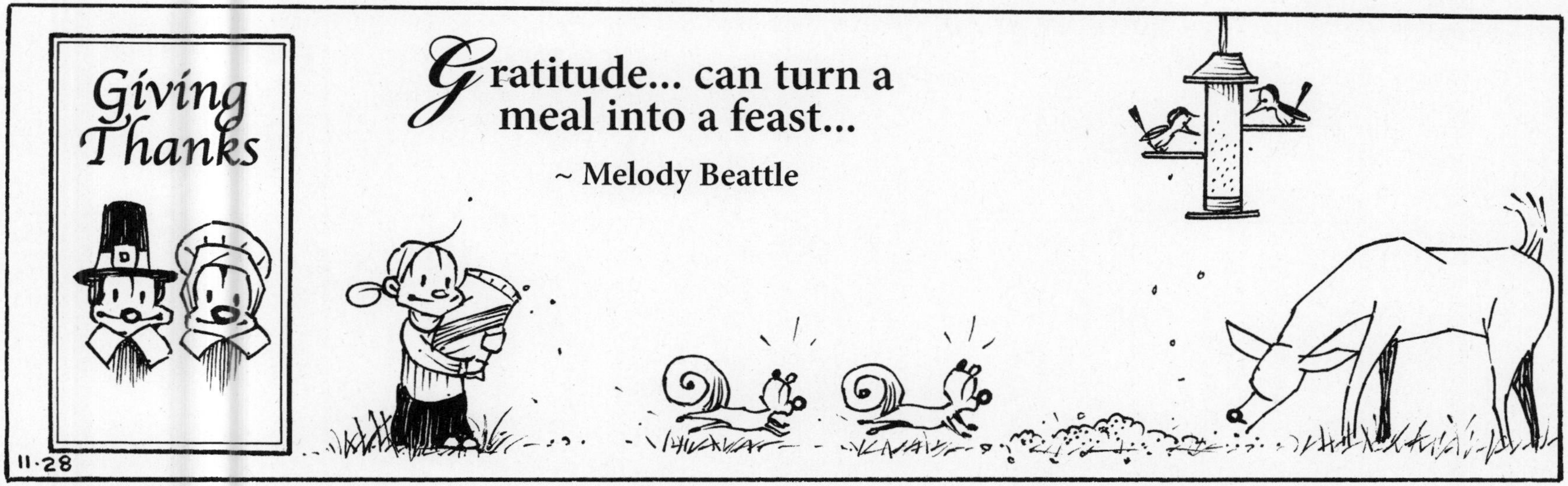
Giving Thanks
Gratitude... can turn a meal into a feast...
~ Melody Beattle
11·28

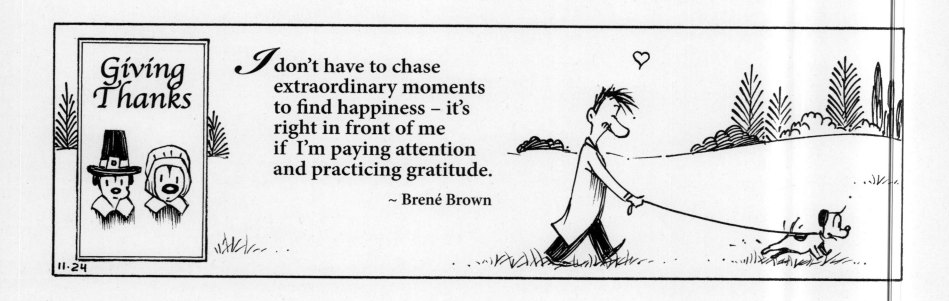

Giving Thanks

11·24

I don't have to chase extraordinary moments to find happiness – it's right in front of me if I'm paying attention and practicing gratitude.

~ Brené Brown

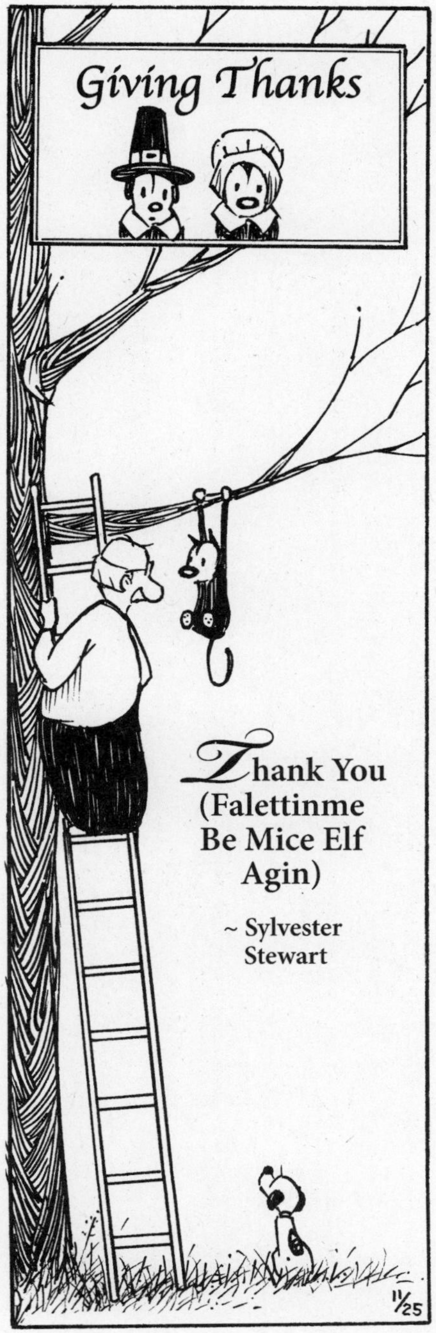
Giving Thanks
Thank You
(Falettinme
Be Mice Elf
Agin)
~ Sylvester
Stewart
11/25

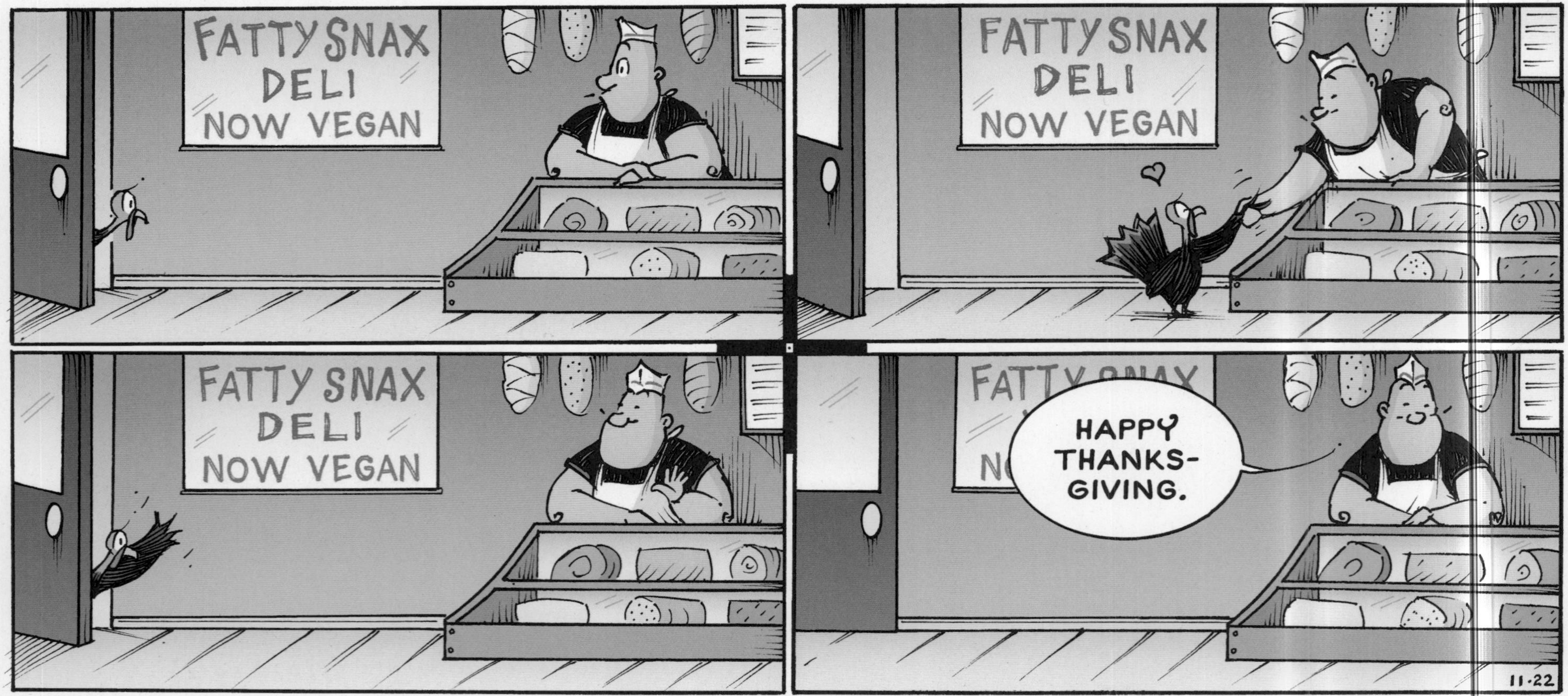
FATTY SNAX DELI NOW VEGAN
FATTY SNAX DELI NOW VEGAN
FATTY SNAX DELI NOW VEGAN
HAPPY THANKSGIVING.
11-22

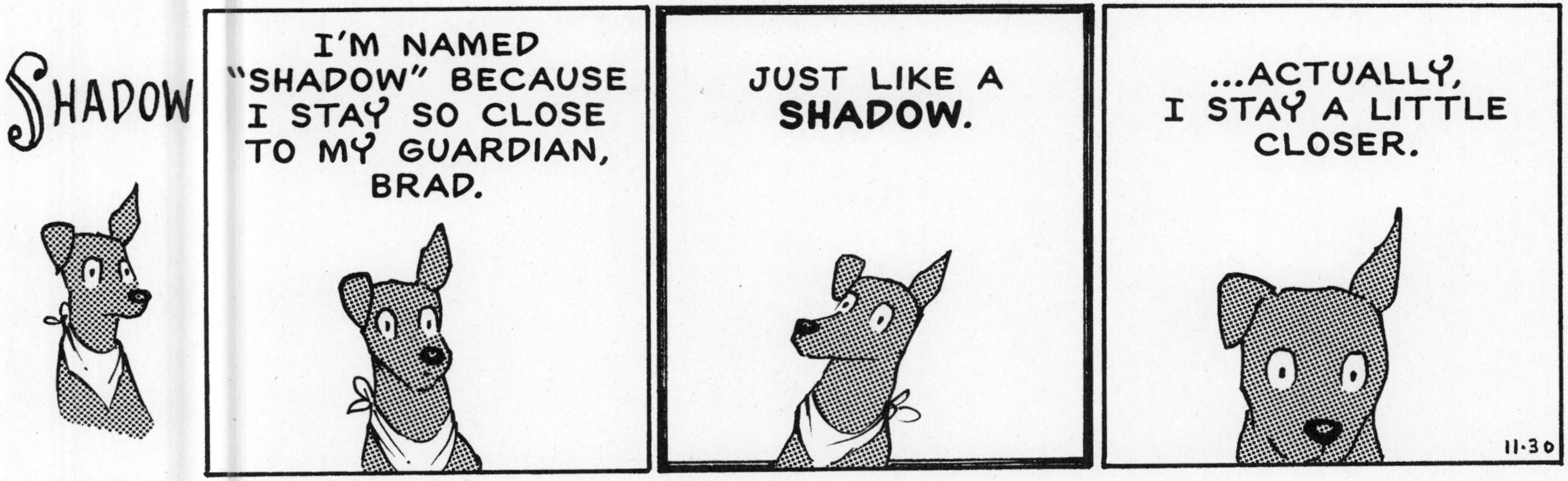
SHADOW
I'M NAMED "SHADOW" BECAUSE I STAY SO CLOSE TO MY GUARDIAN, BRAD.
JUST LIKE A **SHADOW.**
...ACTUALLY, I STAY A LITTLE CLOSER.
11·30

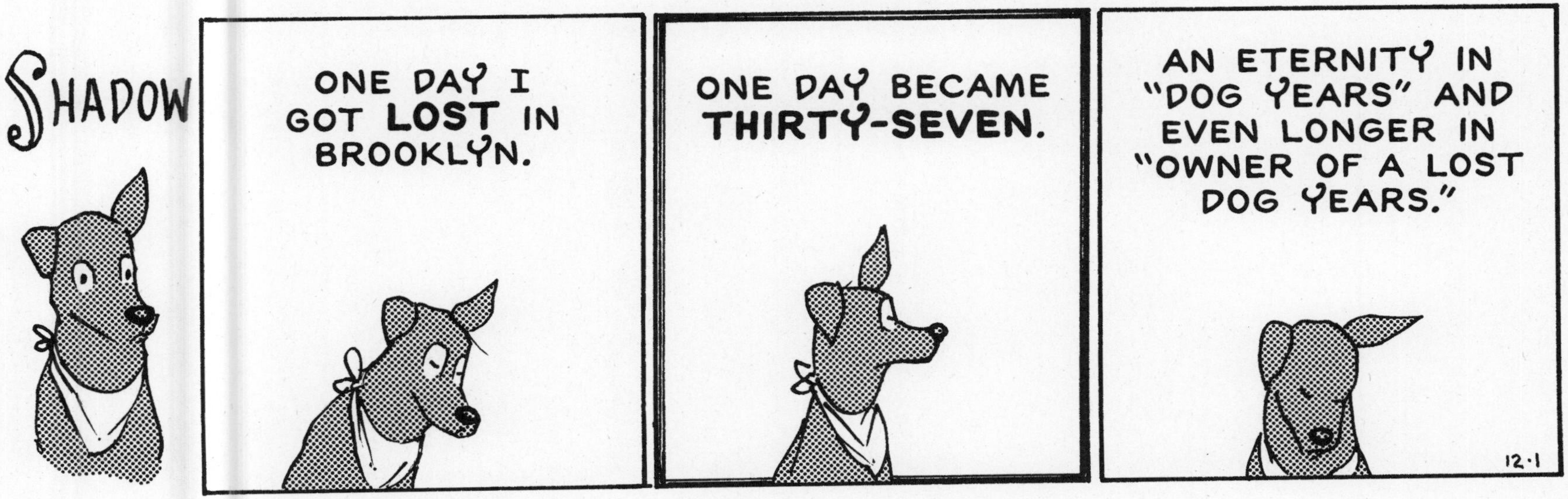
SHADOW
ONE DAY I GOT **LOST** IN BROOKLYN.
ONE DAY BECAME **THIRTY-SEVEN.**
AN ETERNITY IN "DOG YEARS" AND EVEN LONGER IN "OWNER OF A LOST DOG YEARS."
12·1

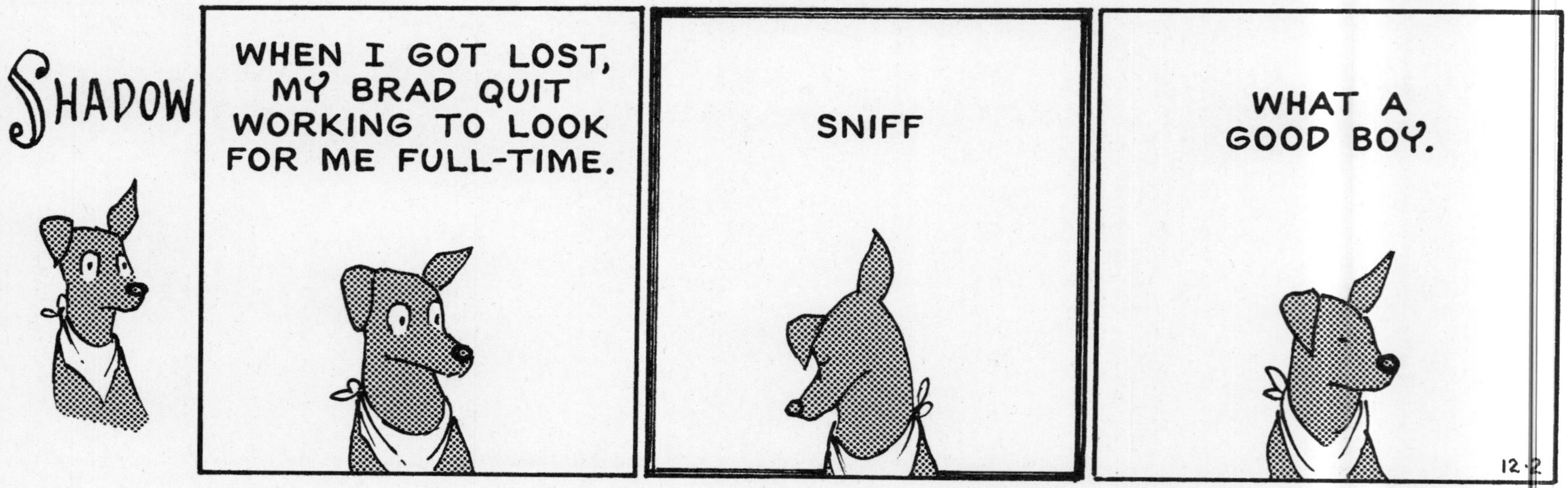
SHADOW
WHEN I GOT LOST, MY BRAD QUIT WORKING TO LOOK FOR ME FULL-TIME.
SNIFF
WHAT A GOOD BOY.
12·2

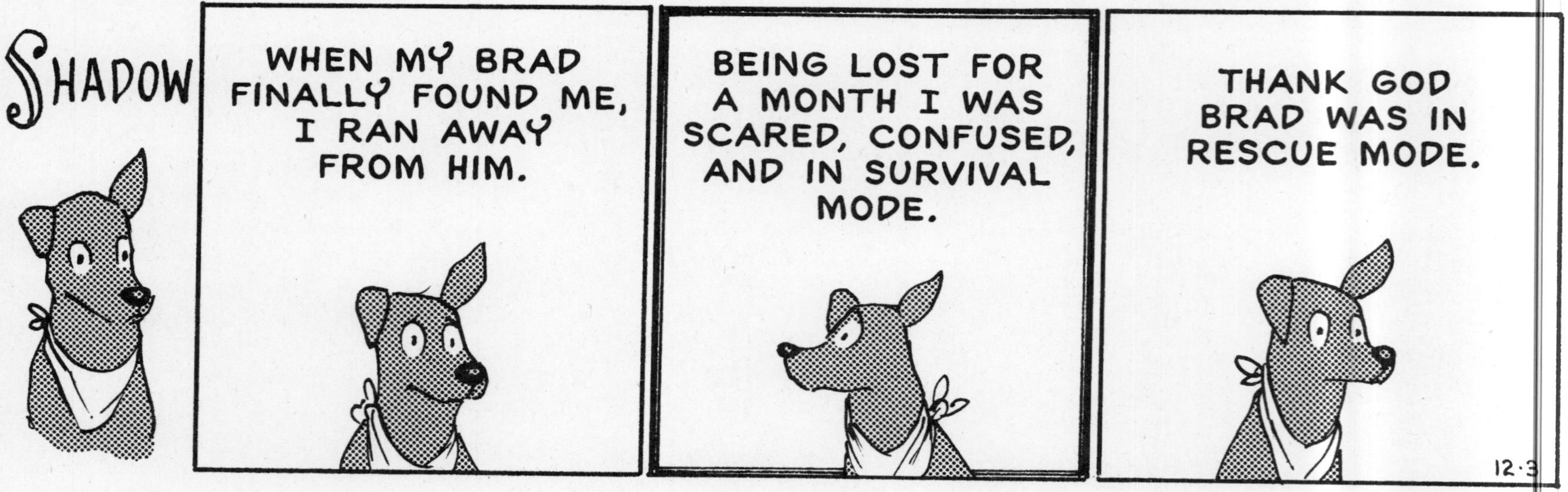
SHADOW
WHEN MY BRAD FINALLY FOUND ME, I RAN AWAY FROM HIM.
BEING LOST FOR A MONTH I WAS SCARED, CONFUSED, AND IN SURVIVAL MODE.
THANK GOD BRAD WAS IN RESCUE MODE.
12·3

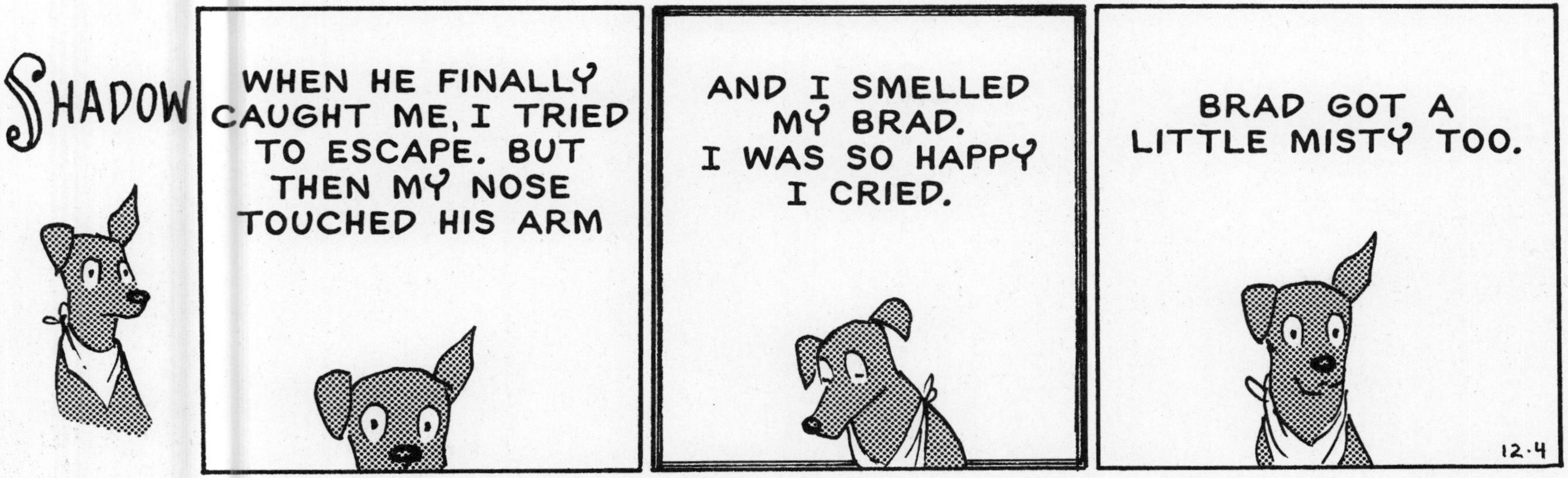
SHADOW
WHEN HE FINALLY CAUGHT ME, I TRIED TO ESCAPE. BUT THEN MY NOSE TOUCHED HIS ARM
AND I SMELLED MY BRAD. I WAS SO HAPPY I CRIED.
BRAD GOT A LITTLE MISTY TOO.
12·4

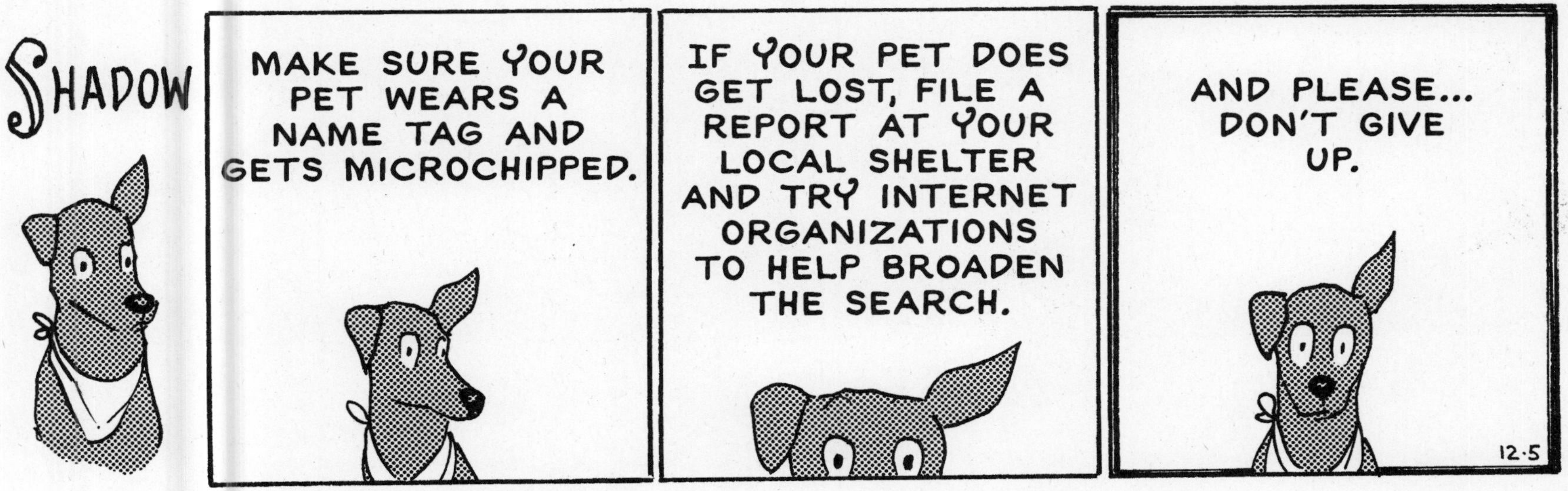
SHADOW
MAKE SURE YOUR PET WEARS A NAME TAG AND GETS MICROCHIPPED.
IF YOUR PET DOES GET LOST, FILE A REPORT AT YOUR LOCAL SHELTER AND TRY INTERNET ORGANIZATIONS TO HELP BROADEN THE SEARCH.
AND PLEASE... DON'T GIVE UP.
12·5

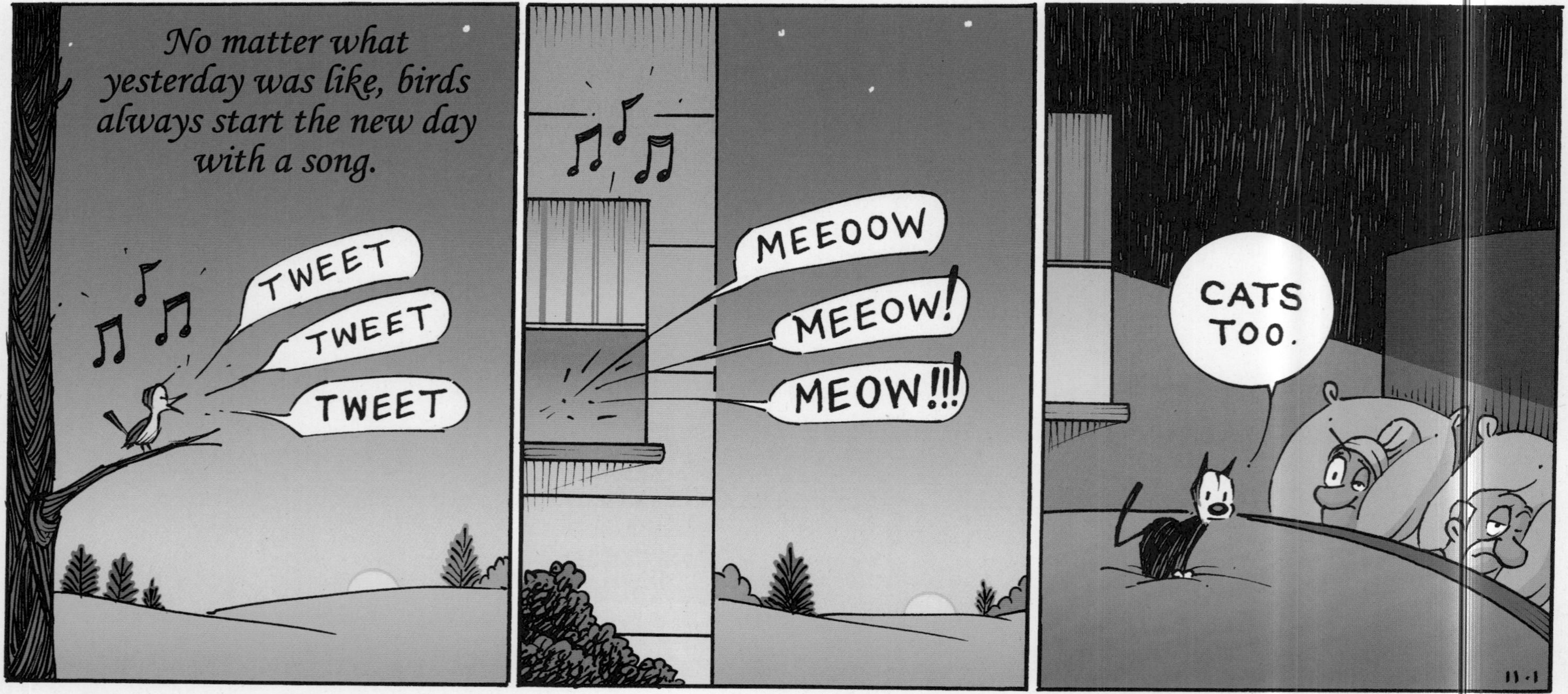
No matter what yesterday was like, birds always start the new day with a song.
TWEET
TWEET
TWEET
MEEOOW
MEEOW!
MEOW!!!
CATS TOO.
11-1

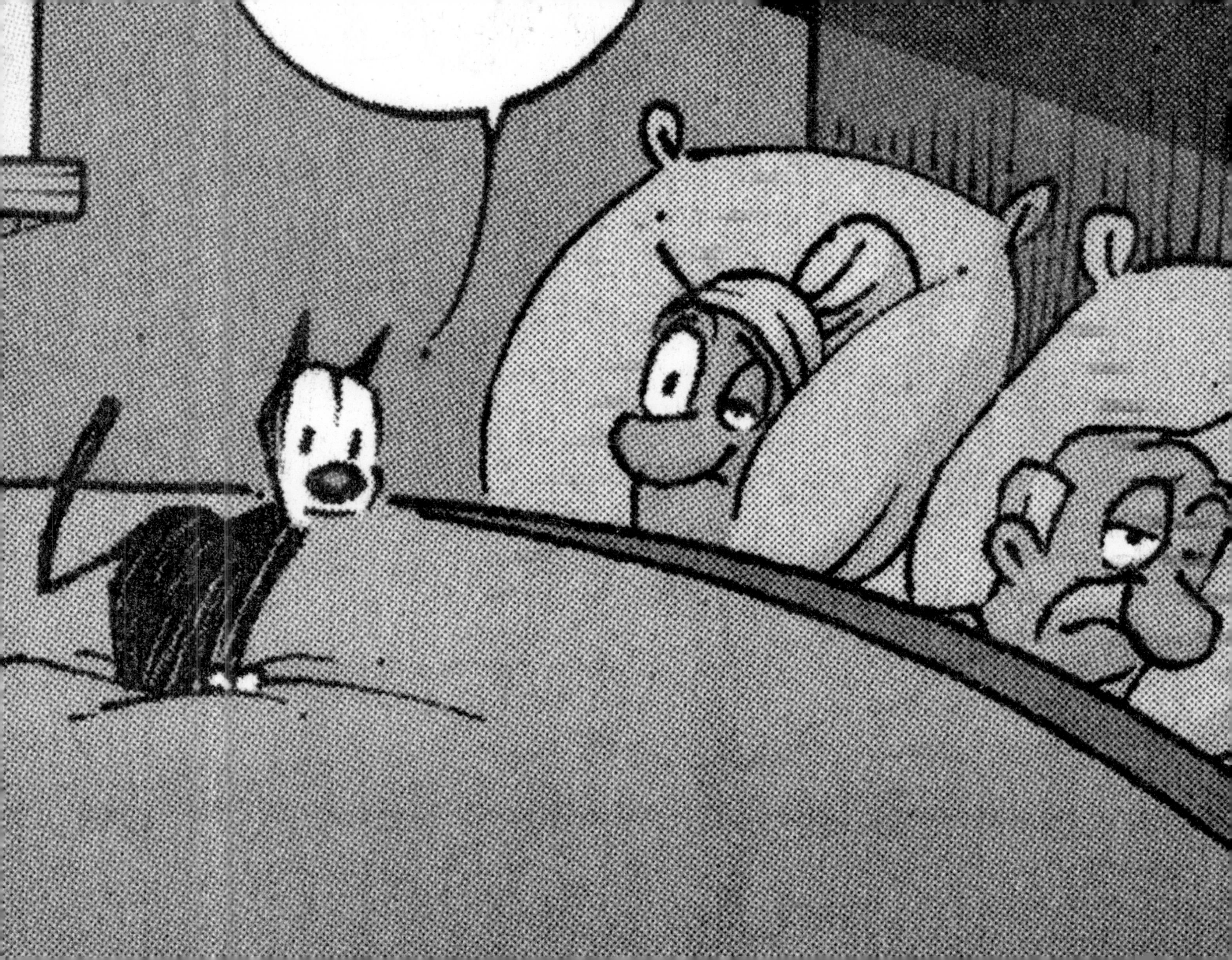

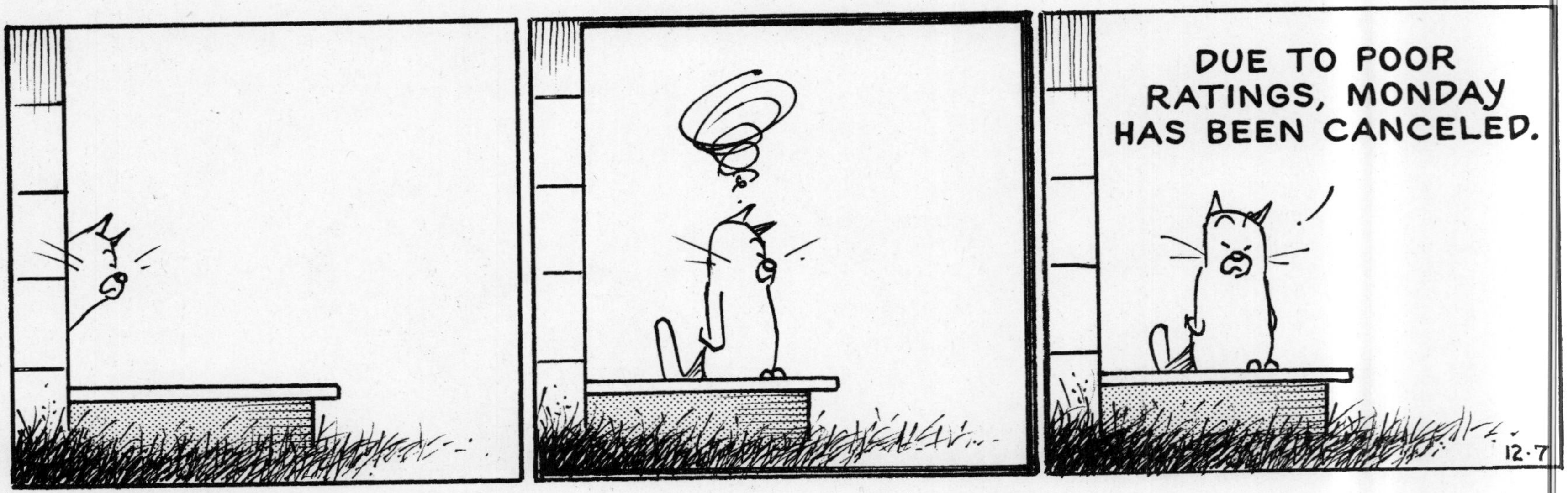

DUE TO POOR RATINGS, MONDAY HAS BEEN CANCELED.
12·7

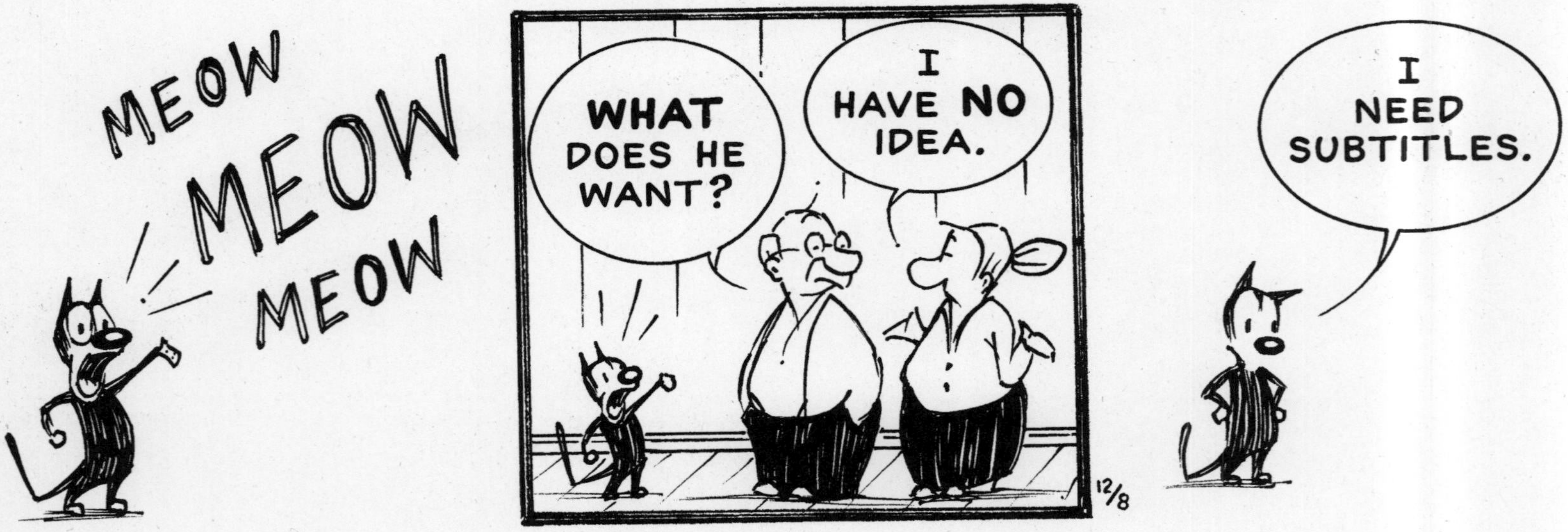

MEOW
MEOW
MEOW
WHAT DOES HE WANT?
I HAVE NO IDEA.
I NEED SUBTITLES.
12/8

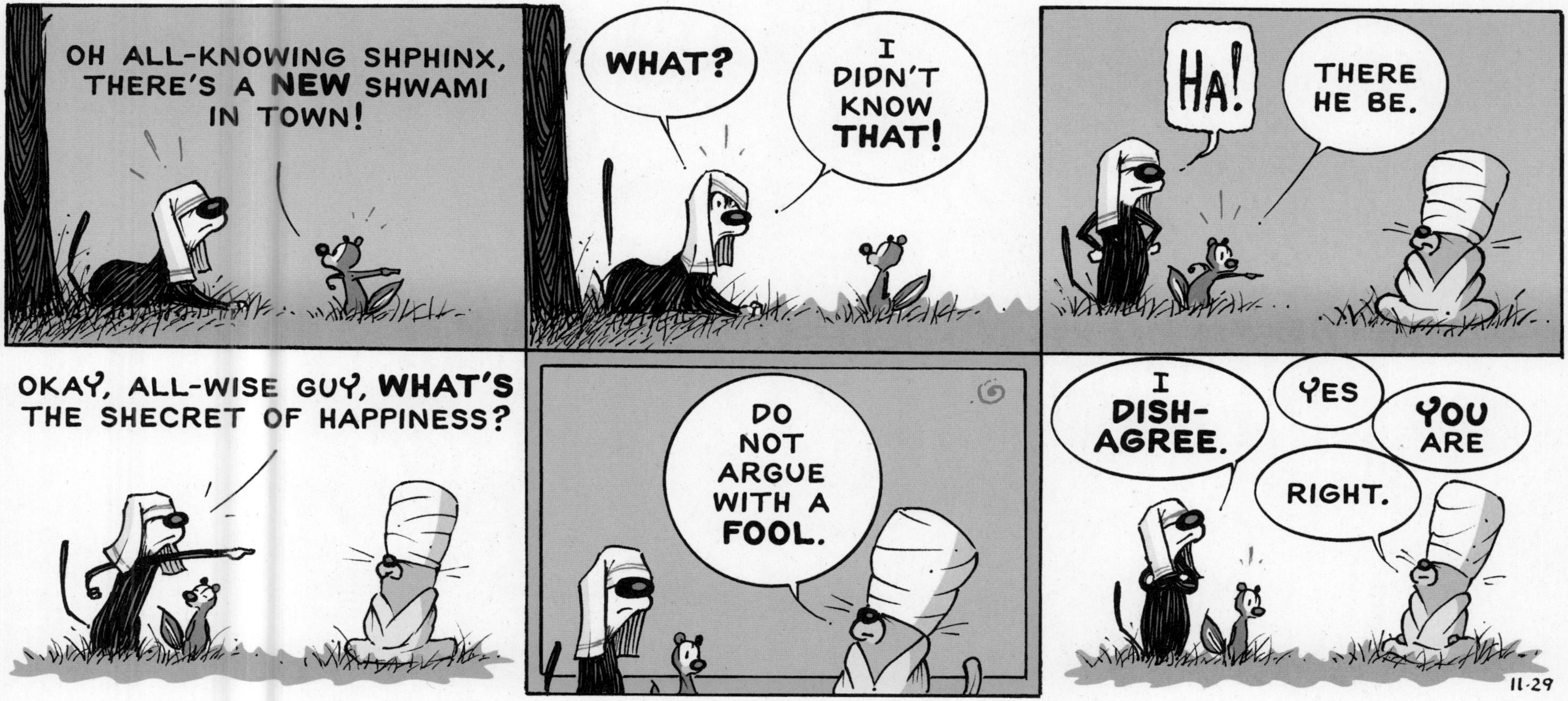
OH ALL-KNOWING SHPHINX, THERE'S A NEW SHWAMI IN TOWN!
WHAT?
I DIDN'T KNOW THAT!
HA!
THERE HE BE.
OKAY, ALL-WISE GUY, WHAT'S THE SHECRET OF HAPPINESS?
DO NOT ARGUE WITH A FOOL.
I DISH-AGREE.
YES
YOU ARE
RIGHT.
11-29

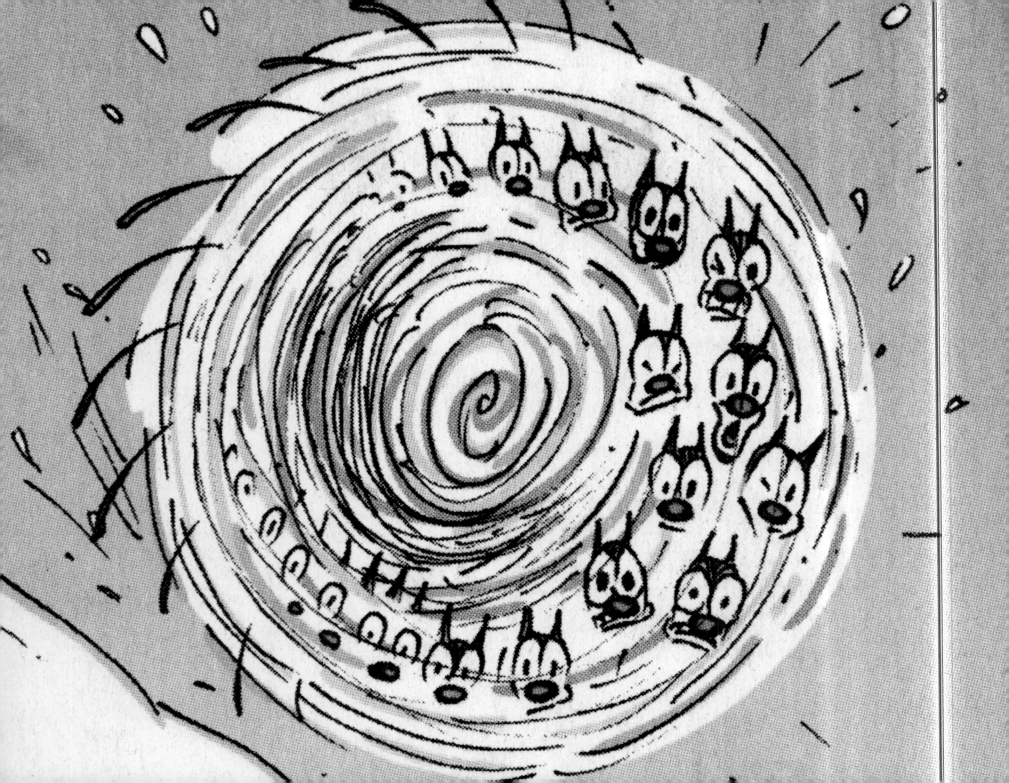

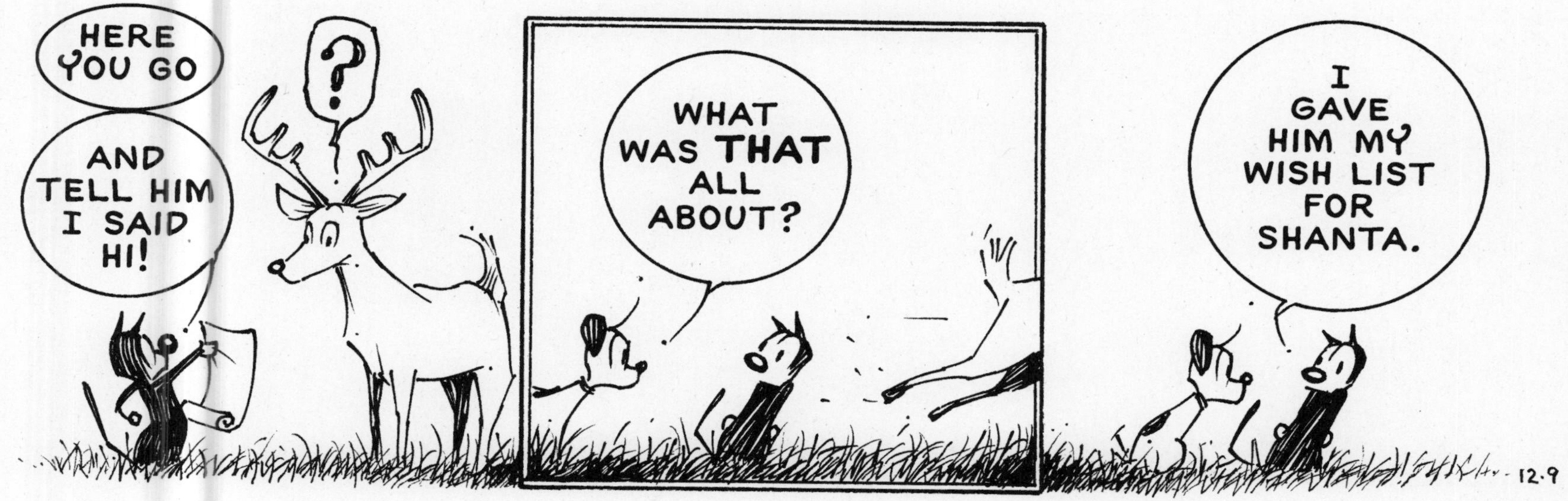
HERE YOU GO
AND TELL HIM I SAID HI!
?
WHAT WAS THAT ALL ABOUT?
I GAVE HIM MY WISH LIST FOR SHANTA.
12·9

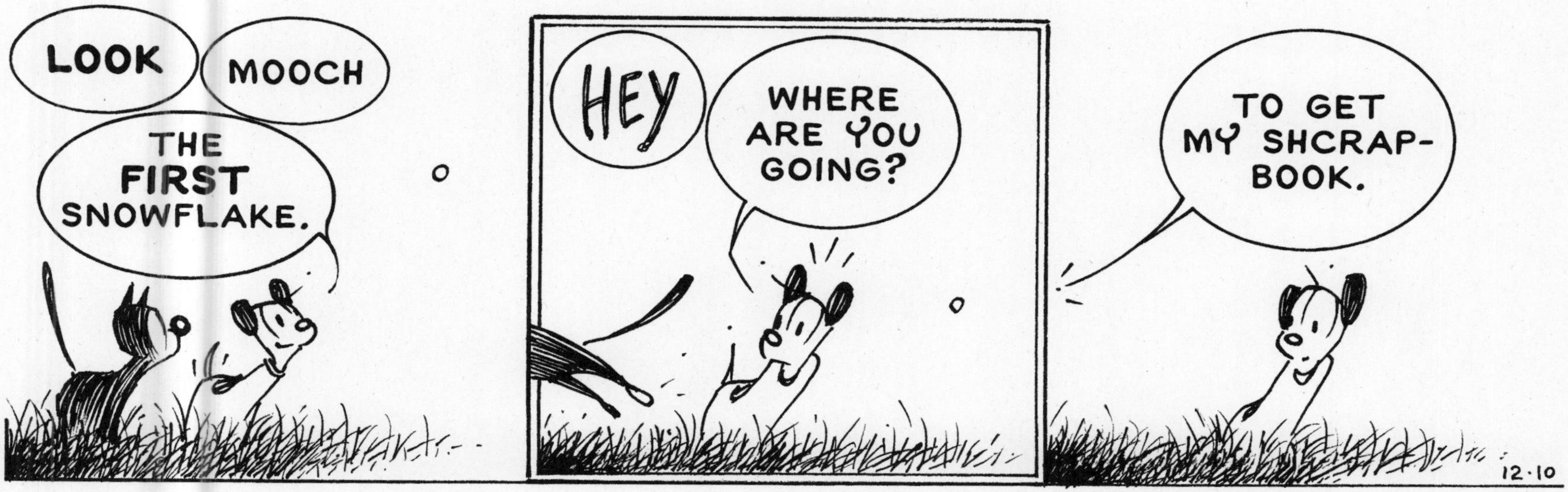
LOOK
MOOCH
THE FIRST SNOWFLAKE.
HEY
WHERE ARE YOU GOING?
TO GET MY SHCRAP-BOOK.
12·10

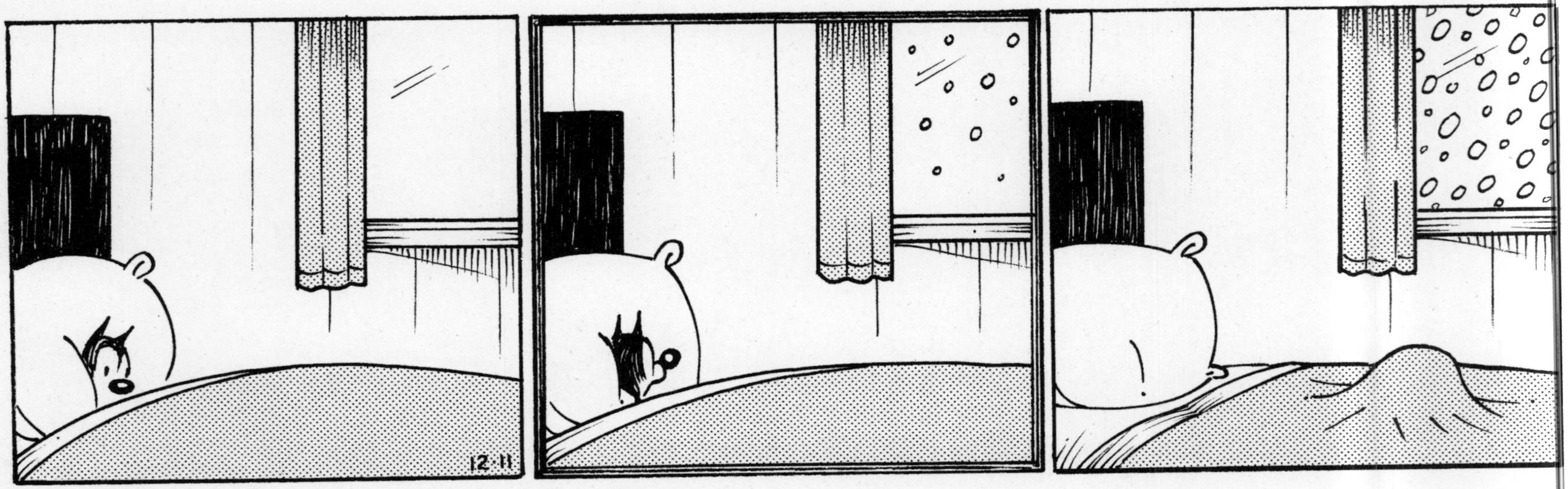
12·11

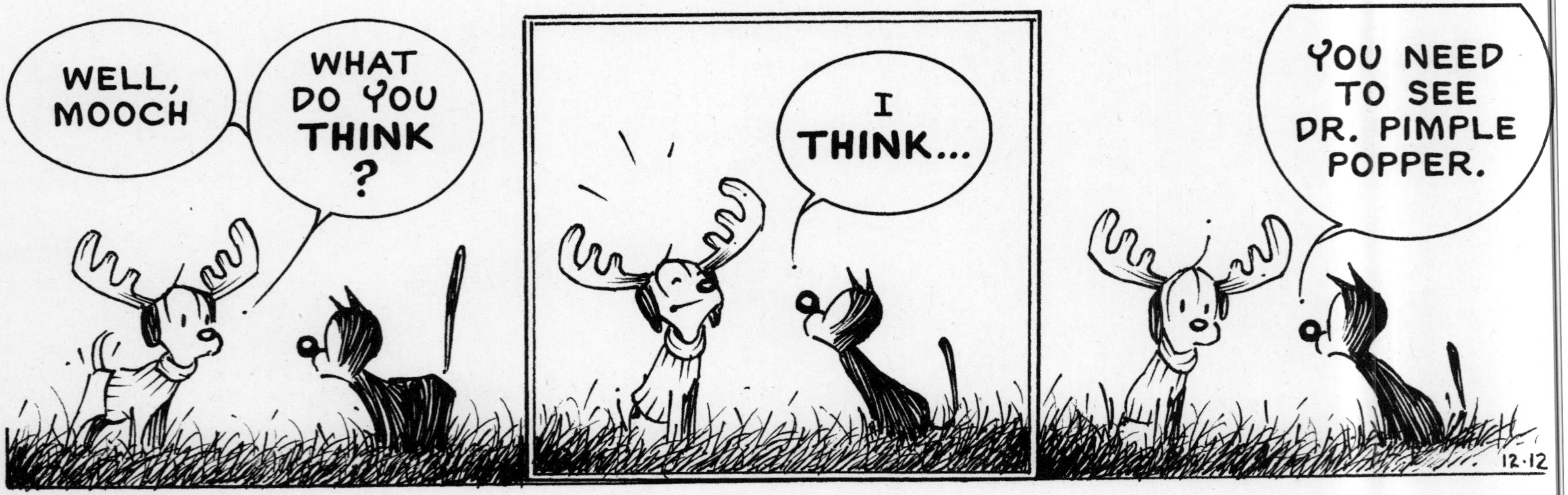
WELL, MOOCH
WHAT DO YOU THINK ?
I THINK...
YOU NEED TO SEE DR. PIMPLE POPPER.
12·12

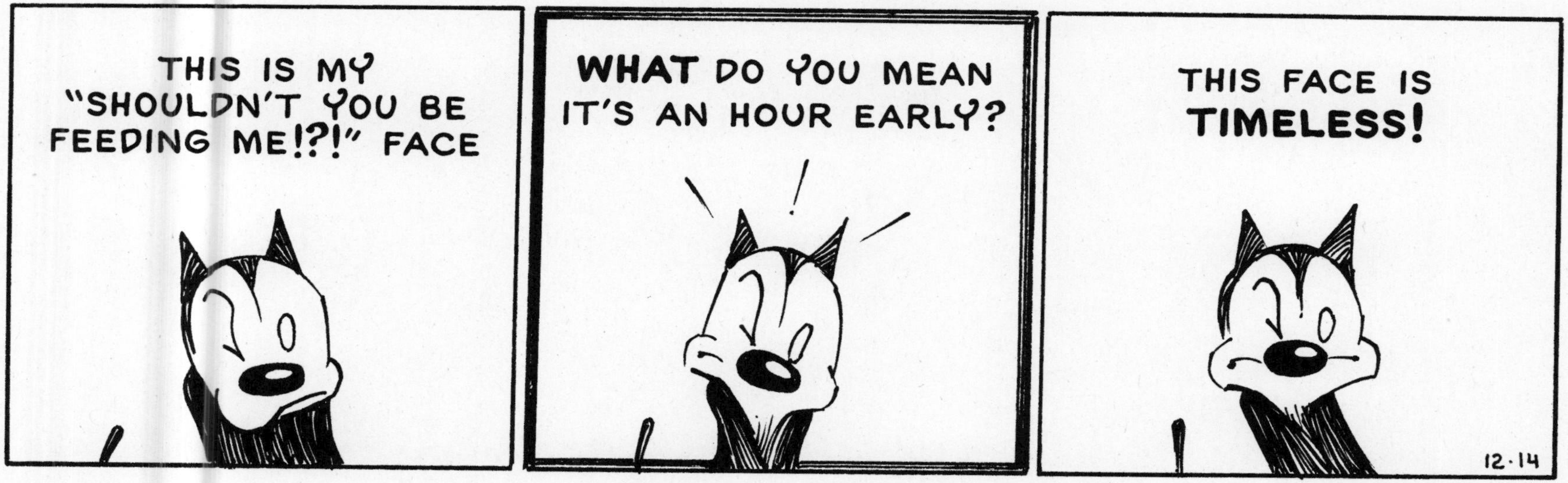
THIS IS MY "SHOULDN'T YOU BE FEEDING ME!?!" FACE
WHAT DO YOU MEAN IT'S AN HOUR EARLY?
THIS FACE IS **TIMELESS!**
12·14

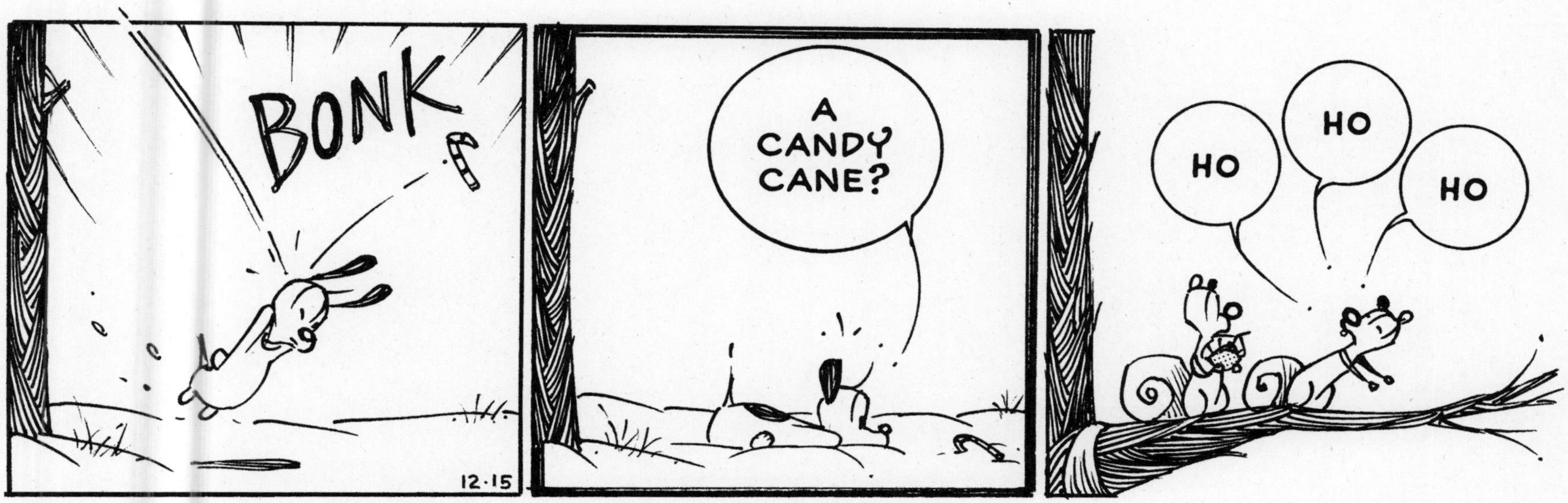
BONK
12·15
A CANDY CANE?
HO
HO
HO

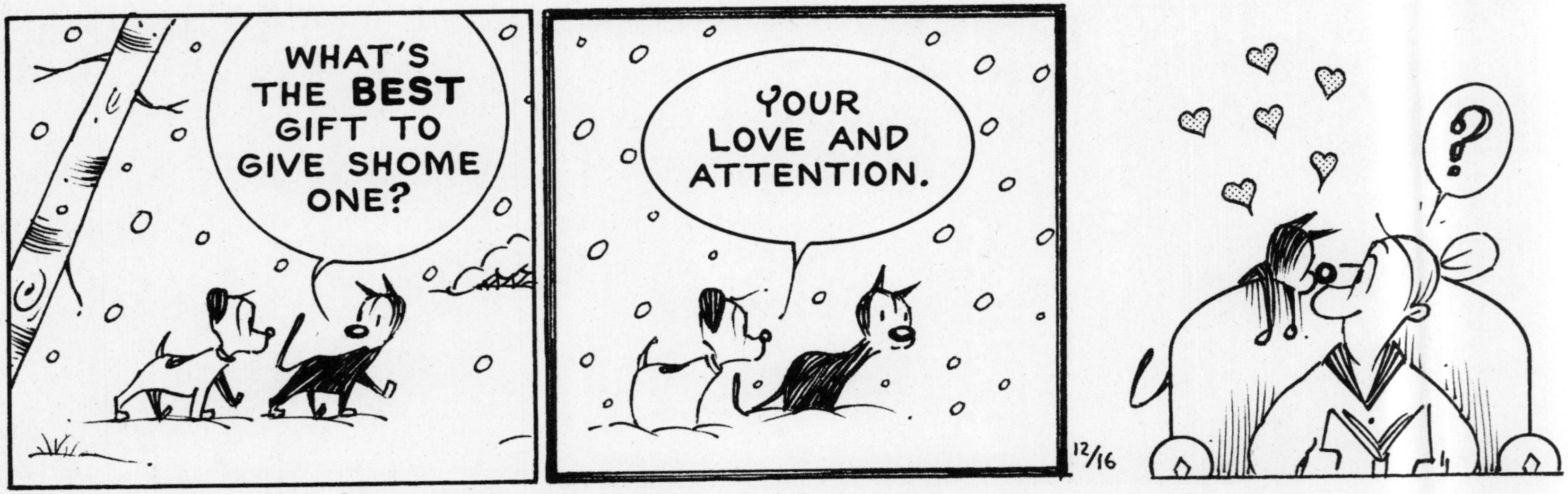
WHAT'S THE BEST GIFT TO GIVE SHOME ONE?
YOUR LOVE AND ATTENTION.
?
12/16

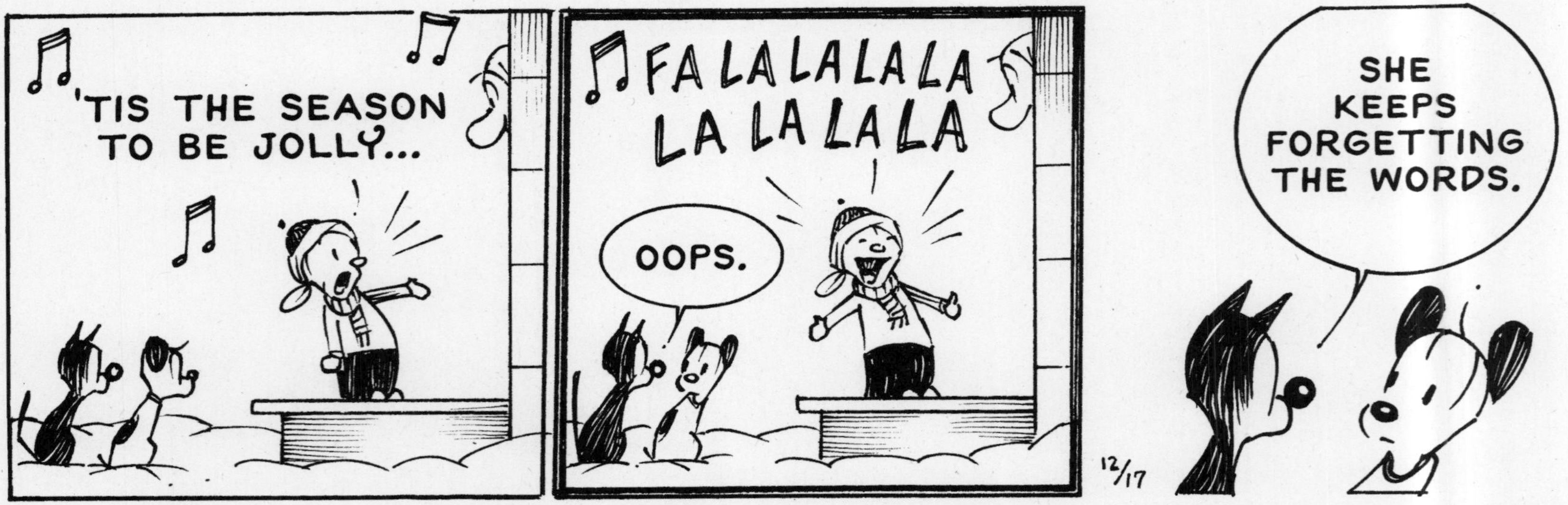
'TIS THE SEASON TO BE JOLLY...
FA LA LA LA LA LA LA LA LA
OOPS.
SHE KEEPS FORGETTING THE WORDS.
12/17

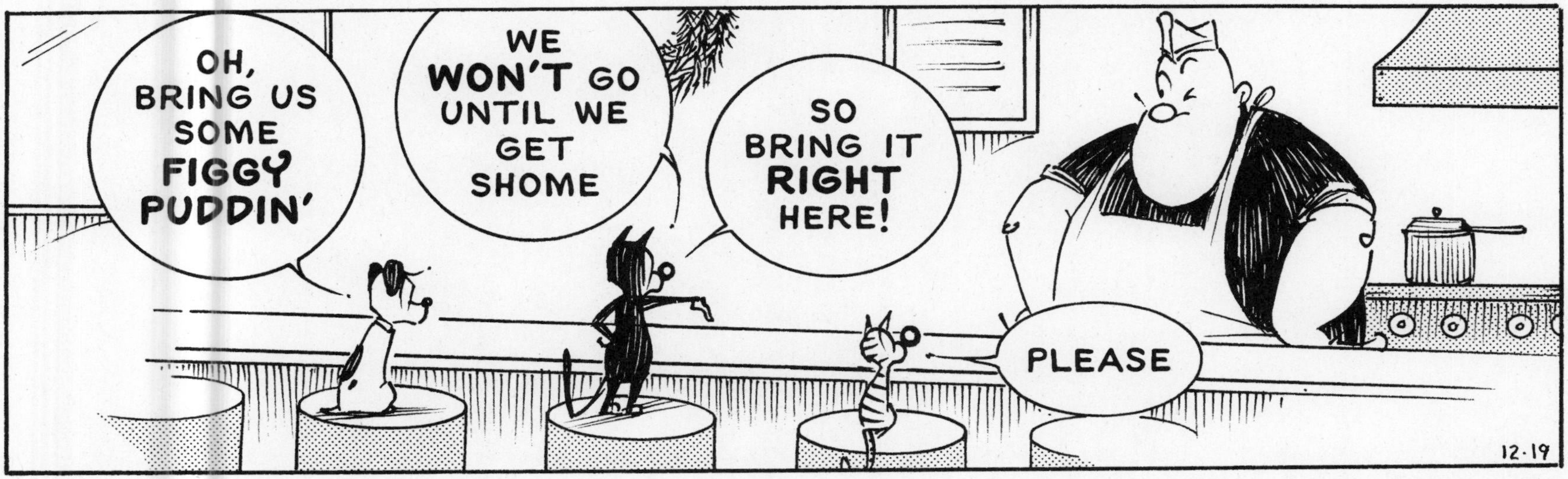
OH, BRING US SOME FIGGY PUDDIN'
WE WON'T GO UNTIL WE GET SHOME
SO BRING IT RIGHT HERE!
PLEASE
12·19

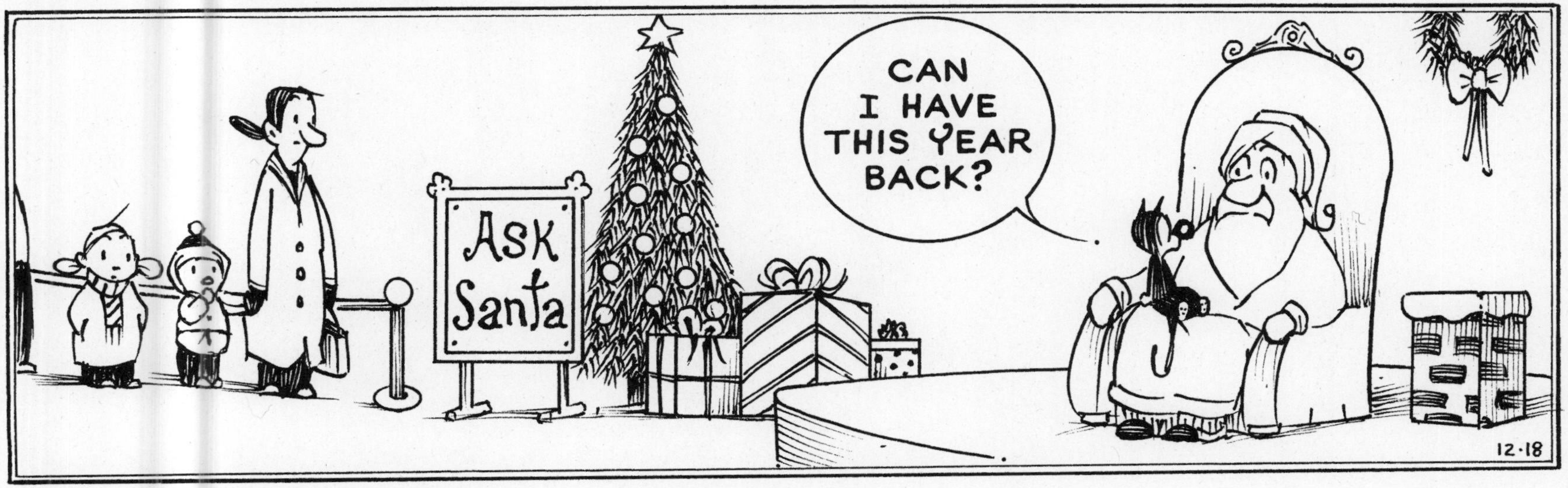
Ask Santa
CAN I HAVE THIS YEAR BACK?
12·18

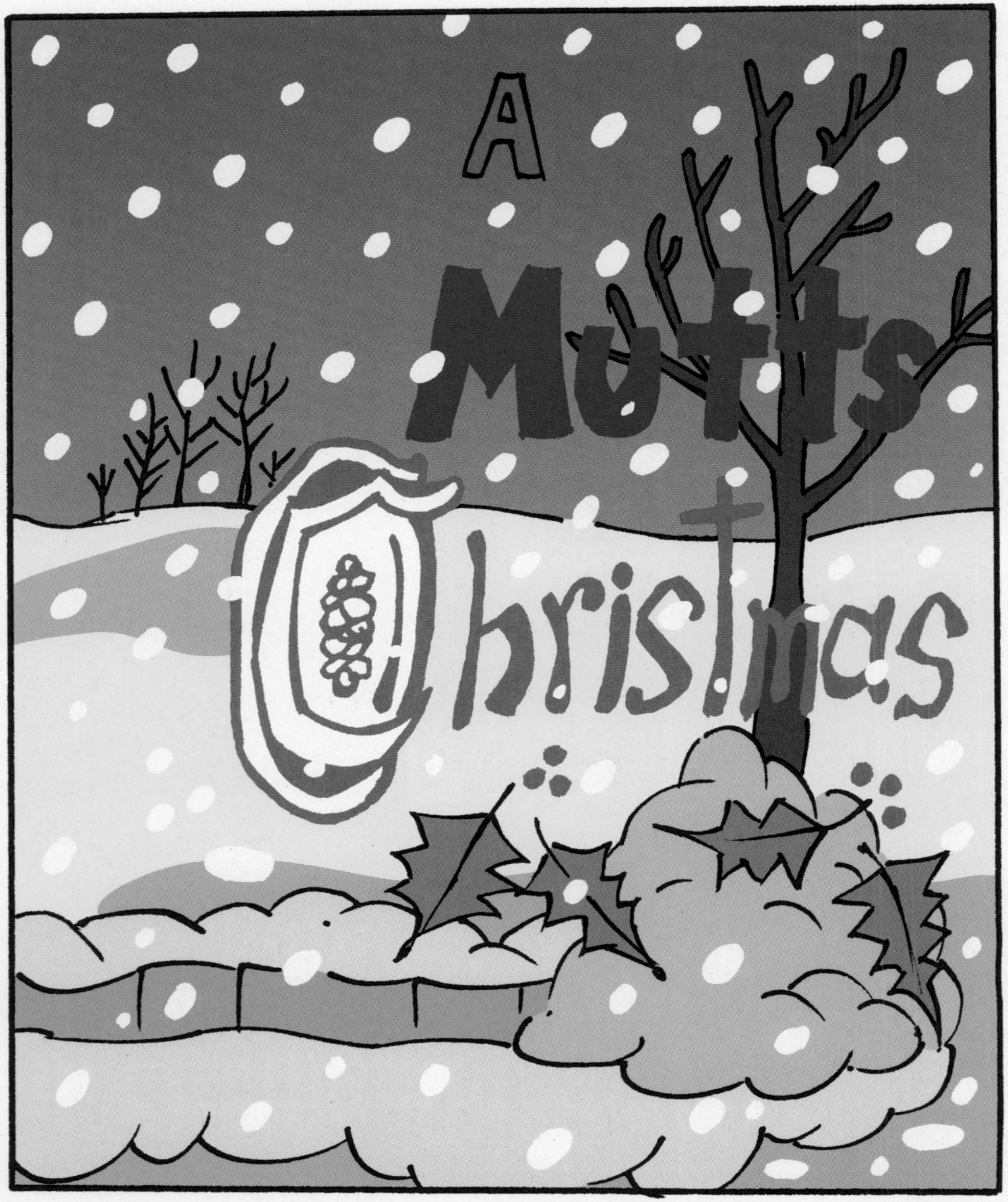
A
Mutts
Christmas

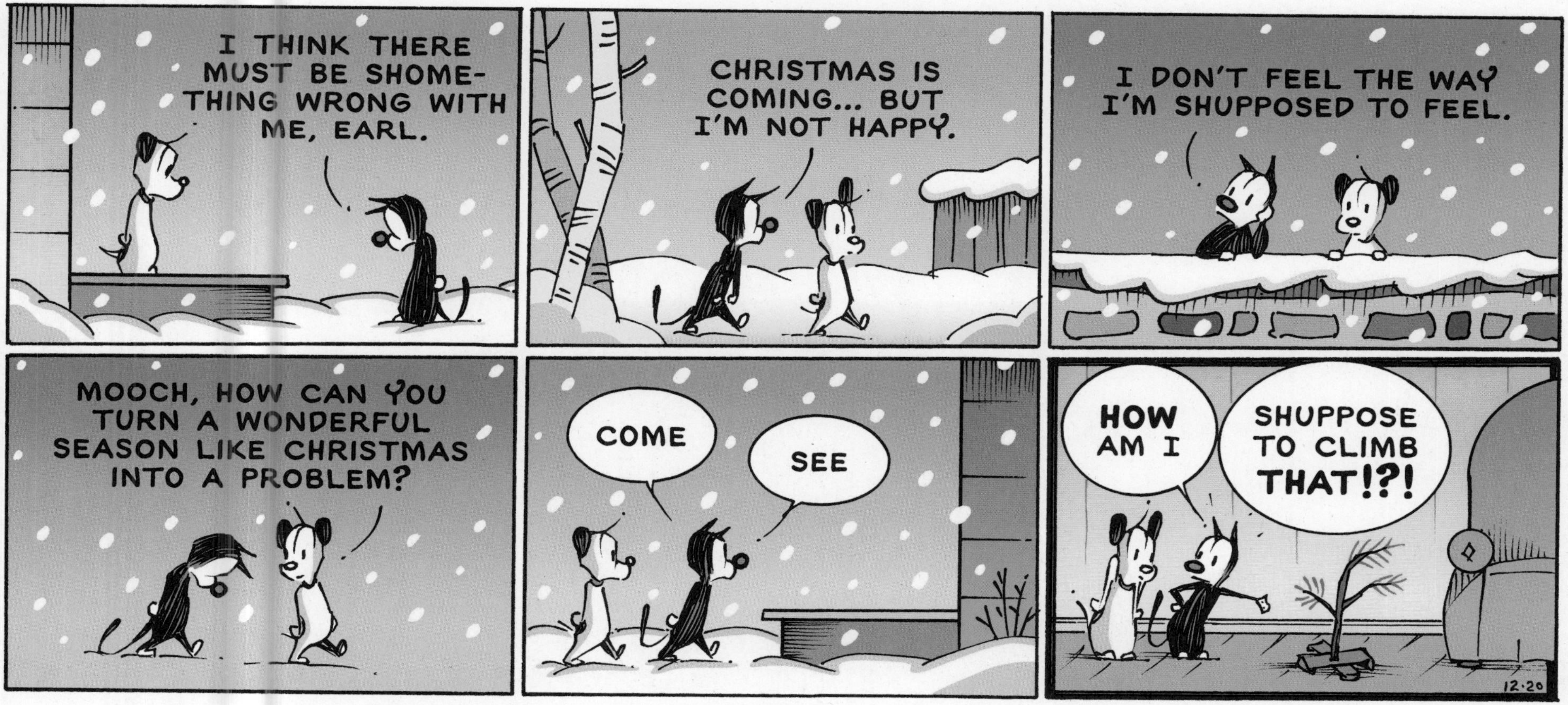
I THINK THERE MUST BE SHOME-THING WRONG WITH ME, EARL.
CHRISTMAS IS COMING... BUT I'M NOT HAPPY.
I DON'T FEEL THE WAY I'M SHUPPOSED TO FEEL.
MOOCH, HOW CAN YOU TURN A WONDERFUL SEASON LIKE CHRISTMAS INTO A PROBLEM?
COME
SEE
HOW AM I
SHUPPOSE TO CLIMB THAT!?!
12·20

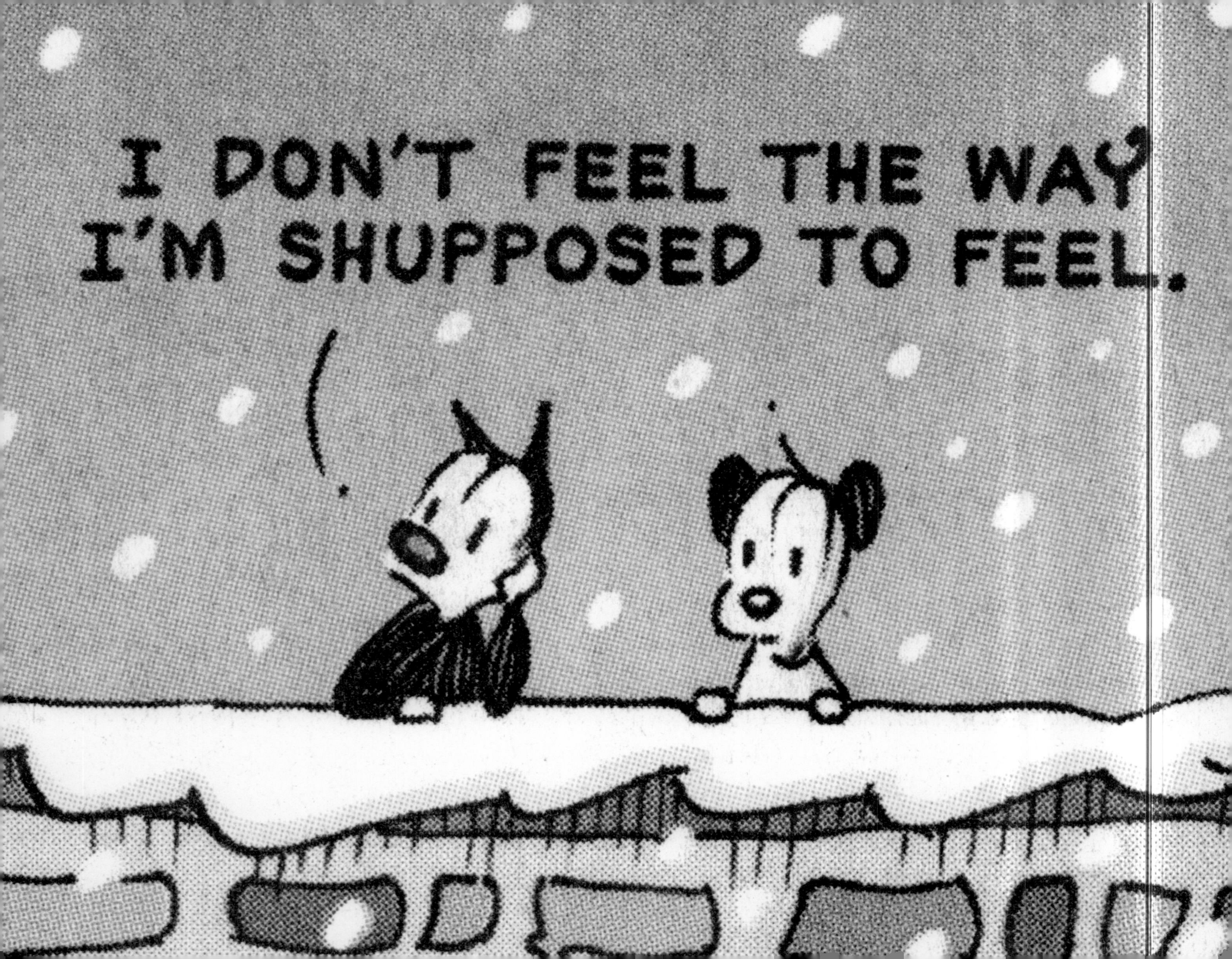
I DON'T FEEL THE WAY
I'M SHUPPOSED TO FEEL.

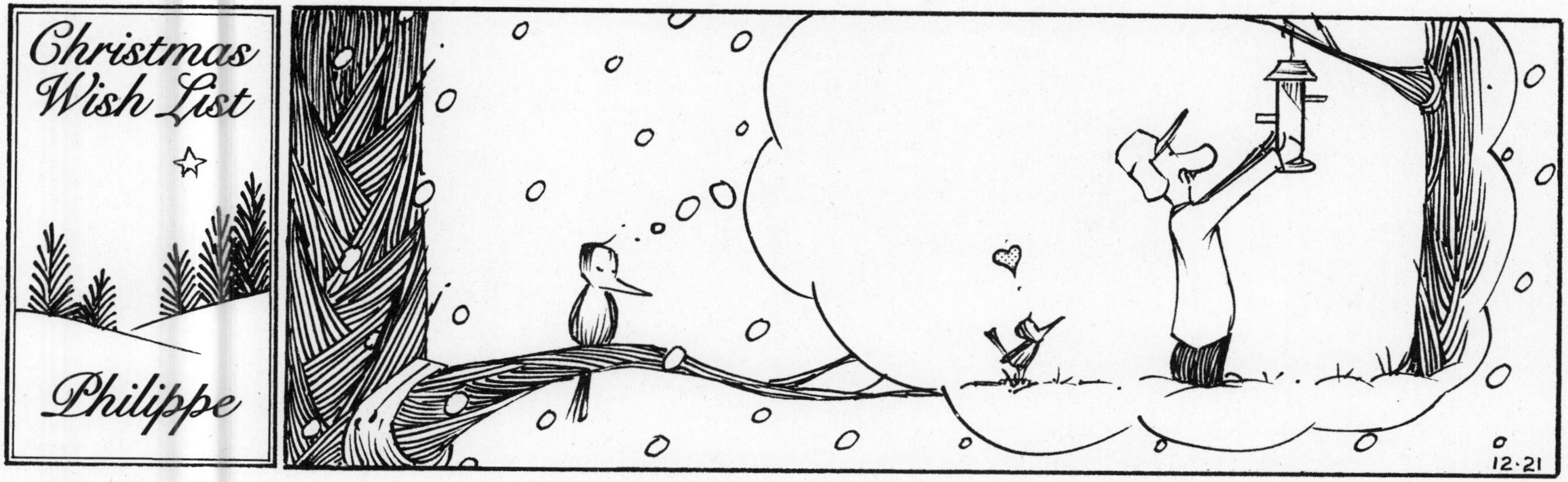
Christmas Wish List
Philippe
12·21

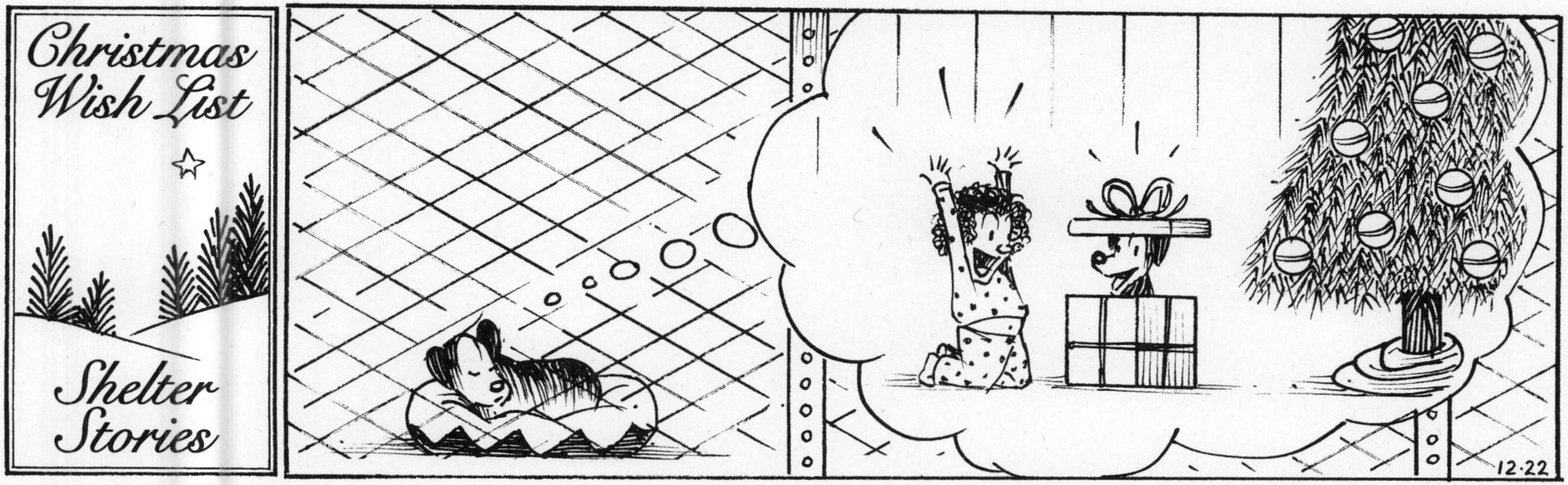
Christmas Wish List
Shelter Stories
12·22

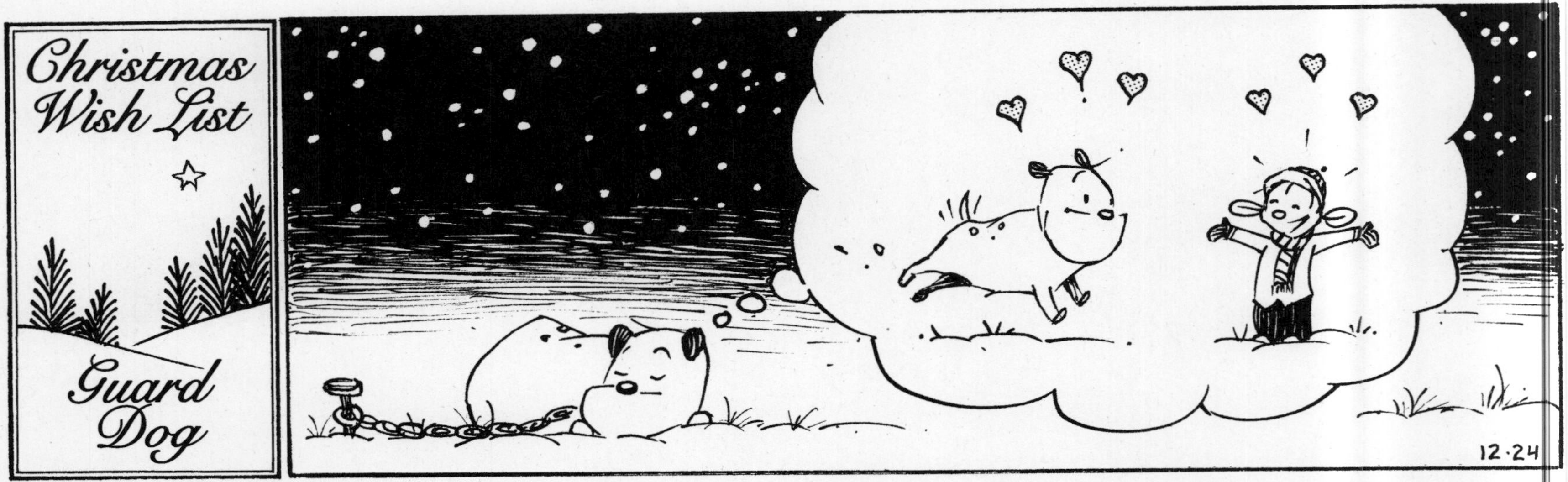
Christmas Wish List
Guard Dog
12·24

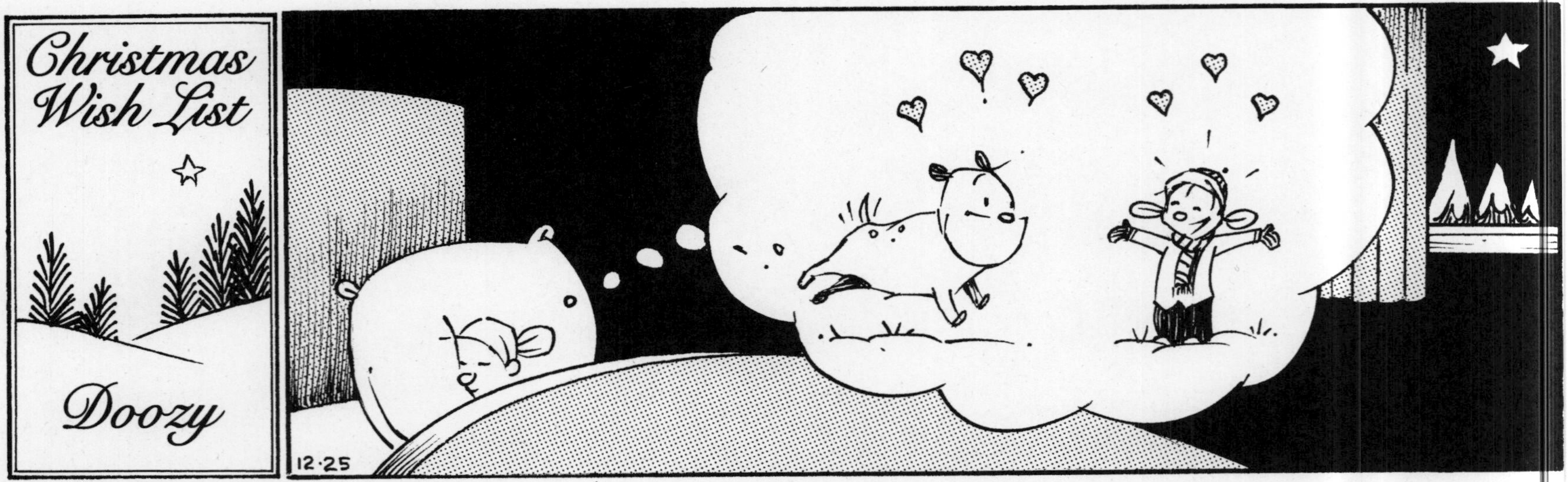
Christmas Wish List
Doozy
12·25

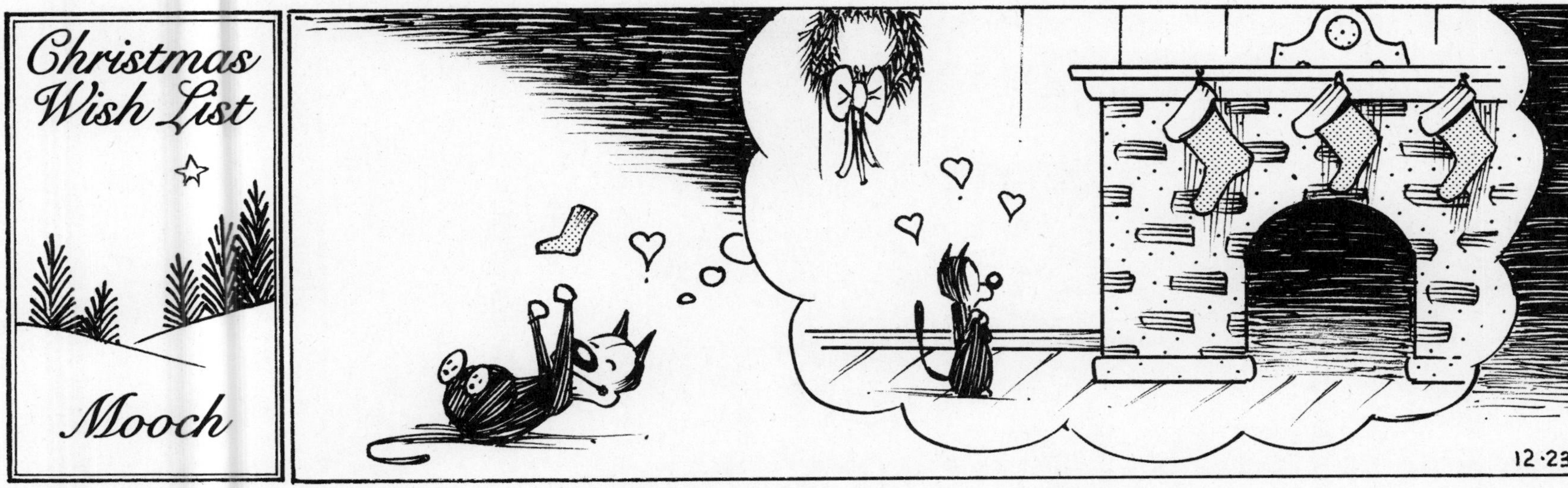
Christmas Wish List
Mooch
12·23

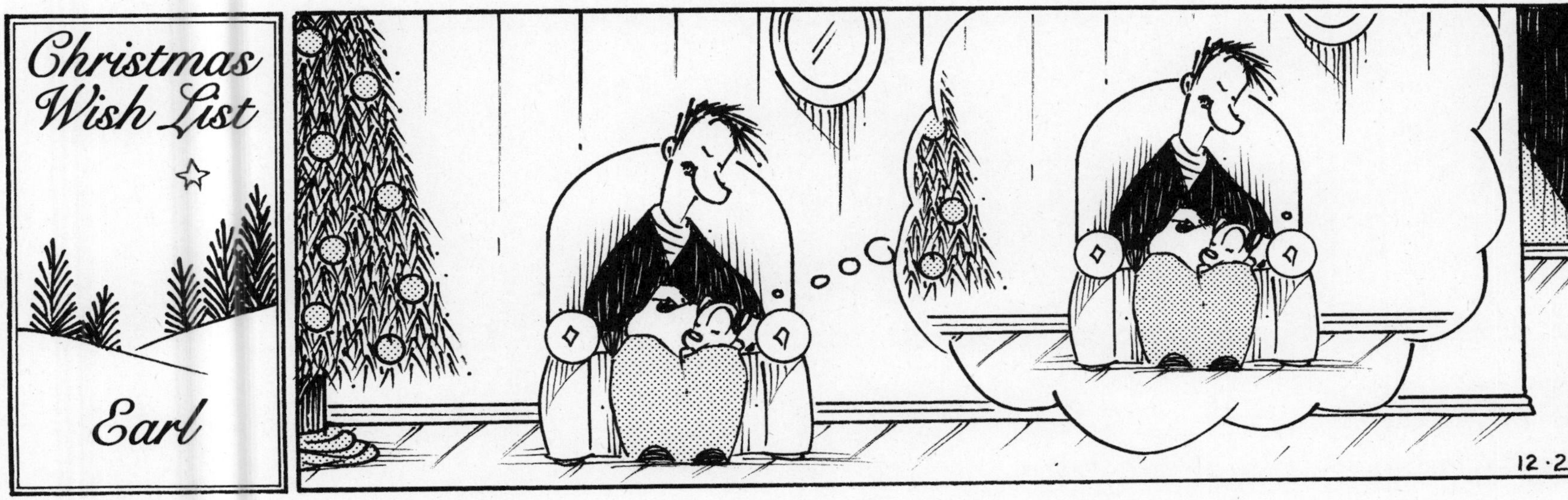
Christmas Wish List
Earl
mutts.com
12·26

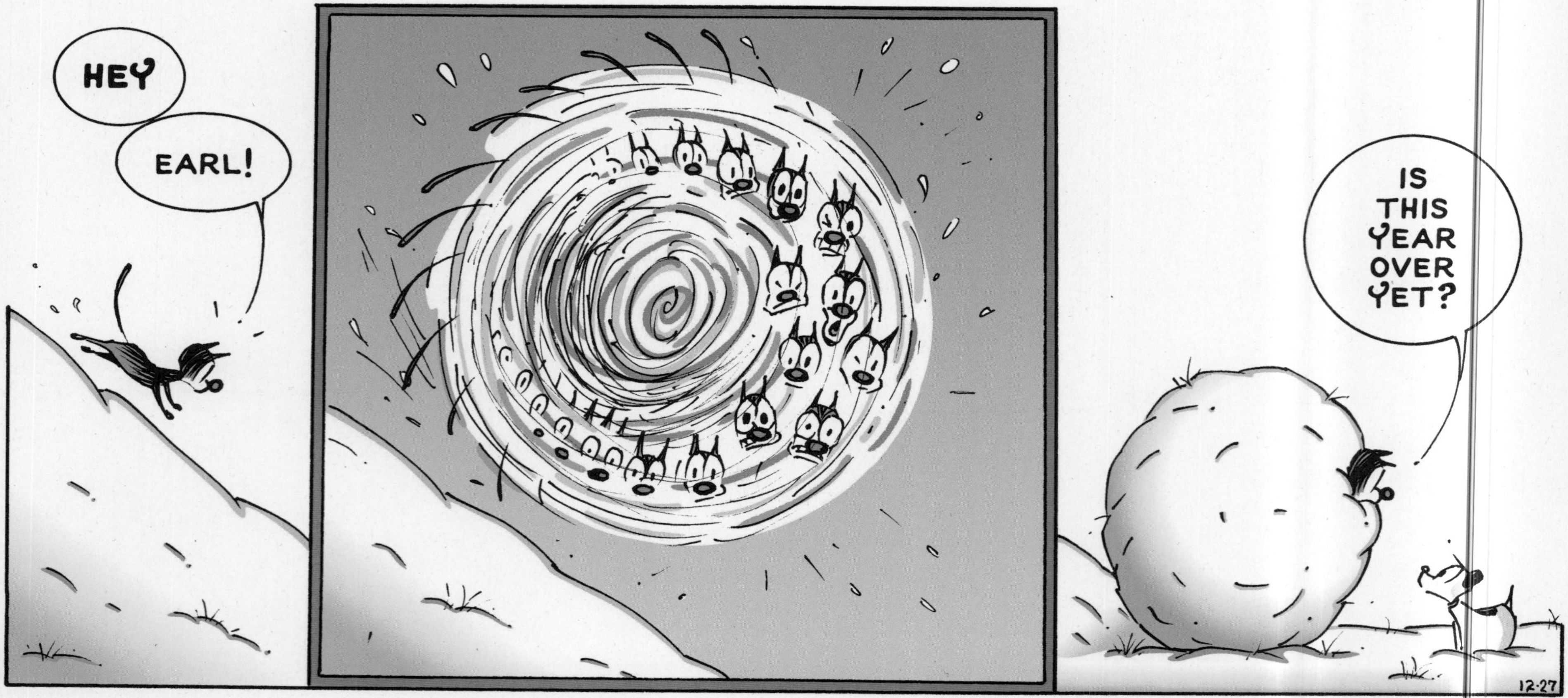
HEY
EARL!
IS THIS YEAR OVER YET?
12-27